The Falcon and the Eagle

Nicholas of Montenegro

The Falcon and the Eagle

Montenegro and Austria-Hungary, 1908–1914

John D. Treadway

Purdue University Press
West Lafayette, Indiana

First paperback edition, 1998
Published in the United States by Purdue University Press
Cover design by David Black

Copyright © 1983 by Purdue Research Foundation
Library of Congress Catalog Number 81-82728
International Standard Book Number 1-55753-146-3
Printed in the United States of America

To My Parents,

Emery and Mabel Treadway

Contents

Preface ix
Acknowledgments xv
A Note on Names xvii

ONE *The Setting* 1
    A Historical Overview 5
    Austro-Montenegrin Relations 8
    Russo-Montenegrin Relations 12
    Montenegro's Relations with the Other Powers
        and Serbia 15
    Montenegrin Politics, 1905–1908 18
    Origins of the Annexation Crisis 19

TWO *The Annexation Crisis, I: 1908* 22
    Montenegro's Initial Response 22
    Efforts at Negotiation 28
    Rapprochement with Serbia 30
    Spič 32
    Military Preparations and Demands 36

THREE *The Annexation Crisis, II: 1909* 40
    Serbia's Capitulation 42
    Montenegro's Capitulation 47

FOUR *From Kolašin to Jubilee: 1909–1910* 51
    The Kolašin Conspiracy 52
    Austro-Montenegrin Détente 55
    Austrian Skepticism 59
    The Proclamation of the Montenegrin Kingdom 61

FIVE *The Malissori Uprisings: 1910–1911* 66
    The Albanian Revolts of 1909 and 1910 68
    The Montenegrin-Malissori Rapprochement, 1910 72
    The Malissori Uprising of 1911 74
    The Resolution of the Crisis 79
    Related Questions 82

SIX *The Road to War: 1911–1912* 87
    Immediate Effects of the Turco-Italian War 88
    Montenegro's Desire for a Border Rectification
        with Turkey 92

Continued Serbo-Montenegrin Enmity   93
Nicholas's Journey to St. Petersburg   95
Aehrenthal's Successor as Foreign Minister   97
Nicholas's Journey to Vienna   100
Turco-Montenegrin Frontier Incidents   101
The Balkan Alliance   105
The Outbreak of War   108

SEVEN *The Outbreak of the First Balkan War: 1912–1913*   112
Austria and Montenegro at the Outset of the War   113
Russian Attitudes   116
The Albanian Question   118
Habsburg Overtures to Serbia and Montenegro   121
Montenegrin Proposals Regarding Albania and Scutari   127
Efforts at Peace: Two Conferences in London   129

EIGHT *The Scutari Crisis: 1913*   135
Serbia's Pullback from Scutari   137
The Palić and Hubka Affairs   140
The Occupation of Scutari   141
More Great-Power Deliberations   143
The Possibility of Joint Austro-Italian Action   148
Montenegro's Capitulation   150
The Crisis in Perspective   156

NINE *From Scutari to Sarajevo: 1913–1914*   159
Montenegro after the Balkan Wars   162
Russo-Montenegrin Relations   169
Closer Serbo-Montenegrin Ties   174
The Question of Unification: Effects on the Triple Alliance   177

TEN *Into Armageddon—The Outbreak of War: 1914*   182
Initial Responses   183
Efforts at Accommodation   186
The Ultimatum   189
Edging toward War   192
Montenegro's Declaration of War   196

Conclusion   201
Notes   213
Bibliography   297
Index   327

Preface

Between 1908 and 1914, Montenegro, the tiny Serb land nestled in the southwestern corner of present-day Yugoslavia, was a mouse that roared repeatedly in European affairs. A poor country whose capital was smaller than many backwater European towns, it was constantly involved in diplomatic crises, many of its own making. "On the map she looks like a mere pin head," remarked one author in discussing Montenegro's past glories. "But the point to that pin became an unendurable irritation in Turkey's side and helped to save Europe from entire domination by the Orient."[1] In time, however, Montenegro became a source of never-ending irritation for the same Europe she had helped save. In 1912, she struck a final blow against Turkey, initiating the First Balkan War. On other occasions, some thought that she might provide the *casus belli* for a much wider conflict.

In his excellent history of the Balkans since 1453, L. S. Stavrianos acknowledged that "the role of Montenegro in South Slav and general Balkan affairs was quite out of proportion to her ridiculously meager material resources."[2] Yet despite the voluminous literature on European diplomacy before the First World War, consideration of Montenegro and her relations with the Great Powers has generally been cursory, often colored by national passions and personal prejudice. Even sober inquiries into the nature of Europe's powder keg have frequently sidestepped Montenegro in order to tackle the seemingly more substantive and controversial case of Serbia. In his detailed study of the origins of the First World War, for example, Sidney Bradshaw Fay dismissed Montenegro in a single sentence, contributing to the myth that she was a negligible quantity.[3]

This study takes a fresh look at the unstable corner of the world where the war began, focusing on Montenegro's relationship with Austria-Hungary and shedding light on many related issues. Montenegro was an important chess piece in matches between Vienna and St. Petersburg for hegemony in the Balkans and between Vienna and Rome for dominance in the Adriatic. Montenegro's actions, interests, and demands often frustrated the cooperative efforts of the Powers to keep the

Preface

peace, challenged the cohesion of the Triple Entente, and exposed the vulnerability of the ostensibly sturdier Triple Alliance. Montenegro's prince and later king, Nicholas I, boldly used the Powers in games of his own and was especially fond of pitting Austria and Russia against one another. In turn, he was often a prisoner of his subjects' strident nationalism in dealings with Austria-Hungary and other states.

Austro-Montenegrin relations consisted of a series of crises and rapprochements, each crisis seemingly greater and more dangerous than the last. Opportunities for peace and friendship periodically presented themselves but were allowed to pass. Austria, whose Balkan policies have been indicted for causing war in 1914, often handled the temperamental Montenegrin ruler and his subjects with insensitive arrogance. Montenegro, whose almost comic penury gave inspiration to Franz Lehár's operetta *The Merry Widow*, strove to fill her empty coffers and extend her frontiers, in the process provoking and antagonizing her much larger neighbor. As it happened, Austria and Serbia started the dominoes falling in 1914, but on several occasions before the July crisis, many people believed that a confrontation between the Dual Monarchy and Montenegro might set Europe ablaze.

This study disputes a commonly held view that Montenegro was merely the handmaiden of Serbia and Russia in their struggles with Austria-Hungary—or, as the fiery chief of the Habsburg general staff once called her, "a trimmer of Serbia in the service of Russia."[4] In pursuing his own goals, Nicholas frequently crossed swords with Belgrade and St. Petersburg. For years, the Montenegrin and Serbian dynasties exchanged epithets with the same vigor with which they purported to champion the cause of a united Serbdom. Similarly, Russia's relations with Nicholas, the man one tsar called his only friend in Europe, sometimes verged on rupture. Montenegro's fluctuating ties with her sister Slav states, despite the fundamental Russophilia and pan-Serbism of her subjects, contributed to and reflected her erratic course and incendiary potentialities in Balkan politics. Ultimately, Nicholas's policies undermined his people's faith in him.

This study also takes issue with the contention, revived in recent years by Fritz Fischer and his school, that in the years immediately before the Sarajevo crisis, Germany was always looking for an opportunity to make war. While generally supporting Austria-

Preface

Hungary's policies in the Balkans, indeed occasionally encouraging her to take bold stands worthy of a Great Power, Germany also frequently restrained Austria, advising her to seek a golden mean in the conduct of her Balkan affairs. Before August 1914, Germany could have taken advantage of any number of crises involving Montenegro to initiate hostilities, but she did not.[5]

Though Montenegro's role in Balkan affairs has been slighted by Western historical literature, it has not been altogether ignored. Most diplomatic histories of Europe and the Balkans give it at least passing reference. One, Luigi Albertini's *Origins of the War of 1914*, 3 vols. (London, 1952–1957), actually devoted numerous pages to Montenegro, but the author's treatment is selective and intermittent. Several works include individual chapters on Montenegro's activities in various crises, among them Bernadotte Schmitt's classic study of the *Annexation of Bosnia, 1908–1909* (Cambridge, 1937); Edward C. Thaden's *Russia and the Balkan Alliance of 1912* (University Park, Pa., 1965); and Ernst C. Helmreich's standard study, *The Diplomacy of the Balkan Wars, 1912–1913* (Cambridge, Mass., 1938). Several articles were generated by the worldwide debate over the war guilt question immediately after the end of the First World War, but in the last thirty years strikingly few articles have been written. One, by Thaden, formed the basis of his aforementioned chapter. Another, by Hans Heilbronner, discussed the merger attempts of Serbia and Montenegro. Two others focused on narrow topics: Helmreich's examination of the Serbo-Montenegrin alliance of 6 October 1912, and Richard Challener's discussion of Montenegro's bizarre attempt to offer the United States a naval station on Montenegrin soil.[6] Happily, Montenegrin scholars have recently given increased attention to their republic's troubled history at the turn of the century, producing several book-length studies. In 1970, Mihailo Vojvodić's monograph on the Scutari crisis appeared, followed the next year by Dimitrije Vujović's survey of Franco-Montenegrin relations during Nicholas's long reign.[7] Both volumes have been of great value to me.

This work is the first comprehensive study in any language of Montenegro's relations with her Great-Power neighbors on the eve of the First World War. In a general sense, it complements the recent intensive and comprehensive reevaluation of European diplomacy before August 1914, a development encouraged by the opening of many European archives to scholarly perusal.

Preface

Most Western-language works on Balkan diplomacy, including Helmreich's study of the Balkan wars and the greater part of Hans Uebersberger's *Österreich zwischen Russland und Serbien* (Graz and Cologne, 1958), have drawn principally upon official and semi-official documentary collections published under the auspices of various European governments after the First World War. In the case of Yugoslav primary sources, most scholars have relied almost exclusively on the German-language edition of *Die auswärtige Politik Serbiens*, which, as Helmreich himself noted, contains only one or two Montenegrin documents.[8] Decades after their publication, these collections are still valuable, and I have drawn heavily upon them, especially *Österreich-Ungarns Aussenpolitik*.[9] I have followed Thaden's lead in utilizing the second series of *Mezhdunarodnie otnosheniia v epokhu imperializma* while investigating the Malissori uprisings of 1910 and 1911.[10]

Yet despite their time-tested usefulness and convenience, these published documents are necessarily selective and must be supplemented with additional information found in several national depositories. The rich holdings of Vienna's Haus-, Hof- und Staatsarchiv—some of whose documents are surprisingly untouched—are fundamental for any student of Balkan affairs and answer many questions raised or left unanswered by *Österreich-Ungarns Aussenpolitik* and other documentary collections. Though Britain's interests in the Balkans were not as great as Austria's, the Public Record Office in London contains many astute and critical analyses of developments and personalities. America's Balkan interests were even more remote, but the National Archives in Washington, D.C., also offers interesting fare for a notetaker's logbook.

Yugoslav archives have been largely ignored by Western historians, many of whom are still waiting for Belgrade to publish an official documentary series. This study has benefitted by an examination of archives and libraries in Belgrade and Cetinje, whose holdings, though not as comprehensive as those of the larger European states, nonetheless shed light on many dark niches of Balkan history. Regrettably, many Montenegrin documents were lost forever during the First World War, and the handful of men who worked in Montenegro's rudimentary foreign ministry were not the dedicated paper collectors commonly found in other European chancelleries. Even if they had been, in patriarchal Montenegro

Preface

the ruler was the chief formulator of policy, and Nicholas was not one to commit the details of his policymaking to paper.

Thus, while Montenegrin documents are useful, it is necessary to rely heavily on foreign reports and reminiscences of dealings with Nicholas and his associates. In the latter category, I note the memoirs of Baron Giesl, Austria-Hungary's minister to Montenegro between 1909 and 1913, and the articles of Gustav von Hubka, a Habsburg military attaché. I am also indebted to the writings of Mary Edith Durham for their many witty and acerbic comments, which gave spice to the frequently dull contents of diplomatic dispatches.[11] Finally, I cite with special commendation the largely untapped resources of the Montenegrin historical journal *Istorijski Zapisi* and its predecessor, *Zapisi,* which have published many important articles as well as numerous documents on Montenegro's foreign policy.

Acknowledgments

I should like to express my gratitude to the faculty and staffs of the various institutions that have permitted me to use their resources, both human and material, in the preparation of this manuscript. In particular, I thank the interlibrary loan divisions of Alderman Library, University of Virginia; Newman Library, Virginia Polytechnic Institute and State University; and the University of Illinois Library at Urbana-Champaign. I gratefully acknowledge the assistance rendered by the staffs of the Svetozar Marković Library, University of Belgrade; the Narodna Biblioteka S. R. Srbije, Belgrade (especially Ružica Radulović); the School of Slavonic and East European Studies and the Institute of Historical Research, both of the University of London; the Public Record Office, London; the National Archives, Washington, D.C.; the Haus-, Hof- und Staatsarchiv, Vienna; the Savezni Sekretarijat za inostrane poslove, Belgrade; and the Državni Arhiv Crne Gore, Cetinje. For their many kindnesses I thank Mary Rose Brandt and Ruth Kurzbauer, formerly with the United States Embassy in Belgrade; Dr. Jovan R. Bojović, director of Istorijski Institut S. R. Crne Gore, Titograd; and the staff of the Fulbrajtova Komisija in Belgrade, especially Bojan Drndić, Maja Grubac, and Ksenija Todorović. I thank the University of Richmond Library for the help graciously given me when I requested it late in this project.

I am grateful for financial support I have received over the past several years, including an NDFL fellowship; a Forstmann Fellowship from the Society of Fellows of the University of Virginia; a faculty research grant from the University of Richmond; and a research grant from the American Council of Learned Societies, financed in part by the National Endowment for the Humanities. I thank especially the Institute of International Education and the International Telephone and Telegraph Corporation for generously sponsoring a year of research and travel in Yugoslavia, Austria, and England. My findings and conclusions do not necessarily represent the views of my sponsors.

I owe much to Enno E. Kraehe of the University of Virginia, who stimulated my interest in European diplomacy many years ago. He was always generous with his time in reading chapters,

Acknowledgments

making suggestions, challenging assumptions, and sharing insights. I am also grateful to Woodford McClellan, Hans A. Schmitt, and Paul Shoup, who took time from their own work to read and criticize mine; to Soloman Wank of Franklin and Marshall College, who kindly answered my various queries concerning Austro-Hungarian diplomacy, and to Mihailo Vojvodić of the University of Belgrade, who shared with me his personal accounts of life in the land of the Black Mountain; to Novica Rakočević of the Istorijski Institut S. R. Crne Gore, who permitted me to read a draft of his forthcoming book on Montenegro before the Great War; and to Radoslav Popov of the Historical Institute of the Bulgarian Academy of Sciences, who explained many of the details of Bulgaria's foreign policy during the Balkan wars.

Over the years, my friends and colleagues have aided me in innumerable ways. I thank them all, especially George Paul, James Piscatori, V. Peter Ziegler, Marla Moore Ziegler, Michael and Margaret Von Herzen, Joe Conn, John R. Rilling, Kenneth F. Meredith, 'Rick Gray, and Jon Kukla. I am deeply indebted to Steve and Lyn Hulland, formerly with the Australian Embassy in Belgrade, who took me into their warm and loving home for several months. Needless to say, I am grateful for the expert assistance provided by my editor, Verna Emery, who did so much to put this manuscript into final form. Most of all I thank my wife, Sandra, whose love, support, example, and sharp editorial eye enabled me to finish. She was an inspiration every step of the way. Finally, I acknowledge the debt I owe my parents, who have sacrificed much for me. Although it took longer to complete than they expected, here, at last, is "the book."

A Note on Names

As the places mentioned in this study frequently have different spellings (indeed, different names) in the various Western and Balkan languages, whenever possible I have used the accepted English form of a foreign toponymy: thus, Vienna instead of Wien; Scutari in lieu of Shkodër or Skodra; Belgrade instead of Beograd. Elsewhere, I have employed indigenous spellings, rendered in Latin type, even when so doing may run the risk of using a current (or traditional) Yugoslav or Albanian form in place of a better known historic name commonly in use at the turn of this century: thus, Bay of Kotor instead of Bocche di Cattaro; Cetinje in place of Cettigné or Cettigne; Shëngjin rather than San Giovanni di Medua; Zagreb rather than Agram. For the sake of avoiding disconcerting anachronisms, I have thought it best to use the old Montenegrin name Podgorica in place of the current Titograd, Berane instead of Ivangrad, and the traditional St. Petersburg in place of Leningrad.

In an effort to rationalize the rendering of personal names, I have given them in their native spelling (when appropriate, with the aid of standard German, Serbo-Croatian, or Albanian diacritical marks), assigning names usually spelled in Cyrillic a precise Latin equivalent: thus, Pašić instead of Pashitch, Mijušković instead of Mioushkovitch, etc. Following standard historical procedure, I refer to ruling heads by their English name equivalents, whenever one exists: thus, Nicholas instead of Nikola, Peter instead of Petar, Francis Joseph instead of Franz Joseph. Russian names are rendered according to traditional and Library of Congress transcription. For Albanian and especially Turkish names, I follow the lead of Stavro Skendi.

Lastly, unless denoted by O.S. (Old Style), all dates are according to the Gregorian calendar.

Common and Historic Equivalents of Certain Place Names

Name used in this study	Alternative
Bar	Antivari
Bay of Kotor	Boka Kotorska, Bocche di Cattaro
Berane	Ivangrad
Bijelo Polje	Biyelo Polye
Bitola	Bitolj, Monastir
Bojana River	Boyana, Buene
Bregalnica	Bregalnitza
Buchlau	Buchlov
Budva	Budua
Cem River	Tsem, Cijem
Cetinje	Cettigne or Cettigné, Tsetinye, Tsettinye, Tzetinje
Constantinople	Istanbul
Crmnica	Tzrmnitza, Tsrmnitsa
Dibrë	Dibra
Djakovica	Djakova
Dobrudja	Dobroge, Dobrudža
Dubrovnik	Ragusa
Durrës	Durazzo, Dyrrhanchium
Edirne	Adrianople
Gerče	Gerche
Gusinje	Gusinye
Herceg Novi	Herceg-Novi, Castelnuovo
Ioánnina	Janina
Kavalla	Kavala
Kolašin	Kolashin
Lezhë	Alessio, Lješ
Ličeni Hotit	Litscheni Hotit
Kotor	Cattaro
Lovćen	Lovchen, Lovtchen, Lovčen
Mitrovica	Mitrovitza
Mojkovac	Moykovatz
Montenegro	Crna Gora, lit. "Black Mountain"
Nikšić	Nikshich, Nikshitch, Nikshiti, Nikshitz
Njeguši	Niegush, Nyegosh, Njegusi, Niegoch
Novi Pazar	Novipazar, Novi Bazar, Novibazar
Ohrid	Ohrida, Ochrida, Okhrida
Opatija	Abbazia
Peć	Ipek
Petrovac	Castellastua
Planinica	Planinitza
Pljevlja	Plevlje, Plevle

Name used in this study	Alternative
Podgorica	Titograd, Podgoricë, Podgoritza, Podgoritsa
Priština	Prishtina, Prishtinë
Prizren	Prisren, Prisrend
Rijeka	Fiume
Rijeka Crnojevića	Rieka
Ržanica	Aržanica
St. Petersburg	Leningrad, Petrograd
Salonica	Salonika, Thessaloniki
Sandžak	Sanjak
Scutari	Shkodër, Skutari, Skodar, Skadar, Skodra
Shëngjin	San Giovanni di Medua, Medova, Singjin
Sjenica	Sienitza
Skopje	Skoplje, Skoplye, Üsküb
Spič	Spizza, Spica, Spitza
Tirana	Tiranë
Tuzi	Tusi
Ulcinj	Dulcigno, Olgun
Vermosh	Vrmoša, Vermoša
Vlorë	Valona
Zagreb	Agram
Zemun	Semlin
Zeta	Zenta

We lack Austria's strength,
but we are a small, courageous people.
We, the falcons of the Black Mountain,
yearn to soar ahead of Austria's eagles.

Nicholas I to Baron Giesl, 1911

CHAPTER ONE
The Setting

"When God finished making the world," runs an old Montenegrin ballad, "He found that He had a great many rocks left in His bag; so He tumbled the whole lot on to a wild and desolate bit of country—and that is how Montenegro was formed." This legend embodies the most important fact about the geography and the history of Montenegro. The barren limestone country around Cetinje was a very inaccessible fortress, and its caves and rocks gave ample opportunity for guerrilla warfare. It was the only corner of the Balkan lands to escape the domination of the Turk from the fourteenth century onwards; here, a few Christian shepherds and goatherds always maintained their liberty. . . . Montenegro remained a small island in the great Turkish sea. That is her essential role in the history of the Balkans.[1]

In 1908, a year of great political upheaval in the Balkan peninsula, Montenegro was not the same small island she had been in centuries past, yet H. C. Darby's pithy paragraph still tells us much about the land of the Black Mountain in the early twentieth century. To begin with, Montenegro was small. Although she had added to her territory and population in the course of many years, more than doubling in size between 1878 and 1880, she was but a dwarf in comparison with her neighbors, the Habsburg and Ottoman empires, or even the other emerging Balkan states. Her population of 275,000 was but a minute fraction of Austria-Hungary's. Indeed, Montenegro had fewer inhabitants than greater Prague, not to mention imperial Vienna or Budapest. Her land mass of some nine thousand square kilometers, approximately the area of the single Austrian crownland of Carniola, could fit roughly seventy times into the confines of the Dual Monarchy.[2]

In 1860, when Nicholas I, the last prince of Montenegro, ascended the throne, the capital of Cetinje consisted of a monastery, a modest official residence, and thirty-four thatched houses. During the next fifty years, it grew greatly in size, but even in 1908, with a population of 5,000, it was one of the least prepossessing capitals in Europe. Many foreign visitors compared Cetinje to villages in their homelands.

The chief commercial towns of Montenegro were Podgorica, Nikšić, Bar, and Ulcinj, the last two being Montenegro's only ports worthy of the name. But despite the existence of a handful of towns with tradesmen, craftsmen, and intellectuals, Montenegro did not have an urban society. Podgorica, the largest town, had 12,000 inhabitants, and only 10 percent of Montenegro's population lived in the seven largest towns. "Christendom's most extraordinary people," as Gladstone once called them, dwelled largely on the land. Like the Scottish highlanders with whom they are frequently compared, they were organized in tribes and clans, and lived according to ancient tribal codes and customs.[3] Montenegro's princes tried to impose their patriarchal, semiautocratic rule on a chaotic, overwhelmingly Eastern Orthodox, society. Along the periphery of the country lived Catholic and Muslim minorities, chiefly Albanians, acquired by Montenegro between 1878 and 1880.

As Montenegro was small, she was also poor. The "chaos of limestone" that gave the country her primitive wildness, her natural fortifications, and for many years her very freedom, also doomed the land to wretched poverty. French writer Pierre Loti, upon seeing Montenegro's landscape for the first time, called it "a veritable petrified sea! The moonlike expanses of an extinguished planet."[4] The more fertile lowlands were largely in foreign hands, Turkish and Austrian, and the soil of the petrified highlands was nearly sterile. Arable land was at a premium, amounting to a very small fraction of the country's total area. Montenegrin peasants generally owned their own land, but this gave them little cause for rejoicing. In more fortunate countries, one-tenth the area of an average Montenegrin plot might have yielded ten times the usual Montenegrin harvest.[5]

Montenegro's wealth lay not in land, but in livestock: sheep, goats, cattle, pigs, horses, and the like. By 1908, this natural asset had increased considerably, even taking into account Montenegro's territorial additions in 1878. Thus, animal husbandry was the principal national occupation. As L. S. Stavrianos has observed, "it was beneath the dignity of a Montenegrin male to do anything else

The Setting

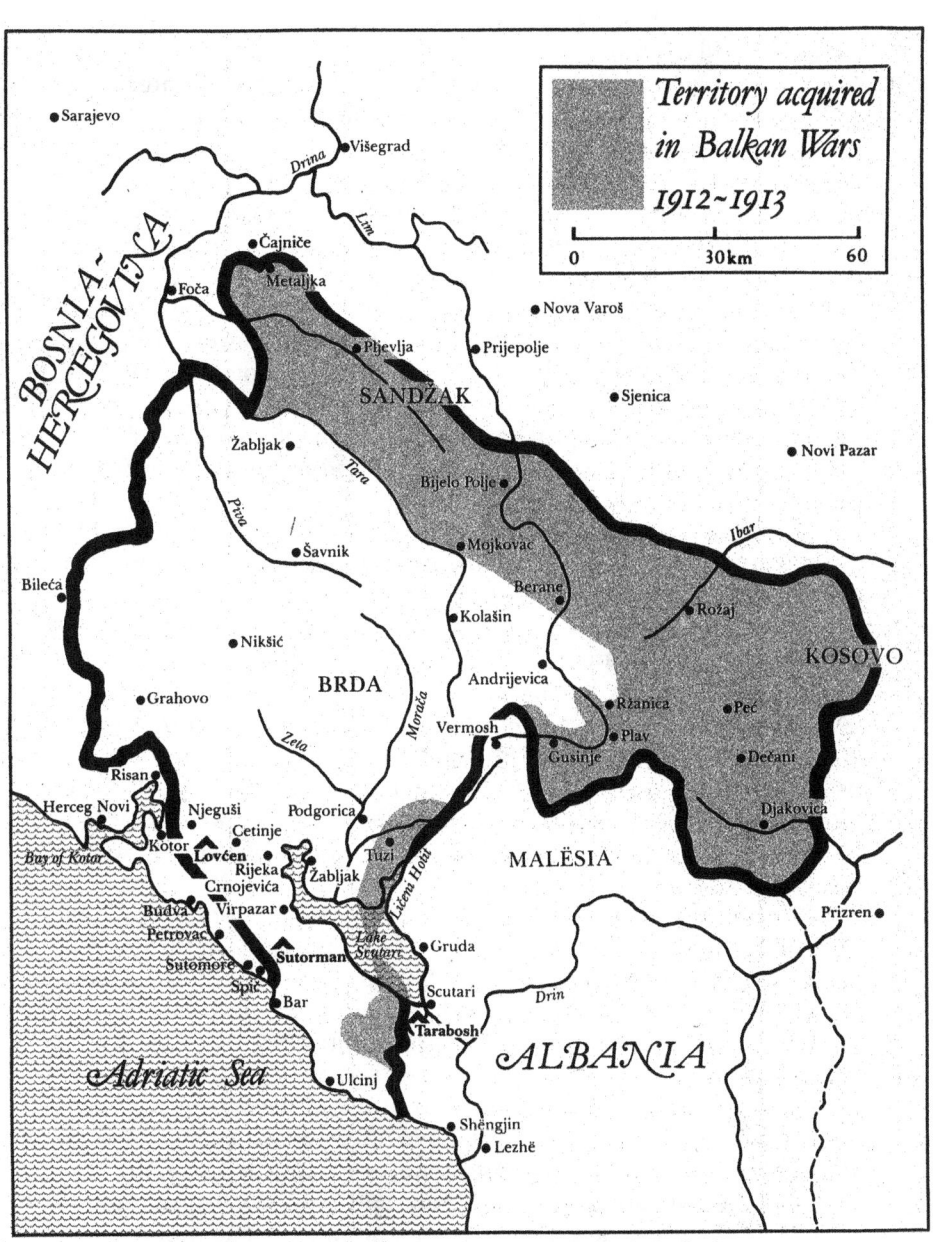

Montenegro, 1908–1914

than tend to his flocks and bear arms. The latter he did with relish and with skill born of constant practice."[6]

In between the numerous wars that punctuated Montenegrin history, the men of the Black Mountain herded their animals, cleaned their weapons, feuded among themselves, and sipped thick Turkish coffee. For the most part, the business of planting, ploughing, and harvesting was left to women. The chief agricultural crop was corn, though other hardy grains, such as wheat, barley, oats, and rye, survived in Montenegro's soil. Olives were harvested in the maritime districts, and in many places fruits, including plums, were grown. The latter frequently went into the making of the fiery national drink, slivovitz. Tolerably potable wine was produced on the plain of Zeta, in the Crmnica valley, and along the coast. Several districts grew fine tobacco, one of Montenegro's prized export crops. Maritime industries did not figure prominently in the economy.[7]

Rural overpopulation and unemployment were major problems. Domestic industry was virtually nonexistent, the Onogošt brewery at Nikšić being a notable exception. What Montenegrin laborers could be found in cities were generally unskilled and unwilling to learn a trade. Foreign enterprises operating in Montenegro relied heavily on imported labor, either from their own countries or from neighboring Hercegovina. Despite this, a small Montenegrin laboring class, baffled by the ways of the modern world but demonstrating the will and strength that would make Montenegro a future bastion of communism, began slowly to emerge. In 1906, the first organized strikes broke out among railroad workers at Bar and printers in Cetinje.[8]

The country's endemic poverty caused many Montenegrins to seek their fortunes elsewhere.[9] In 1905, some sixty-seven hundred Montenegrins left their homeland, bound chiefly for North America. On the eve of the First World War, an estimated thirty thousand were living and working in the United States. The native patriotism of most of these emigrants was very strong, however, and in times of crisis many returned home to bear arms for their fatherland, some bringing with them ideas about parliamentary democracy that were alien to Montenegro's political tradition.

To improve domestic conditions and relieve chronic unemployment, the government sent many students outside the country, especially to Serbia, to obtain a higher education. This action had mixed results. The students brought back needed skills, only some of which could be absorbed by the Montenegrin economy, but they also imported new ideas that questioned the existing state of affairs in their homeland. Many Belgrade-trained students developed a greater loyalty to Serbian institutions than to what they perceived to be the anachronistic and autocratic rule of their own prince. Many joined secret societies, became advocates of a large South Slav state, and called for Montenegro's union with Serbia.

By other objective standards of the day, Montenegro was an underdeveloped and impoverished country. Her rugged terrain made the construction of modern roads difficult. Though blessed with some mineral wealth and extensive but ill-managed forests of beech, pine, and fir in the north and east, Montenegro was unable to exploit these natural resources on her own and turned to foreign capital and entrepreneurs to develop the country. Before 1901, there were no banks in Montenegro, and until 1908, the country did not have its own currency. Even after the introduction of the Montenegrin *perper*, foreign money, especially gold coins, circulated widely.[10]

The poverty of the country did not permit it to pay its own way in the world, a fact which figured prominently in the conduct of its foreign affairs. State revenues derived chiefly from customs duties; monopolies of tobacco, salt, spirits, and oil; and taxes on land, livestock, horses, mills, and (after 1910) alcohol. The government could also claim ten days of labor yearly from each Montenegrin adult or a monetary payment in lieu thereof, but domestic income rarely met state expenses. Long before it became popular in more advanced economies, Montenegro practiced deficit financing. Solvency became a function of other countries' generosity. To escape from this constant state of pauperage was among the principal aims of Montenegro's proud rulers.

A Historical Overview

Much of what was Montenegro in the early 1900s had been part of earlier Slav states.[11] In the Middle Ages, Montenegro had formed part of Stephen Dušan's great Serb empire, but after its disintegration in the fourteenth century, Zeta, Montenegro's immediate predecessor, emerged as an independent political unit. Her territory included much of contemporary northern Albania, stretching along the Adriatic coast, and for a time her capital was Scutari, the principal town on the lake of the same name. Sold to Venice in 1396 and recaptured in 1405, Scutari eventually fell to the Turks. Latter-day Montenegrins would try to reclaim it for their own.

After the battle of Kosovo in 1389, the Ottoman tide engulfed the Balkan peninsula, and many unreconciled Serbs took refuge in Zeta's mountain bastions. For a short while, Zetans escaped the wrath of Turkish occupation, but the Ottomans ultimately encroached upon their territory, seizing their lowland possessions, including the only important towns and the most fertile agricultural land. Desiring security, Zetan ruler Ivan Crnojević moved his court to Cetinje, a more easily defended location in the shadow of Mount Lovćen, which would remain Montenegro's capital for centuries to come. It was this move that many contend marked the end of Zeta and the beginning of Montenegro.

With the decline of Crnojević rule in the late fifteenth and early sixteenth centuries, the Turks claimed Montenegro as their own and even succeeded in having a son of Ivan Crnojević govern the land between 1514 and 1528 as a special Ottoman province. In the course of the sixteenth century, however, the Montenegrins resisted Turkish rule while the Orthodox metropolitans of Cetinje came to exercise greater authority. Until the middle of the nineteenth century, Montenegro was a theocracy, ruled by elected prince-bishops, known as *vladike,* who held temporal and ecclesiastical power in their hands. After the election of Danilo I in 1696, succession was restricted to his family, the Petrovići, who would rule Montenegro until the First World War. As Orthodox bishops were celibate and had no male heirs, for the next 150 years the office of vladika passed regularly, if not always peacefully, from uncle to nephew or great-nephew, until Danilo II (1851–1860) secularized the Montenegrin state in 1852.

The Turks initially offered the Montenegrins a measure of autonomy and religious freedom, but the Montenegrins recoiled at any infringement of their precious liberty. If they were Turkish subjects, they did not act like it, and for the greater part of four hundred years, they waged a determined struggle against Ottoman domination. All Turkish efforts to subjugate the tiny land fell short of the mark. Ottoman levies, demands for tribute, notorious acts of treachery, and punitive expeditions, heightened the struggle for national independence. During the reign of Danilo I, the Montenegrins felt compelled to take drastic measures to "purify" their Orthodox land of Muslim elements. According to legend, on Christmas Eve, 1702, they struck at all Muslims living in the country, and, in the words of a nineteenth-century British clergyman, "when morning dawned not a Mussulman remained alive on the soil of Montenegro."[12] A later, perhaps the most famous Montenegrin ruler, Vladika Peter II Njegoš (1830–1851), wrote an epic poem about these so-called Montenegrin vespers. *Gorski Vjenac (The Mountain Wreath)* stands as one of the finest, most moving works of Serbo-Croatian literature.

Over the years, Montenegrin expansion took place at the expense of the Ottomans. After the battle of Krusi in 1796, Montenegro annexed the Brda region to the northeast of old Montenegro and in 1799 actually secured a fleeting recognition of her independence and sovereignty from the Ottoman sultan. In 1858, Montenegro routed the Turks at Grahovo and acquired the surrounding region and the Šavnik district. In 1878, as a result of the Congress of Berlin, she enjoyed her third major territorial expansion, adding lands on three sides. In 1880, she was awarded the tiny port of Ulcinj, her last acquisition before the Balkan wars (1912–1913).

In 1908, Montenegro's ruler was sixty-seven-year-old Nicholas I, who had served as his country's *knjaz* (prince) and *gospodar* (lord) since 1860.[13] Next to the venerable Francis Joseph, who ascended the Habsburg throne in 1848, he was the longest-reigning sovereign in Europe. Mindful of his country's glorious history of fighting the Turks and the proud heritage of the Petrović-Njegoš dynasty, Nicholas wished to enhance the reputation and strength of his country even further. Toward that end, he diligently paired his numerous sons and daughters with the scions of European royalty, in the process earning for himself the sobriquet "father-in-law of Europe."[14] As Mary Edith Durham recounted, "all that Prince Nikola could do to conquer Europe by 'peaceful penetration' he certainly did."[15]

Although Nicholas did oversee the two-fold expansion of Montenegrin territory after the Congress of Berlin in 1878, he was not satisfied. For him, additional expansion was synonymous with his country's economic and political salvation. Like many others, he believed that if Montenegro could just become big enough, she would be able to survive in the world of the twentieth century. Ultimately, Nicholas aspired to a pan-Serb ideal, desiring nothing less than the resurrection of the medieval Serb empire with himself upon Dušan's throne. Nicholas's dreams had some historic justification, for during most of the previous four centuries, Montenegro had served as the uncontested moral leader of the Serb world. Although the emergence of Serbia in the nineteenth century meant he had a rival for Serb affections, he still clung to his hopes.

Failing the realization of these imperial dreams, Nicholas would have settled for more moderate territorial expansion in line with the territorial limits of the Black Mountain's historical antecedents. His four principal goals were Dubrovnik (medieval Ragusa), Mostar (the capital of Hercegovina), Prizren (the medieval Serb capital), and Scutari. Until the nineteenth century, all of these towns seemed to be fair game. But in 1814–1815 Austria came into the possession of Dubrovnik, and in 1878 she occupied Bosnia and Hercegovina. Cut off by the Habsburgs in the west, Montenegro's prince shifted his eyes quickly to the north, the east, and the south, where the Sick Man of Europe weakly tended what remained of his Balkan flock. Thus, Montenegro's hopes for future territorial expansion hinged largely on the opportunity of adding neighboring Turkish land not occupied by Austria-Hungary. Prizren was a distant goal, Scutari a more immediate one. Unfortunately for Montenegro, Austria and others had their own plans, which did not include Montenegrin expansion. This hostility notwithstanding, an aging Nicholas saw the prize he had long struggled for eluding him and he made desperate efforts to save his dream. These efforts augured ill for the peace of Europe.

Austro-Montenegrin Relations

In the nineteenth and early twentieth centuries, Austria generally obstructed Montenegrin expansion against the Turks; that had not always been the case. Indeed, the dominant feature of early Austro-Montenegrin relations was a common struggle against the Porte.[16] In the course of the seventeenth and eighteenth centuries, Austria, eager to roll back the Turks' Islamic carpet, came to view Montenegro as a useful ally, though one conveniently and consistently forgotten when Turkish wars were over. In the late eighteenth and early nineteenth centuries, the two countries usually found themselves on the same side against French imperialism. In 1805, France occupied the city-state of Dubrovnik and the province of Kotor, which boasted one of the finest natural harbors on the Adriatic. But Napoleon's plans to create a new Slav Illyria disintegrated along with his empire. When French troops withdrew from Kotor, Montenegrin soldiers quickly moved in. Although the Montenegrins claimed Kotor for their new capital, the Concert of Europe decided that Austria should have the strategic bay, and Montenegro, destined to be landlocked for another sixty-five years, had to surrender her treasured coastal tenancy. The loss of Kotor worsened relations between Vienna and Cetinje for years to come, and their common border became a source of diplomatic disputes and the site of occasional skirmishes.[17]

Relations improved in 1848–1849, when Vladika Peter II Njegoš supported the Habsburg emperor in his struggle against Hungarian rebels. For the next few years, Vienna dealt kindly with the Black Mountain, in 1852 sanctioning its secularization, and shortly afterwards intervening in Constantinople to halt a Turkish assault on the country. During the Crimean War, Montenegro's new ruler, Prince Danilo, tried to steer a neutral course, which drove many of his Russophile subjects to revolt and ultimately earned him little Habsburg gratitude. At the Paris peace conference, Austria pursued a singularly self-interested policy, which ignored Danilo and his petitions for territorial adjustments. Vienna also coerced Russia into disclaiming any special interests or rights in Montenegro such as those she had enjoyed in the Danubian principalities. This development caused the Turks to reassert their own claims to sovereignty over Cetinje—claims that were vigorously rejected by Danilo.[18] For the next twenty years, Austria generally stood on the sidelines, as a resurgent France under Napoleon III and a discontented Russia under Alexander II competed for Montenegro's favor, aiding her diplomatically in two short wars against Turkey in 1858 and 1862.

The Balkan crisis of 1876 brought Austria back to the forefront of Montenegrin affairs. On 2 July Montenegro, animated by a revolt against Ottoman rule in neighboring Hercegovina, declared war on the Porte and won several quick victories. When

Russia entered the war, Montenegro's future seemed secure. Indeed, the Treaty of San Stefano negotiated in March 1878, recognized Montenegrin independence while trebling her size, doubling her population, and giving her a considerable stretch of Adriatic littoral. Unfortunately for Cetinje, the Great Powers of Europe overturned the treaty at the Congress of Berlin in June and July, rewriting the peace with Turkey. Austria-Hungary could not deny Montenegro everything that she had been awarded by the first agreement, but she made a concerted effort to reduce Montenegro's gains. As a result, while the new Treaty of Berlin confirmed Montenegro's independence, it only provided for a two-fold increase in territory and reduced her coastal frontage. Even to keep the port of Bar, the Montenegrins had to meet onerous Austrian demands incorporated in Article 29: to neutralize the harbor, to limit the types of vessels anchored there, to forswear the construction of any warships, and to permit Vienna to police their waters. They also had to ask for Austria's permission to build roads and railroads in their new territory. To make matters worse, Habsburg troops occupied neighboring Hercegovina, long an object of Montenegrin irredentism, and acquired the important heights of Spič, which overlooked Bar and thus put the town at a decisive military disadvantage.[19]

Montenegro came into the possession of the port of Ulcinj and additional Adriatic footage a few years later, but Vienna's repeated interference in Balkan affairs rankled in Cetinje. Yet despite this resentment, Austria-Hungary was destined to dominate the economic life of the principality through her geographic position and more advanced economy. Naturally, many officials at the Ballhausplatz hoped that this important economic lever would lead to political hegemony.

Austria-Hungary was Montenegro's chief trading partner, importing raw materials such as timber and minerals, while exporting raw materials for Montenegro's infant industries and much-needed manufactured goods. Austrian towns in Dalmatia, especially Kotor and Budva, were the principal markets for Montenegro's cattle industry, though frequent tariff disputes gave rise to extensive smuggling along the border.

Austria came to play an important role in Montenegro's transportation system as well. The Bohemian firm of Laurin and Klement, subsidized by the Austrian and Montenegrin governments, ran a mail and passenger bus service from Kotor to Cetinje, and thence to Rijeka Crnojevića and Podgorica. Lloyd steamers plied the Bojana River, linking Lake Scutari with the Adriatic, while other Lloyd ships and those of the Ungaro-Croata line called at Bar several times weekly. Austrian engineers and money built roads in Montenegro, but the Montenegrins instinctively mistrusted Vienna's technical and financial generosity. When the Austrians constructed an impressive serpentine road winding from Kotor to the Montenegrin border, the Montenegrins hesitated to complete it. Similarly, in 1908, even when relations between the two countries were unusually warm, Cetinje still declined an Austrian request to build a railroad along the Montenegrin coast.[20]

The border disputes that marred Austro-Montenegrin relations before 1878 continued after the Congress of Berlin. One bone of contention was Mount Dvrsnik in the Grahovo-Krivošije district. A British minister wrote that it was Nicholas's policy "always to keep 'the pot simmering' on the Austrian and Turkish frontier of his Dominions."[21] This was generally true but Vienna also desired certain frontier rectifications in her own favor. Just as Austria possessed the high ground overlooking Bar, so Montenegro controlled the strategic heights overlooking Kotor. If she could not hope to obtain all of Mount Lovćen, Montenegro's most sacred summit, Austria hoped at least to gain possession of the Krstac ridge, which rose some one thousand meters above Kotor.

Thus, in the years following the Berlin Congress, Austro-Montenegrin relations were generally cool, though usually correct. Nicholas travelled to Vienna in 1908 to express his high regard for Francis Joseph, but numerous political, economic, and territorial problems continued to divide the two governments. The principal stumbling block was, as always, Montenegro's desire to expand, and Austria's opposition to it. Austria remained firm in her attempt to insulate her South Slav population from Serbian or Montenegrin influence, hoping to prevent Cetinje or Belgrade from becoming alternative centers of loyalty for her subjects. Moreover, Montenegro's expansionist inclinations clashed with Austria's interest in extending her Balkan imperium, the ultimate goal of which was, for some, possession of the port of Salonica on the Aegean Sea.

When Vienna and St. Petersburg reached a Balkan détente in 1897, Nicholas realized that for a while he would have to tread softly in Balkan affairs. Still, he did not forget his own imperial and expansionist dreams and carefully bided his time.[22]

Russo-Montenegrin Relations

While Austria was considered the traditional foe of Serbo-Montenegrin aspirations, Russia was considered their traditional supporter. Indeed, for 200 years Russia had served as Montenegro's chief benefactress and ally.[23] During the eighteenth century, Russian rulers beginning with Peter the Great had bestowed financial awards upon Montenegro as an expression of their friendship and as payment for services rendered in support of Russia's numerous military ventures against the Turks. In the course of the century, Russian envoys visited Montenegro and invited her youth to take military training in Russia. The first "modern" history of Montenegro was published by Bishop Vasilije in Russia in 1754. The Russians appealed to the common racial and religious heritage of the two peoples and claimed that the war against the Turks was a crusade to rescue the Orthodox Christians of the Balkans from the Muslim yoke. The Montenegrins responded enthusiastically to these overtures. The nature of the relationship was such that for more than six years during the reign of Vladika Sava (1735–1781), a monk named Stephen Mali claiming to be Peter III, the murdered husband of Catherine the Great, successfully established himself as the effective if not the titular ruler of Montenegro. The fact that he claimed to be a Romanov was good enough for most people. As Mary Edith Durham wrote, "Russia was a name to conjure with."[24]

Despite her financial and moral solicitude, Russia's political and diplomatic support, like Austria's, was largely a function of self-interest. When it suited St. Petersburg to ignore Cetinje, she did so without any qualms. Montenegro was not mentioned in the peace treaties ending Russo-Turkish wars in 1711 (Pruth) and 1739 (Belgrade) and was awarded nothing in 1774 (Kuchuk Kainardji) or 1792 (Iaşi). The famous bargain struck by Catherine II and Joseph II in 1781 for the partition of Turkey would have given the western half of the Balkan peninsula to Austria, had it succeeded. In the nineteenth century, Alexander I acquiesced in turning over to Austria the Bay of Kotor. And although he resumed the annual payments to Montenegro that his brother had cut off, Alexander's successor, Nicholas I, was sometimes more concerned with questions of "legitimacy" and the European status quo than in the plight of his coreligionists in the Balkans. At Reichstadt in 1876, the Russians once again demonstrated their willingness to yield considerable expanses of Balkan territory to the Habsburgs.

In the nineteenth century, "official" Russia's cautious approach to the Balkan question was vigorously opposed by the growing legions of Slavophiles and pan-Slavists.[25] Especially during the Eastern Crisis of 1875–1878, journalists, writers, politicians, and others called upon the government to pursue a more active foreign policy to enforce Russia's claim to be the "moral guardian" of the Orthodox and Slavic worlds. The disappointing results of the Congress of Berlin caused St. Petersburg to revert to a more conservative policy and Alexander II to rejoin the League of the Three Emperors. But this did not spell the end of Russian pan-Slavism, which continued to grow in strength. Advocates could be found at all levels of society and government, and a vital contingent made a home for itself in the Asiatic Office of the foreign ministry. In the years ahead, it promoted policies generally in tune with the national aspirations of Serbia, Bulgaria, and Montenegro.

When circumstances merited, the Montenegrins tried to hitch a ride on the pan-Slav chariot. In 1871, for example, Nicholas founded the pan-Slav *Crnogorac* (*The Montenegrin*), the country's first newspaper. Because of its anti-Austrian and anti-Turkish tenor and strident nationalistic propaganda calling for the unification of Serbdom, it was soon banned in the neighboring empires. About the time of the first Three Emperors' League, the nimble Nicholas changed his policies to conform to Russia's; in 1873, the *Crnogorac* was replaced by the milder *Glas Crnogorca* (*The Voice of the Montenegrin*), which remained the semi-official organ of the government until the First World War.[26] Nicholas's ability to change policies with chameleonlike efficiency was a hallmark of his rule as prince and later king. In 1897, when Austria and Russia reached their modus vivendi for the Balkans, Nicholas once again followed Russia's lead.

In the thirty years between the signing of the Berlin Treaty and the Bosnian annexation crisis, Montenegro's relations with Russia were generally good, and Nicholas took steps to keep them that way. Two of his daughters, "girls of Juno-like proportions,"[27] married Russian grand dukes and served as spokeswomen for Montenegrin interests in the Russian capital. Nicholas carefully followed political trends in St. Petersburg. His introduction of a constitution in 1905 was a partial echo of the tsar's decision to grant a duma. For her part, Russia did what she could to keep Montenegro solvent, and on several occasions actually saved the country from bankruptcy and starvation. St. Petersburg contributed large sums of money to Montenegrin royal and state coffers, and engaged in a series of projects designed to lift the country up by its boot straps. Russia subsidized not only the Montenegrin army, but also Montenegrin schools, including a famous girls' school founded by the Empress Marie Alexandrovna. Russians also served as nurses in a largely Russian-financed hospital. In the words of a British diplomat, the Petrović-Romanov tie was of a "particularly close and intimate character."[28]

On balance, then, Russia was Montenegro's truest and most generous supporter in the eighteenth and nineteenth centuries. Alexander III once asserted that Nicholas was his only friend, and the Montenegrins reciprocated this affection by shouting their famous slogan: "We and the Russians—100,000,000 strong!"

But familiarity can be said to breed contempt, and Nicholas, while grateful for Russia's invaluable aid, occasionally felt smothered by Mother Russia's close attentions. Although he had to expect that Russian interference would attend Russian gifts, the prince periodically rebelled at his situation and feigned a "haughty independence toward Russia." The Austrians were the natural beneficiaries of the prince's discontent. When the Russian guardian angel exacted too much in the way of good behavior, Nicholas would duly flirt with the Austrian devil. The Russians, in turn, would move quickly to shepherd "back into the fold the erring and half-starving Montenegrin lamb."[29] It was a game played year after year.

Thus, Montenegro's economic underdevelopment was one of the chief features of her foreign policy and her relations with Austria-Hungary and Russia. The financial appetite of the diminutive state seemed insatiable, due partly to the country's inherent poverty and partly to mismanagement of the treasury, extravagance, and occasional fraud. But if Austria and Russia were the principal targets of Montenegro's financial appeals, other Great Powers were also invited to bail out the principality and participate in its economic development.

Montenegro's Relations with the Other Powers and Serbia

Italy, for one, played an important role in the economic life of Montenegro.[30] In centuries past, the commercial and cultural influence of Venice had made itself felt in Montenegro as it had all along the Adriatic coast. The first printing press in the Slavic world, established in 1493 at Obod, outside Cetinje, had been imported from Venice, and the descendants of the last Crnojević ruler of Montenegro had found the floating city an ideal place to retire. Montenegro's English name is a Venetian variant of the Italian "Monte nero."

After Italy's unification in the nineteenth century, many Italian nationalists, styling themselves the heirs to the faded Venetian empire, campaigned to turn the Adriatic into an Italian lake. Naturally, Montenegro caught their eye, and the Montenegrins, spying a potential new source of revenue, returned the attention. Nicholas added a royal feather to his cap in 1896, when he married his daughter Jelena to the Prince of Naples, later King Victor Emmanuel III. The nuptial union brought Italy and Montenegro closer together and opened the door for large-scale Italian economic penetration of the Black Mountain. The Venetian Compagnia di Antivari soon established itself as an important economic institution in the country, contracting to build and run Montenegro's first railroad, a short forty-two-kilometer stretch between Bar and Virpazar; to operate passenger and postal steamers on Lake Scutari; and to begin the construction of modern port facilities at Bar.

Ships of the Puglia and Servizi Marittimi lines stopped at Bar and Ulcinj, while steamers of the former vied with Austria's Lloyd line along the silt-ridden Bojana River. The Società Commerciale d'Orientale, with shops at Bar and Podgorica, handled food, oil, candles, and soap. The Regia Co-interessata dei Tabacchi del Montenegro ran the country's tobacco monopoly. In 1904, Italians built Montenegro's first radio-telegraph station at Bar.

But despite these significant inroads, Italian entrepreneurs became increasingly frustrated by the backwardness of Montenegro and the provincialism of her officials. The Compagnia di Antivari's fervent hopes for a trans-Balkanic railroad that would use "its" port at Bar as a western terminus remained an idle fantasy.[31] Unable to reap the easy financial reward they had counted on, they were reluctant to pour additional capital into the country, but even their limited investment solidified Rome's political interest in Montenegro. If nothing else, the Italian presence served as a check to Austrian political and economic influence in the country and elsewhere in the Balkans.[32]

None of the other Great Powers had political or economic interests in Montenegro of the same magnitude as those of Austria, Russia, or Italy. Bismarckian Germany, for example, had once felt that the Balkans were not worth the bones of a Pomeranian grenadier. Wilhelmine Germany showed a greater appreciation of the peninsula's possibilities, and her interest in the Berlin-to-Baghdad railway scheme meant that she kept a closer eye on the Balkans than ever before. Even so, the route of that railroad did not cross Montenegro, and Germany was content to let her Austrian ally assume the leading role in relations with that country. Britain's commercial interests in Montenegro were microscopic, confined largely to the Anglo-Montenegrin Trading Company, Ltd., and its successor, the Podgorica-based firm of Hammer and Thomson, which dealt in hides. On the other hand, as an imperial power with world-wide concerns, Britain had more than a passing interest in Montenegro's fortunes. British diplomats proved to be among the most astute political observers in the country. France's diplomatic support for Montenegro had waned after Napoleon III, yet the French still had minor commercial interests in the principality and could not but sympathize with the mountaineers' struggle for economic and political freedom. After 1890, Paris generally took her cue from St. Petersburg in questions concerning Montenegro.[33]

Serbia was the Balkan country most important to Montenegro at the turn of the twentieth century.[34] For over five hundred years, the Montenegrins had embraced the Serbians as brothers, or at least as cousins—long-oppressed members of the same Orthodox Serb family, descendants of Stephen Dušan who had been separated by the Turkish sword. But centuries of separate development had fostered a rivalry and a consciousness of being different. The

Serbians were wont to look upon Montenegrins as boorish louts, uneducated and primitive, while the mountaineers frequently viewed their Serbian relatives as lowland farmers with little backbone for real fighting.

The emergence of autonomous Serbia in the nineteenth century was both a boon and a blow to Montenegro's aspirations. It gave the land of the Black Mountain an important ally in the struggle against the Turks, but also threatened its claim to be the sole heir to Serbia's medieval empire. In the race for leadership of the South Slav world, Serbia seemed to have the upper hand. Geography and economics were two principal factors. Montenegro was located on the periphery of the Balkans; Serbia lay in the very heartland of the peninsula. Moreover, Serbia was larger, richer, and more sophisticated, offering a stronger foundation for a Serb state. Belgrade was a town becoming a city and, in comparison to backward Cetinje, a fitting capital for a new Serb empire.

The feud between the rival houses of Karadjordjević and Obrenović for leadership of Serbia complicated the picture, yet gave Nicholas a degree of latitude he might not otherwise have had. The prince of Montenegro had little regard for Milan Obrenović and was outraged when this Serbian upstart assumed the rank of king in 1882. Three years later, Nicholas enjoyed a measure of revenge by marrying his daughter Zorka to Peter, the mild-mannered and intellectual Karadjordjević claimant to Milan's throne. For a while, the couple resided in Cetinje, where their son Alexander was born. Hedging his bets, however, Nicholas married his second son, Mirko, to Natalija Konstantinović, a relative of the Obrenovići.

While the notorious Milan lived a life of luxury in Vienna and other European capitals, Nicholas and Montenegro sought to assume the moral leadership of the Serb world. But whatever preeminence Nicholas may have achieved was short-lived, as were his dreams of installing himself or one of his sons as king of Serbia. The murders of King Alexander Obrenović and Queen Draga in 1903, and the selection of Peter Karadjordjević as the next occupant of Belgrade's blood-stained throne, virtually sealed the fate of Nicholas's royal aspirations as far as Serbia was concerned. The Montenegrin public greeted the news of Peter's succession with parades, singing, and the traditional firing of guns. But despite these manifestations of sympathy with the new regime and the attendance of Montenegro's Crown Prince Danilo at his brother-in-law's coronation, the "too-closely related dynasties soon began to quarrel."[35] Nicholas grew uneasy as Karadjordjević Serbia quickly replaced Montenegro as Russia's darling and chief agent in the Balkans. St. Petersburg, occupied in the Far East, kept her Balkan wards leashed, but even the tsar could not prevent them from eyeing one another suspiciously. Stormy events in Montenegro would soon destroy the uneasy truce between them.

Montenegrin Politics, 1905–1908

In 1905, Nicholas decided to introduce the trappings of a constitutional monarchy. His motives were mixed: to answer domestic criticism of his rule, to refurbish Montenegro's international image, and to ape the reluctant example of Tsar Nicholas II in granting a duma. If some of the prince's subjects welcomed the new constitution and national assembly, many others mistrusted his purposes, believing that the result would be a sham. They were largely correct. In the words of William Miller: "Parliamentary government did not prove a success. Montenegro in three years had four Cabinets; a group of socialists made its appearance; and the 'spoils system' was introduced."[36] One problem was the unenlightened electorate. In the first round of balloting for the new skupština, some districts actually voted for the prince and the tsar of Russia as delegates! A larger problem was Nicholas himself. After monopolizing power for almost fifty years, he was very reluctant to share it.

The prime minister of the first constitutional government was Nicholas's friend, Lazar Mijušković. Forced to resign in 1906 in the middle of Serbia's trade war (the so-called Pig War) with Austria, his relatively conservative cabinet was succeeded by a more radical one led by Belgrade-educated Marko Radulović. Opponents of the prince, colloquially termed *klubaši* (club members), banded together in the People's Party. Radulović fell early in January 1907, over a dispute with Nicholas concerning army reform. He was followed by Andrija Radović, once very close to Nicholas but who now led the opposition to the prince's policies. Radović's cabinet began inquiries into the administration of Montenegrin finances, an investigation that impugned the integrity of Nicholas and gave him second thoughts about the virtues of parliamentary democracy. As a result, Nicholas forced Radović's resignation and appointed his own government led by Lazar Tomanović, who set out to make the radicals pay for their sins. Many lost their offices, were arrested, or physically assailed, and in the next election, not a single one was returned to the assembly. Yet the tribulations of the *klubaši* were just beginning.

In November 1907, it was announced that a plot had been uncovered to assassinate the prince and overthrow his regime. The radicals were naturally accused of formulating the plan. Radović was convicted of conspiracy and sentenced to long years of imprisonment, but the Cetinje Bomb Affair did not end there. Because many *klubaši* had received their education in Belgrade and pursued Serbophile policies, and because the would-be assassins' bombs uncovered in Cetinje had come originally from the Serbian government's arsenal at Kragujevac, Nicholas accused Belgrade of having a hand in the plot. Serbia closed its legation in Cetinje and relations were broken off, while Russia tried unsuccessfully to mediate the dispute. In short order, Serbia's stock and that of Russia plummeted in Cetinje, at least in official circles. The Dual Monarchy, which had been observing developments from the sidelines, took advantage of the situation to step forward as the prince's champion. For a while, Vienna's tarnished reputation received a much-needed refurbishing. But in the topsy-turvy world of Balkan politics, this state of affairs was bound to be short-lived.

Origins of the Annexation Crisis

Montenegro was only one of many concerns facing Baron Alois Lexa von Aehrenthal when he became Austrian foreign minister in 1906. No matter how interested he might be in maintaining close relations with Cetinje, his first responsibility was to the Habsburg empire as a whole. Aehrenthal, an energetic and aggressive man eager to place his personal stamp on Austria's foreign policy, wished to restore the prestige of the Dual Monarchy, which of late had acquired the nickname as well as many of the attributes of the "new Sick Man of Europe." Thus, Aehrenthal reacted strongly when Austria's Balkan interests were menaced by the Young Turk revolution of July 1908, a revolution which threatened to undo the thirty years of "temporary" Habsburg administration in Bosnia and Hercegovina granted by the Congress of Berlin. To thwart a possible Turkish attempt to reclaim sovereign rights in these provinces as well as to enhance Austria's influence in the Balkans, Aehrenthal acted to obtain for Vienna formal title to Bosnia and Hercegovina. As a gesture toward the Ottomans and the other Great Powers, however, he announced his willingness to end the three-decade Austro-Hungarian occupation of Turkey's Sandžak of Novi Pazar, the narrow corridor of land that separated Serbia and Montenegro.

In plotting a master stroke in the Balkans, Aehrenthal found a willing accomplice in Russia's foreign minister. Like Aehrenthal, Alexander Petrovich Izvolsky wanted to refurbish his country's image and erase the humiliation of the Russo-Japanese War. Each man had something the other desired. Thus in the wake of the Turkish revolution, they concluded an agreement at Buchlau, Moravia, on 15 September, in which the Austrian agreed to support the opening of the Straits to Russian warships in exchange for the Russian's support in annexing Bosnia and Hercegovina. From all that ensued, it would seem that Izvolsky was unclear about the timetable for acting publicly on the "Buchlau Bargain." While Izvolsky leisurely toured Europe, Aehrenthal moved quickly to realize his part of the bargain. When informed of the Austrian's peremptory action, Izvolsky exploded in anger and called for an international conference to overturn it. The proposal gained much support as a means of resolving the unfolding crisis and figured prominently in Montenegro's subsequent plans for territorial aggrandizement, although in the end the conference never materialized.[37]

The annexation of Bosnia and Hercegovina, like many other questions affecting Austro-Montenegrin relations, impinged on Austria's own troubled domestic situation. In particular, the South Slavs, the majority of whom resided in the kingdom of Hungary, were disgruntled with their political powerlessness within the Habsburg system and wanted a greater voice in the conduct of their affairs, preferably within the Dual Monarchy.[38] Increasingly, however, Habsburg South Slavs, now including those of Bosnia and Hercegovina, looked beyond the empire's frontiers for counsel and support. As much by accident as by design, Serbia assumed the role of a potential South Slav Piedmont in the jaundiced eyes of Vienna's policymakers, but Montenegro, too, still commanded the affection and respect of some of the Dual Monarchy's South Slav population.

Aehrenthal proposed to minimize Serbian and Montenegrin influence and maintain "the centre of gravity for the Serbo-Croat peoples within the Monarchy."[39] Precisely how he could effect the annexation without incurring the wrath of Serbia and Montenegro, much less win their open approval, was not clear. But he was determined to proceed with his plan in spite of their feelings, indeed perhaps to spite them by flaunting the empire's power and prestige.

Aehrenthal's scheme flew directly in the face of Prince Nicholas's grand designs. The Montenegrin ruler had long looked upon Hercegovina as Montenegrin *terra irredenta*. According to tradition, his family had emigrated from Hercegovina in the fifteenth century, and Nicholas, despite Austria-Hungary's administration of the province for three decades, still hoped to include his ancestors' homeland in a greater Montenegrin state. Aehrenthal's proposed annexation would preclude realization of this dream. The average Montenegrin shared his sovereign's attachment to the neighboring province and felt a common bond dating back centuries. Montenegrins and Hercegovinians spoke the same dialect of the same language, for the most part worshipped in the same Orthodox church, shared a long and glorious history of fighting the Turk, and crossed relatively freely into each other's territory. Clearly, Aehrenthal could anticipate vigorous and possibly violent Montenegrin opposition should be complete the annexation. Thus matters stood in October 1908.

CHAPTER TWO
The Annexation Crisis, I: 1908

On 6 October 1908, Emperor Francis Joseph formally annexed the provinces of Bosnia and Hercegovina. The action shook all of Europe, especially Russia and her sometime Balkan wards, Serbia and Montenegro. Relations between Cetinje and Vienna soon approached the breaking point. For a long while, it appeared that only an appeal to arms could resolve the annexation crisis.

Montenegro's Initial Response

The unenviable task of informing Prince Nicholas of Vienna's intentions toward Bosnia and Hercegovina fell to the Austro-Hungarian minister in Cetinje, Baron Franz Kuhn von Kuhnenfeld. Unknown to him at the time, the prince had already learned of the impending annexation through Russian sources, and he expected the announcement.[1] Nicholas initially responded to Kuhn's formal communication in surprisingly mild language. He informed the Austrian minister that he was disappointed with the Monarchy's decision but suggested, no doubt to Kuhn's amazement, that the annexation did not have to affect their countries' good relations, particularly if Austria could provide for Montenegro's interests. In short, Nicholas was willing to trade acceptance of the Monarchy's action in return for territory—in this case, part of Hercegovina long "steeped in Montenegrin blood."

Disabusing Nicholas of such fantasies, Kuhn, on Aehrenthal's instructions, offered a counterproposal: if Montenegro maintained a "correct attitude" in the days ahead, the Austrian government

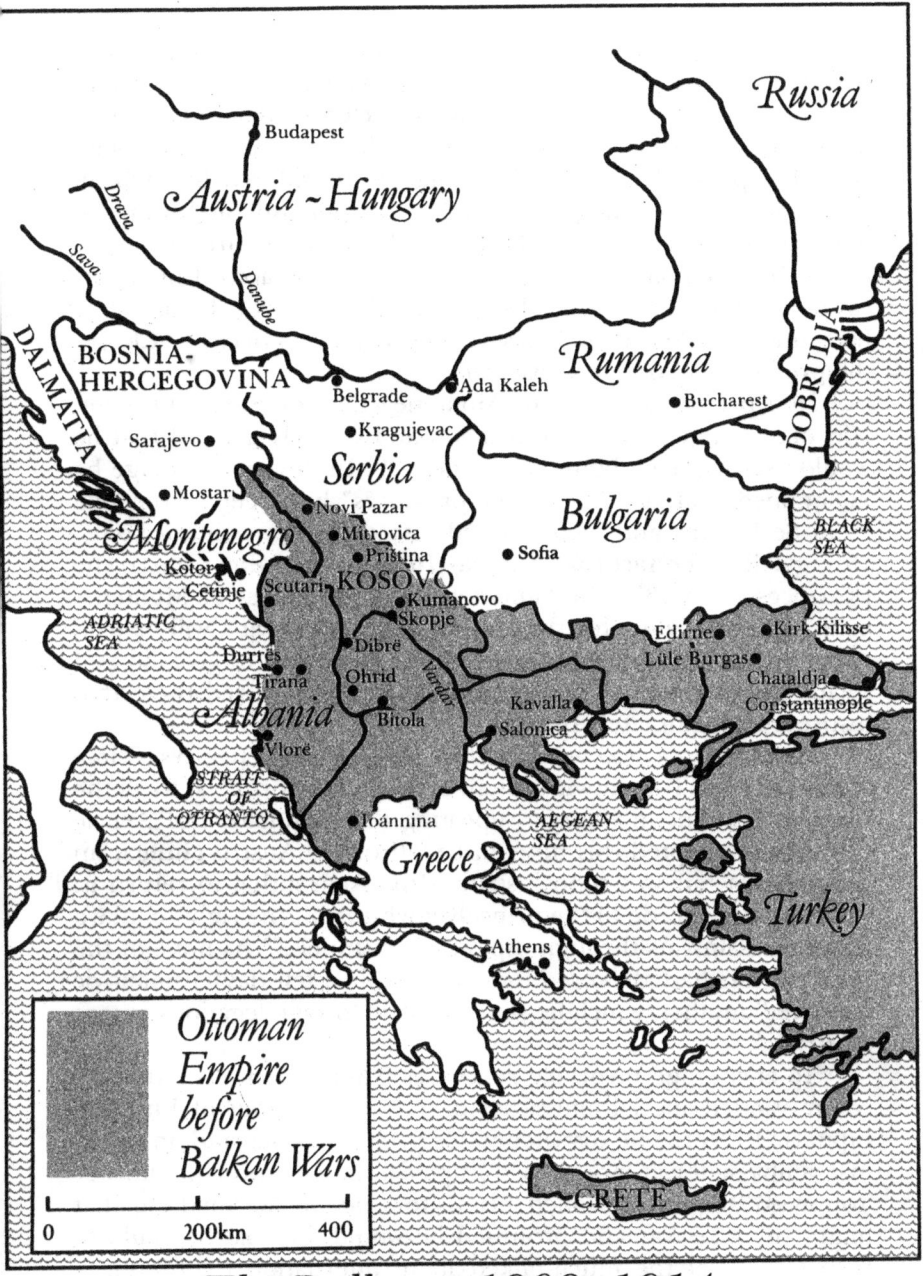

The Balkans, 1908–1914

would be prepared to modify Article 29 of the Treaty of Berlin, which limited Montenegrin sovereignty on her Adriatic littoral and gave Austria-Hungary extensive rights, including that of patrolling Montenegrin waters. Such an offering, however, did not mollify Nicholas, particularly when land that he considered his rightful patrimony was at stake. He lashed out indignantly at Kuhn, denouncing the annexation and claiming that it was in direct violation of the Berlin treaty. If Austria could violate the accord in such a cavalier fashion, so could Montenegro. Henceforth, he asserted, his country would exercise full sovereignty on her own coast.[2] Clearly, the preliminary sparring was over.

In a proclamation to the Montenegrin people on 7 October, Nicholas denounced the annexation and publicly avowed that he would no longer be bound by Article 29. In flowery language he maintained that the "two sister provinces" had been "wrenched from Serb arms and incorporated into a foreign political body." Disregarding the fact that Austria-Hungary had administered the provinces since 1878, he lamented that "the graves of Montenegrins who had fallen for the freedom of Hercegovina will be trod upon by foreign feet." He called upon his subjects to give aid and solace to Serbdom in "this painful hour" and assured them that justice would ultimately prevail.[3]

While the prince aroused his people, Montenegro's Prime Minister Lazar Tomanović sent an official note of protest to all the foreign legations in Cetinje, repeating the repudiation of Article 29.[4] Kuhn accepted this note on behalf of the Austro-Hungarian government but was soon instructed by Aehrenthal to return it: "We cannot concede to the princely government the right to take a position against us through diplomatic channels."[5] As none of the other Powers had answered the note, within a few days Tomanović prepared another, which he sent to all the foreign legations except Austria's.[6]

To encourage favorable responses from the Powers, Nicholas commissioned special emissaries to make the rounds of Europe's capitals. To Rome he dispatched his prime minister and an informal ambassador-at-large, Jovo Popović. Italian foreign minister Tommaso Tittoni cautioned his visitors not to do anything that might provoke war and promised he would do what he could to help Cetinje at the much-talked-about international conference, which Izvolsky hoped would overturn the annexation.[7] Leaving Tomanović behind, Popović then travelled to Paris, where he found the French press stridently on Montenegro's side. Foreign Minister Stéphen Pichon, on the other hand, was more circumspect, expressing sympathy but not offering immediate support.[8] A projected journey to London was obviated by a telegram from Sir Edward Grey to Nicholas, advising him that the British government had no intention of recognizing the annexation. Nicholas took this to mean that Grey was prepared to support Montenegrin claims. To St. Petersburg, the prince sent Lazar Mijušković, the former prime minister, who was also tapped to serve as an observer attached to the Russian delegation at the proposed conference. On 24 October, he handed a beleaguered Izvolsky a list of Montenegrin demands, which included autonomy for Bosnia and Hercegovina or their return to full Turkish sovereignty; the abrogation of Article 29; small territorial cessions, including the district of Spič; and the establishment of free navigation on the Bojana River between Montenegro and Albania.[9]

Meanwhile, the people of Montenegro wasted little time in giving vent to their anger at the annexation, often with violence. Soon after the prince's proclamation, a demonstration occurred in Cetinje that lasted long into the night and continued the following day. Irate citizens, hurling insults, stones, and threats of destruction, marched on the Austro-Hungarian legation. Although police intervention limited the damage to a few broken windows,[10] Baron Kuhn immediately lodged a protest with the Montenegrin government. As a matter of course, the latter tendered its formal regrets and pledged additional security for the legation complex.[11] Promises of such security could hardly mollify the Austrians, however, as they knew the Montenegrin police were in complete sympathy with the populace.

Unsettled by his firsthand experience in the capital and by reports of even more frenzied demonstrations in other parts of the country, the Austrian minister charged Nicholas with deliberate refusal to keep order. The prince made the usual rejoinder that the disturbances were an inevitable consequence of Austria's folly. Kuhn warned that if Nicholas was determined to maintain such an "unhelpful" attitude, Austro-Hungarian arms would be prepared for any eventuality.[12]

In Podgorica, crowds besieged the residence of the Austro-Hungarian commercial agent. When prevented by police from doing serious damage, the protestors moved to another part of town, where they promised support for official Montenegrin policy, whatever it might be, and pledged solidarity with their brothers in Bosnia and Hercegovina.[13] Similar meetings took place in Rijeka Crnojevića, Zeta, Ulcinj, and other towns.[14] In Cetinje, not to be outdone by male incendiaries, Nicholas's youngest daughters, the intrepid princesses Ksenija and Vjera, led a group composed largely of women carrying banners and singing national songs.[15]

By far the most violent demonstration took place in Bar, where a large number of Hercegovinians working on Montenegro's much-prized port and railroad projects eagerly joined and soon assumed leadership of local protests. On 10 October, they informed Habsburg officials that they would not permit Austrian officers travelling on Austrian ships to disembark in the port. Their protests soon assumed a more turbulent character when approximately two hundred workers, accompanied by units of the army and the police, attacked the Austro-Hungarian consulate, tearing down its coat of arms and ripping up its flag. To satisfy Austrian protests, the head of the Bar police, Djuro Ivović was dismissed, only to be promptly installed as the new chief of police in the town of Nikšić.[16]

The site of the largest Hercegovinian emigrant settlement in Montenegro, Nikšić was a hotbed of anti-Austrian sentiment. On 12 October, a popular Hercegovinian refugee, Stojan Kovačević, harangued a crowd of 7,000, inspiring a resolution that exprobrated the "inhuman and barbarous act of the Austro-Hungarian Monarchy," and called on "all Serbs . . . to extend a fraternal hand to their brothers" in their hour of travail. The resolution ended with the familiar slogan "liberty or death." The Montenegrin skupština promptly lauded Kovačević for his aid in preparing the citizens of Nikšić for the struggle ahead. Subsequently, he addressed crowds in other Montenegrin towns, including Cetinje and Podgorica, thereby contributing to popular agitation and indignation.[17]

Popular opposition to the annexation was not confined to the Montenegrin heartland. Demonstrations took place all along the Turco-Montenegrin frontier and in Ottoman territory. In Berane, Pavle Čubrović, armed with instructions from the Montenegrin foreign ministry, headed a meeting attended by the chiefs of the

Vasojević clan, who lived across the frontier. Participants at this conclave selected a central committee, composed of both Serbs and Turks, to direct their anticipated fight against the Austrian army. The Vasojevići, formally Ottoman subjects, joined in condemning the annexation.[18] At Sjenica in the Sandžak of Novi Pazar, another meeting was attended by representatives from the principal Slav towns in the Sandžak—Pljevlja, Prijepolje, Novi Pazar, Berane, Rožaje, Bijelo Polje, and Nova Varoš. The crowd clamored for war with the Monarchy, calling on their Ottoman suzerain to supply them with 30,000 rifles and ammunition. Not all the residents of the Sandžak, however, were as excited about the prospects for an Austrian withdrawal, much less about joining Serbia or Montenegro in a war against Vienna. A large segment of the Muslim population, especially adherents of the "Old Turk" regime, feared that the two Serb states were plotting to divide the Sandžak between them, which in fact proved to be the case.[19]

In Vienna, Austrian officials took pains to prevent similar demonstrations and meetings from taking place among their own Serb population, especially in the newly annexed provinces. Hoping to keep domestic peace by stifling hostile opinion, Habsburg authorities banned the major Montenegrin newspapers, the *Cetinjski Vjesnik* and *Glas Crnogorca,* from Austro-Hungarian territory. This did not daunt the enterprising Montenegrins, who continued distributing their papers under different banners.[20] In Hercegovina, Montenegrins engaged in activities far more dangerous than the dissemination of unfriendly propaganda; they actually prepared for war, encouraging and arming Hercegovinian guerrillas.[21]

Shortly after the first round of speeches and rallies, the merchants of Montenegro joined the popular protest. The first salvo in an economic war between the empire and the principality was fired in November, when the princely government imposed maximum tariffs on the goods of all nations that had not concluded a commercial treaty with Montenegro, a step aimed solely at Austria-Hungary. The empire retaliated by imposing maximum tariffs of its own on all Montenegrin imports. In December, Montenegrin merchants, guided by Nicholas's policies, intensified the conflict by organizing a boycott of Austrian products, which inflicted far more suffering and hardship on themselves and their countrymen than on Austria.[22]

Efforts at Negotiation

Despite his outrage, Prince Nicholas still preferred negotiation to war. As prince, he had to sustain some of the aspirations and demands of his people; he could not openly traffic with the enemy, and thus he had to denounce Aehrenthal publicly. Yet in the earliest moments of the October crisis, while the populace clamored for war and his army prepared for it, Nicholas demonstrated a willingness to negotiate, to compromise, even to recognize the annexation, provided he received something in return: namely, the extension of Montenegrin territory and Austrian renunciation of the rights conferred on her by Article 29 of the Treaty of Berlin.

The prince tried to work his way into Kuhn's good graces. He explained that a threat of resignation by his ministers had forced him to send the official Montenegrin protest note to the Great-Power legations and insisted that he had wanted to tone down its language.[23] Kuhn accepted the prince's excuse at face value, recalling that Nicholas had once called Austrian rule in Bosnia and Hercegovina better than any alternative. Such a man, he told Aehrenthal, was "no fanatic."[24]

Nicholas again broached the question of adjustments along the Montenegrin-Hercegovinian frontier and even asked Aehrenthal's permission to travel to Budapest to discuss the situation personally, representing this proposal as a final effort at compromise, his own contribution toward stopping a sequence of events that he might not be able to control later on.[25] Aehrenthal responded promptly. In a telegram dated 10 October, he discussed the prickly issue of popular agitation in Montenegro, ignoring completely the request for frontier adjustments and mentioning only in passing his continued willingness to discuss an alteration of Article 29. But in order to ensure peace with Montenegro, he was prepared to resort to an old Balkan device: bribery. If Nicholas, who had repeatedly complained of the "inadequacy of the means at his disposal" to influence his subjects, now promised to cooperate, he would have 500,000 crowns placed at his "free disposition."[26]

A wary Kuhn was reluctant to endorse his chief's scheme. From all the information at hand, he surmised that Nicholas would much prefer tangible territorial gains to cash, which he could not show his people.[27] In any case, the question of a monetary gift soon became moot. On 11 October, only one day after Aehrenthal informed Kuhn of the plan, the *Neue Freie Presse* published a mysterious telegram datelined Dubrovnik, which charged that the Austro-Hungarian government had succeeded in buying the prince's consent to the annexation.[28] Nicholas immediately disavowed the allegations and took decisive steps to demonstrate his innocence and patriotism, by ordering a partial mobilization and, in traditional Montenegrin style, by calling on nationals living abroad to return home to defend their fatherland. In private, he told Kuhn that the newspaper's intolerable insinuations, not to mention reports of Austro-Hungarian military activity along the Montenegrin border, had compelled him to take such serious steps. He reiterated his hopes of reaching an accommodation with Vienna and, as a show of good faith, promised to keep Kuhn informed of Montenegrin military preparations.[29]

Aehrenthal was not satisfied by such hedging and warned Nicholas to change his attitude or "we would be forced to consider only our interests and implement our hegemony."[30] These were harsh words, even for Aehrenthal, but he did not hesitate to repeat this policy in Rome and St. Petersburg.[31] Yet while threatening the prince, he simultaneously hinted at economic advantages that might accrue to Cetinje if Nicholas followed Vienna's lead. Recalling the Bomb Affair of 1907, which had done so much to improve Austro-Montenegrin relations, he also played on the prince's fear of internal conspiracy, offering to help contain Montenegrin "subversive elements," which he asserted would be in their "common and monarchial interest." Finally, he appealed to Nicholas's vanity, announcing that he was prepared to confer an Austro-Hungarian regiment on the Montenegrin court, and to arrange a long-awaited reception in Vienna "which would be a natural consequence of this imperial honor."[32] This last gambit promised to have special appeal since Nicholas had demanded an audience with Francis Joseph shortly after the annexation and was ordinarily ready to depart for Vienna on any pretext.

Unfortunately, the timing of Aehrenthal's new overture was wrong. Imperial honors would have been as awkward for Nicholas to accept as the contemplated bribe. The *Neue Freie Presse* article had impugned the prince's patriotism and partially paralyzed his free hand in making policy. The warlike attitude of most of his subjects forced him willy-nilly to assume a more aggressive air. He told Kuhn that while he still hoped for an international conference that would realize his desire for territorial compensation, he would have to "remain true to his honor and the history of his people."[33]

Rapprochement with Serbia

Although Nicholas continued to hope for a satisfactory accommodation with Austria, he realized that the chances of failure were great. Desiring to prepare for all contingencies, he cast his eye about for friends and allies who might assist him should he be forced to take a stand against her. Thus, while petitioning the Ballhausplatz for territorial compensation and assuring Kuhn of his own peaceful intentions, he responded favorably when approached by Serbia with a suggestion for an alliance between the two Serb states.

Relations between Serbia and Montenegro had been strained ever since the Bomb Affair, but common anxiety over the new crisis forced the two governments to make peace. King Peter of Serbia was reluctant to make up with his Montenegrin father-in-law, but he bowed to the will of Foreign Minister Milan Milovanović.[34] In writing Cetinje that Serbia and Montenegro should act "in common, shoulder to shoulder, like true sons of the same family," Milovanović proposed, among other things, that the two countries work for the autonomy of Bosnia-Hercegovina, the partition of the Sandžak between them, and the abrogation of Article 29.[35] On 8 October, he dispatched Jovan Jovanović to Cetinje as a special emissary of the Serbian government, thus setting in motion the wheels of rapprochement.[36]

Only one day after promising to keep Kuhn informed of Montenegrin military preparations, Nicholas sent General Janko Vukotić, his wife's cousin, to Belgrade with suggestions for a Serbo-Montenegrin alliance. As it happened, the general and his entourage, travelling via Rijeka and Zagreb, were halted at the Zagreb railroad station, where Austrian police charged that two of his group were known agitators.[37] The general flaunted a letter of introduction from Kuhn himself but to no avail; the entire party was detained. A surreptitious search of Vukotić's baggage produced a letter apparently concerning Serbo-Montenegrin relations. When the news reached Vienna, the fiery chief of the Austro-

Hungarian general staff, Franz von Conrad von Hötzendorf, sensed clear evidence of espionage and wanted to back the Zagreb police.[38] Aehrenthal, however, saw in the episode only outrageous interference with his office. He had already been told of Vukotić's trip by Nicholas, although he did not know its purpose, and he forced Conrad to back down. Within hours, Vukotić was released and resumed his journey to Belgrade, where he was warmly received on 20 October.[39] Aehrenthal hastened to apologize for the misunderstanding, but the damage had already been done.[40]

In Belgrade, Vukotić and Serbian negotiators established the framework of an offensive-defensive alliance, according to which the two Serb countries promised to coordinate all diplomatic and military ventures that might be necessitated by the annexation crisis. If Austria-Hungary attacked either Montenegro or Serbia, the other was bound to take up arms, even after the expiration of a proposed period for joint offensive action. Among other things, the agreement provided for a division of the recently annexed provinces into Serbian and Montenegrin spheres of influence and theaters of military operations, Serbia assuming responsibility for Bosnia, Montenegro for Hercegovina. The alliance, signed on 24 October, was viewed by the two governments as possibly just the first leg in a triangular military convention including Turkey.[41]

The extent to which Serbia and Montenegro relished the idea of making common cause with the Porte is a matter of some conjecture. Naturally the two Serb states had reservations about doing business with Constantinople, but the situation seemed to warrant extraordinary action. It certainly was worth their while to attempt to come to an agreement with the Ottomans before Berlin and Vienna could induce them to accept the annexation. The initial contact with the Turks was fruitful, and by the end of October a draft convention had been drawn up. But a final accord proved impossible to reach. The Montenegrins did their part to woo the Turks, but ultimately the three countries could not even agree on a general statement of friendship. In the end, Turkey made peace with Austria instead of with her Slav neighbors.[42]

The Serbo-Montenegrin alliance, on the other hand, had an auspicious beginning. At a farewell dinner in his honor, Vukotić toasted the Serbian king and the "essential unity and concord" between Belgrade and Cetinje.[43] Echoing the Montenegrin's sentiments, King Peter saluted the "strong, brotherly bond" that united the two Serb families: "Your mission means that the Prince of Montenegro has recognized his duty. I ask you to assure him that I, too, and my Serbs recognize and assume our duty, and that between the brother-states complete agreement exists regarding the defense of Serb interests."[44] These were heady remarks for two countries that had just been at each other's throat.

The mission of Janko Vukotić was the first tangible representation of the Serbo-Montenegrin détente brought on almost wholly by Austria's action in Bosnia and Hercegovina. For the time being, Serbia and Montenegro terminated their feud and joined hands. The cynical Habsburg ambassador in Belgrade saw in Serbia's acceptance of Vukotić's proposals at least a partial capitulation to the scheming Montenegrin prince, "who was so hated and maligned only months ago." Count Johann Forgách predicted that Nicholas would exploit the alliance to the hilt and then leave poor King Peter holding the bag. Far from being a magnanimous act of forgiveness, Serbia's reconciliation with Montenegro was for him merely "another mistake of foolish Serbian policy." Of course his major complaint was that a Serbo-Montenegrin understanding had been reached at all, and that it might complicate Aehrenthal's efforts to bring the annexation crisis to a speedy termination.[45]

His mission a success, Vukotić departed Belgrade on 26 October. Instead of retracing his steps across Habsburg territory, however, he took the back way home—the long, dusty route through the heart of Serbia and the Sandžak of Novi Pazar. After his unhappy experience in Zagreb, Vukotić was heard to say that in the future he would cross Austrian territory only with sword in hand.[46] The agreement he brought home pleased his sovereign; Nicholas now had an insurance policy he could rely on should he be forced to oppose the Habsburg eagle.

Spič

Like an old bulldog chewing on a favorite bone, Nicholas would not completely give up his notion of extracting some sort of territorial concession from Austria. Ignoring the moral restrictions imposed by his new Serbian alliance and his earlier claims for adjustments along the Hercegovinian frontier, he informed

Aehrenthal in mid-November that his primary objective was now the district of Spič, strategically situated on the Adriatic coast at the southernmost tip of Austria's long and narrow Dalmatian appendage.[47] What made Spič especially alluring to Montenegro was the fact that it overlooked Bar, her principal port, and gave the Austrians an ideal roost for observing and, if necessary, for shelling the most important Montenegrin property on the Adriatic. Moreover, it provided anchorage for the Austro-Hungarian warships that patrolled Montenegrin waters under Article 29 and periodically intimidated the local population.[48]

In arguing for the acquisition of Spič, Nicholas recalled the declarations made by the Austro-Hungarians at the Congress of Berlin to the effect that the Monarchy needed the district to supervise the Montenegrin littoral. The prince cleverly pointed out that since the Dual Monarchy had already agreed in principle to relinquish rights of surveillance along the Montenegrin coast, the original and presumably the only valid reason for holding onto Spič fell by the wayside.[49]

Nicholas pursued his goal while ignoring Aehrenthal's and Kuhn's warnings that to do so was a waste of time. He approached Kuhn from all angles, suggesting first that the cession of Spič would actually be in keeping with Austria-Hungary's commitment to renounce Article 29. Secondly, he stated that relinquishing Spič would assure Vienna of Montenegro's support and free the principality to attend to her peaceful development, which included discussing Aehrenthal's plans for a customs union. He argued that Russia would be satisfied with this solution and Serbia would have to be. Nicholas's third tack was to suggest that if Aehrenthal did not give in now, the prince would wait for the still-discussed international conference to force Vienna's hand. He was convinced that the Entente Powers would support his claims. Finally, he even shook his tiny saber at Aehrenthal, threatening a "blood-letting."[50]

Hitherto inflexible and unresponsive to Nicholas's pleas for territorial compensation, Aehrenthal now queried Kuhn "whether such a territorial gain would, as Nicholas asserts, contribute measurably to the improvement of conditions for the development of Montenegro." The foreign minister also contemplated the intense pleasure he would derive from separating Montenegro from Serbia and thereby throwing all Serbdom into utter disarray. Yet despite these temptations, he was reluctant to commit himself in haste. He thus instructed Kuhn to "impress upon [Nicholas] that every territorial cession on our part—that of Spič or any other area—seems to be unconditionally excluded." The key to Aehrenthal's flexibility was his unprecedented use of the word *seems*.

True to form, he still demanded an immediate change in Montenegro's attitude as a precondition for a "friendly discussion" concerning not only Spič, but also the customs union Nicholas had alluded to earlier. For Austria, a customs union, preferably one along the old Obrenović lines with Serbia, would enable her to exercise more political and economic influence in Cetinje and facilitate the exploitation of the principality's natural resources to their mutual profit. It would also help counter Italy's economic influence. Aehrenthal liked to believe that Nicholas shared his view that "Montenegro can grow only with [Austrian] help."[51]

Aehrenthal's attitude held out the hope of détente with Montenegro, but Nicholas inadvertently nipped the possibility in the bud. As if decreed by the Balkan fates, even before Kuhn could convey his chief's message, Nicholas sent a *pro memoria* to the foreign legations in Cetinje, demanding the "retrocession" of Spič as well as the formal abrogation of all restrictions imposed on Montenegro by Article 29.[52] As he had with an earlier Montenegrin note, Aehrenthal instructed Kuhn to return the offensive *pro memoria* to the prime minister.[53] Tomanović tried to justify his government's actions by explaining that the Montenegrin people were impatient for war, that the demand for Spič was made in order to placate the warhawks, and that without Spič Montenegro was not lord of Bar. To the last assertion, Kuhn replied that Aehrenthal could demand with the same logic that Montenegro cede Lovćen, the mountain that overlooked Austrian Kotor.[54] Indeed, in the future Vienna would do just that.

One month later, Austria was still the only Power to have reacted to Nicholas's *pro memoria*. Despite the fact that the prospects for an international conference were growing dimmer, the prince stuck to his guns regarding Spič.[55] In the middle of December, the Montenegrin skupština sent telegrams to the Italian chamber of deputies and the Russian duma, outlining Montenegro's demands and asking for their countries' help.[56] Then on Christmas Day Nicholas approached the representatives of Italy, Russia, Great Britain, and France, reiterating his demand for Spič.[57]

The prince's Christmas adventure aroused Aehrenthal's curiosity about the attitude of the other four Powers.[58] The British position was the most vexing for the Ballhausplatz and potentially the one fraught with the most unhappy possibilities for Austria's Balkan policy. The British had been among the first to denounce the annexation and had long since encouraged Nicholas's dreams of an international conference that would punish the Habsburgs and reward the Petrovići. The foreign office also had a sympathetic ear for Nicholas's demands for territorial compensation. As one offical wrote, "We have for some time realized how much depends on Spizza [Spič]. . . . The Prince is not unreasonable . . . in asking for Spizza if he undertakes to keep the peace."[59] William O'Reilly, the British chargé d'affaires in Cetinje, agreed, replying that "the one claim put forward as irreducible [namely Spič] seems to be intrinsically a reasonable one."[60]

Of course, the Austrian and German ministers in the Montenegrin capital tried to convince O'Reilly otherwise, insisting that Nicholas was bluffing when he threatened war over Spič. They pointed to the apparent "absurdity of treating the matter of a village and a few hundred acres of ground as a vital question." O'Reilly, however, disagreed: "This country can lose little in a war which it is not likely to lose in any case." He viewed Montenegro's preoccupation with Spič as part of larger concerns—the fate of Bosnia and Hercegovina, the prospects for another Habsburg push toward the south, and the continued existence of the Montenegrin state. To conciliate the prince and his unhappy people, O'Reilly even suggested helping Montenegro obtain the Sandžak of Novi Pazar.[61] Despite his sympathetic interventionism and Sir Edward Grey's apparent endorsement of Montenegrin claims on Spič, the foreign office preferred not to get involved. Grey urged the prince to follow a peaceful course and put his hopes for territorial advantages in the hands of the conference of Powers.[62]

Italy's position provided Aehrenthal with additional solace. Baron Nicola Squitti, the Italian minister in Cetinje, told Kuhn that his government had not replied to either of Nicholas's notes and that Rome "was not inclined to involve itself in a matter which did not concern it directly."[63] Remarkably, even the Russian chargé informed Kuhn that St. Petersburg had not responded to either of the prince's communications.[64] Even so, Montenegro's claims to

Spič lingered on until they were finally stifled by the ultimate resolution of the annexation crisis. Increasingly, the Great Powers sought to extricate themselves and Europe from the international imbroglio as expeditiously as possible. They would not be deterred by a little country's wish for a minute parcel of land.

Military Preparations and Demands

From the outset of the crisis, war had presented itself as a possible sequel to the Habsburg emperor's proclamation of annexation. Austro-Hungarian and Montenegrin troops primed for action along their common frontier. Each side called its own military measures precautionary and defensive and termed the other's provocative.[65] The Montenegrin government wasted little time in preparing for war. Within a week of the annexation, General Mitar Martinović, the war minister, gave confidential orders to have food rations distributed to his troops and to provide each man with at least 220 rounds of ammunition for each rifle. He also activated the Montenegrin Red Cross under the presidency of the metropolitan, Mitrofan Ban.[66] In short order, the Montenegrins sent artillery pieces to the three mountain linchpins of their proposed defense: Mount Lovćen (overlooking Kotor and protecting the most direct approach from Austrian Dalmatia to Cetinje), Grahovo (whose fortifications along the Hercegovinian frontier had only just been completed), and Sutorman (overlooking the port of Bar, where the Montenegrins expected Austria-Hungary to land troops in the event of war).[67] Austria, for her part, strengthened border garrisons and sent gun transports to the frontier, but Aehrenthal refused to allow any additional preparations.[68]

In the wake of the *Neue Freie Presse* article, the Habsburg foreign minister and the Montenegrin prince took an increasingly hard line toward each other. Aehrenthal tried to bully Nicholas into submission. Although reluctant to apply direct military pressure, he demanded an immediate change of heart on Nicholas's part and an apology for past transgressions. Like a riled hedgehog, Nicholas bristled at each Austrian demand and dared Aehrenthal to cross the invisible line between an uncertain peace and certain war.

Austria-Hungary's military response was a point of serious contention between Aehrenthal and Conrad von Hötzendorf. A firm believer in the virtue and utility of the Habsburg military cudgel, the chief of staff feared that if Austria-Hungary failed to exercise her power while she had it, she would inevitably pay a high price for her timidity. In the case at hand, failing approval of an all-out attack on Serbia and Montenegro, he had wanted the annexation to be accompanied by a show of military force sufficient to dissuade the two Serb states from trying to resist the *fait accompli*. Aehrenthal rejected Conrad's demands for strengthening Austro-Hungarian military forces in the Balkans at this time.

Despite the foreign minister's hopes for a speedy denouement, it soon became obvious that Vienna would have to take some military measures, if only for self-defense. Conrad continued to warn Aehrenthal of the dangers inherent in ignoring Serbia's troop levies and Montenegro's recently announced mobilization, especially with the troop strength of Habsburg forces in the provinces along the frontiers of the Balkan States still at peacetime levels.[69] If Aehrenthal did not trust all of Conrad's admonitions, he at least recognized the danger of being caught off guard. On 17 October, while Vukotić was en route to Belgrade, he advised St. Petersburg and Rome of his new, hard diplomatic line.[70] The following day Conrad was given tentative authority to order a partial mobilization, which would send fifteen additional battalions and one naval squadron to the Balkan theater.[71] Unsatisfied, Conrad appealed once more to Aehrenthal, noting that Montenegro's war preparations were much farther along than Austria's. All men capable of fighting had been issued weapons, and heavy guns had been placed opposite Austrian positions. It was hard for him to believe that all these preparations were just for show.[72]

While restraining Conrad, Aehrenthal himself sponsored a dubious diplomatic foray into European Turkey, a move that complemented his stricter approach toward Montenegro. In a secret communication dated 21 October, he made preliminary arrangements to engage Albanian tribesmen, hereditary enemies of Montenegro, on the side of Austria-Hungary in the event of "Montenegrin aggression" against the Monarchy. According to the plan, in the event of trouble the Austrian consul general in Salonica was to distribute arms, munitions, and money to agents from Scutari, the principal city of northern Albania, who would in turn give them to Albanian warriors on the Montenegrin frontier. Aehrenthal was willing to work with either the Catholic or Muslim Albanians, whichever group could be won over more easily.[73]

Such a precautionary step was not enough to satisfy Conrad's obsession with security. He asked Aehrenthal whether his inadequate preparations meant he had received from Nicholas a secret pledge renouncing war against Austria. Aehrenthal replied in the negative. He was simply playing his own professional hunches. "I believe," he explained to Conrad, "that under present conditions [Nicholas] is acting to maintain his standing in the eyes of Serbdom. On the other hand, I believe that there is too much at stake—and too little to be won—for him to risk engaging us in open hostilities."[74] Thus, he again turned down Conrad's demands for definite military action, afraid that even a partial mobilization might force the prince to resort to even more extreme measures. Archduke Francis Ferdinand forcefully seconded Aehrenthal's repudiation of Conrad, informing the foreign minister that Conrad's lust for war had to be suppressed and war itself avoided at all cost.[75]

The deteriorating situation soon necessitated a change of policy. In the wake of the Serbo-Montenegrin rapprochement, Aehrenthal conceded the necessity of making certain adjustments in Austro-Hungarian forces in the Balkans. These consisted largely of a partial implementation of Conrad's so-called "Brown Mobilization," which called for raising the complement of the 15th Army Corps headquartered in Sarajevo and rotating several army battalions to southern Dalmatia.[76] In defending his new tack, Aehrenthal pointed out that increased guerrilla activity in Bosnia and Hercegovina justified calling up more troops.[77] Despite the open sympathy of a large portion of Austria's newly annexed border population with the raiding parties, he reasoned that he was "obligated to give our frontier population every measure of protection to which their belonging to the Monarchy entitles them." He told his diplomats, and through them the governments to which they were accredited, that Austria-Hungary's military activities should not be misconstrued as a partial mobilization or a deliberate concentration of military forces along the Serbian and Montenegrin borders.[78]

As early as 22 October, Conrad had set out his war plans for the following spring. In his "Foundations for Concrete Preparations for War for the Year 1909," he treated Montenegro with the respect due a worthy foe. He realized that it would be an arduous task to dislodge the Montenegrins from their age-old mountain redoubts and feared that intrepid Montenegrin troops could wreak havoc on Habsburg possessions in southern Dalmatia, especially Dubrovnik and Kotor.[79] To keep Montenegrin forces at bay, he contemplated employing five and a half divisions, or 68,000 men, roughly one-fourth the entire population of the mountain principality.[80]

By the end of 1908, it appeared that if Conrad had not won his tug of war with Aehrenthal, then at least his counsel was being taken more seriously in Vienna. Josef Redlich, parliamentarian and historian, recorded that all parties were against Aehrenthal.[81] Ominously, the chief of staff made preparations for hostilities to begin as early as 1 March 1909.[82] The new year boded ill for peace.

CHAPTER THREE
The Annexation Crisis, II: 1909

While Field Marshal Conrad honed his saber, Aehrenthal continued to seek a peaceful solution to the problem he had created for himself and Europe. As he confided to Josef Redlich, the situation was so bad that he had decided to come to terms with the Ottoman Empire.[1] By New Year's Day 1909, negotiations with the Porte were well under way.

The protests of Serbia and Montenegro notwithstanding, Turkey was the party most injured, at least in juridical terms, by the Habsburg annexation of the two former Ottoman provinces. The Young Turks, whose revolution a few months before had helped precipitate the annexation, were outraged by it. They mobilized troops and attempted a boycott of Austro-Hungarian goods. They even seriously contemplated a military alliance with their traditional enemies, Serbia and Montenegro. These efforts proved fruitless, however, and in the end the Young Turks were as amenable to German entreaties and Great-Power pressure as their "decadent" predecessors had been.[2]

On 12 January 1909, Kiamil Pasha, the Turkish grand vizier, and his cabinet approved an Austro-Hungarian program that satisfied Turkish interests and restored friendship with the Dual Monarchy. Under this accord Austria promised to compensate Turkey for the loss of Bosnia and Hercegovina in the amount of 2.5 million Turkish pounds and to renounce all rights of occupation in the Sandžak of Novi Pazar. On 26 February, the Young Turk regime signed a formal treaty agreeing to these terms, thereby accepting the annexation. Although the Porte delayed final ratification until 5 April, Aehrenthal had scored an important diplomatic triumph and had every reason to hope that Turkey's acceptance of the annexation would quickly bring other claimants to a peaceful settlement. Events, however, did not proceed quite that smoothly.[3]

As 1909 began, Austria-Hungary's relationship with her Slav neighbors worsened. Symptomatic of the deteriorating situation was a diplomatic confrontation between Aehrenthal and Milovan Milovanović, the Serbian foreign minister. On 2 January, the Ballhausplatz learned that in a fiery address to the Serbian skupština Milovanović had accused the Habsburg Monarchy of desiring "to enslave the people of the two Serb lands."[4] Though Milovanović tried to play down the use of the verb "to enslave,"[5] Aehrenthal demanded a formal apology, which he received.[6]

Emphasizing the dangers of the moment as well as revealing the serious rift between the Austrian foreign minister and the chief of staff, *Danzers Armee-Zeitung* published a sensational article that called for war with Austria's enemies. The military publication, which shared and reflected Conrad's warlike point of view, boldly stated that "the hour has struck. War is inevitable. Never was a war more just." Precisely which country Austria should take on first did not seem to matter much to the army paper, which believed that "we are being driven to war; Russia drives us, Italy drives us, Serbia and Montenegro drive us." The article finished with a rhetorical flourish that could only make Belgrade and Cetinje (not to mention other capitals) ponder Vienna's true intentions: "Our blood throbs in our veins; we strain at the leash. Sire, give us the signal!"[7] Only with difficulty did Aehrenthal succeed in keeping Conrad and his supporters in check.

Shortly after Milovanović's humiliation came the news of the Austro-Turkish protocol, a rude shock to both Belgrade and Cetinje. In Montenegro, British chargé William O'Reilly characterized the understanding as "the event of the past month."[8] Both Serbia and Montenegro felt betrayed by Turkey, whose sympathy they had courted and whose support they had counted on.[9] Prince Nicholas worried that Turkey's defection to the Austrian position would make it more difficult for Montenegro to win her case for compensation. He remained firmly convinced, however, that the proposed international conference, whenever it met, would overturn the Austro-Turkish agreement.[10]

Turkey's defection hardened Montenegro's resolve to act in concert with Serbia, and vice versa. On 22 January, Prime Minister Tomanović emphasized Montenegro's demands in common with

Serbia's before an angry session of the Montenegrin parliament.[11] On the twenty-ninth, the Serbian chargé d'affaires at Bar queried Nicholas about the possibility of a joint Serbo-Montenegrin memorandum stating their countries' minimum terms for a settlement of the crisis.[12] Despite these good intentions, events would soon force Serbia to act independently of her Montenegrin ally.

Serbia's Capitulation

At the end of January, four months ahead of schedule, the Serbian government issued orders for the callup of new recruits. Toward the end of February, policymakers in Vienna talked of Aehrenthal's "Kriegspolitik" and speculated on what would take place "after the war."[13] Redlich, who shared Conrad's preference for preventive military strikes, believed that the Habsburg Empire could not hold onto her Balkan dominions without "hitting Serbia on the head at least once."[14] For him, as for Conrad, the time for military action was ripe. That war would take place in the spring was taken almost for granted, and very few believed that a Balkan conflict could be localized.[15]

Sir Edward Grey aptly captured the gravity of the situation: "[it] is getting so ominous that in the interests of peace whatever settlement first appears practicable should be encouraged."[16] For the next three months, the Concert of Europe tried through diplomatic channels to find Grey's "practicable settlement." The Powers bickered and bartered among themselves. They debated issues of principle and morality, and just as often argued over questions of prestige, honor, and national interest, both in the Balkans and elsewhere. No country wished to lose face, but it remained to be seen if any was really prepared to resort to arms.[17]

One major obstacle to peace, as far as Austria was concerned, was Serbia's "irreducible" demand for territorial compensation. Aehrenthal consistently rejected any such claim, whether made by Montenegro or Serbia.[18] Unfortunately for his program of peace, the Russian foreign minister continued to lend support to Belgrade's—and by extension to Cetinje's—territorial aspirations. The Powers found themselves at an impasse. Then on 27 February, one day after the signing of the Austro-Turkish agreement, Izvolsky made what one historian has styled "the great surrender in the interest of peace."[19] Yielding reluctantly to Franco-German pressure, he informed Belgrade that "the Powers [were] not disposed to support the idea of a territorial aggrandisement of Serbia."[20] Aehrenthal informed the British ambassador in Vienna that the action taken by Russia was a step in the right direction.[21]

Serbia's response to Izvolsky's action was generally conciliatory. Milovanović did the bidding of his Russian mentor and dispensed with his demand for a slice of Bosnia. On the other hand, he continued to hedge on the issue of negotiating directly with Austria-Hungary, something Aehrenthal insisted on.[22] It was clear that Belgrade believed, or wanted to believe, that the Powers could still salvage something for it. Aehrenthal, however, considered Serbia "a purely private concern of Austria-Hungary."[23] He would be satisfied with nothing less than a Serbian declaration made without intermediary.[24]

The Powers kept Prince Nicholas informed of the steps being taken in Belgrade. On 3 March, for example, the Russian chargé d'affaires travelled to Rijeka Crnojevića to inform the prince of a second démarche presented by Izvolsky on 1 March, urging Serbia to take up negotiations directly with Vienna. Baron Squitti, the Italian minister, hoped that Nicholas would draw the correct conclusions from the new Russian policy and thus ease himself out of a difficult situation. He even advised the prince that he could in no way count on Italian support for his territorial aspirations. Nicholas petulantly responded: "We will march nevertheless!" Squitti countered that to do so would be folly.[25]

Despite his martial rhetoric, Nicholas invited Kuhn to his palace the very next day for talks, the first time in five months that the Austrian minister had been asked to the royal residence. The prince spoke in general terms at first but mentioned his long-standing hope for an eventual border rectification in Montenegro's favor. Kuhn discounted this stale suggestion, but the two nevertheless parted company on friendly terms. The minister wired the Ballhausplatz that his visit might be interpreted as the "beginning of sobering" on the prince's part.[26] Perhaps the time was right for a spring thaw in the frigid relations between their two countries.

Aehrenthal eagerly read the report of Kuhn's visit, which he hoped would be the first step in reaching an understanding with Montenegro independently of Serbia. He instructed Kuhn to see the prince again as soon as possible and remind him that the sooner Montenegro altered her attitude vis-à-vis the empire, the sooner Vienna would be prepared to consider the "desires and interests" of the principality.[27] This line of argument, of course, was anything but new; Kuhn had conveyed the same message to Nicholas on countless other occasions. Aehrenthal hoped, however, that circumstances had changed sufficiently for the prince to consider his words in a new light.

Meanwhile, the Montenegrin government brooded over the Russian démarche in Belgrade and decided to reply with a note of its own. Although annoyed that Serbia had answered Izvolsky without consulting Cetinje first, it deliberately patterned its note on the Serbian model,[28] with one important difference: Cetinje continued to deny the legality of the annexation and reserved "freedom of action" regarding any decisions of the Great Powers.[29] It was no secret that the ruling circle in Cetinje was disappointed in Serbia's decision to submit to Russian pressure and surrender all claims to territorial compensation.[30]

Montenegro's attitude left Kuhn little room to work with, especially as Nicholas had complained to Squitti that his subjects would not permit him to negotiate secretly with Austria.[31] Aehrenthal, however, urged Kuhn to press on. "The situation may be cleared up," he advised, "and in the event of a negative outcome, all of Europe will see that we are not to blame." He asked Rome and St. Petersburg to exert pressure on Cetinje as well as Belgrade in order to bring about a settlement.[32]

On the evening of 10 March, Kuhn met again with Nicholas. At first, the prince expressed the fatalistic view that it was too late to reach an agreement with Austria, but when Kuhn pointed out that the Austro-Turkish protocol, as well as the Great-Power proposals under consideration in Belgrade, presented Nicholas with an escape route, the prince demurred. Once again he stated he would leave all such matters in the hands of his precious conference. Significantly, he left the door open for the possibility of a bilateral agreement, but only if Aehrenthal was in a position to offer "a palpable, advantageous solution which would give him a bridge to return on." A dejected Kuhn concluded that the "palpable, advantageous solution" entailed the transfer of a piece of Habsburg territory.[33] Despite all that had happened in five months, Nicholas stood by his original demands.

The chances for an Austro-Montenegrin truce, however small, vanished overnight. Serbia was responsible. On 10 March, the same day that Kuhn and Nicholas talked about building bridges, she responded to Russia's second note with a partially conciliatory, partially provocative note of her own, which met with Aehrenthal's angry disapproval.[34] The proud Balkan land was still unwilling to prostrate itself completely before Austria. To force Belgrade's hand, Aehrenthal cautiously approved Conrad's demands for calling up additional troops and for transporting fifteen extra battalions to the Serbian frontier.[35]

The Austrian military build-up caused Nicholas to order countermeasures. In response to Austro-Hungarian naval maneuvers off the coast of Spič, he sent additional troops to Bar.[36] Aehrenthal, anxious to detach Montenegro from Serbia, assured Nicholas via Rome that the seventeen ships were only on regular maneuvers and although these had not been previously scheduled, they warranted no cause for alarm.[37] Rather than provoke Vienna unnecessarily, Nicholas accepted this explanation and cut the size of his intended mobilization at Bar from six battalions to one.[38] Still, the prospects for peace did not appear good. In Vienna, people spoke of war in the present tense.[39]

On 28 March, Austro-Hungarian authorities closed the border with Montenegro, except for the road leading from Kotor to Cetinje.[40] The following day, Vienna took one more step toward armed conflict, ordering "Yellow Mobilization." Also known as "Mobilization B" (for Balkans), this provided for the full utilization of five of the empire's fifteen army corps against both Serbia and Montenegro.[41] According to one historian, "Conrad left the Council with the conviction that now, at last, the reckoning with Serbia, which he had so often urged, was about to begin."[42] According to another, "only complete submission on the part of Serbia would avoid an appeal to arms."[43]

Great-Power diplomacy, however, thwarted Conrad's militaristic designs. At the eleventh hour, Germany submitted a clever but complicated formula that permitted the Powers to approve the annexation by exchanging telegrams rather than meeting in formal conference. This solution appealed to a majority of the Powers, who preferred to deal only with the question of Bosnia-Hercegovina and not with a host of other issues that a conference might raise.

Russia, on the other hand, stood to gain from a meeting of the Powers, and Izvolsky was understandably reluctant to commit himself to Germany's plan. German chancellor Bernhard von Bülow, therefore, resorted to a power play designed to force the Russian's hand; he demanded a simple yes or no answer.[44] Failing a satisfactory reply, the chancellor stated that "we should then draw back and let things take their own course."[45] To many observers and later historians, this meant war—a war Russia would be morally obliged to take part in but one for which she was singularly unprepared. Izvolsky also feared that Aehrenthal might embarrass his government by exposing his own dubious role in the "Buchlau Bargain" to the whole world, should he not cooperate. Faced with such dismal prospects, he had no choice but to confront Belgrade with the unhappy truth: Russia would not support Serbia in case of war. The disheartened Serbs had to take seriously the advice offered them by Alexander Guchkov, the Russian Octobrist leader: "Do not begin any war now, for this would be your suicide; conceal your purposes and make ready; the days of your joy will come."[46]

Abandoned by Russia and faced with occupation or worse at the hands of Austria, Serbia at last "yielded to the Concert of Europe which had become the agent of Austria's success."[47] On 31 March 1909, the Serbian government delivered a written declaration, the substance of which had been prepared by Aehrenthal and communicated to Belgrade by an approving British foreign office. Serbia accepted without reservation modification of Article 25 of the Treaty of Berlin (affecting the status of Bosnia and Hercegovina), which had been agreed upon by the Great Powers. Moreover, she pledged "to abandon the attitude of protest and opposition which she has maintained in regard to the annexation since last autumn" and "to live henceforward with [Austria-Hungary] on a footing of good neighborliness."[48] To the casual observer as well as many a veteran diplomat, the pledges to abandon her protest and be a good neighbor were merely two sides of the same coin. For Aehrenthal, however, the former implied more than a mere promise of friendly relations; it was a token admission of guilt on Serbia's part. He had long demanded just such a clause in Serbia's written declaration to him, and in the end he got what he wanted. He would demand a similar statement from Montenegro, but the result would be unexpectedly different.

Aehrenthal accepted Serbia's declaration "with satisfaction," and informed the European capitals that he considered the Serbian controversy to be at an end.[49] Needless to say, Conrad held another opinion.[50] A few weeks later, Austro-Hungarian and Serbian armies began to demobilize. Aehrenthal now turned his full attention to the matter of Montenegro, the last obstacle on his road to total victory.

Montenegro's Capitulation

News of Serbia's capitulation had a profound effect in Cetinje. Kuhn reported widespread disillusionment and uncertainty. Prince Nicholas made one last appeal to Sir Edward Grey, wiring him that Montenegro had decided to place her fate in his hands.[51] Grey, however, having done his duty with regard to Serbia, was more than content to let Italy bear the burden of dealing with Montenegro.[52]

As early as 25 March, the Italian foreign minister had worked out a scheme for bringing the recalcitrant principality to heel.[53] Tittoni's plan called for Austria to direct a note to Rome, which would then be transmitted to Cetinje for the consideration of the Montenegrin government. The essence of the proposal called for the abrogation of paragraphs 5, 7, 8, 9, and 10 of Article 29 and the alteration of paragraph 6 to read: "The port of Antivari [Bar] shall retain the character of a commercial port; no works can be erected there which will transform it into a military port."[54] This was precisely what Aehrenthal had offered at the outset of the crisis in October, although Nicholas still desired the abrogation of Article 29 *in toto*.

The Austrian foreign minister agreed to the project in principle but insisted on a note from the Montenegrins along the lines of the Serbian capitulation.[55] Moreover, he wanted it sent directly to his office rather than through Italian channels.[56] Tittoni agreed to use his influence and, if necessary, to send a special envoy to Cetinje to ensure that Nicholas "accepts what is offered him and keeps quiet."[57] This step was not needed; a warning in the form of an Italian démarche proved to be adequate. Tittoni actually encountered far more difficulty dealing with Vienna than with Cetinje.

On 2 April, Baron Squitti, seconded by the British representative, addressed Italy's démarche to the Montenegrin government. Tittoni requested that Montenegro relay the following message, or a similar note, to Rome for transmittal to Vienna:

> The government of the prince is ready to conform to such decisions as may be taken by the Great Powers in respect to Article 25 of the Treaty of Berlin; it will maintain henceforth relations of friendship and good neighborliness with the Imperial and Royal Government of Austria-Hungary.[58]

Tittoni neglected to ask Nicholas to respond directly through Austrian offices, an omission that irritated Aehrenthal. It made no real difference to the Italian foreign minister how the Montenegrin note was transmitted to Vienna, just as long as it was sent. But Aehrenthal insisted on the Montenegrin capitulation being made directly.[59] Tittoni gave in and agreed to advise Cetinje to adhere to Aehrenthal's prescription.[60]

Another problem was Aehrenthal's demand that Montenegro pledge to give up her hostile attitude toward the Habsburg Empire as a precondition for the abrogation of Article 29. Serbia had grudgingly agreed to such a stipulation, and Aehrenthal saw no reason why he should grant Nicholas special dispensation. He called the Montenegrin pledges "absolutely necessary" for a peaceful solution to the crisis.[61] On 2 April, he demanded that Tittoni amend the second clause of his model note to Cetinje to read:

> It [the Montenegrin government] undertakes from the present to abandon the attitude of protest and opposition which it has observed with respect to the annexation of Bosnia and Hercegovina since last autumn and in addition it undertakes to maintain henceforth relations of friendship and good neighborliness with the Imperial and Royal Government of Austria-Hungary.[62]

If Tittoni had followed Grey's scrupulous example in the case of Serbia, he would have transmitted the Austrian demands precisely as set forth by Aehrenthal. The Italian, however, had his own way of doing business. Having acceded to one of Aehrenthal's picayune demands, he was not going to submit to another. Thus, he omitted the seemingly *sine qua non* modification from the text of his initial note to Cetinje and refused to send it subsequently. The prince of Montenegro, of course, would not concede anything that was not demanded of him.

Squitti had expected Nicholas to come to terms in short order, but the Montenegrins would not be rushed. Three days after receiving Tittoni's note, they were still arguing among themselves over the wording of their reply and especially over the future status of the port of Bar, an issue central to the question of Montenegro's sovereignty over her own Adriatic littoral. Despite the delay, Squitti remained confident that Nicholas would bow to the dictates of reason and the ultimate threat of force.[63] Izvolsky, for his part, counselled Montenegro to keep the peace and not to ask for Spič or any other compensation. On 6 April, Montenegro, like Serbia before her, finally capitulated.[64]

Delicately circumventing a ticklish situation, Tomanović directed notes conforming to Tittoni's textual exemplar to both the Italian and Austrian representatives. In the note to Squitti, Nicholas and his cohorts also indicated their willingness to accept Bar's continued existence as a commercial, nonmilitary port.[65] The last holdout had thus submitted to the will of the Powers, and it appeared to all that Austrian diplomacy had won a great triumph.

Typically, Aehrenthal was not wholly satisfied with this denouement. He had desired to reproduce Serbia's capitulation exactly and was annoyed that Montenegro had somehow escaped the totality of her prescribed fate. Tittoni's handling of the negotiations, which Nicholas described as "the gentle art of mediation," had soured the sweet taste of victory for the Austrian.[66] Baron Kuhn suggested that he remind Nicholas that his acceptance of the revision of Article 25 implied the cessation of his hostile attitude toward Austria-Hungary.[67] But for all his obstinacy, the foreign minister realized he could not make any more demands on Montenegro or on the other Powers. Montenegro enjoyed a sympathetic world audience and to be uncompromising over such a triviality would have been "neither wise nor useful." Emperor Francis Joseph agreed completely.[68] Aehrenthal thus accepted the Montenegrin note as written.[69] He also masked his anger with Tittoni and extended his personal thanks to the Italian foreign minister for his part in bringing the annexation crisis to a relatively happy conclusion.[70]

On 8 April, Baron Kuhn formally conveyed Austria's acceptance of the Montenegrin note. He reported that as far as he could tell the resolution of the crisis was well received by the Montenegrin government and people. Both Nicholas and Tomanović expressed their hopes for a quick lifting of the border quarantine and a speedy normalization of trade. In a demonstration of his good faith, Nicholas ordered Montenegrin troops to pull back from the Austro-Montenegrin frontier and the Lovćen plateau. He then set out for a short respite at Rijeka Crnojevića.[71]

One week later, Nicholas received Kuhn and O'Reilly together at the palace. He told them that during the crisis he had been "disgusted with the policy of Russia," and while he would "preserve a grateful recollection of past benefits," he would never put his faith in Russia again. In deliberately exaggerated language, he asserted that "it was now evidently the fate of Montenegro to be the satellite of Austria-Hungary, and he was glad that the resumption of good relations now enables him to ask the Government of the Dual Monarchy for the assistance which the Principality required for its development." In return, Nicholas pledged his country's assistance against all foreign powers, save Russia, which, despite his harsh words, retained her special place in Montenegro's pantheon.

At the conclusion of this unusual session, Kuhn assured O'Reilly that the prince's words really had no special significance, that Nicholas had said no more on this occasion than he had any time prior to the annexation.[72] But therein lay their real importance: things were at long last back to normal. For all practical purposes, the crisis was over. Montenegro had submitted to the demands of the Powers and in return assumed almost complete sovereignty over her Adriatic coast for the very first time. Now, both sides began the semifiction of resuming normal if not cordial diplomatic relations. The truth was that Austria-Hungary trusted the little Balkan principality as much as Montenegro trusted her—not very much at all. As if to underscore this point, the most cynical of all Habsburg policymakers, Conrad von Hötzendorf, continued to generate his war plans, in which Montenegro figured prominently—never as a prospective ally, but always a future casualty of Habsburg arms.[73]

CHAPTER FOUR
From Kolašin to Jubilee: 1909–1910

Montenegro's diplomatic situation changed little between the spring and autumn of 1909. The tiny Balkan land still chafed at the treatment accorded it during the annexation crisis by Austria-Hungary and the other Great Powers, including its traditional Russian benefactor. For several months it also continued to extend an olive branch to Serbia in the wake of the two countries' cooperative efforts earlier in the year. Then in the fall of 1909, two domestic questions emerged that ultimately had international ramifications and abruptly altered the principality's relations with both Vienna and Belgrade.

The first involved a plot to overthrow Prince Nicholas and his government. Although this conspiracy, led by members of the liberal opposition, was swiftly suppressed, the resulting crisis assumed international proportions. Nicholas and many of his countrymen, recalling the Bomb Affair of 1907, saw Belgrade's hand in the plot. Mutual recriminations and invective soon flew between the two Serb states, and Serbo-Montenegrin relations, which had grown so close over the annexation issue, were strained to the breaking point.

In the second instance, Nicholas schemed to realize a life-long dream and in the process launched his small ship of state on a new mission in international waters. Ten years before, on the fortieth anniversary of his accession to the Montenegrin throne, he had assumed the style and title of "royal highness."[1] Late in 1909, with his fiftieth jubilee only months away, the dean of Balkan rulers longed for full royal honors that would make him the formal equal of his son-in-law, King Peter of Serbia. His aspirations reflected the interplay of an old man's vanity, jealousy of Peter, and fear for his dynasty and state. Nicholas thus set out to make himself a king and his country a kingdom. Austria-Hungary agreed to Nicholas's jubilee project and for a short while was acclaimed as Montenegro's friend.

The Kolašin Conspiracy

At the time of the annexation crisis, feuding Montenegrin factions had temporarily set aside their political differences in the face of what they believed to be Habsburg aggression. Those members of the liberal People's Party who had not been imprisoned during the Cetinje Bomb Affair in 1907 halted their attacks on the prince and temporarily supported his program to resist Austria. Unfortunately for these *klubaši*, Nicholas did not reciprocate their good will. The memories of the Bomb Affair were still too fresh, and Nicholas refused to moderate his autocratic rule in gratitude for loyalty in an hour of crisis. He continued his propaganda campaign against the *klubaši* and refused to grant amnesty to their leaders.[2]

Confronted with such obstinacy, the liberals decided to resume their struggle for a more democratic government rather than come to terms with the existing one. Protest soon turned into conspiracy. In Podgorica, a group of young revolutionaries quietly plotted to infiltrate regional governments throughout Montenegro; their aims were to foment open rebellion within a year, free their comrades in jail, and oust Nicholas. Leading the rebels was Major Nikola Mitrović, a postal official.[3]

Early in October 1909, one of Mitrović's subordinates, army lieutenant Petar Djinović, heard a rumor that the government had uncovered the conspiracy. Without consulting his fellow conspirators, he called his company together and marched on a munitions depot at Kolašin, hoping to raise the standard of revolt before Cetinje could act. In so doing, he brought on the catastrophe he was trying to forestall. Nicholas was soon informed of the uprising and ordered loyal troops to surround the depot. Prevented from reaching its goal, Djinović's company quickly scattered. The end was predictable. The conspiracy disintegrated; arrests and reprisals followed.

On 12 November, a little more than one month after the abortive uprising, a military tribunal rendered severe judgments: seven rebels were sentenced to death and thirty-three to varying terms of imprisonment. Those who counted on the prince's mercy were disappointed. Only a fortunate few were freed for lack of evidence.[4]

The Kolašin trial dealt a hard blow to Montenegrin liberals. The government had tightened its hold by acting quickly and uncompromisingly. Henry Beaumont, the new British minister in Cetinje, observed that "the affair seems to have been magnified by the government in order to eliminate certain undesirables."[5] Yet Count R. de Sercey, the French minister, reported that the trial had led to a degeneration of the domestic political situation. Not content with exercising a strangle hold on the People's Party, the government used terror against the populace at large. Sercey contended that no one even dared allude to the affair in public.[6]

The Kolašin conspiracy trial, like the Bomb Affair of 1907, did not remain an exclusively Montenegrin event but sent reverberations far beyond the tiny country's mountain recesses. Harsh sentences imposed on the generally pro-Serbian *klubaši* evoked a sharp reaction in Belgrade. Crowds demonstrated while Belgrade's *Dnevni List* lashed out at Nicholas and his "tyrannical regime." Montenegrin students in Belgrade reviled their prince even more viciously than they had two years earlier.[7]

The Montenegrin response to events in Serbia was equally swift and vituperative. Beaumont reported that "the half-dozen people who make up the official world" in Cetinje were angry that their Serbian counterparts had not suppressed the demonstrations. Indeed, many suspected the connivance of the Belgrade government. A series of articles in the Montenegrin press attacked Nikola Pašić, the Serbian prime minister. The *Cetinjski Vjesnik*, for example, accused him "not only of having countenanced the recent demonstrations—but of having constantly tolerated and even encouraged conspiracies against Prince Nicholas."[8] The Montenegrin papers charged the Serbian government with conducting anti-Montenegrin propaganda and denounced Belgrade-educated Montenegrin students and adherents of the People's Party as agents for Greater Serbia.[9]

While most members of the official Montenegrin community postulated that Serbia was behind the abortive conspiracy, many Serbs suspected that Austria-Hungary was the real villain. In fact, some were convinced that Nicholas had made an anti-Serbian pact with the Habsburg devil. Serbian nationalists as well as other Yugoslav political groups and journals wildly reported that the anti-Serbian rhetoric of the Montenegrin government was part of a deliberate Austrian policy to throttle the national strivings of Serbs, Croats, and other South Slav peoples.[10]

Cynical Serbs were not the only ones trying to find or concoct evidence of Austria's hidden hand in the events in Cetinje. In a letter to the French foreign minister, Sercey recounted Austria-Hungary's "well-known goals and methods" in the conduct of her Balkan policy—i.e., fostering quarrels and internal crises in the Balkan states. Precisely how Austria-Hungary was involved this time Sercey was not sure, but drawing on sensationalist accounts in the Viennese press, he suspected that the Ballhausplatz wanted to drive a wedge between members of the prince's family.[11]

The *Neue Freie Presse* had reported, in what Beaumont termed "exaggerated language," that the Kolašin conspirators had intended to replace Nicholas with his son Crown Prince Danilo.[12] To make matters worse, the Vienna daily also gave currency to subsequent rumors that Nicholas intended to disinherit Danilo in favor of his second son, Prince Mirko. These reports annoyed Nicholas to such an extent that steps were taken to have official retractions printed in both the *Neue Freie Presse* and Italy's *Tribuna*.[13]

If Aehrenthal was behind the ramblings of the Austrian press —and there is no evidence to suggest that he was—then the alleged plan to set Petrović against Petrović failed miserably. Nicholas told the British minister that he was irritated by the Austrian reports of dissension within his family. Moreover, he said he would never forgive the Habsburg Empire for the annexation of Bosnia and Hercegovina, or for the "inadequate" compensation awarded Montenegro. Yet, all these grievances notwithstanding, he trained his guns on Belgrade, not Vienna.[14]

At home, the Montenegrin sovereign pointedly snubbed Todor Petković, the Serbian representative at Cetinje. On the occasion of a visit by the French fleet to Bar at the end of 1909 (the first such visit since the lifting of Article 29's restrictions), Nicholas invited the French, Russian, and Bulgarian legations to send representatives to the welcoming festivities. Petković, however, had to stay behind. Sercey, who had wanted the fleet's visit to symbolize France's affection for all South Slavs, called Nicholas's stand "impolitic." Like Nikolai Diachenko, the Russian chargé d'affaires, he was disturbed by the acrimonious relations between their two would-be Balkan protégés. Both Sercey and Diachenko intervened several times in early January to urge "moderation and conciliation toward Serbia." They appeared to be making some headway in their efforts to cap the Montenegrin volcano when news of a new plot against Nicholas filtered into Cetinje.[15]

A confidant in the Serbian capital swore that two young men had told him they intended to assassinate Nicholas sometime in the spring; the prince sent agents to Belgrade to ferret information about the supposed conspiracy. These investigators concluded that Stojan Protić, the Serbian finance minister and Pašić's alter-ego, had masterminded the plot. Baron Wladimir Giesl von Gieslingen, Kuhn's replacement as Habsburg minister in Cetinje, reported that the Montenegrin ruling circle took for granted the Serbian king's knowledge of the scheme.[16]

Once again Petković was the target of Nicholas's wrath, and this time the prince ordered him to leave the country. Before the Serbian minister had started down the long, winding road to Kotor, however, the Russian government succeeded in restraining Nicholas. The prince relented and allowed Petković to remain in Cetinje—at least for the moment. As things turned out, when Petković did leave the Montenegrin capital months later, it was not under an order of expulsion.[17]

By February 1910, the anti-Serbian animus had reached a new crescendo in Cetinje. Articles and commentaries directed against the Serbian government filled columns long reserved for another adversary. Unwittingly assigning a peacekeeping rationale to Austria's long-standing policy of keeping the two Serb states apart, one member of the Montenegrin government confided to Giesl that "if we were neighbors with Serbia, we would have come to blows long ago."[18]

Austro-Montenegrin Détente

Many contemporaries as well as later scholars perceived in the Kolašin conspiracy and its aftermath an intricate piece of Habsburg handiwork. They believed that if Austria-Hungary had not engineered the Serbo-Montenegrin rift in the first place, she had certainly acted swiftly to exploit it. This interpretation has limited validity. For the most part, the Austrians were content to watch the internecine feud from afar, preferring to let the Montenegrins and the Serbians fight among themselves without being directly involved. Of course, Aehrenthal was not one to ignore an opportunity to gain political capital at no risk to himself. Hence, at the request of Prince Nicholas, he followed the French example in dispatching an Austro-Hungarian naval squadron on a goodwill mission to Montenegro.[19]

At 8 A.M. on 1 March, the Austrian naval force dropped anchor at Bar, signalling the start of a four-day festival. A delegation, limited to twenty-four by the sparse facilities of the only hotel in the capital, made its way to Cetinje where it was feted by a gregarious prince. Nicholas and the squadron commander exchanged warm toasts; Giesl reported a ridiculous remark made during the celebrations that if a plebescite had been held, two-thirds of Montenegro would have voted for Austria-Hungary.[20]

Although Nicholas played the good host and called for closer relations with Austria, especially through the signing of a commercial treaty, it was his son Prince Mirko who made the most concerted effort to cultivate better relations with Vienna. Having missed a dinner at the Austro-Hungarian legation in honor of the visiting naval officers, Mirko later called on Giesl, ostensibly to apologize for his absence but using the occasion to praise Austria-Hungary and to make a play for Giesl's trust. Although the annexation had "destroyed a dream," he began, Montenegro had come to terms with the *fait accompli*. As far as she was concerned, a chapter of history was closed and a new direction in foreign relations had to be followed, one dictated by certain geopolitical realities: namely, that "Russia is far away; Austria is close." Mirko unabashedly asserted his faith in Austria-Hungary's good intentions: "We cannot do without the close cooperation and friendship of Austria. We also know that your government is not hostile toward us." Ironically, these were sentiments that Aehrenthal had long communicated to his representatives in Cetinje for official Montenegrin consumption but that until now the Montenegrins had consistently ignored, sidestepped, or rejected.

It seemed clear that Montenegro, or at least Mirko, wanted something, a suspicion confirmed by the prince's pronouncement that Montenegro would greet any sign of Austrian friendship with "thankful joy." As soon as Austria-Hungary reciprocated Montenegro's trust, he promised to help pull down the guns positioned atop Mount Lovćen. Mirko's remarks revealed a connection between his wooing of Vienna and his father's ongoing feud with Belgrade. In part disclaiming his own Serb birthright, he drew a marked distinction between the Montenegrins and their erstwhile brothers-in-arms: "Montenegrins are not Serbians, neither cowards, nor traitors, nor regicides. . . . We do not want to have anything to do with Serbia." He even went so far as to reject his father's cherished dream of becoming king of Serbia.

Mirko's diplomatic thrust also clearly stemmed from worries within the Montenegrin court over daily reports of anti-Petrović activity in Belgrade; he carefully sought a measure of Austrian protection. He confided that the government had received news of a fresh attempt to be made on Nicholas's life in a few weeks. "There are only four of us," he observed, "with my son, five; a single bomb can kill us all." Assuring Giesl that his representations were made without the knowledge or permission of his father, he asked for Vienna's assistance in making sure that such a tragedy did not come to pass. As most conspirators and would-be assassins from Serbia would have to traverse Habsburg territory, he asked that Austro-Hungarian border officials and police be especially vigilant for the next few days.[21]

Unaccustomed to such mellifluous language from a Montenegrin, Giesl promptly submitted Mirko's request to Aehrenthal. Impressed by the prince's attitude, the foreign minister still advised Giesl to be skeptical of anything Mirko said.[22] In the end, nothing came of the feared assassination attempt.

One month later, in an after-dinner conversation at the Austro-Hungarian legation, Crown Prince Danilo, who like his brother was noted for periodic Austrophilia, spoke his mind on another topic. Danilo, who had once mentioned the possibility of celebrating his father's fiftieth jubilee by raising Montenegro to the rank of kingdom, now asked Giesl to write to Francis Ferdinand for the latter's personal approval of the project.[23] Although the crown prince must have known that a report of his conversation with Giesl would be duly transmitted to the Ballhausplatz, he explained that he did not want to bother Aehrenthal at this time because he considered the affair a private and familial matter. Similarly, he did not wish to write Francis Joseph because the aging emperor belonged to "an entirely different generation." "Write the heir to the throne," he requested, "that I swear he is the first and only person I have asked for counsel in this matter. For me there exists neither the tsar of Russia, nor the king of Italy, nor any other sovereign." Sounding like a Montenegrin version of Milan Obrenović, Danilo promised that should God will that Francis Ferdinand and he succeed to their respective thrones, he would always seek his Habsburg friend and mentor's advice on all political questions.

Giesl refrained from answering Danilo's request until he had consulted Aehrenthal, but he treated another question broached by Danilo with boldness. The crown prince mentioned that it was the wish of the princely family that an unspecified Austrian archduke might grace the jubilee planned for the fiftieth anniversary of Nicholas's reign. With an eye toward mending dynastic and diplomatic relations between the two countries, especially at no cost to Habsburg honor, Giesl reminded the prince that in the midst of the annexation crisis, Montenegro had ignored the sixty-year jubilee of the Habsburg emperor; before the present request could even be considered in Vienna, Montenegro would have to make good the slight. With a reference to Francis Joseph's eightieth birthday celebration in Ischl, Giesl hinted that it should prove an easy matter for the Montenegrins to find the "right form of redress."[24]

Danilo thanked Giesl for his remarks and apparently transmitted them to Nicholas. At his next meeting with the Austrian minister, Nicholas found an opportunity to mention the emperor's birthday: "Isn't it true that His Majesty's eightieth birthday will be celebrated on 18 August in Ischl?"[25] Within a few days, Aehrenthal let it be known that a proposal to elevate Monenegro to the rank of kingdom would be sympathetically received in Vienna.[26] Danilo expressed his appreciation for Aehrenthal's prompt, though formally unsolicited, approval, informing the foreign minister that no firm decision had yet been reached on the matter. Pretending that his father was not the project's ultimate architect, he added that the final decision would be made by the government and would reflect the will of the people.[27]

Aehrenthal delayed communicating Danilo's personal message to Francis Ferdinand for two or three weeks until the latter's return to Vienna. The archduke said he was touched by Danilo's affectionate words but avoided giving his personal opinion. He proffered instead his warmest regards and echoed Aehrenthal's earlier pledge that the Austro-Hungarian government would sympathetically entertain any measure taken "in the interest of the [Montenegrin] dynasty and state."[28]

Prince Nicholas himself subjected Giesl to yet another round of intensive pro-Austrian politicking, asserting that Montenegro "owe[d] so much to the [Habsburg] Monarchy, which was always our benefactor." Pandering to Aehrenthal's personal animosities as well as his professional pride, he berated Russian diplomats in general, Aehrenthal's arch-antagonist, Izvolsky, in particular. "A Russian diplomat will never be capable of cheating an Austrian," he averred. Indeed, the prince maintained that only one Russian, former foreign minister Nikolai Giers, had been sensible enough to advise him to stay on good terms with Austria-Hungary.[29] Nicholas had come full circle since the annexation crisis.

When the Austrian naval squadron visited Montenegro early in March, Prince Nicholas had emphasized his long-standing interest in concluding a commercial and maritime treaty with Austria-Hungary. In the spring of 1910, Aehrenthal consented to resume talks. After months of negotiation between Giesl and a trio of Montenegrin financial experts, a tentative agreement was eventually reached the following February.[30] Similarly, in mid-summer a joint commission met in an attempt to delimit the Austro-Montenegrin border between Grahovo and Krivošije, the site and source of much dispute since Austria's acquisition of the Kotor region in 1815.[31] Nicholas's new approach to Vienna seemed to be bearing fruit.

Austrian Skepticism

Whether Nicholas or Danilo was the driving force behind the movement to have Montenegro promoted to the rank of kingdom was not initially clear. At first, Giesl assumed that Danilo was trying to arrange a spectacular anniversary present for his father. But in patriarchal Montenegro, it was virtually inconceivable that the crown prince could have acted without his father's knowledge, permission, or direction. Officials at the Ballhausplatz wondered as well whether Danilo was telling the truth when he maintained that his country had first consulted Austria about the jubilee project. What in retrospect appears a singularly unimportant issue, at the time touched Austrian pride deeply and served to test whether Montenegro's words of affection carried the force of conviction.

When he first raised with Giesl the possibility of changing Montenegro's international status, Danilo had made it clear that he wanted to consult Archduke Francis Ferdinand before broaching the subject with any other European leader, including the tsar of Russia.[32] As early as 13 April, however, almost two weeks before the archduke's delayed response to Danilo's inquiry, Giesl had heard rumors that Nicholas had turned to St. Petersburg for approval.[33] On the nineteenth, Danilo denied these stories, swearing that Montenegro had not been in contact with the Russian emperor, through either official or family channels.[34]

Italy's relationship to the royal Montenegrin project was similarly clouded. On 18 April, Aehrenthal wrote Giesl that Duke Giuseppe Avarna di Gualtieri, the Italian ambassador, had informed him that Montenegro had raised the question in Rome, and that Marquis Antonio di San Giuliano, Tittoni's successor as foreign minister, had given his approval.[35] On the nineteenth, however, Danilo told Giesl a slightly different story, insisting that Italy had acted on her own initiative, and that San Giuliano had given his consent at the same time he had made his initial inquiry about the "Montenegrin rumors."[36]

Obviously at least two stories existed concerning both Russia and Italy. Giesl decided to take Danilo at his word, but Aehrenthal, more familiar with the wiles of Montenegrin princes, would not.[37] He warned his minister of the extravagant language Nicholas's sons often used: "I know he [Danilo] is often favorably disposed toward us and likes to show it. . . . I would not place in doubt the value of maintaining good and attentive relations with [him]. . . . My only intention is to facilitate the correct evaluation of [his] often exaggerated . . . assurances."[38]

It was Aehrenthal's opinion that Danilo's friendly words were meant to convey the impression that Montenegro had turned to Austria-Hungary alone, which she had not. Even before Danilo had consulted Giesl about the royal project, Aehrenthal discovered, Nicholas had confided in Baron Squitti. The Austrian foreign minister also guessed that Montenegro had consulted her traditional Russian ally, despite pledges to the contrary.[39] Aehrenthal's conclusions reflect the most probable chain of events.[40]

Whatever the case, Aehrenthal and Giesl could take a measure of satisfaction in knowing that they were not the last ones to be apprised of what was afoot. As early as 22 April, Giesl had reported Nicholas's definite intention to assume the royal title.[41] But it was not until the middle of May that the prince informed the British minister of his plans. Beaumont transmitted the prince's explanation to the foreign office: "In finally yielding to the wishes of his subjects, he was actuated by no personal ambition, but seeing that all the other Balkan States were governed by sovereigns of kingly rank, although their existence as independent States was shorter than that of Montenegro, he thought it fitting that the country over which he ruled, however small, should not be in an inferior position to Rumania, Serbia, and Bulgaria." As far as Beaumont was concerned, however, the principal motivating factor in Nicholas's decision to become king was the fact that his detested son-in-law, Peter of Serbia, already was one.[42]

The Proclamation of the Montenegrin Kingdom

Although there were other matters of importance before the Montenegrin government and Cetinje's tiny diplomatic community in the summer of 1910, Montenegrin officials and foreign diplomats spent an inordinate amount of time preparing for the principality's elevation to kingly status. Not all diplomats were keen on the anniversary project. The French chargé d'affaires disparaged the Montenegrins for the additional expenditures required to finance the festivities and the new royal court.[43] Yet no government, including the French, was willing to deny the prince his moment of glory and thereby deny itself an unusual opportunity to court his favor. Despite the academic debate between Aehrenthal and Giesl over Montenegrin favoritism and duplicity, all the Great Powers gave their consent to the Montenegrin project.

The ongoing Petrović-Karadjordjević dispute clouded the issue of Serbia's representation at the jubilee in Cetinje. The Montenegrins harbored mixed emotions about a possible visit by King Peter. On the one hand, they felt it was fitting and proper for Peter to pay homage to Nicholas, who was, after all, an old ally as well as his father-in-law. Yet they would have been hard pressed to welcome with open arms a man so recently vilified in the Montenegrin press and loathed in official circles. From Peter's standpoint, the problem was just the reverse. A visit to Nicholas, a man he disliked, might be misconstrued as a sign of weakness; he, the king of Serbia, would not go to a Montenegrin Canossa. By the same token, he could ill afford to slight Nicholas to his face. The problem generated lively speculation: would Peter visit Cetinje, and if so, under what conditions?

On 17 June, the British ambassador in Vienna relayed to London the contents of an article in the day's *Die Zeit*. The article reported that Peter would not be attending the jubilee celebration in Cetinje and noted a Montenegrin rejection of a demand purportedly made by Petković that all those sentenced in connection with the Kolašin conspiracy should be pardoned. Furthermore, it reported that the Montenegrins had threatened not to receive Pašić, the Serbian prime minister, if he were to accompany his sovereign to Cetinje. Pašić, in turn, was supposed to have threatened to resign should the king go without him. Peter's reported solution was to send Crown Prince Alexander in his place.[44]

Despite the story, the British minister in Cetinje insisted as late as 5 July that Peter's trip was still up in the air. While conceding that the article contained certain elements of truth, he denied the charge that Petković had *demanded* a full pardon for the Kolašin conspirators as a precondition for the Serbian king's visit. He did admit, however, that Petković was trying to arrange just such a pardon.[45] One day earlier, Sir James Whitehead, the British minister in Belgrade, had refuted another of the newspaper's claims, namely that Nicholas had threatened to refuse to receive Pašić: "Although Prince Nicholas has been guilty of many small breaches of international etiquette, he ha[s] not yet transgressed the rules as far as that."[46]

As it turned out, *Die Zeit*'s article of 17 June accurately predicted the course of events. At the end of July, Peter, citing reasons of poor health rather than political differences, declined the invitation to participate in the Cetinje celebration. At the same time it was announced that Crown Prince Alexander would represent his father. Peter sought to soften the blow by writing Nicholas a cordial note.[47]

On Sunday, 28 August, the Montenegrin skupština passed a resolution elevating the principality to the rank of kingdom and Nicholas to the rank of king. As he had indicated to Giesl in April, Nicholas affixed his signature to the legislative act. Thus, on the fiftieth anniversary of his reign as prince, he assumed the title Nicholas I, king of Montenegro, a 101-gun salute marking the occasion.[48]

If one royal son-in-law opted to remain in Belgrade, another, King Victor Emmanuel of Italy, chose to make the pilgrimage to Lovćen. King Ferdinand of Bulgaria also honored Nicholas with his royal presence, while Greece sent her crown prince.[49] Grand Dukes Nicholas and Peter (two more sons-in-law) represented the tsar. Despite Danilo's earlier request for a visit by an Austrian archduke, Austria-Hungary was represented by her regular minister, as were Germany, France, and Great Britain. Instead of special missions, these nations sent gifts and congratulatory messages.[50] The tsar used the opportunity to name Nicholas a field marshal in the Russian army and dispatch Russian warships to Bar.[51] To add to the festivities, the new royal couple celebrated their golden wedding anniversary a few days early.[52]

The Serbian delegation led by Crown Prince Alexander was well received in Cetinje, but the visit did not repair the breach between the two Serb houses. Colville Barclay, the British chargé in Belgrade, speculated that, if anything, the jubilee celebration had served to increase the jealousy between Peter and Nicholas. But if Peter was unhappy with Nicholas's assumption of the royal title, many other Serbian citizens were furious. The very day that Nicholas became king, a nasty demonstration erupted at the National Theater in Belgrade, where a special performance of the Montenegrin poet-king's drama, *Empress of the Balkans*, was being given in his honor. Barclay observed that "the era of a rapprochement between Servia and Montenegro, which had so suddenly dawned when the annexation of Bosnia and Herzegovina was announced . . . can now be said to have come to an end with the proclamation of Montenegro into a kingdom."[53]

Austria-Hungary was the principal beneficiary of the dispute between Cetinje and Belgrade. Beaumont noted that "while all other missions have been completely eclipsed by the display made by Russia," the Montenegrins were paying special attention to the efforts made by Austria-Hungary.[54] Francis Joseph's "autograph letter of congratulation was so specially cordial that alone of all congratulatory letters from Sovereigns of States, it was at once published in full in all the Montenegrin papers."[55]

The Viennese press reciprocated Montenegro's good feelings. Commenting on the newly forged relationship between the Habsburg Empire and the new Balkan kingdom, the British ambassador in Vienna noted that "there is an evident desire to be friendly, and all the principal journals speak in warm terms of the Prince's patriotism and clever statesmanship, as well as of the progress made by Montenegro under his rule."[56] For the time being, it seemed as though Austria-Hungary and Montenegro had put behind them the ill feelings generated by the annexation. Aehrenthal had every reason to congratulate Nicholas on his latest accolade, and the king in turn had every reason to be content with the unusually cordial treatment now accorded him by the Monarchy.

The new Austro-Montenegrin relationship was not completely problem-free. Border incidents, which had troubled Austro-Montenegrin ties in 1909, continued in 1910.[57] Although both sides recognized the need to delineate their frontier and agreed to form a border commission, little was actually accomplished.[58] The Montenegrins continued to accuse Austria of building fortifications on contested territory. On 15 July, the potentially explosive nature of the problem became apparent when two Austro-Hungarian officers strayed across the poorly marked border near Vršuta and were apprehended. Although Montenegrin authorities released the men in Cetinje two days later, Giesl grumbled that the Montenegrins had acted hastily and that the soldiers had not been treated "like officers."[59] Nicholas apologized, not wanting the incident to spoil his jubilee, and Aehrenthal was content to let the matter rest. One month later, however, the Austro-Hungarian war ministry still called for satisfaction. Aehrenthal wisely denied it revenge.[60]

A second, more serious problem was a belated Russian jubilee present to Nicholas, designed to stem Montenegro's drift toward Vienna. In late November and early December, Russia and Montenegro concluded a military convention in which St. Petersburg promised to pay Cetinje an annual subsidy of 600,000 rubles and provide the Montenegrin army with instructors, arms, and munitions. If the 600,000 ruble outlay was less than half of what the Russians had originally considered, it still represented a handsome source of regular income for Nicholas's impoverished forces. Even so, it was not an outright gift. Nicholas had to pledge to behave himself, to conclude no offensive alliance without Russia's permission, and to place his small army at Russia's disposal upon request. If he failed to meet any of these obligations, St. Petersburg reserved the right to suspend the subsidy and other forms of assistance.[61] At first glance, it appeared that with the closing of the military convention Russia had drawn Montenegro irrevocably into her diplomatic orbit and dealt a fatal blow to the brief Austro-Montenegrin rapprochement. But happily for the Ballhausplatz, Nicholas soon demonstrated that even in financial questions, he was willing to bite the hand that fed him.

CHAPTER FIVE
The Malissori Uprisings: 1910–1911

Mary Edith Durham, the intrepid English writer and champion of Albanian causes, concluded that little good would come of Nicholas's new royal standing. "One point both Montenegrins and Albanians agreed upon," she related. " 'A king must have a kingdom. The Powers would not otherwise have allowed him to be king. Soon there will be war.' "[1]

Even as Nicholas and his sons negotiated with the Powers over his assumption of the royal mantle, a crisis brewed in neighboring Albania, where revolt against Turkish rule raged throughout 1910 and 1911. Montenegro, Albania's hereditary foe, responded to the situation by taking the Malissori (Catholic Albanian highlanders) under her wing, as always with an eye toward enlarging her own territory. Ultimately, Nicholas became an outspoken champion of Albanian interests. By the summer of 1911, it appeared likely that he would provoke a military confrontation with the Ottoman Empire, one fraught with dangerous implications for the territorial status quo and the uneasy peace prevailing in the Balkans. The Powers, especially Russia, with strong diplomatic support from Austria-Hungary, took steps to thwart the realization of Durham's pessimistic prognosis.

Many people were perplexed by Austria-Hungary's great interest in Albania. Conrad von Hötzendorf described the land as "a mostly swampy coastal fringe, where malaria rages for months on end, and which has only a few usable harbors."[2] Yet Conrad himself offered two explanations for Albania's importance. First, she represented a bulwark against Slavic, more particularly Serb, expansion.[3] Secondly, Vlorë, one of her "few usable harbors," was a strategic port that commanded the Straits of Otranto, the narrow separating the heel of Italy's boot from the Balkan peninsula. In the event of war, Vlorë could conceivably serve as an Austrian or Italian Gibraltar.[4] In the words of one Italian, "whoever possesses the port of Vlorë will be the absolute ruler over the Adriatic."[5] This theory, subscribed to by both Italy and Austria-Hungary, gave rise to an intense rivalry between the nominal allies. Italy tried to establish her presence on the eastern shore of the Adriatic, while Austria-Hungary tried to circumscribe the Italian beachhead. Harried officials at the Ballhausplatz despaired at this complication in the already unstable Balkan situation.[6]

Austria's interest in Albania had begun in the seventeenth century, when the Turks awarded the Habsburgs a "religious protectorate" over the Catholics of the Ottoman Empire, including the Malissori tribesmen of northern Albania. Subsequent treaties and agreements in the eighteenth century renewed and expanded Austria's right to build and support churches, schools, and religious institutions. Until the middle of the nineteenth century, Vienna took a rather desultory interest in the affairs of her Albanian ward; but after her exclusion from Germany in 1866 and her expansion into the Balkans in 1878, Austria's interest in her "protectorate" became more animated.[7]

Toward the end of the nineteenth century, expansion-minded Italy initiated a challenge to Austria's cultural hegemony by founding Italian schools in Albania. Albanian was spoken in most of these, but in 1888 Italy established two elementary schools in Scutari, traditionally a center of Habsburg influence, with Italian as the language of instruction.[8] The Mürzsteg agreement of 1903 fanned the smouldering rivalry. Many Italians feared that the resulting Austro-Russian program of reform for troubled Turkish Macedonia would leave their nation without a voice in Balkan affairs.[9]

Italian activity notwithstanding, Austria-Hungary had every reason to feel secure in the belief that northern Albania belonged to her sphere of influence. The Habsburg Monarchy maintained its traditional role as protector of the indigenous Catholic population, much as Russia championed the cause of the Orthodox in the Ottoman Empire. Durham described the relationship this way:

> The Catholics [of northern Albania] relied upon Austria with amazing faith. If a Turkish army dared approach the Christian mountains, there were folk who believed that the Emperor Franz Josef himself, upon a warhorse, would ride at the head of his troops to their rescue.[10]

If the Catholics put their trust in the Austrians, so did the Habsburgs rely on the Catholics of Malësia to resist Slavic expansion. This they did as a matter of course, with little prompting from Vienna.

There was no love lost between the Albanians and the Montenegrins who shared the same limestone mountain ranges. Following the decision of the Congress of Berlin to award Montenegro tracts of Ottoman-Albanian territory, the Catholic Albanian tribes fiercely opposed Cetinje's attempts to annex the towns of Tuzi and Gusinje. Their resistance was so great that "the frontier floated on blood."[11] In the end, the Albanians held on to Tuzi and Gusinje, while the Montenegrins received the Albanian port of Ulcinj as compensation.

The Montenegrin-Albanian border remained one of the most dangerous in the Balkans. Albanians continually raided Montenegrin lands, stole sheep for sport, ambushed unsuspecting Montenegrins, and used their neighbors' mountains for a firing range. Montenegrins retaliated in like fashion.[12] At the time of the annexation crisis, Aehrenthal initiated plans to take advantage of this ancient enmity by enlisting the Albanian tribesmen as a rear guard in case of war with Montenegro. Durham reported that Austria apparently had promised the Catholic highlanders 10,000 rifles, amid rumors that a victorious Monarchy would return Ulcinj to the Albanians.[13] True to Aehrenthal's expectations, the Albanians were ready to march.

Given Austria-Hungary's preeminence in northern Albania and that region's traditional hatred for Montenegro, it seemed fanciful to suppose that the two mountain foes could become friends overnight. Aehrenthal felt confident that, for all her turmoil, Albania remained an oasis of relative constancy as far as Austrian policy and influence were concerned. "Then," as Durham aptly observed, "the unexpected happened. It always does in the Balkan Peninsula."[14]

The Albanian Revolts of 1909 and 1910

An overwhelmingly Muslim land, Albania had once been considered the jewel in Turkey's European crown. At the turn of the twentieth century, she was still perhaps the most loyal of the empire's European dominions, despite her own internal anarchy. According to one authority,

> The rule of the Sultan was only nominal, and his representatives, deprived of all effective authority, were limited to appeasing the very strong unrests which would attract the attention of Europe. In order to fulfill this task, the Ottoman authorities did not command, but implored, promised, and yielded.[15]

The Young Turk revolution of 1908, with its enigmatic catchword "constitution," promised something better to Albania: an indigenous administration, an unfettered cultural development, and a happier, more secure existence.[16] A general truce was declared throughout the land, and the people celebrated the arrival of constitutional rule with feasts, parades, and the customary firing of guns into the air.

Initially the Albanian patriots collaborated with the Young Turk regime, but relations soon deteriorated.[17] The Albanians had hoped for an autonomous existence within a larger Ottoman family, demanding the right to speak and write their own language, to establish and run their own schools, and to administer their own lands. Turkey's policies of centralization and Ottomanization antagonized Albanian nationalists, transforming zealous supporters of the Committee of Union and Progress (the Young Turk party) into bitter opponents. The Turks went so far as to deny the very existence of a separate Albanian nationality.[18] Reluctantly, the Albanians came to the conclusion that they had substituted one nefarious Turkish regime for another: "The leopard does not change his spots nor the Ethiop his skin. The Turk is always a Turk."[19]

According to one critic of Ottoman rule, "no administration, however efficient, could possibly succeed in northern Albania unless liberally endowed with tact. The Turks possessed none."[20] As early as April 1909, Albanian soldiers participated in a revolt in Constantinople against Young Turk rule. The same year the Young Turks demonstrated their authority by crushing an incipient revolt among the Albanians of Kosovo vilayet, who refused to pay taxes or submit to compulsory military service.[21] The Kosovars served as an attractive target for the Young Turks because they were largely Muslims who supported the deposed sultan, Abdul Hamid. Djavid Pasha, the Turkish divisional commander at Mitrovica, achieved his immediate objective in quelling the revolt, but his brutal campaign, especially against the Muslim highlanders, only confirmed the Kosovars' worst fears about the intentions and methods of the new regime. Subdued for the time being, they awaited another opportunity to strike at Turkish authority.[22]

That moment came the following year. In March 1910, while Austrian ships visited Bar and Nicholas's sons charmed Giesl, revolt broke out anew in Kosovo. Protests in Priština over municipal tax levies gave way to fighting, and before long the Albanian tribes of Kosovo had concluded another domestic truce to fight the Turks.[23] By early April, the uprising had assumed dangerous proportions.[24]

The Porte resolved to dispose of the Albanian threat as expeditiously as possible in order to demonstrate the new government's vitality and strength. Margrave Johann von Pallavicini, the Austro-Hungarian ambassador in Constantinople, remarked that an "energetic and successful use of state power in Albania" could put the so-called Albanian question as well as the prestige of the Ottoman government in a new light.[25] If successful, it might mean that the Sick Man of Europe was not terminally ill. Aehrenthal agreed that "a militarily strong Turkey [was] the best guarantee for peace in the Balkans," but he doubted whether force of arms alone could resolve the Albanian problem. In an unusually farsighted letter, he wrote that a corresponding development in administration and the economy would constitute the touchstone of the Young Turk regime.[26]

Only one year after the annexation crisis, many countries still distrusted Austria's Balkan policies, and some believed that Aehrenthal had inspired the Albanian revolt for his own selfish purposes. Unfortunately for the Ballhausplatz, the *Neue Freie Presse* gave credence to a Serbian rumor that Albanian rebels had raised the Austro-Hungarian flag—in Serbian eyes, indisputable proof of Austria's "connivance" in the uprising.[27] Some months later, Miroslav Spalajković, the general secretary of the Serbian foreign ministry, admitted his government's conviction that "Austria-Hungary alone could be at the bottom of the whole affair."[28]

In fact, Austria's attitude toward the revolt was one of strict reserve and nonintervention.[29] As indicated in a letter to Pallavicini, Aehrenthal wanted the Albanians, especially the Catholics, to be treated as fairly as possible, and he worked to ameliorate the harsher aspects of Turkish rule. By the same token, he hoped that Turkey, Germany's new associate, would put her own house in order before the rebels turned publicly to Vienna for assistance, or before other governments, notably the rapacious Balkan states, could exploit the crisis.[30]

His worries concerning Albania's Balkan neighbors were not without foundation. Sofia and Belgrade—not to mention Cetinje—were already preparing for "eventualities."[31] The Serbian minister in Constantinople informed Pallavicini that if atrocities were committed against the Christian population of Kosovo, "we could not restrain our people for long."[32] Marquis Antonio di San Giuliano, the new Italian foreign minister, tried to allay some of Aehrenthal's fears by assuring him that Italy did not intend to occupy "a centimeter" of Albanian soil. But Kajetan Mérey, the Austro-Hungarian ambassador in Rome, doubted whether the Italians would let an opportunity pass to increase their influence in Albania at Turkey's and Austria's expense.[33] Everything hinged on the effectiveness of the Porte's response.

Unable to suppress the Albanian revolt with the troops at his disposal, General Shevket Turgut Pasha, the commander of Turkish forces in northern and eastern Albania, called for reinforcements; by early June he had mastered the military situation.[34] Albanian rebels were still at large, but the Porte smugly asserted that the tactic of striking with great military force had justified itself.[35] Aehrenthal was less confident in the long-term effectiveness of a military solution and urged a policy of reconciliation.[36] But the stubborn Turks preferred a program of Ottomanization and pacification aimed at closing Albanian schools and clubs, suppressing Albanian papers, arresting and exiling Albanian nationalists, and disarming the entire Albanian population.[37]

The Ottoman war minister naïvely asserted that the Turks could disarm the sons of Scanderbeg without serious incident, and in fact intended his troops to bypass Scutari on a casual march from Kosovo into central Albania. The Malissori tribesmen, however, frustrated his optimistic plans, refusing to comply when ordered by the vali of Scutari to pay taxes and surrender their weapons. First the tribes of Hoti and Shali, then the Grudi and Kastrati, sought refuge across the border—in the land of their hereditary enemy, Montenegro.[38]

The Montenegrin-Malissori Rapprochement, 1910

When Kosovo rose in revolt in March 1910, Field Marshal Conrad von Hötzendorf predicted that Montenegro would have a hand in the development of events.[39] Few doubted that Nicholas would try to manipulate the crisis.

In April, while pledging his troth to Austria-Hungary in connection with his father's royal promotion, Crown Prince Danilo assured Baron Giesl that Montenegro shared Aehrenthal's pacific wishes in the Albanian matter. He dismissed as insignificant the faction of his countrymen, led by General Vukotić and Prime Minister Tomanović, that opposed any kind of intercourse with Austria and tried to redirect Austrian suspicion by questioning the designs of Bulgaria and Serbia. Citing "confidential reports," he apprised Vienna that these two Balkan states were preparing to mobilize their armies and even mentioned a Serbian call to march on Kosovo.[40] Such tidings only underscored the gravity of the crisis.

Austria was not the only Great Power to distrust Montenegro's intentions. In mid-May, the Russian, French, and Italian governments, intent on arresting Montenegrin adventurism, advised Cetinje to maintain a peaceful attitude with regard to Albania. Tomanović assured the representatives of the Powers that Montenegro would do so, at least while existing conditions prevailed. Chagrined by the Great-Power action, Nicholas denied charges that he had disseminated guns and ammunition among the Albanian insurgents or had engaged in any extraordinary road construction near the Albanian border. He insisted that his was a "wait-and-see" attitude. Giesl thus concluded that Montenegro would enter into war against Turkey only if the situation in Albania deteriorated markedly *and* if she were not alone.[41] This was not particularly assuring because no one knew how long the Turkish military could hold the Albanians at bay, and Danilo had already indicated that the Balkan states were ready to work together. Aehrenthal correctly suspected that Nicholas would act to take advantage of the situation "one way or another."[42] The king's denials to the contrary, it appeared that he already had.

A Montenegrin functionary, a secret member of Nicholas's persecuted opposition, informed Vienna that his government was forging a new relationship with the Malissori. In May, an agreement had been concluded with certain Albanian tribal leaders, who promised to put in the field 4,000 men, virtually the entire male contingent of the four principal tribes, if Montenegro entered into war with Turkey. For the moment, external pressures and a healthy respect for Turkey's military capability prompted Montenegrin restraint, but the Montenegrin informer warned that a significant change in Turkey's fortunes would induce the king to pursue a more active policy.[43]

Catholic Malissori were not the only Albanians involved in the rapprochement with Montenegro. Rebel leaders from largely Muslim Kosovo, notably Isa Boletin, also figured prominently. Boletin openly intended to use Montenegro as a base for forays into Albania. Nicholas initially observed a singular neutrality by ignoring the Kosovar's presence on Montenegrin soil, and only on 15 June, after numerous protests from the Turkish ambassador, did he escort Boletin and thirteen followers away from the Albanian border. The Montenegrin government called this measure a "spontaneous act of friendship" for Turkey.[44] Aehrenthal was not duped by Montenegrin semantics. At the end of June he remarked that

> the smallest Balkan state has given thought to exploiting the Albanian confusion for her own end, and . . . even though she momentarily rejects direct intervention, still follows conditions in the neighboring Albanian lands with intense interest and maintains communications with them which enable her to return to a more far-reaching plan of action at a moment's notice.

He feared that Turkey's campaign to disarm the Albanians would drive the latter further into the arms of the Montenegrins, a state of affairs which would be neither natural nor "in Turkey's or our own interests."[45]

The Russians, in the process of concluding a military convention with Montenegro, were in the best position to press Nicholas to do the bidding of the Powers and facilitate the repatriation of the Albanian refugees. Happily for Austria, St. Petersburg saw no point in prolonging the Albanian turmoil and advised Nicholas to cooperate. Sergei Arseniev, the Russian minister in Cetinje, threatened to withdraw Russian political and material aid if he did not.[46]

Nicholas quickly met the demands of the Powers, in part because he did not want to lose Russian aid, in part because he had his own reasons for wanting his Catholic guests to go home. The cost of feeding and sheltering, not to mention arming, more than twenty-five hundred refugees was considerable. The Montenegrin treasury, hard pressed to meet regular accounts, did not have spare cash for extraordinary humanitarian ventures, especially when an immediate return on the outlay seemed improbable. His own long-range plan for exploiting Albanian difficulties still gestating, Nicholas realized that the Catholic bands would not make any real headway against the Turks before the year's end. Winter was just around the corner; fighting would cease until spring. The king did not want to subsidize the Malissori when they could do him no good.[47]

For the time being, Nicholas chose to work for an understanding between the Turks and the Albanians. His first effort at playing "honest broker" resulted in a firm Turkish refusal to meet Malissori demands to return their arms, rescind their tax increases, and reopen Albanian national schools.[48] His second effort, however, was more successful. In mid-November, fourteen Malissori chiefs presented him with an even longer list of demands, among them a general amnesty, the restriction of Malissori military service to the vilayet of Kosovo, the selection of their municipal officers from among Albanian candidates, the legalization of their language, and indemnification for sequestered or confiscated property, including weapons. Curiously, Sadreddin Bey, the Turkish minister who had rejected the first set of demands, gave his tentative approval to the second, commending it to his government.[49]

On 18 November, Nicholas read the formal reply of the Porte, which approved most of the demands though it refused to reimburse the tribesmen for the loss of any weapons. The king communicated the note to the Malissori and politely urged them to accept the Porte's terms and return home. The majority did his bidding. Although another revolt broke out shortly in the Dibër mountains of Albania, the Malissori crisis of 1910, a dress rehearsal for a larger crisis the following summer, was over.[50]

The Malissori Uprising of 1911

The Turco-Albanian agreement of November 1910 proved to be no more than an uneasy armistice. With winter's end, the tribesmen of Malësia took up arms once again. In March, they attacked Turkish outposts on the Albanian-Montenegrin frontier, surrounded the important fortress of Tuzi, and even threatened Scutari.[51] The Powers soon questioned Montenegro's involvement in this second revolt.

As they had the year before, the Montenegrins disavowed any complicity in the uprising or in plans to meddle elsewhere in European Turkey. Nicholas assured the Ottoman ambassador that his government was observing "the strictest neutrality,"[52] while his eldest son claimed that "we Montenegrins most sincerely desire peace."[53] Despite these denials, it became increasingly clear that Montenegro did have a hand in the new revolt. In particular, General Vukotić aided the rebels by passing out weapons, which the Malissori used against the Turks.[54] Montenegrin troops also captured twelve Turkish soldiers on their own initiative and took them to Podgorica.[55]

Colville Barclay, the British chargé d'affaires in Belgrade, reported that the Montenegrin king had consulted the Serbian government, with which he was otherwise barely on speaking terms, about the possibility of a joint Serbo-Montenegrin venture in Macedonia. Such a venture implied Montenegrin activity in northern Albania as well. Under pressure to keep the peace, Belgrade responded that it "did not think the moment opportune;" it did not, however, altogether rule out joint action at a later date. Whitehall took steps to discourage any such activity.[56]

From Dubrovnik, the British vice consul cynically observed that "it is true that His Majesty's utterances are not always taken seriously, owing to the habit which he has of suiting his expressed opinions to the views of the person whom he is addressing."[57] Even so, George Moses, the American minister to Greece and Montenegro, reported this disturbing royal admonition to the Russians: "I know the mission of Montenegro and I shall be faithful to it; but I cannot permit the massacre of Christians to take place on my frontier, and if it occurs I shall have to do my duty."[58] All the Great-Power observers, including Austria-Hungary's ambassador to Berlin, concluded that the wily king was playing a devious "double game."[59]

Pallavicini wrote from the Golden Horn that Nicholas was walking a tightrope between his own personal territorial aspirations and the desiderata of his new Albanian clients. As Sir Fairfax Cartwright, the British ambassador, reported from Vienna, "It is recognized here that the King is in a difficult position because it is suspected that he nurses the ambition of becoming some day Prince of an autonomous Albania, and for that reason he cannot afford to lose the sympathies of the Albanians by treating them harshly at the present moment under pressure from Constantinople." Pallavicini believed that Nicholas "would temporize and await events so as not to compromise himself too much either in favour of the Turks or the Albanians, until the one or the other obtained the upper hand."[60] Durham was somewhat bolder than Pallavicini, accusing the king of planning the insurrection "as part of his effort to obtain a kingdom."[61]

One cannot lightly dismiss Nicholas's territorial ambitions in northern Albania or his overtures to Serbia for a joint mission in Macedonia. He did not aid the Albanians merely to be a good neighbor. The Albanians had risen in revolt against the Turks many times before, but never had they enjoyed the solicitude Nicholas now offered them. His expansionist aspirations in Hercegovina foiled by Austria-Hungary in 1908, the king had no alternative but to forage for territorial plums in other orchards, all of which happened to be tended by Ottoman overseers. Scutari, the medieval capital of Zeta, was the most inviting fruit of all, and within easy striking distance. A second but more distant prize was Prizren, Stephen Dušan's medieval capital. Its liberation from Muslim hands had long been a dream of Serbs everywhere. Nicholas himself had penned a song that Durham described as enshrining "in a few verses the Great Servian Idea—the song that every Serb schoolchild knows, 'Onward, onward, let me see Prizren.' "[62] Both Scutari and Prizren were populated by Albanians, Catholic as well as Muslim. Aware of Nicholas's territorial aspirations, the Powers of Europe looked on apprehensively as he manipulated the Albanian rebellion.

As Montenegro's intentions were suspect, so were Austria's. Serbia still blamed Aehrenthal for the "Albanian troubles," and Italy doubted the sincerity of the foreign minister's pledges of nonintervention in the Albanian imbroglio.[63] The British ambassador in Vienna, however, rightly discounted the possibility of the Austrian government's having encouraged the rebellion in any way:

> To have done so would mean that Aehrenthal had suddenly and completely changed his policy, and I have no reason to assume that he has done this. The two main factors in Aehrenthal's policy are to do everything that is possible to maintain good relations with

The Malissori Uprisings: 1910–1911

Turkey and likewise with Italy. For him to intrigue in Albania would be to arouse at the same time the ill-will of both those two countries against the Dual Monarchy, and Aehrenthal would gain nothing tangible in return for such action. Austria does not want Albania but she will never allow Italy to set foot on that side of the Adriatic.[64]

As it had done the year before, the Ottoman government called upon Shevket Turgut Pasha to bring the rebellious Albanians to heel. Shortly after his arrival in Scutari, on 11 May, he proclaimed martial law and offered a pardon to all rebels (chiefs excepted) who returned to their homes within a period of five days.[65] On the third day, however, the impatient general ordered his troops to seize the important height of Dečić, overlooking Tuzi.[66] A truce was now out of the question. In their Podgorica declaration of 18 May, sixty Albanian chiefs rejected Turgut's demands and refused to lay down arms until the Porte honored its previous commitments.[67]

During a month of intense fighting, Turgut Pasha's forces sought to encircle the rebel strongholds with a pincers movement emanating from Turkish bases in Scutari and Gusinje. According to British accounts, they destroyed "every village, house, or church in their path."[68] By the end of June, the Catholic insurgents, joined by the powerful Mirdite clans, were trapped, victims of superior power and numbers.[69] They had but three choices left to them: to surrender, to die where they were, or to flee across the border into Montenegro. Most chose the last option. Once again, Montenegro became a haven for a large body of insurgent forces determined to make war on the Ottoman empire. Once again, Podgorica became the unofficial capital of Catholic Albania as King Nicholas welcomed the Malissori with open arms.

Despite continued fighting, the Turkish government prematurely announced on 12 June, that the revolt was over.[70] At the same time, it took a conciliatory position vis-à-vis the Albanians. Having subdued the foe with sword and torch, the Porte now proposed to win its enemy over with a promise of amnesty and monetary compensation.[71] On 18 June, coinciding with a goodwill visit by Sultan Mehmet V to Kosovo, Turgut Pasha communicated an imperial decree of amnesty, which also offered 10,000 Turkish pounds to any rebel who surrendered to Turkish authorities and turned in his arms within ten days. Moreover, the government promised monetary compensation for property lost, damaged, or destroyed during the recent military operations. Although attracted by the financial offer, the wary Albanians would have nothing to do with a package that required them to surrender their precious weapons.[72]

Amid reports of renewed conflict, Albanian leaders met in the Montenegrin village of Gerče on 23 June. Aided by the popular Albanian patriot Ismail Kemal Bey, who had found his way to Cetinje earlier in the month, they responded to Turgut Pasha's proclamation by drawing up the "Gerče Memorandum," also known as the "Red Book," in which they addressed their grievances and aspirations not only to Constantinople, but also to Europe, Great Britain in particular. Offering a program for all of Albania, not just the Catholic north, they demanded not political independence but rather the right of autonomous national development within the Ottoman Empire. They sought the right to bear arms, amnesty, economic assistance, and political, linguistic, and educational reforms.[73] These Albanian demands soon appeared in several European newspapers.[74]

The sultan, who hoped that the rebels would tire of fighting and be pacified by his government's concessions, signed his amnesty decree on 3 July. The rebels, however, stood by the Gerče Memorandum and rejected the amnesty, which did not address their principal grievances. Demonstrating more flexibility than at any other time within the past two years, the Turks took this display of recalcitrance in stride and made an additional gesture designed to appease the insurgents. They recalled Turgut Pasha, who conveniently became a scapegoat.[75] Although his departure signalled a victory of sorts for the Albanians, it still did not satisfy any of their formal demands as outlined in the Gerče manifesto.

This omission was soon remedied. Abdullah Pasha, Turgut's successor, arrived in Albania laden with substantive proposals, some of which conformed to points in the memorandum, including an offer of concessions for the Catholic highlanders. The Porte offered amnesty, reduced taxes, educational and economic reforms, the right to bear arms, and military service limited to Albanian lands.[76] Considering the Porte's previous intransigence and hostility, it was a very appealing package. But the Malissori, hardened by past dealings with the Turks, still refused to budge from their

Montenegrin sanctuaries or make peace with the Porte.[77] The Turks concluded, as did the Great Powers, that King Nicholas and his government were chiefly responsible for the obstinacy of the Albanians. The crisis now entered a new phase, with the Montenegrins, more than the Albanians, the objects of Turkish and foreign pressure.

The Resolution of the Crisis

In the spring of 1911, the Turkish government accused Montenegro of fomenting the Albanian revolt and threatened retaliatory action.[78] Responding to Montenegro's appeal for a Great-Power guarantee against such Turkish threats, Russia assured the Porte that Montenegro's military preparations along the Albanian frontier were merely defensive and advised it not to provoke a military encounter.[79] At the same time, St. Petersburg cautioned Nicholas to maintain strict neutrality regarding the Albanian revolt.[80] Although grateful for Russia's démarche in Constantinople, Nicholas took umbrage at Russia's interference in Cetinje, especially the pressure being applied by Minister Arseniev.[81]

Aehrenthal also attempted to defuse the Montenegrin time bomb by inviting Nicholas to visit Vienna.[82] He knew that Vukotić or any other Montenegrin leader would be reluctant to engage in any provocative action in the king's absence. Nicholas, however, would not be pried away from his mountain command post.[83] Although Aehrenthal continued to pressure the Albanians, the Turks, and the Montenegrins to come to terms with each other, he was more than willing to let the Russians assume the lead in trying to resolve the crisis. At home, the Austrian clerical press and other opponents of the foreign minister's cautious *Balkanpolitik* attacked him for his "apparent abandonment . . . of Austria's right of protection of the Christian population in Albania." Critics demanded that he intervene forcefully on behalf of the Malissori, as they believed Russia had done earlier on behalf of Montenegro. Disgusted with the "stupidity" of the Turkish government, Aehrenthal eventually met his critics halfway.[84] On 8 June, both the semiofficial *Fremdenblatt* and the *Neue Freie Presse* ran important stories that chastised the Porte for its "relentless suppression of the rebellion." The papers contended that "cooperation with Albania and not constant warfare should be the aim of a sensible Turkish policy."[85]

Turkey's mid-June volte-face in dealing with the Catholic highlanders could not have come at a better time for Aehrenthal, who again urged Nicholas to stop encouraging the insurgents and to use his influence to have them accept Turkish terms.[86] Cartwright reported Aehrenthal's hope that the other Powers would follow the example of Austria and Russia in making strong representations at Cetinje.[87] In the face of such warnings, Nicholas argued that he could not in good conscience order or advise the Malissori to return to Albania unless one of the Powers guaranteed that Turkey would carry out her program of amnesty and reform.[88]

Britain's Sir Edward Grey could appreciate Nicholas's arguments, no matter what the motives behind them. He also realized that to secure an international guarantee, however desirable for Albanian interests and peace in the Balkans, would be no easy task: "It is a matter in which only the Powers most nearly interested by geographical position or racial sympathy could take the initiative."[89] Thus, he relied on Austria or Russia to take the first step. He knew that France, already embroiled in Morocco, and Germany, covetous of good relations with the Ottoman Empire, would recoil from pursuing a policy that might appear to the Turks as unwarranted intervention in their internal affairs. Yet he believed that neither France nor Germany would ultimately refuse its support should an understanding be reached among the other Powers.[90]

Russia seemed prepared to take the initiative when Nicholas arranged a meeting in Cetinje between Sadreddin Bey, the Turkish minister, and the Albanian chieftains.[91] The councillor of the British embassy in St. Petersburg reported the view of the Russian foreign ministry that "the Turks were now in direct relations with the Albanians, and if they could not come to terms with the chiefs that was their own affair."[92] Grey now appeared determined to obtain the elusive Great-Power guarantee on his own,[93] but he had barely taken his first step when the German secretary of state informed him that Berlin would "not consider itself able" to join any collective action in Constantinople.[94]

King Nicholas had raised Russian hopes for peace by facilitating the initial Turco-Albanian parley, and also by dispatching a special messenger to St. Petersburg. On 19 June, Lazar Mijušković travelled to the Russian capital to affirm Nicholas's pacific intentions, and, simultaneously, to obtain Russian financial assistance in meeting the costs of feeding, clothing, and possibly arming the Albanian refugees.[95] Mijušković's embassy met with some success. Acting in the absence of Sergei Sazonov, Deputy Foreign Minister Anatol Neratov agreed to pay the cost of maintaining the refugees, but he stipulated that Nicholas would receive his money only after the Malissori question had been peacefully resolved.[96]

In Cetinje, Minister Arseniev and Colonel Nikolai Potapov, the Russian military attaché, advocated stronger measures to control the king. After a conversation with Nicholas on 16 June, Arseniev concluded that the Montenegrin ruler was merely awaiting payment of the Russian military subsidy before attacking Turkey. Arseniev suggested tightening Nicholas's purse strings until the king could be made to see reason; on 28 June, Neratov reluctantly approved this plan.[97] Accordingly, less than half of the 1,104,000 crowns deposited in the Russian mission's account at the Bank of Montenegro was made available to the Montenegrin government.[98] When Nicholas ordered the arming of Montenegrin reservists and their transfer to Podgorica, Potapov pointedly informed the Montenegrin war minister that the king was disregarding, indeed violating, the intent of the Russo-Montenegrin military convention of 1910. The attaché ordered the removal of a Russian advisor from the Albanian frontier and informed the Montenegrin minister that Russia might even refuse to foot the bill for the Podgorica encampment.[99]

Still, Nicholas did not yield. On 4 July, he ordered the mobilization of troops at Podgorica. One week later, Janko Vukotić told Mary Edith Durham that "all was ready, and he could take Scutari in ten days."[100] In mid-July, Prime Minister Tomanović tried to ascertain the probable attitude of Serbia, Bulgaria, and Greece in the event of a Turco-Montenegrin war.[101] Despite the apparent gravity of the situation, Neratov refrained from applying more pressure, allowing Turkey to make the next move.[102]

On 20 July, spurred to action by Austria, Russia, and Italy, the Porte tendered another, presumably its final, peace proposal, this time including an offer of a minor frontier adjustment in Montenegro's favor around Lake Scutari. Turkey asked Neratov to persuade Nicholas not to interfere with the return of the Malissori and to use his influence to persuade the Albanians to accept the Turkish amnesty.[103] On 26 July, Arseniev took the ultimate step to bring Nicholas to reason. He informed the monarch that Russia would withhold *all* support, financial and material, unless Montenegro complied with St. Petersburg's "requests."[104] Nicholas indignantly told Baron Squitti that he would rather "starve than continue in this slave relationship," but in the end, the pauper king capitulated.[105]

With an eye toward preserving his subsidy and the tsar's appanage, Nicholas reluctantly agreed to advise the Malissori chiefs to accept the Turkish concessions and go home.[106] Thus, one day he championed the Albanians; the next he threatened to take away their arms and food unless they did his bidding.[107] Never, Durham bitterly recorded, had a people been "more shamelessly betrayed" than the Albanians.[108] But in reality, they, like Nicholas, had no other choice. Despite her wild rhetoric, Durham realized this, and at Vukotić's request, helped persuade her Albanian friends to accept the Ottoman offering.[109]

On 3 August 1911, the Turks and the Malissori signed a peace agreement at Podgorica. Within two weeks, all Albanian refugees had departed Montenegrin soil, save fifty or so die-hards who refused to return to Turkish rule. In Durham's words, "with brutal haste, men, women, and children were hunted back across the border like so much cattle." Sometime later, she discovered that formerly teeming Podgorica had become desolate: "Soldiers, officers, insurgents, correspondents—all had disappeared like a dream; or was the present calm but a dream—the hush before the storm?"[110] Albanian unrest continued, especially among the Mirdite population, but the Malissori crisis of 1911 was at an end.

Related Questions

As might have been expected, the crisis caused a serious clash between Aehrenthal and Conrad von Hötzendorf. Aware that the Turco-Albanian conflict might lead to war with Montenegro, Conrad was eager to implement military preparations for the "eventual intervention of the Monarchy."[111] For the time being, he suggested the mobilization of a single army corps, but in the long run he contemplated taking advantage of a Turco-Montenegrin war to exploit Austria's so-called right of occupation in the Sandžak, an act that would put an end to Serbian and Montenegrin dreams of establishing a joint frontier.[112]

Despite this preoccupation, Conrad's letter to Aehrenthal of 18 July was more restrained than usual. Cognizant of the foreign minister's policy of nonintervention in the Malissori crisis, he acknowledged that a military solution was not necessarily the best one, suggesting that a more desirable course of action would be for Austria to end the conflict and concentrate on refurbishing her standing among her erstwhile Albanian friends.[113]

The last suggestion carried with it the implied criticism that Aehrenthal's policies had allowed Austria's stature to deteriorate. Outraged by what he deemed an unjustifiable and impudent intrusion into his personal domain, Aehrenthal left no doubt as to who was in charge of the Dual Monarchy's foreign policy. Calling attention to the fact that Austria-Hungary had surrendered her "right of occupation" in the Sandžak more than two years before, he repudiated the field marshal's scheme. He guaranteed that Vienna would not play the role of spectator if and when either Turkey or Montenegro moved to take up cudgels, but stated that he preferred to work for peace rather than war. Having initiated an "exchange of thoughts" with Rome and St. Petersburg, Aehrenthal intended to act jointly with other Powers to prevent the outbreak of hostilities. His object, as always since the end of the annexation crisis, was to maintain the status quo.[114]

Conrad expressed satisfaction that Aehrenthal at least acknowledged the possibility of war and gave his unsolicited approval to a declaration of the Powers on the Albanian question. Nonetheless, he suggested that Austria would have to back a declaration with force, an oblique reminder that he would need time to prepare for any military activity.[115] Aehrenthal reminded Conrad that a Great-Power declaration had not yet been agreed upon, and in any case, it would not be made unless war actually broke out between Montenegro and Turkey. He emphasized that Austria-Hungary would support any future declaration with diplomacy, not military action.[116]

Despite the Malissori crisis and in part because of it, the summer of 1911 marked a high point in Austro-Russian relations. The Russians were engaged in the process of re-evaluating their international policies and commitments and did not want an Albanian crisis to sidetrack their endeavors. Aehrenthal appreciated their intervention in Cetinje and concluded that the tsar, like himself, had no great faith in the king of Montenegro. In mid-June, he wired his ambassador in the Russian capital that he hoped for an Austro-Russian rapprochement, perhaps even a return to the halcyon days of 1903.[117] In his opinion, Sazonov and Neratov were "calm and rational people—not Izvolskys. I deal directly with Petersburg over the Balkan policy and we understand each other. It is not an entente with Russia, but we have pleasant relations. That must suffice for now."[118]

During the Malissori crisis, Vienna and St. Petersburg pursued similar, if not identical, policies designed to maintain peace in the Balkans. Neither Aehrenthal nor his Russian counterpart wanted a Balkan brushfire to rage out of control. In the end, the Habsburg foreign minister received accommodation at little or no cost. The Russians on the other hand, who almost singlehandedly coerced Nicholas into giving up his warlike notions, bore the brunt of the Montenegrin government's umbrage.

Clearly, Russia's handling of the Malissori crisis did not "strengthen the ties between Cetinje and St. Petersburg" to the extent that one scholar has suggested. If "King Nicholas followed Russia's advice to do everything in his power to maintain peace," it was because he had to, not because he wanted to.[119] Alexander Izvolsky aptly expressed Russian bitterness toward Montenegro's behavior. In mid-July, the former foreign minister characterized Nicholas's policy in Albania as "Austrophile," one that was "neither Slavic nor good"; he accused Giesl of having "bewitched" the Balkan land.[120]

Russia's unilateral intervention at Cetinje in May had disturbed the Montenegrins, but Arseniev's July threat to terminate Montenegro's subsidy had completely outraged them. In reaction, Nicholas informed Giesl and Squitti that he was taking steps to free Montenegro from Russia's pecuniary vise.[121] With much emotion he told the Austrian minister: "In 1702 we freed ourselves from the Turks; today, after 209 years, from the Russians."[122] Giesl recognized the king's words for what they were: a thinly veiled appeal to Austria-Hungary for money. Indeed, Nicholas announced that he would now have to turn to Vienna for a loan.

Echoing his king, Lazar Mijušković denounced his country's "morally demeaning and shameful" relationship with Russia and advised Giesl that the Montenegrin government was searching for ways to free its country from the heavy Russian yoke. It wished to remain Russia's friend but to stop serving as her "watchdog." Mijušković did not appeal directly for Austrian assistance but mentioned his desire for all of the Great Powers to aid the poor Balkan land. He proposed a lottery be organized in the Great Power states, the proceeds of which would go into the Montenegrin treasury. Approaching the budgetary problem from all angles, he even suggested cutting back on domestic expenditures by phasing out Montenegro's small standing army and reverting to the old militia system.

Giesl was amazed at the speed with which the Montenegrin chameleon changed colors. By cutting off all ties with Russia, a course of action that would have been repugnant to the vast majority of his subjects, Nicholas might recklessly and unnecessarily traumatize his impoverished land, which was simply incapable of generating more tax revenue. In so doing, he would imperil his own rule.[123] Giesl was by this time familiar with the temporary Russophobia that periodically gripped Montenegrin leaders; he advised Aehrenthal that it would be premature for Austria-Hungary to take a firm stand on the Montenegrin requests. Following his chief's example in the Malissori crisis, he counselled a wait-and-see attitude.[124]

Three weeks after the termination of the Malissori affair, Dušan Gregović, the former chargé d'affaires in Constantinople, became the new Montenegrin foreign minister. His appointment, however, did not herald a loss of confidence in Tomanović, the king's principal political confidant, who stayed on as prime minister. As Count John de Salis, the British minister in Cetinje, correctly concluded: "Foreign affairs will doubtless continue to be guided by the King as in the past."[125]

On 18 September, the new foreign minister met with Aehrenthal in Vienna to discuss a coinage convention between their two countries, and the troublesome Austro-Montenegrin frontier.[126] Inevitably, they also discussed the Malissori uprising. Gregović confessed that he had been one of the many Montenegrins who had believed that his country had little to lose in a war with Turkey. Upon hearing this, Aehrenthal facetiously advised his visitor that in the future he should first ask for Vienna's appraisal of Montenegro's chances for success in war. That way she could avoid another bout with insolvency and ignominious dependence on Russia.

Though acting primarily in the capacity of his master's voice, Gregović also delivered a personal message from Danilo, who, as ever, wished to give evidence of his political sympathy for Austria-Hungary. Echoing Giesl's earlier conclusions, Danilo observed that as long as his father reigned, Montenegro could hardly be emancipated from Russia's baneful influence. Despite his occasional harsh words and hurt feelings, his father was so enchanted by Mother Russia and so beholden to her, that "even if he wanted to, he would not be in the position to break radically with [her]." For the time being, he asserted, Cetinje would try to maintain a healthy distance from the clutches of the Russian bear, but both Danilo and Gregović feared the consequences of a renewed pro-Russian course, which they felt was inevitable.

Aehrenthal acknowledged Danilo's message by reaffirming Vienna's interest in perpetuating the Petrović-Njegoš dynasty. But, as he had told Giesl many times, it was Nicholas and not Danilo who directed the Black Mountain's foreign policy. At heart, Aehrenthal doubted the sincerity of Danilo's commitment to a pro-Habsburg course. To his way of thinking, it was virtually impossible for any Montenegrin government, present or future, to sell the Russophile Montenegrins on long-term Austro-Montenegrin friendship and cooperation. Consequently, he viewed the current complaints about Russian exploitation as yet another game in which Cetinje played Austria and Russia against each other. As far as Aehrenthal was concerned, the Dual Monarchy's relations with the tiny Balkan kingdom were correct; it would be up to Montenegro to keep them that way.[127]

CHAPTER SIX
The Road to War: 1911–1912

No sooner had the Albanian question been set aside than a new crisis erupted in North Africa, one with even more serious implications for peace in the Balkans. After France had tightened her hold on Morocco in 1911, the Italian government moved to realize its imperial ambitions in Tripoli. On 27 September 1911, claiming mistreatment of her nationals and Ottoman biases against her economic ventures, Italy delivered an ultimatum to the Porte, giving it twenty-four hours to choose either Italian occupation and administration of Tripoli, or war. Despite a conciliatory Turkish response to these demands, Italy declared war when the time limit expired on 29 September.[1]

Although Rome informed Vienna of its decision regarding Tripoli only one day before delivering its ultimatum, the Italian foreign minister took pains to allay Aehrenthal's concerns over the possible effects of the altercation. In August, Aehrenthal had made it clear that he feared any action in Tripoli might provoke a military conflict with dangerous reverberations on the Balkan peninsula.[2] San Giuliano, aware of this possibility, tried to convince his Austrian counterpart that there was no real danger, particularly if Italy restricted her activities to the Mediterranean.[3] Aehrenthal, having recently weathered another in a succession of never-ending Balkan crises, could hardly have been comforted by the Italian foreign minister's misplaced optimism.

Although displeased by Italy's actions, Aehrenthal promised not to obstruct her path; at the same time, he reserved freedom of action in dealing with future developments. "I must express the hope," he wrote, "that Italy, in the execution of the action, will avoid everything that could have the effect of spreading the conflict to the Balkans and to keep in mind the fact that the origins of the Triple Alliance trace back principally to the desire to maintain the status quo in the Balkans."[4] Britain's Lord John Morley echoed Aehrenthal's fears when he remarked that the *Panther* was a lamb in comparison with the present crisis.[5]

Despite Aehrenthal's hopes for peace, the Turco-Italian War ultimately unleashed the desires of the ambitious Balkan states, which conspired among themselves to dismember European Turkey. Naturally, Montenegro joined these conspirators. The bombardment of Tripoli late in September thus set in motion a chain of Balkan wars that reordered the peninsula, and eventually the whole of Europe. In the words of G. P. Gooch and Harold Temperley, "Italy's difference with Turkey over Tripoli inaugurate[d] a period of actual war, and thereafter one or other nation [was] almost continuously in conflict until Europe plunged into Armageddon in 1914."[6]

Immediate Effects of the Turco-Italian War

Balkan affairs were relatively tranquil on 27 September 1911, when Italy delivered her ultimatum to the Porte. The most newsworthy events were the possible state visit to Austria of King Peter of Serbia and the marriage of his daughter to a Russian prince.[7] Within days, however, the Balkans were drawn into the vortex of the crisis. Aehrenthal soon faced the formidable task of containing the territorial rapacity of the various Balkan states and preventing any brushfire on the peninsula from developing into a pan-European conflagration.[8]

Aehrenthal reaffirmed his desire for peace to the British ambassador and the chargés d'affaires of Germany, Russia, and France at a diplomatic reception on 28 September. He warned his colleagues that, because of Turkey's "negligence" and Italy's "rashness," they had no choice but to help him control the situation. To this end, the Austrian foreign minister suggested that the Powers insist that the Golden Horn maintain the status quo in the Balkans,[9] while he spoke personally to the representatives of Bulgaria, Serbia, and Greece and cabled Sofia, Belgrade, Athens, and Cetinje.[10]

Other Great-Power statesmen, and the Balkan leaders in particular, were also cognizant of the possibilities of the moment. On 28 September, the same day as Aehrenthal's reception, Milovan Milovanović, the Serbian foreign minister, accurately projected the course of events. He confided to Stefan von Ugron zu Ábránfalva, the Austro-Hungarian minister in Belgrade, that if the conflict between Italy and Turkey became protracted, repercussions on the peninsula would be inevitable. Montenegro would make far-reaching demands for Turkish territory, and Bulgaria would soon follow her example.[11] Milovanović, however, like the foreign ministers of other Balkan states, assured Vienna that *his* country would join such a movement only in the most remote instance.[12]

Policymakers in Vienna were not taken in by these assurances, sensing that the Balkan states could not possibly resist the opportunities presented by the Turco-Italian conflict. The Austrians also knew that suspicion and rumor flourished on the peninsula and worked against any Balkan country keeping even its most well-intentioned pledges. The situation posed by the Sandžak of Novi Pazar confirmed Austria's misgivings.

Vienna became concerned when reports of a general arming of Muslims in the Sandžak and along the Serbian border caused the Serbians to fear for the safety of the Christian population.[13] Aehrenthal reminded the Serbian minister, Djordje Simić, that these reports were unsubstantiated, while assuring Milovanović that there was no cause for his government to take any precipitate action.[14] Instead, he urged the Serbians to employ their good relations with the Porte to obtain explanations and assurances;[15] at the same time he advised the Turkish government to refrain from taking any hostile measures along an already precarious frontier.[16] Aehrenthal's diplomatic actions prevented an immediate crisis but did not lay to rest the question of the Sandžak.

As the issue of armed Muslims fell by the wayside, the Austrian military attaché in Belgrade raised another aspect of the ever-ticklish Sandžak problem that touched upon Austria's relations with her Balkan neighbor and, ultimately, the maintenance of the status quo in the region. Major Otto Gellinek reported to his chief, Conrad von Hötzendorf, that Serbia, long covetous of the Sandžak, now feared that Austria would attempt to reoccupy it.[17] Serbian newspapers printed reports from Zagreb, Sarajevo, Pljevlja, and Višegrad of Austrian troop transport and deployment, trips of ranking officers to Vienna, tight security on the Bosnian frontier, and the like—all pointing, in Serbian eyes, to an imminent Austrian reoccupation.[18] The Serbian government commenced a partial mobilization,[19] and though reports of Austria's action proved to be false, many Serbs remained disquieted.[20] In November, after the Italian annexation of Tripoli, rumors began to circulate about the formation of yet another secret Serb nationalist group, the Black Hand.[21]

The Montenegrin government reacted calmly to the Turco-Italian crisis throughout the fall of 1911, while Nicholas sought to turn the war to his own advantage. Still dreaming of uniting Montenegro and Albania under his crown, he offered his services to Rome in the form of an invasion of Turkish Albania.[22] This proposal rejected, the king displayed his talent for duplicity by instructing his foreign minister, Dušan Gregović, to assure Vienna that it was his intention to honor Aehrenthal's request for peace in the Balkans.[23] The German minister received additional assurances from Nicholas himself that Montenegro would go along with Austria-Hungary "through thick and thin."[24]

On 17 October, Giesl reported that the inflammatory rumors about Austria's designs on the Sandžak were being taken seriously in the various Slav embassies in Cetinje, particularly the Russian.[25] Yet so strong were Nicholas's public pledges of peace, that some cynical diplomats also believed that an agreement had been signed in Vienna between Aehrenthal and Gregović providing that in the event of an Austrian reoccupation of the Sandžak, Montenegro would acquire Scutari, Berane, or some other slice of Turkish territory. The Montenegrin government lent credence to this view by remaining silent.[26] Aehrenthal was delighted, believing that fear and doubt about his true intentions might contribute to peace. As he explained to Giesl,

> Serbia and Russia especially—but also Italy—have presently a great interest in keeping the peace in the Balkans. The more these states believe in the possibility of the intervention of our troops in the Sandžak, the greater will be their fear to exploit complications in the Balkans to the point of crisis, and the more vigorously they will work not to destroy the peace.[27]

The rumors concerning the Sandžak became an article of faith not only with the Serbs, but also with Nicholas. Although he knew that no agreement had been signed between his country and Austria, he set out to achieve an analogous understanding. In a remarkable interview on 31 October, he pleaded with Giesl to travel to Vienna and to present Aehrenthal with a secret treaty that would "secure the political future of the [Montenegrin] kingdom."[28] In an almost comical display of monarchial obsequiousness, he prostrated himself before the Austrian eagle and explained just how far he was willing to go to demonstrate his loyalty: "I pledge myself and my land—and this should be written down in a convention—always to follow Austria-Hungary's advice. . . . I place my army of 40–50,000 . . . at the service of Austria-Hungary against every enemy except Russia and Serbia—*I will even march against Italy.*"[29] In return for his support, Nicholas desired nothing less than an Austrian endorsement of his territorial claims in northern Albania—provided that Turkey fell apart. He concluded: "I shall do everything Austria-Hungary wants—for example, place a kingdom of Montenegro united with northern Albania under the protection of Austria-Hungary."[30]

Although certain aspects of Nicholas's proposals undoubtedly appealed to Aehrenthal, the Austrian rebuked the king for his incessant scheming, which threatened the status quo. But after applying the verbal whip, Aehrenthal extended Nicholas another financial carrot. Reminding the king that Austria-Hungary, through the flotation of loans, the construction of roads and railroads, and the like, had repeatedly demonstrated her heartfelt concern for Montenegro's well-being, Aehrenthal explained that he was prepared to continue this beneficent policy, if Nicholas observed Vienna's interest in peace. Hoping to add savor to his remarks, Aehrenthal intimated that a customs union between their two countries could probably be arranged within three or four years.[31]

Throughout November, Nicholas gave evidence of trying to keep the peace. In partial reward, he was permitted a loan of 3.5 million crowns from the Boden-Credit-Anstalt of Vienna to meet a deficit estimated at one million crowns.[32] Then, from Constantinople, Pallavicini reported rumors of Montenegrin intrigues in Albania and Italian intrigues in Montenegro, rumors that San Giuliano vigorously denied and for which there is no evidence.[33] But even an unsubstantiated rumor was enough to put Aehrenthal on edge. He warned Gregović that "different indices" seemed to show that Montenegro was not keeping her word.[34] Although the situation was not critical, it would soon become so.

Montenegro's Desire for a Border Rectification with Turkey

In mid-December, Nicholas hatched a new project that clearly had the potential of disrupting the status quo. He proposed that Montenegro and Turkey exchange territory, specifically Turkish-held Ržanica for the Montenegrin lake region, including the districts of Velika, Mokra, and Jezerski Vrh.[35] Montenegro coveted the Ržanica sector because it was a Turkish wedge that divided her northeastern territory and hampered commerce and communications in the region. The fact that Nicholas was trying to take advantage of Turkey's troubles elsewhere to secure a relatively innocuous exchange of land was far less disturbing than the manner in which the proposal was made. The king informed Assim Bey, the Turkish minister, that if the Porte did not agree to the new border regulation, it might regret the consequences. Understandably, Constantinople took umbrage at this poorly veiled threat, and after denouncing the plan in Cetinje, turned to the Powers for assistance.[36]

The Ottoman ambassador in Vienna requested that pressure be brought to bear on Montenegro to tone down her statement.[37] Almost simultaneously, the German undersecretary of state proposed a joint Austro-German démarche at Cetinje to advise the Montenegrins to refrain from any futher provocative acts or words.[38] Although generally sympathetic to the gist of the proposal, Aehrenthal did not want his allies to gain prestige at the Golden Horn at the expense of his own in Cetinje. Citing a comprehensive report by Rudolf Weinzetl, the Austro-Hungarian chargé at Nicholas's court, he told Berlin that Montenegro's territorial proposals were motivated less by anti-Turkish animus than by a genuine desire to correct what seemed to be an "injustice and inconvenience."[39] Nonetheless, Aehrenthal refused to endorse Nicholas's demands. Ržanica was inhabited largely by Albanians, whose incorporation into Slavic Montenegro would fly in the face of established Austro-Hungarian policy. He hoped instead that the Turks would be satisfied with Weinzetl's report, which included a statement by their own minister in Cetinje that the situation was not that serious. On the other hand, if Constantinople still requested the application of Austro-Hungarian pressure, or if Montenegro developed an "incorrect attitude," then he was prepared to take part in Germany's démarche.[40]

Nicholas naturally believed that the Powers should intervene on his behalf, rather than Turkey's, to redress a wrong and remove a threat from his border. Parrying Giesl's contention that a Turkish attack was not in the cards, he argued that his policy had to be calculated on the basis of just such a possibility. If Turgut Pasha were to be reappointed head of Turkish forces in Scutari vilayet, he suggested, the danger of attack would be very real indeed.[41]

Even without Turgut Pasha, conditions along the Turco-Montenegrin border continued to deteriorate. In January 1912, one of a series of frontier skirmishes moved an increasingly bellicose Gregović to warn British chargé Lucas-Shadwell, ordinarily the vice consul in Dubrovnik, that the Montenegrin government would make "one last attempt" to come to terms with Turkey, indicating that the people living along the frontier "would welcome war if they could provoke it." At this juncture, the British representative took Gregović's harsh words with a grain of salt: "I do not think that great importance should be attached to these utterances of the Minister of Foreign Affairs, as the King alone directs foreign policy and if His Majesty inspired this alarming and pessimistic statement it is possible that he did so with the object of securing the support of the British ambassador at C[onstantino]ple in his efforts to obtain a rectification."[42] In the months ahead, Turkey would negotiate a frontier settlement with Montenegro, but instead of serving as the prelude to peace, it became a pretext for war. In the meantime, the Turco-Montenegrin border remained an unsettled issue.

Continued Serbo-Montenegrin Enmity

One of Aehrenthal's greatest fears in the early stages of the Turco-Italian War was the prospect of a Serbo-Montenegrin rapprochement. Happily for him, it appeared as though relations between the two Serb states were as unfriendly as ever. Despite the alluring possibility of a joint action against Turkey, the two countries continued to fire propaganda salvoes at one another.[43] The Serbians were disturbed by Austria's loan to Montenegro, but they were outraged when in December the patriarch of Constantinople selected Gavrilo Dožić, a Montenegrin, over their own candidate as the new metropolitan of Prizren. The incident, if seemingly trivial, was important in the eyes of the Orthodox Serbians and Montenegrins, one more link in the chain of enmity.

A few years before, with the aid of Russia and the acquiescence of Serbia, Nicholas had successfully lobbied in Constantinople for the appointment of the Archimandrite Nicephor to the bishopric of Prizren, the holy city of Serbdom. The radical cabinet of Milovanović, however, soon grew dissatisfied with Nicephor, forced his resignation, and campaigned for the selection of Vasilije Radenković, a former Serbian guerrilla, maliciously labeling Dožić "that Austrian candidate."[44] In late December, however, the patriarch chose Dožić, a decision that raised cries of protest in Belgrade. The Montenegrin response to Serbian calumnies was so vehement that the British representative in Cetinje observed that "if the two countries had a common frontier war would be inevitable."[45]

Comforting though this might be to Aehrenthal in the existing situation, he did not choose to reverse Austria's age-old policy of trying to keep the two Serb states apart. Afraid that Montenegro's anti-Serbian feelings might seek an outlet close to home, he strengthened Austria's forces along the Austro-Montenegrin border.[46] Despite the Austrian military presence, or because of it, a conflagration soon flared up—not along this border, but along Montenegro's smouldering frontier with Turkey.

Just as the Austrians were pleased by the continued enmity between Montenegro and Serbia, so was the rest of Europe relieved in December when Aehrenthal finally succeeded in dismissing Field Marshal Conrad von Hötzendorf from his post as chief of the Austro-Hungarian general staff. Austria's most famous advocate of preventive strikes against any or all of the empire's foes, Conrad had devised numerous plans of action against Russia, Serbia, Montenegro, and even Italy. Late in 1911, with the main body of Italian forces engaged with Turkey, he advised implementing his plan against Italy in retaliation for Rome's attempt to reach an accommodation with St. Petersburg at Racconigi in 1909 behind the backs of its allies. The fact that Italy had neglected until the last minute to tell Vienna of her intention to occupy Tripoli and now threatened to upset the status quo in the Balkans, contrary to the letter and spirit of the Triple Alliance, served as sufficient pretext for

Conrad. That an Austrian strike against Italy would also upset the balance of power in the Balkans seemed inconsequential to him, though clearly not to the foreign minister.[47]

Conrad's bellicose attitude served at least one useful purpose: it made the Italians (as well as the Serbians and the Montenegrins) think twice before breaking their pledges not to disturb the Balkan status quo. On the other hand, it made them extremely distrustful of Vienna's real intentions and gave rise to rumors such as that mentioned earlier concerning the Sandžak. The *Neue Freie Presse* reported that Conrad's dismissal gave proof of Austria's peaceful intentions and the firmness of her resolve to stand by her allies. The conservative *Reichspost*, however, argued that "Count Aehrenthal will never, never be able to find a justification for the loss of this man."[48] In only one year's time, the *Reichspost's* demands for Conrad's reappointment would be met. Aehrenthal himself would pass from the scene, and Conrad would be granted an imperial reprieve to take up where he had left off. Until then, Nicholas could rest secure in the knowledge that the wings of Austria's most powerful hawk had been clipped.

Nicholas's Journey to St. Petersburg

At the end of January 1912, Nicholas prepared to set out on a long-deferred trip to St. Petersburg, his first court visit since becoming king. Before leaving Cetinje, he invited Baron Giesl to discuss this trip and the new, disturbing reports from Albania. Only one week earlier, he had been unusually optimistic about the chances for keeping a lid on the bubbling Albanian cauldron; on the eve of his departure, however, he painted a somber picture of the prospects for peace. Echoing Squitti's sentiments, he predicted that with the coming of spring, the Muslims of Kosovo and the Catholics of northern Albania would rise in their annual revolt. The result would be predictable: Montenegro would have to play host to migrant Albanians in an unsolicited encore of the events of the past two summers. Giesl suspected that one of Nicholas's principal aims in going to Russia was to request assistance for just such a contingency. Moreover, he was sure that the king would also direct a similar financial appeal to Vienna. In the minister's opinion, Nicholas counted on being paid to keep the peace, or at least not to make war.⁴⁹ He and Aehrenthal could only hope that Russia would use her influence to restrain Montenegro from embarking on any Balkan misadventures.⁵⁰

The king's original itinerary took him to St. Petersburg via Rijeka, Venice, Munich, and Berlin.⁵¹ In Venice, he planned to await the arrival of Crown Prince Danilo, whom he had dispatched to Sofia, ostensibly to attend ceremonies celebrating the majority of Bulgaria's Crown Prince Boris.⁵² After spending four or five days in St. Petersburg, the king intended to travel incognito to the Habsburg capital, where he hoped for audiences with both Francis Joseph and Aehrenthal. He had his heart set upon an official Habsburg reception, but in the cold month of February, the king's vanity had to yield to the emperor's poor health.⁵³

Nicholas began his journey on 30 January. Despite his numerous pledges to keep the peace, the monarch's parting remarks to the crowd that had assembled to wish him well were not reassuring:

> You will doubtless say to me what a Montenegrin Voivode said to one of my ancestors who was starting for Russia. . . . "I entreat you to make the Czar swear on the altar-stone that he will not forget us as one forgets the watch-dog tied at the door of the sheep-fold, and say to him that we can no longer remain in our present unhappy condition of poverty, hemmed in and crushed on all sides."⁵⁴

Prime Minister Tomanović, usually a spokesman for the party of caution and restraint vis-à-vis Turkey, spoke to Giesl with evident resentment of the manner in which Russia had treated Montenegro of late, especially with regard to the Malissori refugee problem. Bitterly he recalled that the Montenegrin government had to turn to Austria-Hungary for a loan the Russians had refused to provide.⁵⁵

Despite its pomp and ceremony, Nicholas's departure was marred by rumors of a new Serbian-based conspiracy to depose him and establish a constitutional government with Prince Mirko at its head. Lucas-Shadwell reported that "Slav politicians at . . . [Dubrovnik] are inclined to think that the story of the conspiracy is not entirely groundless. Such a movement might come from Bulgaria or the United States, where there are Montenegrin revolutionaries."⁵⁶ Although the evidence of an anti-Petrović conspiracy is overwhelming, that for a specific assassination attempt is not. In any case, Cetinje remained calm in the king's absence.

Gregović reported that the meeting in St. Petersburg with Sazonov was "satisfactory in every respect."[57] The Russians had treated the king with great respect, but they also brought "strong pressure" to bear on him to keep the peace.[58] The British minister heard that they had even threatened to discontinue their subsidies as in 1911 unless "Montenegrin foreign policy were brought into close touch with Russian views."[59] The day after his return to Cetinje, the king appeared amenable. He made "ostentatious overtures" to the Turks and entertained the Turkish commandant of Scutari in Podgorica for five days. Soon afterwards, a mixed boundary commission made considerable headway toward resolving the volatile frontier question.[60] All the while, Nicholas walked a tightrope. He wanted it known that he was complying with Russian "orders," yet he clearly did not want to alienate his own Malissori clients.

Upon his return, Nicholas also became somewhat more solicitous of Austria-Hungary. In February, he dusted off a proposal of the previous autumn to have Austrian—not Russian—jurists help reform Montenegrin courts and judicial institutions.[61] Shortly thereafter, the Austro-Montenegrin trade treaty signed in February 1911 went into effect, and it was announced that an Austrian firm had contracted to build a section of the projected Risan-Nikšić railroad between Grahovo and Trubel. The irritated Russian chargé d'affaires at Cetinje wrote to Sazonov about a possible alliance between the Dual Monarchy and the tiny kingdom. Such was not the case, but the improvement in Austro-Montenegrin relations gave Aehrenthal's successor at the Ballhausplatz one less problem to worry about.[62]

Aehrenthal's Successor as Foreign Minister

On 17 February, Aehrenthal died of leukemia, a disease that had slowly sapped his strength and impaired his ability to run the affairs of the Ballhausplatz. His death was not greatly mourned in Cetinje, where memories of 1908 burned fresh in the minds of all.⁶³ The unofficial list of candidates to succeed Aehrenthal was long, including such illustrious names as Baron Stephan Burián, the joint Austro-Hungarian finance minister, and Count Nicholas Szécsen, the Austro-Hungarian ambassador in Paris. For better or worse, Francis Joseph selected one of the individuals recommended by the dying Aehrenthal: Count Leopold Berchtold von und zu Ungarschitz. Ironically, Berchtold was also Sazonov's first choice. Little did the Russian know that in two years' time the two would be bitter enemies in a world at war.⁶⁴

Berchtold assumed his new position reluctantly, after a short period of semiretirement.⁶⁵ Like his predecessor, he became foreign minister following a tour of duty in St. Petersburg. But whereas Aehrenthal had earned a well-deserved reputation for ruling the Ballhausplatz with an iron hand, Berchtold soon proved less sure of himself. Some critics called him pliable; others, spineless. In his postwar memoirs, Heinrich Kanner, former editor of *Die Zeit*, related that whenever confronted by a tough question, Berchtold would press a button calling the appropriate section chief to provide the right answer for him.⁶⁶ Some observers were also disturbed by the new foreign minister's close relationship with Archduke Francis Ferdinand, one of Aehrenthal's most frequent opponents.⁶⁷

Fortunately, Berchtold's first several months in office were not marred by a major European crisis. He continued Aehrenthal's policy of working toward an end to the war between Italy and Turkey but did not have to contend with a Balkanic eruption such as would face him in the autumn. In March, Pallavicini reported from the Golden Horn that relations between Turkey and the Balkan states were correct, if not cordial.⁶⁸ The German emperor was likewise convinced that Russia had no intention of stirring up trouble in the Balkans for fear of unleashing another revolution at home.⁶⁹ When William conferred with King Victor Emmanuel in Venice, in part to discuss renewal of the Triple Alliance, the two monarchs exchanged optimistic evaluations of the Balkan situation. The Italian king mentioned that his Montenegrin father-in-law had received admonitions from the Great Powers, and he speculated that Nicholas would not do anything which might incur their wrath.⁷⁰

Mary Edith Durham's assessment of the situation was more

realistic. War was in the air. "Daily," she wrote, "I saw Montenegro shoving towards war, and the Turks steadily fortifying Scutari." On 10 March, Petar Plamenac, soon to be foreign minister, replaced Jovan Popović as Montenegrin chargé in Constantinople. Plamenac later boasted that he had been transferred to the Golden Horn for the express purpose of declaring war on Turkey.[71] Following another frontier clash with Turkish troops on 17 May, Nicholas himself asked Durham to begin raising funds for the wounded that would soon have to be treated. In Podgorica, she was asked to stay to see the first shot fired in the war against the infidel.[72]

If the Montenegrins were preparing for war with Turkey, they had not yet made any moves to improve their ties with Serbia, a necessary ally. In fact, Serbo-Montenegrin relations worsened in March 1912, when King Peter transferred the remains of members of the Serbian royal family, including those of Zorka, his wife and Nicholas's eldest daughter, from Cetinje to the new Karadjordjević mausoleum at Topola in the Serbian heartland. Nicholas complained bitterly about the "unceremonious behavior" of the Serbians, and the British minister observed that the event could only increase tension between the two families.[73]

Animated by the hostility of their respective dynasties, the Montenegrin and Serbian presses roared invective in almost daily battle. In the words of Count de Salis, "during the spring and early summer the press controversies between the two countries were unusually bitter. . . . The 'Cettinski Vjesnik' carried on an unequal struggle with the Belgrade press." In July, the Belgrade *Pravda* even reproduced the text of a nonexistent treaty between Montenegro and Austria-Hungary, which promised the former much of Albania, Old Serbia, and Macedonia. As late as 31 July, the *Vjesnik* printed a scathing attack on the personal integrity of Nikola Pašić, the Serbian prime minister. Then suddenly the newsprint cannonades ceased. On 7 August, the *Vjesnik* focused its attention on the miserable situation in European Turkey and rumors of a Serbo-Bulgarian alliance. The British minister concluded that "the day may be worthy of note as indicating the earliest possible moment at which steps can have been taken with a view to an understanding with Servia and the admission of Montenegro to the Balkan alliance" that was then in the making.[74]

Nicholas's Journey to Vienna

Nicholas and King Ferdinand of Bulgaria announced in May that they would travel to Vienna to conduct talks, presumably with the new Habsburg foreign minister. The visits came as something of a surprise to Vienna, because neither monarch had been formally invited, but Francis Joseph graciously agreed to receive them both.[75] At least one Balkan monarch thought the trip was a good sign; as far as King Carol of Rumania was concerned, the more lectures the Montenegrin ruler received on the virtues of keeping the peace, the better. On the other hand, he was suspicious of Ferdinand's intentions in the Austrian capital, fearing an appreciation of Bulgaria's stock there at Rumania's expense.[76]

On 6 June, after assembling a royal entourage acceptable to Vienna, Nicholas and Giesl steamed out of Bar aboard the Austro-Hungarian ship *Gäa*.[77] The following morning the king was greeted by a cannon salute as the ship passed the naval base and fortifications at Pula. From Trieste, where the ship docked at 8 P.M., the king's entourage departed for Vienna aboard an imperial train. Tight security was maintained owing to rumors of yet another plot on the king's life. Upon alighting at the Südbahnhof in Vienna, Nicholas was greeted by Francis Joseph himself, who promptly delighted his visitor by naming him commandant of an Austrian infantry regiment. After a short welcoming ceremony, the two sovereigns made their way to the Hofburg.[78]

Both Berchtold and Francis Joseph counselled Nicholas to keep the peace and urged the king "to abstain from encouraging in any way Albanian unrest." Nicholas duly assured his hosts that he was doing his best to keep their trust. To the Italian ambassador, however, he gave evidence of markedly different sentiments. Reproaching Italy for promising at the outset of the Tripolitan venture not to upset the Balkan status quo, he asserted that he had hoped to wear his Cross of Savoy on the field of battle and, more especially, on his grand entrance into Salonica! The ambassador believed that the king's sputterings were uttered merely for effect, but Berchtold wondered whether Nicholas's favors could be purchased for as little as the honorary command of an infantry regiment.[79]

Six days after embarking on his curious embassy, the king returned home. He seemed satisfied with his visit, but many were puzzled as to why he had undertaken it. It seemed out of character for the king to have left his base of operations when conditions were so unsettled; in addition, nothing substantive had been achieved. His meetings with Francis Joseph and Berchtold had amounted to little more than an "exchange of courtesies." Equally strange was the *Cetinjski Vjesnik's* subsequent hostile response to a rather conciliatory article in the *Neue Freie Presse,* commending Montenegro for her "moderation" during the annexation crisis. The British minister in Cetinje noted sardonically that in replying to the Austrian paper, which "was attempting, though perhaps unskillfully, to flatter King Nicholas, the inspired organ of the Montenegrin Government should have thought proper to adopt, especially at the present moment, a somewhat bellicose attitude towards Austria-Hungary."[80] In his memoirs, Giesl noted that the entire visit had been a "gross deception."[81] It would soon become apparent how correct he was.

Shortly after returning home, Nicholas made sweeping changes in his cabinet. Long-time Prime Minister Tomanović unexpectedly yielded his portfolio to General Mitar Martinović, the king's aide-de-camp and head of the military. For a short while, Martinović also assumed the responsibilities of foreign minister. Despite a wholesale reshuffling of cabinet posts, the British minister advised Whitehall that no change in Montenegrin foreign policy was likely.[82] De Salis ignored the fact that Nicholas had appointed a military man as head of his government, one with little political or diplomatic experience and commonly known to favor a policy of action against Turkey.

Turco-Montenegrin Frontier Incidents

Only weeks after this change of the ministerial guard, Turco-Montenegrin relations took another turn for the worse. A number of frontier clashes and a snag in procedures formalizing a border protocol ended the short period of tranquility that had followed Nicholas's visit to Vienna. On 11 June, the joint boundary commission finally agreed to a border rectification in the neighborhood of Ržanica. The Montenegrins acted quickly to ratify the agreement, but the Turks delayed.[83] Rumors soon reached Constantinople that

Montenegro was preparing to issue an ultimatum calling for the acceptance of the border protocol within four days. Plamenac denied this as well as the suggestion that Montenegro was trying to use a frontier incident between Montenegrin and Turkish troops at Govedje Brod near Podgorica to force her own way on the border treaty.[84] Henceforth, such skirmishes occurred almost daily. If Montenegrin soldiers did not fire across the boundary, Montenegrin peasants did.

Unable to bring decisive military force to bear because of the war with Italy, the Turks tried another time-tested medium of control: bribery. At Nicholas's request, the Ottoman government had agreed some time before to purchase the summer residence of the Montenegrin diplomatic representative in Turkey, a comfortable house at Emirghian on the Bosphorus, for the not inconsiderable sum of 500,000 francs. Although Nicholas had not yet been able to produce the requisite documents of ownership, Rustem Bey, Sadred-Din's unpopular successor in Cetinje, informed Weinzetl that the Turkish government was still prepared to make an initial payment of some two hundred thousand francs, the balance to be paid in annual installments, perhaps in excess of the already generous sale price. Rustem Bey denied that the Turks were afraid of Nicholas; they merely thought that it would be wise to "win" him over to a more sympathetic position. In fact, in early June, the king had received a payment of some ten thousand lira.[85]

Turkey's attentions were not directed solely at the Montenegrin ruler. Recounting the fact that Prince Mirko had once talked the late Sultan Abdul Hamid into an annual subvention (and in fact still desired one from the Young Turk regime), Rustem Bey suggested that the Porte should grease the palm of Crown Prince Danilo, whose influence with his father was believed greater than Mirko's and who was first in line to succeed to the throne.[86] Notwithstanding Rustem Bey's solicitude, the Montenegrins could not be bought this time—at least not by the Turks.

On 4 August, Montenegrin and Turkish troops clashed at Mojkovac, northeast of Kolašin. After attempting unsuccessfully to have Turkish forces withdraw peacefully from contested territory, the Montenegrins forced them out, in the process destroying a number of Turkish blockhouses. Although the evidence seemed to indicate that it was the Turks who had violated Montenegrin sovereignty in the first instance, Rustem Bey, his policy of appeasement crushed, addressed two notes to the Montenegrin government on 6 August demanding an official apology for the incident and threatening dire consequences if Cetinje should not comply. Acting with unusual speed and circumspection, the Porte moved to defuse a potentially explosive situation and disavowed the actions of its minister. On 8 August, Rustem Bey telegraphed his resignation to Constantinople and left Cetinje forthwith.[87]

The Montenegrins soon presented a note to the signatory Powers of the Treaty of Berlin formally requesting their intervention in the border dispute. The Italian minister at Cetinje and his colleague the Austrian chargé Weinzetl (Giesl had gone to Vichy on a two-week vacation for reasons of health) both voiced objections to the wording of the last paragraph note, which called for a time limit for settling the question. This might be misconstrued by the Turks as the ultimatum Plamenac had already disallowed. To emphasize their demands, the Montenegrins ordered the dissolution of the mixed boundary commission, which had been meeting to settle the prolonged dispute. The Porte, however, refused to recognize the peremptory Montenegrin step and ordered Colonel Ali Riz Bey and his staff to remain in Cetinje.[88]

On the night of 14 August, Turkish troops attacked the largely Christian population (Vasojević tribe) of the district of Berane, just beyond Montenegro's northeastern border with Turkey. Many were killed, and it was reported that upwards of three thousand sought refuge from Turkish brutality. Montenegrin troops were immediately transferred to the area to face Turkish units soon reinforced by troops commanded by the infamous Djavid Pasha. The Powers set to work to prevent the latest incident from escalating into the opening round of a Balkan war.[89]

So vociferous were the Turks in their condemnation of Montenegro that the Powers were inclined to believe that the Porte was in fact the aggrieved party. The Turkish foreign minister "assert[ed] very positively that . . . [the] incident near Berane was deliberately provoked by [the] Montenegrin Gov[ernmen]t. . . ." and accused the Montenegrins of occupying Turkish territory.[90] Thus, when Sir Edward Grey advised the Turks to remove their troops from the border, he demanded that the Montenegrins withdraw immediately from "Turkish territory and from the neighborhood of the frontier."[91] On 21 August, a Cologne newspaper published a report that "Montenegro seemed to be the aggressor on the occasion: that all the Powers, including Russia, were strongly urging Montenegro to keep the peace . . . and that it was impossible for them to permit quite a secondary state like Montenegro to attempt to play the part of Providence."[92] The German secretary of state for foreign affairs also believed Montenegro to be the guilty party.

On 23 August, the Great-Power diplomats in Cetinje made "energetic representations" to the king and government. Simultaneously, Giesl and de Salis urged Nicholas to withdraw his troops from the frontier. The king forcefully denied the stories concocted in Constantinople about Montenegro's occupation of Turkish territory as "absolutely untrue," and urged the Powers to intervene at the Golden Horn if they wanted to see justice done and prevent the slaughter of innocent Christians.[93] As if to underscore his innocence, Nicholas agreed to suspend military operations and again asked the Great Powers to take up the question of the border protocol with the Porte.[94] The Powers soon concluded that in the case at hand, Montenegro had acted in good faith. In Constantinople the British representative, Charles Marling, intimated to the Turkish foreign minister that London now possessed information that "showed fairly conclusively that Montenegrin troops had not crossed [the] frontier, that great excesses had been committed by Turkish troops, and that several villages had been destroyed." According to the Briton's account, the foreign minister's response was "shuffling and evasive."[95]

Almost as quickly as it had arisen, the Berane crisis wound its way to an uncertain conclusion. The Turks refrained from committing any "objectionable" atrocities and the Montenegrins duly withdrew their troops from the border. Even so, it was reported that the Turks, instead of removing their forces, actually reinforced them.[96]

In August, the Powers accomplished little toward bringing Montenegro and Turkey closer together. On the eighteenth, an ominous note was sounded when A. Kolushev, the Bulgarian minister to Cetinje, suddenly left his post, allegedly for personal reasons. When Kolushev arrived in Sofia shortly thereafter, Bulgaria's Prime Minister Ivan Geshov tried to scotch rumors that the visit had a political significance and was related to the Turkish crisis.[97] Toward the end of the month, King Nicholas invited Giesl and other dignitaries on an excursion to the top of Lovćen, the important mountain whose fate would soon be the center of Europe's diplomatic attention. Although he had withdrawn his troops from Berane, the king repeatedly cast covetous glances in the direction of Albania while reflecting on Montenegro's chances in the war he said could not be avoided. To Giesl it seemed that all of the Balkan states were searching for a *casus belli*.[98]

The Balkan Alliance

As the summer of 1912 drew to a close, it was increasingly clear in the chancelleries of Europe that the Balkan states were acting more in concert than ever before. For the time being, they joined in a common front directed principally against Turkey, whose Balkan dominions they wished to divide among themselves. They hoped as well to foil the policies and practices of the old Concert of Europe, which seemed determined to sustain the Sick Man of Europe beyond his natural time.

The godfather of the Balkan alliance was Nikolai Hartwig, the Russian minister in Belgrade, ably assisted by A. V. Nekliudov, his counterpart in Sofia. Hartwig was a Russian pan-Slavist, whose appointment to Belgrade in 1909 after a turbulent tenure in Tehran, complicated Aehrenthal's task of keeping Serbia at bay. In the biting words of Durham, "[h]e had successfully worked the ruin of Persia. He was now to compass that of Turkey. Hartwig was a man to stick at nothing."[99]

A series of agreements between Serbia and Bulgaria became the cornerstone of the Balkan alliance. Ever since 1908, the Russians had been eager to put together an alliance to combat what they feared was an Austrian *Drang nach Süden,* but for a variety of reasons, principally the long-standing jealousies between the two Balkan states, their efforts had come to nought. The outbreak of the Turco-Italian War had given Hartwig another opportunity, one which he zealously seized, often against the directions of his foreign ministry. Hartwig realized his hopes with the signing of a Serbo-Bulgarian treaty on 13 March and a military convention on 12 May. Mention of Macedonia, which each country claimed as its own, was left deliberately vague.[100]

Montenegro's interest in a Balkan alliance antedated the Serbo-Bulgarian rapprochement. In November 1911, for example, when rumors had abounded concerning Austria's intentions vis-à-vis the

Sandžak, the *Cetinjski Vjesnik* had spoken "warmly in favour of a confederation of the Balkan states as a suitable safeguard against the particular danger (the Austrian) which menace[d] them for the moment." The Montenegrin newspaper even went so far as to indicate that just such a confederation was in the making, sponsored jointly by Great Britain and Russia—a most preposterous charge so far as it pertained to England.[101]

It was altogether fitting that Montenegro's affiliation with the Balkan league of 1912 should come by way of her close association with Bulgaria. In 1910, at the time of the fiftieth jubilee celebration, King Ferdinand had traveled to Cetinje to honor the Montenegrin sovereign. Even then certain observers had commented upon the special relationship developing between the two countries.[102] Indeed, a Greek journalist had contended that Ferdinand and Nicholas had reached an agreement providing for the cession of the western third of the Sandžak to Montenegro (something which did eventually transpire) should Turkey agree to part with it "of her own will or under duress."[103]

Durham suggested that it was Nicholas who took the first step in the direction of entente with Bulgaria by approaching Ferdinand through a Dutch journalist by the name of Baron de Kruyff. With great circumspection, de Kruyff relayed the fruits of his discussions with Ferdinand to a Montenegrin agent waiting for him in Trieste. This occurred about the same time Nicholas made his overtures to the Serbian government for joint action in Macedonia.[104]

In May 1912, the Serbians, as angry as ever with their cousins across the Sandžak, rejected the idea of letting Montenegro join the Serbo-Bulgarian alliance; Sazonov advised Sofia not to pursue the issue.[105] The Bulgarians, however, had minds of their own and were inclined to reach an agreement with Montenegro, even a bilateral one, without the explicit blessings of Belgrade or St. Petersburg.

The initial meeting, which led to a Bulgarian-Montenegrin alliance, took place neither in Sofia nor in Cetinje, but in Vienna, "right under the noses, so to speak," of Count Berchtold and the Emperor Francis Joseph, on the occasion of the official visits of Kings Ferdinand and Nicholas in June.[106] This was the great deception Giesl had hinted at earlier. Actually, by the time Nicholas and Gregović had moved into the Hofburg, Ferdinand and Geshov had departed the Austrian capital for Berlin, but they left behind

S. Danev, the president of the Bulgarian sŭbranie, and M. D. Rizov, the Bulgarian ambassador in Rome who was summoned for the occasion to negotiate clandestinely with the Montenegrins. Rizov seemed especially qualified to talk to the visitors from Cetinje as he was married to a Montenegrin and had served as his country's minister at Nicholas's court from 1903 to 1905.

Both sides quickly came to an agreement on the major issues, Gregović expressing his government's willingness to act with Bulgaria in the sense of the Serbo-Bulgarian treaty, and even proposing initiating hostilities with Turkey earlier than that agreement had provided for. The principal difficulty proved to be the financial assistance Montenegro required from Bulgaria to do her part, which was not agreed upon until August.[107] In the meantime, Bulgaria sought to complete arrangements with Greece and Serbia.

Geshov's denials to the contrary, Kolushev's sudden trip to Sofia in August 1912 had indeed been motivated by political rather than personal concerns. He took with him news of Montenegro's desire to conclude a final agreement as quickly as possible and Nicholas's plea for immediate action against Turkey. At a famous crown council held at Ferdinand's hunting lodge on 26 August, about the same time Montenegro withdrew her forces from the Berane salient, the Bulgarian leaders acceded to Nicholas's request and agreed to confront Turkey with an ultimatum they believed she could not possibly accept. In Helmreich's words, "the hub of the whole was Sofia, and as the hub turns, so turns the wheel. Sofia pressed for a war with Turkey."[108]

In September, Bulgaria and Montenegro agreed upon a draft of a military convention that provided for war against Turkey no later than 28 September. As it turned out, Montenegro was the only one of the Balkan allies ready to begin on schedule and the timetable had to be set back. Montenegro and Serbia used the additional time to conclude a belated agreement of their own. Meeting in Switzerland, their negotiators hammered out the details of an offensive-defensive alliance by 2 October; their agreement called for a joint declaration of war against Turkey no later than 14 October. The alliance was hastily ratified in Belgrade and Cetinje on 6 October.[109]

Most of the Powers were unaware of this new danger to peace in the Balkans. Sazonov, one of the few who knew of the Balkan accords, seemed confident that he could still control events on the peninsula. Poincaré, however, when informed some time later of the contents of the Serbo-Bulgarian treaty, remarked that "[Russia] perceives today that it is too late to stop the movement which she provoked, and as I told Sazonov and Izvolsky, she tried to apply the brake, but it was she who started the motor."[110]

The Outbreak of War

By mid-September, it was obvious to all observers in Cetinje that Montenegro was readying for war. Once again, Montenegrin and Turkish troops exchanged fire, this time near Tuzi and Planinica.[111] As the Powers had not responded to the Montenegrin government's earlier note demanding intervention at Constantinople, Nicholas let it be known that he no longer felt bound to honor his previous pledges to keep the peace. Yet with uncustomary and unsettling reservation, he refrained from flashing his verbal rapier. To add to the uncertainty of the moment, the crown prince departed for Italy on 16 September on a mission whose goals were unclear. Giesl feared that the king intended to express himself with deeds rather than words and warned Berchtold that only forceful Great-Power action could nip a catastrophe in the bud.[112] The Powers, largely unaware of the Balkan league's far-reaching machinations, believed the crisis hinged upon two closely related problems: whether Turkey could mollify her rebellious Albanian subjects and also come to terms with Nicholas.

Nicholas and a variety of other European observers had been correct in predicting the annual Albanian uprising. With the coming of spring in 1912, Isa Boletin had again led his Kosovars in revolt, this time with surprising results. The Albanians won victory after victory over the Turks. After Albanian irregulars entered Skopje and threatened to march on Bitola and Salonica, the Turks agreed to grant sweeping concessions that promised autonomy in the largely Albanian vilayets of Kosovo, Scutari, Ioánnina, and part of Bitola. This program conformed in large measure to Berchtold's own proposals for decentralization of Turkey's European dominions.[113]

If the Muslim Albanians were more or less pleased by the prospect of an autonomous Albanian under Ottoman suzerainty, their Balkan neighbors were not. They had their own designs on Turkey-in-Europe, including Albania. Nor were the Catholic Albanians very impressed by the Porte's generosity, having heard such promises before. For months the Montenegrins had surreptitiously enticed and incited their Malissori neighbors, and now their efforts paid off.[114] In early September 1912, Nicholas had apparently tried to solidify his support with the Catholic Albanians by offering Prenk Bib Doda, a disaffected member of the Young Turk central committee, Montenegrin support for an autonomous Albanian entity in the north with Christian priests and a Catholic governor. All Nicholas asked in return was Albanian support for Montenegro's proposed drive on Scutari.[115] Now, to Turkey's chagrin, the Montenegrins courted Albanian favor in the open. The Turkish foreign minister complained to Pallavicini that the Montenegrin king had formally received ten Catholic Albanians in Cetinje, who afterwards were feted in the company of Montenegrin ministers. The focus of their mutual celebration seemed to be an upcoming annexation of Catholic Albania by Montenegro. Under such circumstances, it was understandable that the Turks were reluctant to make binding commitments to Montenegro.[116]

Late in September, Serbia, Greece, Bulgaria, and Montenegro revealed that they were planning to present the Great Powers a collective démarche. To head off such a presumptuous move, Sazonov promptly instructed his representatives in the Balkan capitals to use their influence to stop delivery of the note. Berchtold followed Sazonov's lead, while contemplating the Russian foreign minister's suggestion of more formal action against the impetuous Balkan states.[117] On 1 October, Giesl carried out instructions from Berchtold and advised the Montenegrin government to keep the peace. By this time, however, King Nicholas had given the order for a general mobilization of his eleven-brigade army;[118] similar orders were issued in Belgrade, Sofia, and Athens.[119]

In Vienna, Conrad's successor as the chief of the general staff, General Blasius Schemua, concluded that Turkey had "neither the strength nor the will nor the time" to carry through her proposed reforms, and that Great-Power intervention, even if it were possible, probably could not stave off a war the Balkan states seemed determined to wage. In keeping with the requirements of Conrad's famous Mobilization Plan B, Schemua requested permission to increase troop strength along the borders of Serbia and Montenegro.[120]

Simultaneously, Sazonov asked Turkey not to station any redifs on her Balkan frontier and implored the Balkan states to halt their mobilizations; Berchtold seconded Russia's intercession.[121] Yet Sazonov believed, undoubtedly with good reason, that even stronger measures would have to be taken to restrain Turkey and especially the Balkan constellation. Everything, even the cherished program for internal Ottoman reform, would have to take second place to the more immediate problem of defusing the international crisis.[122] In Vienna, Berchtold had an exceptionally cordial meeting with the Russian ambassador, during the course of which he assured Giers that Austria-Hungary was prepared to join Russia and the other Powers in making a collective démarche in the Balkan capitals.[123] San Giuliano voiced his approval for the plan and stated his belief that all was not yet lost; if the Powers could curb the *Kriegslust* of King Nicholas and the Bulgarians, then Serbia and Greece would surely back down.[124]

Giesl complained to Berchtold that events were moving so quickly he barely had time to absorb and record them. On 2 October, the Austrian minister pessimistically reported that there was hardly a "weak hope" left for peace. The king seemed to want war, and even if he desired to back down, he could not, as he had placed himself squarely in the middle of the war party. On 1 October, Nicholas discussed the crisis with Giesl while driving through the bumpy streets of Cetinje. Insisting that he was not an ambitious man and sought no glory in war, the king boasted that he would prefer to take on the Turks singlehandedly, rather than in league with his Balkan allies. The king's assurances that he would not fire the first shot did little to allay Giesl's growing apprehensions.[125] The same day, two proponents of peace, Lazar Mijušković and old Vojvoda Plamenac, visited Giesl. Mijušković intimated that should Montenegro lose her war against Turkey, Nicholas's dynasty would be in serious trouble; republicans were already waiting in the wings.[126]

On Wednesday, 2 October, the king in "half humorous, half ironical" tones, suggested that Giesl, for twenty years a military attaché in the Balkans, assist him in drawing up plans for Montenegrin military operations against Turkey. On 5 October, another Turkish negotiating team arrived in Cetinje in a futile attempt to reach an eleventh-hour settlement. The following day Nicholas confidentially informed Giesl that he would "strike out" at Turkey in the next few days.[127] At General Vukotić's house, rakija flowed in anticipation of a new war; the confident general went so far as to outline his battleplan for Durham: Generals Bošković and

The Road to War: 1911–1912

Martinović would capture Scutari and then join his forces in the conquest of Prizren. As Durham recalled, "no mention was made of when the other Balkan states were to come in. Bulgarian support was certain. Madame Yanko begged me to go with her husband and photograph his entry into Prizren." Similarly, General Martinović invited the Englishwoman to Podgorica to witness the opening shot of the war.[128]

Like their leaders in St. Petersburg, the Russians in Cetinje were divided over which course of action Montenegro should take. Some, like a teacher at the Russian Institute, were confident that the Russian army would intervene to save the day, as it had in 1877, if the Montenegrins ran into trouble. Others, like one young officer affiliated with the legation and the cadet school, insisted that the tsar was in no position to aid his headstrong Balkan wards.[129] "The Montenegrins are absolutely mad!" he exclaimed to Durham. "You must use all your influence to stop them. They must not make this war! We have already told them so most severely. They are mad, I tell you—we cannot and must not have war now."[130]

On Tuesday, 8 October, the Powers finally delivered their démarche in the Balkan capitals. In the absence of the foreign minister, Giesl and Alexander Giers, the Russian minister, took their declaration to the king himself. Nicholas politely listened to what they had to say and then tendered a negative reply.[131] He had already empowered his chargé in Constantinople to inform the Turkish government "that in view of frequent incidents on [the Turco-Montenegrin] frontier his Government had decided to leave [the] solution of all questions pending between the two countries to the arbitrament of war."[132] At noon Nicholas and Mirko departed Cetinje for army headquarters at Podgorica. It was obvious that this was no ordinary trip. Their departure was witnessed by Queen Milena, the princesses, and the ministers of the allied Balkan states, amidst a cacophony of guns, bells, and cheers.[133]

Despite the fighting that had already occurred all along the Turco-Montenegrin border, Nicholas desired to have an "official opening" for his war. On the morning of 9 October, his entourage gathered on a hill above Podgorica to see the ceremonial first shot fired. By striking out before his allies, the king assured himself of a "certain moral weight" in the Balkan world.[134] At least the old man kept one promise to the Powers; he did not fire the opening shot. That honor fell to his youngest son, Prince Peter.[135]

CHAPTER SEVEN
The Outbreak of the First Balkan War: 1912–1913

The shelling of Planinica, which Nicholas staged with such ceremony, forced a hasty Turkish retreat, and Montenegrins had their first taste of victory only hours after they had begun their attack. On 12 October, General Janko Vukotić, commander of the Eastern Army, took Bijelo Polje; four days later Berane fell. General Radomir Vešović, the commander of Vukotić's right flank, similarly disposed of Plav and Gusinje.[1] Naturally, the generals hoped that all of their battles would be as gratifying, but their juggernaut soon ran into difficulties. Montenegro's impetuous warriors had not taken sufficient time to consider the logistics of a tough military campaign, and the army soon experienced shortages of basic items, ranging from maps to food supplies. Durham was dumbfounded by the inadequate provisions for the wounded—150 hospital beds, no more having been deemed necessary. Unfortunately, the Montenegrin style of attacking the enemy head-on quickly filled the hospital wards to overflowing.[2]

Montenegro's principal goals in the campaign were Scutari and Prizren. Hoping to conquer the former in a giant pincers movement, General Mitar Martinović approached the city from the southwest, along Lake Scutari's southern coast, while General Blažo Bošković and Crown Prince Danilo attacked along the lake's northern littoral. They intended to take Scutari and then join Vukotić's troops for a push into Kosovo vilayet. Events, however, did not proceed as planned.

Montenegrin forces came within sight of Scutari two weeks after the start of the war and everyone, including the Austrians, expected the city to fall to Nicholas's troops.[3] Martinović slowed down his advance, presumably to give Danilo the honor of taking the city; in so doing he gave the Turkish defenders, led by the very capable Hussan Risa Bey, valuable time to prepare for a long siege. The Montenegrins soon found they could not take the city by themselves and reluctantly turned to Serbia for assistance. In the meantime, Nicholas's troops occupied the area around Shëngjin, Scutari's natural port on the Adriatic, while the Serbs, who declared war on 18 October, deprived Nicholas of Prizren. In Durham's pointed words, "the scheme of the three divisions of the Montenegrin army meeting at Prizren had . . . passed into Nevernever Land, along with King Nikola's dream of sitting there upon the throne of Stefan Dushan."[4]

Montenegro's war aims conflicted with the aspirations of Albanian nationalists, but in the struggle at hand Nicholas considered his country's historic rights superior to their ethnic claims. That both Scutari and Prizren were overwhelmingly Albanian cities meant far less to him than the fact that they had once been Serb cities. Having championed the cause of the Malissori in 1910 and 1911, he now rode roughshod over the hopes of these Albanian tribesmen. Although he still claimed to be looking after Albanian interests, his rhetoric did not bear any resemblance to the often harsh realities of his actions. If it was true that Montenegro was "liberating" the Albanians from the Turkish yoke, it was only true because she intended to incorporate these newly "freed" people in a greater Montenegrin kingdom. Some Malissori tribesmen welcomed the Montenegrins initially, but most were repelled by their "liberators' " chauvinism and egoism. Indeed, a majority of those who defended Scutari against Nicholas were Albanians rather than Turks.[5]

Austria and Montenegro at the Outset of the War

Once hostilities began in earnest, Berchtold's concern was to keep them removed from areas vital to Habsburg interests. For many years, the Sandžak of Novi Pazar had been one such area, and on the eve of war it was generally held to be one still. At the end of September, for example, the German military attaché in Belgrade had reported his belief, based on a conversation with a leading Habsburg military official, that the Austro-Hungarian general staff had already decided to implement the now infamous Plan B if either Montenegro or Serbia intervened in the Sandžak.⁶ Before long, the Austro-Hungarian foreign ministry laid any such plans for military intervention to rest.

Anticipating the expansion of the Turco-Montenegrin war into a Balkan-wide affair, the leading officials of the Ballhausplatz met on 16 October to review Habsburg aims in the region. They were in a somber mood. For the Habsburg officials—at least for most of them—the Sandžak was no longer a vital area of interest. Although Serb expansion into the corridor was certainly not desirable for Austria-Hungary, it was also not worth going to war to prevent. In a lengthy session, they reached the tentative conclusion that Austria-Hungary would resort to arms only if one of the Great Powers should attempt to establish itself on the eastern shores of the Adriatic or Ionian Seas.

Even if the section chiefs were to succeed in maintaining the Sandžak as a buffer between Serbia and Montenegro, they recognized the possibility of Serbian and Montenegrin armies joining forces south of the corridor. Far better than to seek expansion in the Sandžak or elsewhere in the Balkans, they concluded that the Dual Monarchy should work to secure its lines of communications in the peninsula, protect Albania against Serb expansionism, and obtain border adjustments for the Monarchy wherever possible. Indeed, they suggested using the Sandžak as a bargaining chip to obtain regulation of the Austro-Hungarian frontier along the corridor or around Mount Lovćen as "compensation" for Austrian "consent to the aggrandizement of Montenegro to the south" or possibly the economic union of either Montenegro or Serbia (and eventually both) with the Monarchy.⁷

The following three days Habsburg officials held additional conferences at the Ballhausplatz. On 19 October, the day after Serbia, Bulgaria, and Greece entered the war, they confirmed their decisions of the sixteenth, agreeing that Austria-Hungary should attempt to conclude a customs union with Montenegro and secure rectification of the Austro-Montenegrin frontier in return for "permission" to acquire the Sandžak and other districts.⁸

Thus, Austria-Hungary altered her Balkan policy in mid-October but she refrained from publicizing the fact. As far as most of the rest of the world was concerned, nothing had changed.⁹ Fearful of the consequences of Montenegrin intervention in the Sandžak, Squitti and Alexander Giers, his Russian counterpart, advised Cetinje to channel military operations elsewhere.[10] Nicholas was already mindful of Austria's traditional concern; even before the outbreak of war, he had promised Giesl that he would seek the approval of Vienna before moving troops into the Sandžak.[11] If Serbia took a similar view, Berchtold reasoned, all would be well. Giesl was convinced that despite the incendiary potentialities of hotheads like Minister of Interior Jovan Plamenac, only a Serbian incursion into the region would place Montenegro on the offensive.

To keep Nicholas on this course, Giesl favored a warning from Vienna that Montenegro must not cross a line running through Berane, Ibar, Mitrovica, and Priština or support guerrillas beyond it. The line was surprisingly generous, leaving much room for campaigning, but at a safe distance from the Bosnian border and the Sandžak proper.[12] Berchtold, however, hesitated to interfere that much; he favored a simple warning to keep military activity away from the Austrian border and an unofficial reminder of the Powers' recent démarche in support of the territorial status quo in the Balkans. His instructions to this effect did not even mention Giesl's plan.[13]

Giesl was satisfied with Montenegro's immediate reaction: copious assurances of the inviolability of Novi Pazar, the recall of officers from the Sandžak frontier, and the shift of General Vukotić from Bijelo Polje to targets in the south, which Giesl believed would keep the army too busy to enter the Sandžak—unless of course the Serbians intervened first.[14] At the end of October, this is exactly what happened, and just as the Austrian minister had feared, Nicholas, too, entered the Sandžak.[15] For Giesl, it was a case of "opportunity making the thief."[16]

On 29 October, Princess Ksenija, the king's daughter and personal secretary, informed Giesl and the other foreign representatives that despite "recommendations" that he join Vukotić's forces in the southeast, Major Mašan Božović had occupied Pljevlja at the invitation of a delegation of its notables, who called for Montenegrin troops to restore order between the Muslim and Christian populations.[17] Giesl termed this explanation a "lame attempt" to cover up, stating bitterly that in war, orders, not recommendations, are usually given to troop commanders. And if, as the Montenegrins suggested, Božović had not received the king's "recommendations" in time, the Montenegrin government had not made an effort to redress the error by ordering a withdrawal from Pljevlja.

Austro-Montenegrin relations were not limited to diplomatic questions of present or future territorial tenure. A host of Austro-Hungarian humanitarians soon arrived in Montenegro to help ease the pain and trauma of war.[18] They cared for Turkish prisoners, numbering in the thousands, at Nikšić and elsewhere in the interior of the country. One philanthropic group provided a considerable quantity of food for the Turks, whose diet otherwise would have been restricted to whatever meager portions the Montenegrins would have been able to spare. In the beginning at least, King Nicholas was effusive in his praise of this Austrian solicitude.

Elsewhere the Austro-Hungarian Red Cross worked hard to aid casualties of war. In Tuzi, one Austrian physician reported attending ten Turkish prisoners, all with their noses cut off, the youngest being a lad of fifteen. If the Montenegrins could not make headway in their march on Scutari, it appeared that they found other ways to vent their frustrations. Nicholas, of course, emphatically denied that Montenegrins were responsible for any excesses committed in northern Albania, preferring instead to blame all cases of mutilation, rape, and pillage on the indigenous Malissori population—his staunch allies of yesterday and potential subjects of tomorrow.[19]

Russian Attitudes

For Austria-Hungary, one of the most disconcerting facets of the Montenegrin declaration of war was the shift it signalled in Russo-Montenegrin relations.[20] Until the declaration of war, Giers, the Russian minister in Cetinje, had gone out of his way to act in concert with Giesl and the Great Powers. He had even shared a number of his confidential telegraphic instructions with the Austrian minister. After 8 October, however, this relationship changed. Although Giers had not taken any overt action in support of the Montenegrin war effort, Giesl rightly detected his vacillation between two divergent Russian policies: an official position of working for peace in the Balkans and an unofficial one of appealing to popular enthusiasm, thereby indirectly fueling the Serbian and Montenegrin war machines.

Giers's "unofficial" proclivities mirrored the Russian public's widespread dissatisfaction with official government policy. In St. Petersburg and Moscow, major newspapers vigorously criticized Sazonov's so-called "Austrophilia." The *Novoe vremia*, for example, cited the "unnatural conjunction between Russian and Austro-Hungarian diplomacy which bodes no good." Some papers called for Russian volunteers, reminiscent of 1877.[21] The citizens of Cetinje apparently forgave Giers for his part in the démarche of 8 October. Appealing for a more sympathetic Russian attitude, they manifested their own pro-Russian inclinations by demonstrating in front of the legations of Montenegro's Balkan allies and also the Russian embassy.[22]

The appearance in Cetinje of Grand Duke Peter Nikolaievich and his wife, supposedly visiting Montenegro in an unofficial capacity although clearly dispatched with the tsar's personal authorization, only tended to confirm Giesl's suspicions. Moreover, Russia's military advisors, who initially had been ordered by their government to stay clear of the field of battle, began to make their presence felt. Unlike most of the other military attachés, who kept a proper distance from the front by confining their visits to main headquarters, General Potapov traveled to Scutari to "observe" the situation first hand.[23]

Although usually precise in carrying out Sazonov's exact directives, Giers was unquestionably pan-Slavic in his sympathies. This attitude, however, did not guarantee his or his country's support for Nicholas personally. As time wore on, Giers grew convinced that the king was more trouble than he was worth and that Montenegro's only salvation lay in a union with Serbia. Accordingly, he worked toward that end, at cross purposes with Austrian policy.

Initially, it appeared that Izvolsky, the Russian ambassador in Paris and Aehrenthal's old nemesis, might move closer to Austria-Hungary as a result of the Balkan conflict. Applauding Poincaré's decision to endorse the démarche of 8 October, he told the Austro-Hungarian ambassador in Paris that in his opinion it would be best for Russia to continue her common front with Austria-Hungary. His unusual Austrophilia, however, proved short-lived. Engendered by his fear of a Turkish victory, it dissipated quickly when it became apparent that the Balkan allies had the upper hand.[24] Performing a volte face, he soon joined most of his fellow Russian diplomats in championing the territorial claims of the Slavic states.

The Albanian Question

The rapid Balkan victories brought the fate of Albania once again to the forefront of Great-Power concern. Afraid that the victorious Balkan allies would overrun the country and carve it up among themselves, the Ballhausplatz contemplated ways to secure its autonomy. On 21 October, Berchtold and Count Alex Hoyos traveled to Italy to discuss various issues, including the Albanian problem, with San Giuliano and Victor Emmanuel; they agreed at this meeting to champion the cause of an autonomous Albania.[25] On 23 and 24 October, the Bulgarians and Serbians swept to great victories at Kirk Kilisse and Kumanovo. A few days later, the Bulgarians shattered Turkish defenses at Lüle Burgas and marched to the famous Chataldja lines defending Constantinople. These startling and swift victories caused both sides to accelerate their plans.

In Vienna, officials hurriedly proposed a governmental structure and sketched possible future boundaries for Albania. During the last week of October, a ministerial council charted a desired course for Austria's future Balkan policy. In an excellent summary of the council's lengthy memorandum, Alfred Pribram wrote that

> Albania is given pride of place and great emphasis is laid on the fact that the most important question for Austria-Hungary—a question that must in case of necessity be decided by the sword—was to prevent any Great Power, or for that matter even a small Power like Servia, gaining a foothold on the east coast of the Adriatic or the Ionian Sea. An autonomous, or in the event of the abolition of Turkish sovereignty an independent, Albania would serve this purpose. This new State should be given as much territory as possible in order that it might be viable and capable of development.[26]

Alfred von Kiderlen-Waechter, the German secretary of state for foreign affairs, and William II were quick to endorse the Austrian plan as "moderate and very reasonable."[27]

No matter how reasonable it was, Austria's plan challenged the historic and territorial aspirations of the Balkan allies, all of whom laid claim to some part of Albania. The Serbians, in particular, made an Adriatic port one of their foremost war aims, and Serbian troops were in the process of crossing the rugged Albanian mountains to occupy the Albanian coast. Berchtold's appeals to restrict military operations on Albanian soil fell upon deaf ears.

Poincaré suggested that the Powers adopt a policy of disinterestedness in the Balkans and let events take their natural course. The Ballhausplatz quickly rejected this proposal, and the semiofficial *Fremdenblatt* even threatened intervention if the Balkan states did not heed Vienna's warnings.[28] In preparation for such a contingency, a ministerial council on 29 October had ordered an increase in military strength in the three southern provinces of the empire.[29] Yet in an address to the foreign affairs committee of the Austrian parliamentary delegation on 5 November, Berchtold insisted that his intentions were pacific: "We are prepared to make large allowances for the new situation created by the victories of the Balkan states and thus lay the foundations of a lasting and friendly understanding with them. On the other hand, we have also the right to demand that the legitimate interests of the Monarchy shall suffer no harm from the new settlement of things." Thus, Berchtold formally dropped demands for a status-quo-ante settlement, the first Great-Power statesman to recognize publicly that the clock could not be turned back.[30] Moreover, he emphasized that his program for Albania was not inflexible and that he would take into account future developments.

Given her past intransigence, Austria's new program was unexpectedly moderate, but the Balkan states were determined to realize their own aspirations and paid scant attention to Berchtold's call for Albanian inviolability. The other Powers, too, were slow to embrace the Austrian program; Russia in particular held out for a Serbian port. The Serbian cause was backed by a number of Austrian liberals, including Josef Baernreither, and the Czechs, Karel Kramář and Thomas Masaryk.[31]

Blithely ignoring Berchtold's strictures, the Montenegrins began to occupy the port of Shëngjin, opposite Scutari. A perturbed Berchtold quickly instructed Giesl to inform Nicholas that while he did not want "to disturb Montenegrin military operations in any way," a lasting occupation of the Albanian coast would be inconsistent with plans for an autonomous Albanian entity.[32] He requested Rome to make similar representations in the Montenegrin capital, explaining carefully to San Giuliano that the Austro-Hungarian démarche referred specifically to the Albanian coast and did not rule out Montenegrin expansion in other directions.[33]

Nicholas pointedly snubbed these representations, arousing Berchtold's ire. In the course of a bumpy car ride from Virpazar to his headquarters on 12 November, Nicholas petulantly responded to Giesl's message, arguing that "Shëngjin is the lung of Scutari; one cannot be separated from the other." Clearly, he intended to keep both, all the while denying that his troops were already in the area. "Perhaps they were Malissori," he suggested to Giesl, adding vaguely that the latter case "would give me even more to do—but I have my plan." After arriving at Rijeka Crnojevića, the king justified his evasiveness on the grounds that Giesl's message had been tendered verbally and was not signed or in "proper form." To Giesl's rejoinder that it was nonetheless an official communication, he answered that he considered it "null and void," and refused any further reply.[34] The following day, Squitti gave Nicholas an identical message, adding that the integrity and autonomy of Albania were important to Italy, too. Once again, the king rejected the message.[35]

Much to Giesl's amazement and chagrin, his dispatch to the king was soon published by the *Cetinjski Vjesnik*, which unabashedly reported the Montenegrin government's policy of noncompliance.[36] Berchtold angrily responded to this flagrant attempt to disregard an official communication from a Great Power, warning Nicholas that his attitude toward the démarches would have an ill effect on future Austrian policy toward his kingdom.[37]

The following day, apparently having tired of his game, Nicholas apologized for his behavior and the publication of the note, saying that he had been suffering from a fever and a sore foot.[38] He then presented Giesl with a series of wild suggestions; most of these the Austrian discounted as nonsense, although some of Nicholas's ideas would resurface in the days ahead. One proposal was to arrange a marriage between the Montenegrin king's youngest son, Prince Peter, and an Austrian archduchess. A second was to have an Austro-Hungarian warship carry Nicholas to Vlorë to be crowned king of Albania. While Montenegrin troops continued their occupation of the Albanian coast, Giesl could hardly take Nicholas's overtures seriously. In response to the Montenegrin's request to preserve the confidentiality of his suggestions, Giesl sarcastically answered, "Rest assured, Sire, I will consider them as null and void."[39] Berlin soon followed Vienna's lead with a warning of its own.[40]

Despite this pressure from the Triple Alliance, Montenegro continued her military activities along the Adriatic coast. By mid-November, Shëngjin was in Montenegrin hands and Lezhë seemed only a stone's throw away. But Serbian forces arrived in Lezhë before Nicholas's troops and set up their own administration. The Montenegrins had to be content with guarding one end of the bridge over the Drin River leading into the town, while their allies undertook the occupation of the remainder of the Albanian coast as far as Durrës. The arrival of the Serbians made the Albanian problem that much more serious. Berchtold believed that they would be far harder to dislodge from the Adriatic beachheads than the Montenegrins.[41]

Habsburg Overtures to Serbia and Montenegro

Austro-Serbian relations suffered another jolt in November when Belgrade demanded the recall of Oskar Prochaska, the Austro-Hungarian consul in Prizren, whom it accused of inciting the Turkish and Albanian populations against Serbian forces. In the wake of Prizren's occupation, communications between Prochaska and the Austrian foreign ministry were interrupted. For a while no one knew whether the diplomat was still alive; rumors circulated that Serbian troops had physically abused him. Even after Vienna learned that Prochaska was unharmed, some government officials called for military action to teach the Serbians a lesson.[42]

Like Aehrenthal before him, Berchtold strove to keep the hounds of war leashed, but Chief of Staff Schemua and other Austrian generals gained Francis Joseph's approval for military preparations in southern Hungary and along the Russian border. The latter preparations were in response to the tsar's decision not to dismiss the third-year troop levy as previously scheduled at the end of October. Throughout November, both Austria and Russia increased their troop strengths, both sides stopping short of ordering a general mobilization, a step tantamount to declaring war.[43] Amidst growing fear of a European conflict, the Powers decided to hold an international conference to resolve the Serbian problem and other outstanding issues.[44]

Despite the Prochaska affair and the provocative Serbian advance to the sea, Berchtold still hoped to reach an accommodation with Belgrade. In the Austrian program for the Balkans unveiled in October, he had supported the territorial aggrandizement of one or the other Serb states, "entering into a lasting relationship of friendship, alliance, customs union, or the like," because "a Serbia or a Montenegro attached to our sphere of interest or power would be the simplest and perhaps the only way to secure for ourselves in the future a link with Salonica or Albania."[45] In retrospect it is hard to see how an Austro-Serbian rapprochement was a real possibility, but, nonetheless, Berchtold communicated his version of the "good neighbor policy" to Pašić. Should Serbia not accept his overtures, he would then approach Nicholas.

Minister Stephan von Ugron proposed closer economic relations, Serbia's retention of her territorial gains in the Balkan interior, and an outlet on the Adriatic—through Bosnia—or perhaps a port on the Aegean.[46] But as Albertini has pointed out, the program suffered from an important contradiction: it "attract[ed] Serbia into the orbit of the Monarchy and . . . [yet] oppos[ed] one of her chief aspirations," namely, her own Adriatic port.[47]

Pašić was slow to respond to Vienna's overtures because he did not want to settle for an Obrenović-like arrangement concocted by the Ballhausplatz. On 25 November, he infuriated Berchtold by stating in the *Times* that "it is essential that Serbia should possess about fifty kilometers from Alessio to Durazzo. This coastline would be joined to what was formerly Old Serbia. . . . For this minimum Serbia is prepared to make every sacrifice, since not to do so would be false to her national duty."[48]

Pašić emphasized to Redlich, Masaryk, and others who came to Belgrade that Serbia desired better economic relations with Austria-Hungary but not at the price of her own Adriatic port. He stated his willingness to travel to Vienna to discuss the matter with Berchtold, but an invitation was never forthcoming. Berchtold had already agreed with the other Powers to discuss at an international conference the questions Pašić wanted to resolve bilaterally.[49] He could not reach a separate agreement with Pašić even if he wanted to; to do so would entail surrendering one of his own nonnegotiable demands for a purely Albanian coastline.[50]

In face of Belgrade's recalcitrance, Berchtold turned to Nicholas. The result was a scheme that did the foreign minister little credit and ran the risk of embarrassing him in the eyes of Europe. On this occasion, Berchtold was willing to dicker behind the backs of his allies, especially the Italians. The essential element of Berchtold's plan—agreed to by the leading officials of the foreign ministry on 19 October—was an offer to yield Scutari to the Montenegrins in exchange for the coveted heights of Mount Lovćen, which overlooked the vulnerable Dalmatian town and naval base of Kotor.[51]

In outlining his program to Giesl, Berchtold argued that Lovćen had only "offensive importance" for Montenegro, but could have crucial "defensive significance" for the Monarchy. This was a dubious assertion because Lovćen was the gateway to much of Montenegro, including the capital of Cetinje. Berchtold also contended that Lovćen's cession would constitute adequate proof of Montenegro's intention to pursue a pro-Austrian policy. Should the Montenegrins surrender their mountain bastion, they would have little choice but to appease their giant neighbor. Austrian possession of Lovćen would enhance Kotor's position as a strategic naval base, and carry with it the risk of alienating Italy, whose long coastline was vulnerable to a sea attack and who already mistrusted Austria's intentions in the Adriatic. But this was a risk Berchtold seemed willing to take.

In addition to the Scutari-Lovćen exchange, Berchtold contemplated extensive economic agreements between Montenegro and Austria, including the customs union Aehrenthal had frequently alluded to. The Austro-Montenegrin trade treaty, concluded the previous February, permitted the duty-free import of Montenegrin cattle into Kotor; Berchtold now proposed opening the entire Monarchy to Montenegrin goods on a most-favored-nation basis.

Berchtold advanced good reasons why the Montenegrins should permit their country to become an economic adjunct of Austria-Hungary. Smuggling could be eliminated; Montenegrin timber, minerals, and other natural resources could be exported to the two countries' mutual benefit; and, with the income from an expanded market for her exports, Montenegro could look forward to a "blossoming future." Berchtold further mentioned that the new arrangements would enable Nicholas to assimilate his newly acquired territories with much greater ease. Finally, the Monarchy would compensate the impoverished king for the loss of tariff revenue by guaranteeing him a regular income, which would render unnecessary his well-known reliance on Russian gifts.

In return for this bounty, Berchtold requested his pound of flesh. Austria's rights in Montenegrin waters for the purposes of transit, fishing, and coastal trade would have to be guaranteed. The foreign minister also sought the future merger of the Austro-Hungarian and Montenegrin rail lines, especially along the Adriatic coast, the ultimate aim of which was the creation of a network by which Austrian trains could reach Albania by traversing Montenegrin territory.

The object of this comprehensive project, or so Berchtold told Giesl, was to liberate Montenegro from Russian economic vassalage. But the line between the kind of economic freedom he proposed and a new economic vassalage to Austria was exceedingly thin. Even Berchtold doubted whether Nicholas would be willing to accept so many conditions to assure himself of Scutari. Accordingly, he asked Giesl to assess the king's mood before commissioning him to relay the details of the project to the palace. Unsure of the king's reliability, Berchtold suggested that Giesl might first talk to Danilo, who in the past had given evidence of a pro-Austrian posture and might be willing to put in a good word with his father.[52]

Giesl did not approve of his chief's proposed Montenegrin package, especially its economic and commercial components. He believed Nicholas wanted immediate results and would not sacrifice Russia's celebrated, if temporarily suspended, annual subvention of more than two million crowns for the slow, albeit rational, economic growth of his country. It was well known that the Montenegrin monarch was uncomfortable with economic questions and usually deferred to the judgments of his financial advisors. Giesl was also certain that Danilo would offer Austria no assistance in converting Nicholas to Berchtold's scheme. The Austrian minister informed Berchtold that the crown prince's sporadic Austrophilia was now a thing of the past; in fact, he was, as Giesl wrote, ensconced in Gruda, allegedly under the baneful influence of Russia's resident grand duke, Peter.

Giesl was convinced that Nicholas would reject the Scutari-Lovćen exchange and possibly inform his allies, and all of Europe, of Austria's overtures. For this reason, he believed it would be a foolish and dangerous mistake to let the wily king "look at our cards," especially if the knowledge thus obtained could be used to mobilize European opinion against the Monarchy. He also thought that if Nicholas even suspected that Berchtold was willing to surrender Scutari, he would promise him anything in order to get it and then go his own way. Although an unbiased observer examining Berchtold's economic proposals for the first time might have been tempted to reach another conclusion, Giesl bitterly complained that in Montenegrin eyes "Austria-Hungary is good only to be exploited; every page of the history of Montenegro in the last three years is proof of this assertion."[53]

For Giesl, only the application of Austro-Hungarian military power or diplomatic pressure could combat the "intoxicant of victory . . . the sensation of fundamental emancipation from Europe . . . the boundless feeling of potency" that seemed to grip the Montenegrin leaders. Giesl thus put forth a counterproposal, one he advised issuing to Nicholas under his name so that neither the foreign minister nor the Austrian government would be held liable for any possible repercussions. Giesl's proposals contained a list of military requirements Austria would expect Montenegro to meet, most particularly the cession of Lovćen; it also provided for strong retaliatory action should Montenegro not comply—a possible naval demonstration of the coast of Shëngjin and the seizure of Krstac, the important ridge overlooking Kotor. The Montenegrin government would thereby be confronted with a *fait accompli,* which would have to be sanctioned in return for permission to stay in Scutari.[54]

Wisely, Berchtold rejected this scheme, believing that any military action on the part of Austria-Hungary would be premature and would only arouse the instant hostility of Europe. A territorial exchange, such as he had suggested, was one thing; forcible seizure was something else. Modifying his own recent program, he recommended that Giesl not insist on the cession of Lovćen or even a shifting of the Austro-Montenegrin border to the crest of the mountain. It would be enough to move the frontier somewhere beneath the crest, only as far as necessary for the safety of Kotor.[55]

On 22 November, five days after Berchtold had dispatched his new proposals to Giesl, the minister finally talked with Nicholas. Giesl flatly informed the king that he would not be permitted to retain Scutari or its immediate environs indefinitely. Although Nicholas listened to the Austrian's strictures with "equanimity," he also warned Vienna that "if the Monarchy tries to drive me out with force, I will fight to the last goat and the last cartridge."[56] He promised to consider Berchtold's proposals, both territorial and economic, and to send an aide to discuss them further. Nicholas made it quite clear, however, that should an Austro-Montenegrin understanding on northern Albania not be reached, he would wait "sword in hand" in Scutari for the Austrians to try to evict him.[57]

Nicholas sent Lazar Mijušković, whom Giesl characterized as the "only man in Montenegro with whom one can rationally talk economics," to discuss Berchtold's proposals with the Austrian minister on the following day. Mijušković was disturbed that Berchtold would not support Montenegro's claims in the highlands of Albania. While he found some merit in the foreign minister's economic ideas, they still sounded to his ear more like "economic enserfment" than "economic liberation." The customs union might be worked out, Mijušković said, but only if Austria would extend the same offer to all of Montenegro's Balkan allies.[58]

As far as the sensitive Austro-Montenegrin border was concerned, Mijušković told Giesl that his government was willing to discuss the exchange of territories of equal value anywhere along the frontier, except Krstac, which was not negotiable under any circumstances. He first explained that the Krstac ridge was only of marginal importance in Austria-Hungary's defense preparations (could the Austrians really expect Montenegro to threaten or attack the Dalmatian lowlands for long?), but it was of critical importance to Montenegro's. Moreover, Lovćen was the sacred mountain that gave the country its name; its separation from Montenegro was unthinkable. To surrender it would cost Nicholas his crown, and the Petrović-Njegoš dynasty its throne.[59]

Thus, Berchtold's elaborate scheme to gain Lovćen and realize an almost century-old Austrian dream came to nought. The result was clearly commensurate with his poor planning. As if to punish Montenegro for her obstinacy, he henceforth took the position that Scutari must belong to Albania. On 28 November, Albanian nationalists in Vlorë, led by Ismail Kemal, proclaimed the independence of Albania, including Scutari. Austria-Hungary and Italy both heartily approved this action.

As it turned out, Giesl was correct not to trust the discretion of the king or his advisors. They kept Pašić, for one, informed of the Austro-Montenegrin discussions and saw to it that the British minister in Cetinje was equally cognizant of the state of affairs. On 25 November, de Salis informed Grey of the negotiations.[60] The British foreign secretary was thus prepared when later that year Montenegro tried to turn Berchtold's overture to her own advantage. An attempt to win Scutari diplomatically for Montenegro soon threatened to drive a serious wedge between Austria-Hungary and Italy.

Montenegrin Proposals Regarding Albania and Scutari

On 27 November, Mijušković again visited Giesl to discuss the king's fervent hope of being awarded the future throne of Albania. "With more rhetoric than logic," as Giesl put it, the king's confidant enumerated several criteria that must be met by any Albanian prince. He would have to be a foreigner, as no Albanian candidate was likely to be qualified or acceptable. Second, he could not come from a major European ruling house. Third, he would have to be a "pliant" man, because as a "tool" of the Great Powers, he would have to answer to their directives. Last of all, he would have to be a capable administrator, to oversee the creation of the new Albanian government. Only Nicholas, Mijušković claimed, met all of these criteria and therefore was "the most natural and practical solution." He would be a popular, or at least an acceptable, choice not only to the Malissori and the Mirdites, with whom he had had a close working relationship, but also the other Albanians, Christian and Muslim alike. Mijušković also asserted that the other members of the Balkan alliance as well as the Great Powers would sanction Nicholas's candidacy because Montenegro was "the weakest and [therefore] the least dangerous among the Balkan lands."

Predictably, Giesl discounted the entire proposal and hotly disputed most of Mijušković's points. In his opinion, the people of Albania, whether living in the north or the south, whether Malissori, Mirdite, or Muslim, would not be any happier under the rule of a Slavic prince than they had been under that of the Ottoman sultan. Moreover, he doubted seriously whether the other Balkan states, particularly Serbia, would approve Nicholas's candidacy. The Powers, for their part, wanted a politically independent Albania, one administered in accordance with Albanian national interests. It was doubtful whether such an Albania could be achieved by giving the sceptor to Nicholas. Instead, Giesl asserted, the Powers would choose a prince on the basis of "justice and practical interests;" Austria would see to it that the prince was not a puppet of Russia.[61]

On 29 November, Nicholas called Giesl to Rijeka to discuss a wide range of issues and to explain Crown Prince Danilo's controversial decision to abandon his command of Montenegrin forces (allegedly because of severe intestinal disorders).[62] In Danilo's absence, the king assumed supreme command of the army, although General Vukotić actually served as chief of staff. Nicholas tried to convince Giesl how important Scutari and Shëngjin were for both Montenegro's and his own future, arguing that the fate of his dynasty was at stake. He worried about the rising tide of pro-Serbian sentiment among his subjects, fostered in large measure by the persecuted Narodna Stranka (People's Party). Every Serbian success unanswered by Montenegrin arms seemed to raise the level of public dissatisfaction with his rule. Only by gaining Scutari and northern Albania, he argued, could he redeem himself in the eyes of his people.[63]

This argument, which would become a familiar one in the days ahead, did have some basis in fact. That the king was gradually losing the affection and respect of many of his subjects was no secret, but the extent to which his throne was endangered was another question—a matter of much speculation and occasional machination in Vienna and St. Petersburg.

With little warning and dubious sincerity, Nicholas chose this moment to suggest a new scheme—an alliance with Austria-Hungary against Serbia. This proposition may not have indicated his true feelings for the Monarchy, but it did reveal something about his distrust of his Karadjordjević ally. Precisely what kind of relationship the king had in mind remained obscure. A "common defense" against a "common enemy" could take on many different forms. The king, however, made one thing clear: he was turning Berchtold's economic and commercial proposals on their head, so that the benefits that would have accrued to Austria-Hungary might now flow to Montenegro. In return for an agreement, he asked Austria-Hungary to keep the peace on Montenegro's Dalmatian and Hercegovinian frontiers. He also sought Habsburg economic assistance in the form of monetary grants, the construction of streets and railroads, the equipping of harbors, and the like, to enable Montenegro to stand up to Serbia. When the Balkan war concluded, Nicholas stated, he would ask Austria-Hungary to step "ostentatiously" to Montenegro's side and defend her territorial claims in the Sandžak. In return, the king promised support for Berchtold's autonomous Albanian state, provided that it did not include Scutari or Shëngjin.

When Giesl noted that it was Austria's intention to have Scutari incorporated into Albania, Nicholas responded: "I will not hear talk of that. . . . I will stay in Scutari." Giesl, annoyed by the king's infinite audacity, told him that only a European forum could decide the fate of Albania. For Giesl, the king's new proposals were as senseless as his recent claims to the throne of Albania, or his dubious threat to abdicate and move to the United States if he could not remain paramount in the Serb world.

Nicholas was a shrewd man who liked to prepare himself and his country for every contingency. Once again he had sought to wheedle Habsburg assistance with no strings attached, all the while avoiding anything that would imperil his profitable, though evervacillating, relationship with Russia. His realism, however, was often checked by other facets of his personality and politics. As Giesl noted, he was "a dreamer, a chauvinist, and also an egoist from the first water," a person who "sees only through his own glasses and believes himself to be a focal point of world politics." He would soon make good this unvoiced claim.[64]

Efforts at Peace: Two Conferences in London

The month of November 1912 had been a troubled one for Europe. The troops of the Balkan alliance had reached the outskirts of Constantinople; and despite Vienna's vociferous protests, the Slavs had secured long stretches of the Adriatic coast. As December approached, the scales of European war and peace hung in a delicate balance. The semimobilized armies of Austria-Hungary and Russia eyed one another anxiously across their common border; Germany, Italy, and Austria-Hungary renewed ahead of schedule their Triple Alliance—for the fifth and final time. Francis Joseph reappointed the saber-rattling Field Marshal Conrad von Hötzendorf to his old post as Austro-Hungarian chief of staff.[65] Yet the clouds of war had a silver lining. Having sued for peace, the Turks concluded an armistice on 3 December with the Serbians and Bulgarians. To many it seemed that the Balkan war might be drawing to a close, and with it the threat of a wider conflict. The Powers arranged a peace conference in London, known as the St. James Conference, and invited all belligerents to participate. Although Nicholas doggedly continued his campaign against Scutari, he agreed to send a delegation, consisting of Lazar Mijušković, Jovo Popović, and Lujo Vojnović.

Hopes for peace in the new year were quickly dashed. Turkey refused to surrender Edirne, the Aegean islands, and Crete; thus, following another nationalist coup in Constantinople, the Balkan war began anew. In this second round of fighting, the Turks fared as badly as they had in the first. In March, the Greeks finally took Ioánnina and the Bulgarians, aided by Serbian forces, occupied Edirne. Of the major Ottoman fortresses in European Turkey (Chataldja aside), only Scutari remained unconquered.

Concurrently with the troubled London peace conference, another diplomatic assembly convened in London in December—the Conference of Ambassadors. For almost eight months, it brought together members of the two rival European alliance systems, who sat as the Concert of Europe. They discussed a wide range of issues, including Serbian access to the sea, the disposition of the Aegean islands, and the formation of an autonomous Albanian state. France, Russia, Germany, Italy, and Austria-Hungary were represented by their ambassadors in London, Great Britain by her able foreign secretary. It was largely because of Sir Edward Grey's impartiality, deft management, and tireless devotion to the cause of peace that this conference accomplished as much as it did and preserved peace among its members through more than sixty sessions.[66]

Wasting little time, at its first meeting on 17 December, the Great-Power conference endorsed a program for a neutral, autonomous Albanian state, one guaranteed by the Powers and capable of independent economic development. This program for Albania dealt a death blow to Serbia's aspirations for her own port on the Adriatic; but in exchange for Russian cooperation, the other Powers acquiesced in Serbian commercial access to the sea through a neutral Albanian free port, possibly Durrës, to be connected to Serbia by an international railroad. This was a far cry from what Pašić had demanded, but at least it assured Belgrade free transit of goods, including military wares, in time of peace. Although these broad outlines were quickly agreed to, months would pass before the decisions of the Great Powers would take effect. They disagreed among themselves over the details of the program, and both Serbia and Montenegro were understandably loathe to surrender their precious Adriatic beachhead to a nonexistent Albanian entity. If a separate Albania was destined to come into being, Montenegro was still determined that it should not have Scutari.

In London, Lazar Mijušković, one of the delegates to the St. James Conference, tried to undermine Great-Power opposition to a Montenegrin Scutari. What he could not achieve through reasoned argument, he set out to accomplish by exposing Austrian hypocrisy to the world. He informed the Italian ambassador of Berchtold's earlier proposals for a Lovćen-Scutari exchange. Unfortunately for Mijušković and his king, the scheme to embarrass Berchtold, sabotage Austro-Italian negotiations over Albania, and win Scutari for Montenegro fell short of the mark.[67]

Rome was duly upset by the intimations of Austrian perfidy and accused Berchtold of crassly ignoring Article 7 of the Triple Alliance, which provided for consultation on Balkan questions and reciprocal compensation for every advantage, territorial or other, which Austria or Italy might obtain beyond the existing status quo.[68] The Italian press was especially vocal in its condemnation of Austria, the *Corriere della Sera* contending that "the question of Scutari is not an ethnic one for her as she [Austria] claims, but is purely a political question." *La Provincia di Padova* proclaimed: "With the occupation of Lovćen, the gulf of Boka would become an Austrian Bizerta."[69] Nor were the Italians the only ones disquieted by Mijušković's revelations. St. Petersburg issued a stern warning to Cetinje not to go through with any territorial exchange, and Berlin, citing Italy's "faithful support" for Vienna in years past, warned Berchtold not to disrupt the Triple Alliance.[70]

Berchtold claimed innocence in the matter, but obstinately refused to relinquish all claim to the mountain—perhaps the only step that would have satisfied Italy. On 29 December, he categorically (and falsely) denied that Giesl had ever received instructions to negotiate for Lovćen, informing the Italian ambassador that if Austria ever came to acquire the mountain, it would only be after preliminary agreement with Italy. One week later, he again assured Avarna that he would do everything in his power to meet his treaty obligations. Yet while assuring the Consulta of his honorable intentions, he added provocatively that Article 7 referred only to the maintenance of the status quo in European Turkey; when that equilibrium disappeared, Article 7 would cease to function.[71]

The Austro-Hungarian ambassador in Rome demonstrated a similar attitude in his dealings with the Italians. Instead of minimizing the issue of Lovćen, he proposed an Aegean island as a future Italian quid pro quo for Austria's acquisition of the mountain. In a misguided attempt to allay Italian fears about Montenegrin security in the event of a new Austro-Montenegrin border, he also suggested moving Montenegro's capital from Cetinje to Nikšić, in the less-exposed interior of the country.[72]

Despite such insensitive remarks, Rome was moved to accept Berchtold's solemn denials and a public *dementi* in the Austrian press. Following warmly tendered advice from his German ally, San Giuliano agreed to support Vienna's position on Scutari and to work in St. Petersburg for the city's inclusion in the future Albanian state.[73] Thus, Berchtold escaped relatively unscathed from Mijušković's trap.

Not only did the Montenegrin effort to embarrass Austria fail to change anyone's mind on Scutari, it also raised serious questions in Montenegro about the wisdom of the king's secret diplomacy. When pressed by the Russian minister for an explanation of Montenegro's dealings with the Austrians, an embarrassed Prime Minister Martinović claimed ignorance in the matter. Nicholas, for his part, tried to clear himself by shifting some of the blame to Mijušković, noting in a royal apologia that his loyal aide had taken too seriously a casual observation that Austria could be embarrassed by bringing up the question of Lovćen.[74]

In the wake of the Lovćen affair, Austria was obliged to pursue her "Scutari-for-the-Albanians" campaign more vigorously than ever. On the other hand, she did not rule out "compensation" for Cetinje, including the regulation of the Bojana River, which would lower the level of Lake Scutari and give Montenegro important arable land. Russia was agreeable to the idea of compensation, but did not give up her effort to obtain Scutari for Montenegro.

Later in January, Grey discussed the Scutari question with the Montenegrin delegates to the London peace conference. They still argued that it was absolutely necessary for Montenegro to hold the city and warned that if Austria marched against Montenegro, Russian opinion "would be very strongly moved." The significance of Scutari was clear to Grey: "if Austria marched against Montenegro, Russia would march against Austria; Germany would then march against Russia, and France would march against Germany: all this on account of Scutari. It would be intolerable." He continued:

> ... the question of Scutari was a bomb which might set the whole of Europe on fire, and we must prevent it from bursting. I know very

well how strong Montenegrin feeling was about it. But others also had strong feelings, and we must find some way of reconciling the various peoples who were interested. Montenegro would gain a considerable amount of territory in any case, and it would be a pity for her to press the question of Scutari to the point of a European war.[75]

The Powers tried to take the matter out of Montenegro's hands. But sketching the frontiers of a state even as small as Albania was a troublesome affair, and the deadlock over the fate of key Albanian cities, including Scutari, that had begun in December continued well into the new year. Russia demanded that the towns of Prizren, Peć, Dibra, Djakovica, and Scutari should all go to the Serb states, while Austria-Hungary, initially at least, claimed them for Albania.[76]

In time, Djakovica and Scutari became the principal problems. After much acrimonious debate and mutual recrimination, a breakthrough was finally achieved in March. Berchtold, wanting to settle the Scutari question before the Montenegrins actually occupied the city, decided to concede Djakovica.[77] To ensure the greater part of the Albanian heartland, including the all-important coastline, for Albania, he was willing to sacrifice much of the arid periphery. But his concession was not made gratis. Berchtold required first, that Montenegro (now aided by units of the Serbian army) should give up her siege and yield Scutari to the Great Powers; secondly, that Serbian troops withdraw immediately from the Albanian coastal region; thirdly, that the Powers recognize the already agreed-upon borders for northern Albania; and finally, that they secure protection for the minorities, chiefly Catholic and Muslim Albanians, under Serbian and Montenegrin jurisdiction. The Russians, happy to gain Djakovica, were more than willing to meet Berchtold half way.[78]

The principal problem was now how to induce Montenegro to accept the decision of the Powers. Warhawks in Vienna clamored for the application of military force. They were angered by Nicholas's intransigence and the "Skodra affair," in which a Montenegrin officer had insulted the captain of an Austro-Hungarian vessel.[79] But the Conference of Ambassadors, anxious to preserve its unity of purpose and action, disapproved any unilateral intervention.[80] It decided instead that if Nicholas continued to resist, the Powers would hold a joint naval demonstration off the Montenegrin coast.[81]

Nicholas responded quickly to a 28 March resolution to this effect. On 30 March, his troops defiantly renewed their artillery attack on Scutari. An incensed *Neue Freie Presse* exclaimed: "Montenegro answers with bombs!"[82] A crisis of the first order was in the making.

CHAPTER EIGHT
The Scutari Crisis: 1913

Nicholas's renewed attack on Scutari prompted the European Powers to initiate a naval demonstration along the Montenegrin coast. The crisis was front-page news throughout April and early May, as all of Europe wondered whether the international naval action would succeed in bringing the recalcitrant Balkan kingdom to its knees and in the process eliminate the growing possibility of a general European war.

In a final attempt to avoid a showdown between Montenegro and the Concert of Europe, Sir Arthur Nicolson advised Jovo Popović, the Montenegrin delegate in London, to "accept without delay" the decision of the Powers, for even if Scutari were to fall, he argued, Montenegro would eventually have to bow to Europe's will and evacuate the town. Popović and his countrymen did not agree. They believed that they could challenge the Powers and win, but if necessary, they were prepared to die.[1]

Eager to begin the demonstration, Berchtold on 1 April ordered a division of Austrian ships to Bar, where they would await the arrival of the other contingents.[2] After initial hesitation, Germany sent the cruiser *Breslau* to join the Austrian ships; the Italians, although annoyed by Berchtold's haste, followed suit.[3] In St. Petersburg, Sergei Sazonov faced difficult choices. He wished to remain true to the decision of the London conference, but he did not dare alienate public opinion, which had already threatened to oust him should he not support Montenegro's claim to Scutari.[4] To appease pan-Slav sentiment, he declined Russian participation in the naval demonstration but on 2 April approved such action by his French and British allies. With Russia's sanction, their warships sailed for Bar, and the naval demonstration was under way.[5]

Although five of the Great Powers had agreed to participate in the demonstration and the sixth had sanctioned it, their diplomats still debated details of the operation, such as the authority of the naval commanders and the extent of their zone of operation.[6] At first the commanders, led by British Admiral Cecil Burney, possessed a large measure of independence. But when on 5 April they demanded Nicholas's immediate submission and threatened a total blockade of the Montenegrin coast should he refuse, Grey, Nicolson, and others decided to tighten the chain of command over the operation. Henceforth, the commanders could take no action without consulting their respective governments.[7] The Powers also debated the scope of their blockade. Berchtold wished to cover the entire Montenegrin-Albanian coast from Bar to the important Albanian port of Durrës. The French and others argued for a more restricted zone. After heated discussion, the conference decided to limit its operations from Bar to the Drin River, a point just beyond Shëngjin, the Adriatic port closest to Scutari.[8] This decision came too late to prevent Serbian troop landings at Shëngjin—landings that encouraged the Montenegrins to continue their resistance—but the Powers hoped through their naval demonstration to prevent any similar action in the future.[9]

The naval blockade formally began at 8 A.M. on 10 April, the Powers terming it "pacific" and emphasizing that the squadron should fire only if fired upon. The British admirality was firm in delineating the blockade's limits: "[It] does not imply any kind of warlike action such as the occupation of places on the coast, or the landing of men, in which you should restrain from joining."[10] The naval demonstration scored its first success almost immediately: Serbian troops on Greek transport ships in Salonica harbor were ordered to disembark, and the Greek government announced that henceforth its ships would not convoy Serbian soldiers to the Albanian theater.[11]

The Montenegrin government officially decried the presence of the squadron as a violation of Montenegrin sovereignty and a breach of the Powers' so-called neutrality.[12] Nicholas dismissed the threat posed by the maritime action with feigned indifference, though he threatened to fire on the warships should they move against Montenegro. Rumors abounded in Berlin that he was surrounded by hawkish ministers and generals, who were more determined than he to take Scutari, and that the king had been intimidated by threats of a palace coup if he did not cooperate. Berchtold, for one, took no stock in this gossip; he remained convinced that Nicholas alone was responsible for Montenegrin obstinacy.[13]

Serbia's Pullback from Scutari

Despite the blockade, the struggle for Scutari continued. Captain Gustav von Hubka, the Austro-Hungarian military attaché in Cetinje, reported that the city was in grave danger and that only quick and energetic measures could avert disaster for Austrian policy.[14] A Russian transport laden with ammunition and war matériel had reached the Montenegrin coast before the blockade had begun. With Serbian troops and these supplies, the Montenegrins outside Scutari were in a strong position.[15]

Berchtold was furious at the continued presence of Serbian troops on Albanian soil, over one hundred ten thousand, by Austrian count. Since the earliest days of the war, he had endeavored to diminish Serbia's influence in what he considered an Austrian sphere. He now stepped up his pressure on the Serbians, hoping that if they could be induced to withdraw from the campaign, the Montenegrin siege would collapse, and he could avoid the embarrassment of having the city occupied by Slavic troops.[16] His scheme worked, at least in part. Pressed by the Austrians and sobered by the resolve of the Powers, the Serbian government formally announced on 11 April that it would terminate all hostilities and pull back from Scutari.[17]

As Pašić expected, the king of Montenegro was outraged by this decision. Although it gave Nicholas a convenient excuse to end the siege and blame his action on Belgrade, he chose not to take that course.[18] Publicly, he continued his aggressive stance. Privately, however, he hinted at the possibility of a settlement should the Powers be daring enough to attack Montenegro directly. He wrote his representatives in London and Paris that "the siege of Scutari will be continued until its conquest or occupation by [a] detachment of the Great Powers or the bombardment of a Montenegrin harbor. In the last two cases, Montenegro would be assured of an honorable withdrawal."[19] It was unclear whether the wily king meant what he said or was merely baiting the Powers.

The Serbians complied with the letter of their agreement to pull back from Scutari, arranging to remove their soldiers on the same Greek ships that had transported many of them to Albania.[20] Despite Berchtold's fervent hopes, the evacuation did not ease the pressure on the troubled city. The Serbian army left behind a great deal of military hardware, which the Montenegrins gleefully appropriated. With no end to the siege in sight, the city soon reached the verge of collapse.[21]

While Austria continued her push for strong coercive measures to rescue Scutari, the other Powers considered less drastic alternatives, believing that the desired capitulation could be achieved with patience and an inviting carrot. San Giuliano, Sazonov, and Stéphen Pichon, the French foreign minister, suggested that financial and territorial inducements might bring success with Nicholas, as they had so often in the past.[22] Berchtold believed that it would be demeaning for the European concert to cajole and wheedle a lesser state, especially one as exasperating as Montenegro. But as a clear majority of the Powers favored some appeasement, he had little choice but to acquiesce.

Austria remained unequivocally opposed to any kind of territorial compensation on the grounds that the Powers had already agreed upon the northern contours of the future Albanian state. Berchtold thus rejected attempts to sacrifice even the smallest section of Albanian soil for a resolution of the crisis.[23] He was more receptive to proposals for financial assistance, however, having been advised by Giesl that a financial offer, coupled with the naval demonstration, just might work. Giesl believed that the Montenegrin people doubted their country could win Scutari without Serbian assistance; some, he claimed, even felt that Montenegro's ultimate survival depended upon political union with Serbia. If Nicholas failed to take Scutari, or to win some equivalent prize with which to placate public opinion and boost his sagging popularity, he could be overthrown. The political upheaval that would ensue might then result in Montenegro's merger with her Serbian neighbor. To avoid this possibility, Giesl suggested giving Montenegro "the possibility of an economic independence . . . [albeit] under the guarantee of [international] financial control." Such a course might be distasteful, but it would prevent a less desirable alternative—a Serbian Montenegro.[24]

As a consequence of Giesl's report and the advice of his German ally, Berchtold agreed to the idea of international financial support for Montenegro, but he insisted that any financial award not be called compensation.[25] Ever wary of the Montenegrin king's guile, he also demanded certain guarantees and controls, namely, that the loan should be underwritten by all the Powers together and that Nicholas submit to the demands of the London conference prior to receiving any funds.[26]

Under the chairmanship of British Prime Minister Asquith, the conference on 17 April endorsed a Franco-Italian plan for a loan in the amount of 30 million francs (1.2 million pounds sterling) to enable Montenegro to normalize her financial situation and defray some of her expenses resulting from the war. Although Popović had told Nicolson that his government would not submit to pressure or accept compensations, the Powers continued to hope that their financial offer would work.[27]

When Count de Salis informed Nicholas of the proposed financial aid, the king coldly rejected it, asserting that the only money he would accept was that due him from Turkey as war reparations.[28] The British representative discounted Nicholas's refusal, contending that "when the right moment comes, . . . the King will take the money. At present he feels he risks nothing by keeping up the comedy of defiance for a while longer."[29] Crown Prince Danilo indicated that his father might consider lifting the siege if the Powers provided adequate territorial, not financial, inducement. Much to Austria's chagrin, some of the Powers were willing to listen to Nicholas's territorial claims.[30]

While the London conference hammered out the details of its financial proposal, the situation inside Scutari worsened. Thousands in the city were ill; many died each day from starvation.[31] Fearing that the city would capitulate and that a Montenegrin massacre of the inhabitants would follow, the Austrian foreign minister advocated strong steps. He demanded "as a minimum" for his approval of the financial aid program the landing of international detachments and their occupation of the Montenegrin ports of Bar and Ulcinj.[32] He also proposed resupplying beleaguered Scutari from the ships of the international squadron.[33] Should the other Powers not agree, Austria-Hungary would have no choice, in his view, but to act on her own.[34]

Berchtold's call for action received a cold shoulder in London. Asquith and Nicolson argued that to supply Scutari or to land troops in Montenegro would be tantamount to an act of war, a step the conference was not willing to take.[35] Austria's demands were thus quickly rebuffed. Instead, on 21 April the ambassadors at London took up a French proposal to have the Porte cede Scutari directly to the Powers, an action that would pull the rug out from under Nicholas, as well as give him another excuse to bow out gracefully.[36] Despite Nicholas's apparent indifference to financial assistance, the conference decided to issue a formal démarche containing an official offer of a loan.

The Palić and Hubka Affairs

While the London conference sought a diplomatic resolution of the Scutari crisis, already strained Austro-Montenegrin relations deteriorated even further in the face of two unpleasant incidents. The first stemmed from reports that Montenegro was conducting a terror campaign against Catholics in her newly conquered territories.[37] Berchtold was outraged by stories of forced conversions of Catholics to Orthodoxy at gunpoint and the violent death of a Catholic priest.

In March, Montenegrin authorities had killed Father Luigi Palić, a Franciscan, whom they had accused of seditious activities. Although a mixed Austro-Montenegrin commission had concluded that there was insufficient evidence to substantiate either the Montenegrin version (according to which Father Palić had been shot while trying to escape) or the Catholic version (which contended that he had been criminally manhandled and brutally murdered), Berchtold was not satisfied.[38] Contending that Cetinje had not even bothered with the trappings of legality in dealing with Palić, he advised the Austro-Hungarian vice consul in Djakovica to leave the town and directed Giesl to make a series of demands on the Montenegrin government in atonement for Palić's death. Most importantly, he demanded freedom of religious choice and movement for the Catholics on Montenegrin soil.[39]

A second incident that marred Austro-Montenegrin relations took place on 21 April. The Montenegrin government, allegedly for temporary military considerations, unexpectedly interrupted postal and telegraphic communications with Austria-Hungary, causing Giesl to send Hubka to the nearest Austrian telegraph station in Kotor, to pick up and deliver messages.[40] Between the Montenegrin town of Njeguši and the Austrian border, a trench dug across the narrow road forced his legation car to stop. According to Hubka's account, only the alert driving of his chauffeur had prevented a serious crash. Apparently undaunted by this experience, Hubka sent the car back to Cetinje and tried to reach Kotor on foot, whereupon he was stopped by Montenegrin soldiers. Only the irate intervention of Giesl, who threatened to leave Cetinje at once, enabled Hubka to continue his journey. Giesl's remonstrations, however, did not put an end to all of Hubka's troubles; on his return from Kotor, Montenegrins along the road threw stones at him.[41]

Berchtold protested these actions, which he argued violated the fundamental rights of diplomatic representation. He demanded a Montenegrin apology and a formal investigation.[42] The Austrians struck back by refusing to allow gasoline destined for Nicholas's automobiles to cross the border and by forbidding horses to enter Dalmatia from Montenegro unless accompanied by a veterinarian's certificate.[43] Giesl called for even stronger measures: "[an] ultimatum threatening the reoccupation of the Sandžak and [the] breaking off of diplomatic relations."[44]

The Montenegrin government did agree to hold an investigation and punish the guilty, but it ignored Austria's demand for a formal apology.[45] A stalemate thus ensued. The Palić and Hubka affairs would not be resolved to Austria's satisfaction until the Scutari crisis itself was settled.

The Occupation of Scutari

On the night of 22–23 April, after the Montenegrins had seized the strategic heights of Tarabosh overlooking Scutari, Essad Pasha Toptani, the crafty Albanian-born commander of the Turkish garrison, surrendered the city.[46] For the first time since 1405, the ancient capital of Zeta was again in Montenegrin hands. Heinrich von Eckardt, the German minister in Cetinje, duly noted that Scutari had not been conquered, but rather that Essad Pasha had "offered [its] capitulation."[47] Although Essad insisted that he had done so because of the city's internal plight, many contended that he had not yet run out of food and was still in a position to resist a Montenegrin assault.[48]

Observers were correct in their assessment that the surrender of Scutari was the result of a mutually advantageous bargain between King Nicholas and Essad Pasha.[49] Nicholas had agreed to allow Essad and his army of some twenty-five thousand men free passage out of the city and to permit them to take rifles, field guns, banners, ammunition, and other supplies.[50] He also offered a bribe of undisclosed amount and a promise to recognize Essad as king of Albania in exchange for the would-be monarch's formal cession of Scutari,[51] thereby circumventing the decisions of the Powers concerning the town and frustrating Austria's insistence that it be awarded to Albania.[52]

On the morning of 24 April, Montenegrin troops under Janko Vukotić took control of the city's fortifications. The next day, Essad greeted Crown Prince Danilo at the entrance to the town and formally surrendered. Montenegrin flags soon flew defiantly over the town and its fortress. Two hours after midnight on 23 April, twenty-one cannon shots were fired over Cetinje, the long-awaited signal that Scutari had fallen. Despite the hour, the whole town celebrated. Men, women, children, and even wounded soldiers poured into the streets. As demonstrations of joy continued the following day, drunken citizens shot guns into the air and called out, "Down with Austria! Down with Baron Giesl! Down with all the Great Powers!" Later Hubka recalled that a donkey attired in an old dresscoat was paraded through the streets, an anti-Austrian placard around its neck. Giesl reacted furiously, demanding nothing less than the occupation of Cetinje.[53]

In Belgrade, too, the fall of Scutari excited public opinion and anti-Austrian sentiment. As Ugron reported, "with genuine South Slav passion, the fall of Scutari . . . is seen as a triumph of the Serb cause."[54] Symptomatic of the outpouring of hatred against Austria-Hungary, the Belgrade daily *Politika* reported a discussion, perhaps apocryphal, between a high Serbian government official and an army officer. The official allegedly asserted: "Now we don't have anything more to fear. We have secured our future." The officer replied: "By God, I fear, I fear that someone [else] could fall on Austria-Hungary and destroy her before we do!"[55] Official Belgrade's accolades were somewhat more muted. Ever jealous of its smaller cousin, it quickly emphasized that Montenegro's glory was Serbia's, too—that the capture of the city was made possible by Serbian arms and advisors. On the other hand, in an effort to minimize the Montenegrin accomplishment, officials pointed out that Scutari had given in without a real fight.[56]

Vienna's reaction to the fall of Scutari was predictable. On 24 April, Heinrich von Tschirschky und Boegendorff, the German ambassador in Vienna, described the mood in the city as one of "smothered rage, the feeling of having been led by the nose by Russia and her friends. Poor Berchtold is execrated in the sharpest terms." He added his own opinion that it was "high time for the Monarchy to demonstrate to Europe and still more to its own nationalities that it is not a dead carcass to be disposed of by others as they pleased."[57] Similarly, the British ambassador in Vienna wrote that Austrian reaction to the fall of Scutari resembled that of the British government when it received news of the fall of Khartoum:

> On all sides it is said here that prompt action is necessary and that any further delay is out of the question. We are reaching the most critical moment in the whole of this long crisis, the moment when the Powers will either find the means of continuing to work together, or that at which they will have to part company and each go its own way in the pursuit of what it may consider to be the defence of its own interests. Austria-Hungary has reached the point of the parting of the ways.[58]

More Great-Power Deliberations

The ambassadors' conference in London originally scheduled for 24 April met a day earlier. Dismayed and irritated by the news from Scutari, the ambassadors showed unusual harmony in insisting that the will of Europe be enforced. They swiftly formulated a démarche informing Cetinje that the fall of Scutari in no way modified their intentions regarding the fate of the city and advising Nicholas to surrender without delay.[59] This unanimity, however, did not extend to their discussions of the coercive measures that should be taken against Montenegro should the Balkan kingdom ignore their advice.

Some of the conference participants believed that the fall of Scutari would actually make it easier for the Montenegrin king to give in; Berchtold disagreed. He wished the conference powers to land troops, to bombard Montenegrin ports, or to allow Austria to assume the "moral obligation" to enforce the will of Europe in her own way.[60] The Germans backed their Austrian ally, urging Britain to take the lead in a military intervention.[61] The British did not believe that the situation warranted immediate military action, and still hoped that a financial or territorial lure could eventually induce Nicholas to surrender Scutari. Piqued by the conference's rejection of his suggestions, Berchtold repudiated his previous decision to participate in the loan to Montenegro—at least until Scutari was evacuated. Thus, he removed the last nonmilitary measure from Austria's armory of alternatives.[62]

The collective démarche agreed upon at the 23 and 25 April sessions of the London conference was delivered to Montenegro on 27 April. This was another day of celebration in Cetinje. Not only had Danilo returned in triumph from Scutari with Turkish flags, cannon, and the key to the city, but it was also Orthodox Easter Sunday. Although the Powers had hoped that Nicholas would quickly agree to their démarche acting foreign minister Dušan Vukotić explained to the ministers that during Easter only messages of the utmost urgency could be received or answered. The envoys, including the Russian minister, were outraged by this behavior.[63]

Despite Vukotić's disquieting lack of concern, Nicholas was aware that at least one of the Powers (namely Austria) was nearing the end of its patience; he thus decided to engage in some Easter diplomacy, consulting Eckardt and Giesl in an effort to learn what action was being contemplated.

With Giesl, Nicholas touched upon various ways in which the Powers might "facilitate" a Montenegrin decision to evacuate Scutari. As he had at the time of the withdrawal of Serbian troops, he suggested that the Powers collectively, or Austria independently, land a detachment of troops on the Montenegrin coast, whereby the "forceful action of Europe" would be demonstrated and provide him with an excuse to disengage from Scutari. Further, he suggested an idea which he had earlier abhorred—the exchange of Lovćen for Scutari. Although Vienna still coveted the Montenegrin massif, Giesl realized that the timing of the offer made it impossible to accept. The king could not be trusted to be discreet. In addition, Austria-Hungary had already committed herself irrevocably to saving Scutari for Albania and knew that such an exchange would alienate Italy and probably shatter the Triple Alliance.[64]

Giesl informed Nicholas that he could not negotiate a settlement with the Powers and warned him that he had but one choice left: unconditional surrender. As he had with Squitti earlier, Nicholas feigned indignation at Giesl's reference to financial assistance and refused to indicate whether he would go along with the Powers' 27 April démarche. Such an important issue would have to be considered by the Montenegrin skupština, and Nicholas doubted that it would be able to address the question until the following Monday. Giesl rightly concluded that the monarch was stalling for time.[65] While Nicholas tried to hold the Powers at bay, Dušan Gregović, the Montenegrin court marshal in Scutari, was scheming to organize a plebiscite there for the city's incorporation into Montenegro.[66]

Sir Edward Grey chose this crucial moment to return from a brief vacation and to interject his influence. As Britain was not directly affected by the outcome at Scutari, he could not countenance her taking part in military action against Montenegro. He was willing to agree, however, to one or more of the Powers taking measures to implement conference decisions in which Britain had joined. At the thirty-seventh meeting of the London conference on 28 April, he proposed one final warning to Montenegro before such stringent measures should be taken. If Nicholas withdrew from Scutari, "reasonable compensations" would be in order; otherwise, the Powers would leave him to his destiny. The disheartened French ambassador, Paul Cambon, put it another way: "If Nicholas submits to the Powers, Sir Edward Grey hopes to make him certain concessions; if not, he'll abandon him to Austria." The French, Russian, and even the Italian ambassadors asked Grey to modify the wording of his proposal, hoping to restrain Austria, but Grey was determined to submit it to the cabinet for discussion in its existing form. Karl Max Lichnowsky, the German ambassador, eagerly seconded the proposal and called on the Powers to approve it as soon as possible.[67]

Grey hoped that the new proposal would mollify the Austrians, but it did not. Count Albert Mensdorff, once more frustrated in his efforts to have the ambassadors approve immediate coercive measures, announced that his government would reserve for itself the right "to seize in a given moment the necessary measures for the implementation of the will of Europe." Berchtold believed that should Austria take such a step, "the other Powers w[ould] decide in any event to cooperate with us on land or at sea in the action that is becoming necessary." Yet for all his saber-rattling, Berchtold did not say that Austria had already decided to act. He played a clever game with the concert, hoping that by keeping the other Powers guessing, he would move them to embrace the measures he wanted.[68]

In St. Petersburg, Sazonov implored Berchtold to act with caution, particularly as reports he had just received indicated that the greater part of the Montenegrin army in Scutari had been pulled out, leaving only five battalions in the city.[69] Such news did little to pacify Berchtold, who wanted all Montenegrin soldiers out of Scutari; it did even less to calm Conrad, who told the German military attaché that the troops leaving Scutari were being transferred to the Austro-Hungarian border.[70] As 1 May approached, most observers guessed that Austria would launch an attack. Although Baron Karl von Macchio of the foreign ministry had told Tschirschky that the Monarchy would wait at least until the Thursday session of the conference, Vienna newspapers reported that the army was ready to march at any time.[71] Grey desperately tried to delay Austria's "given moment," wiring his counterparts in the other European capitals to consider the ramifications of premature Austrian action.[72] On the morning of 1 May, however, Berchtold and Conrad presented their respective plans to Francis Joseph. The foreign minister advised a limited action directed against Scutari; the field marshal called for all-out war against Montenegro, and, if necessary, Serbia and Russia.[73]

The Montenegrin government complicated Grey's efforts to achieve a peaceful settlement. On 30 April, it denounced and rejected the Great-Power démarche of 27 April requesting the surrender of Scutari, and on the following day, a crown council voted unanimously to continue resistance.[74] Nicholas, however, behind the scenes, held out some hope to Grey by suggesting, in a *pro memoria* delivered by Popović to Whitehall, that he now might be willing to withdraw from Scutari in exchange for adequate territorial and financial compensation. Grey was very encouraged by Popović's visit, believing that the Montenegrin king was weakening.[75] As he told the ambassadors' conference on 1 May, "the communi-

The Scutari Crisis: 1913 147

cation volunteered spontaneously by the Montenegrin delegate is a fait nouveau and seems to indicate that King Nicholas is beginning to realize how serious the situation is. In view of this H[is] M[ajesty's] Gov[ernmen]t cannot say that the last resort has yet been reached, and, in the circumstances, an effort, even if it be the last, is worth making to avoid a resort to force."[76] Grey hoped that Nicholas's action would bolster support for his 28 April suggestion to the conference that the Powers make one more attempt to settle matters with the gospodar. Even Mensdorff was encouraged by the new development and supported Grey's idea of one final démarche, with the provision that the Powers agree to a time-limit for a response.[77]

In light of Nicholas's recent communication, the British foreign office asked that Austria refrain from taking any independent action before the next conference meeting, scheduled for Monday, 5 May. The Russians also advised Vienna to postpone any coercive measure until the Powers had had time to tender their final proposal and Cetinje had had time to respond.[78] Grey sent an urgent telegram to Nicholas, conveying the essence of the proposal he hoped the Powers would approve and warning the king that this would be his last opportunity to conclude a peaceful settlement of the Scutari question. The alternative was the unpleasant prospect of a separate Austrian military action, not to mention the forfeiture of any economic assistance.[79]

Over the weekend of 2–4 May, officials in the Great-Power capitals prepared for the crucial conference meeting on Monday. The foreign ministries of Austria and Russia were particularly busy as diplomats struggled to formulate policy while the Scutari crisis came to a head. Berchtold ultimately decided not to participate in the Powers' new démarche. He was angry that they had not addressed the concrete coercive measures to be taken if Montenegro refused to withdraw, established a time limit for a response, or ruled out economic compensation as a quid pro quo for evacuation.[80] The Russians, on the other hand, gave their approval, but they had not made up their minds what to do in the event the diplomatic overture failed and an Austrian attack resulted. Sazonov indicated that if Vienna's action was confined solely "to obtaining evacuation of Scutari, he trusted that [the Russian] government would be able to control public opinion. But if it assumed larger proportions he could not answer for consequences."[81] In the interest of peace, he advised Berchtold to reconsider the entire matter and not risk war for the sake of a vacuous "prestige policy." Otherwise, he contended, Austria, not Montenegro, would be acting against the will of Europe.[82] The situation was clearly tense. Sir George Buchanan, the British ambassador in St. Petersburg, wrote Nicolson: "Isolated action by Austria seems now inevitable and, as the possibility of such action has ever since the beginning of the crisis constituted the chief menace to European peace, the political outlook is blacker than at any other period of the crisis."[83]

The Possibility of Joint Austro-Italian Action

While Buchanan predicted that Vienna would soon take independent military action, others believed that Austria might try to induce Rome to join her. Indeed, unbeknownst to the London conference, secret Austro-Italian discussions on the subject of coordinating military action against Montenegro had been under way for several weeks.

Shortly after the Great-Power naval demonstration had begun, Berchtold quietly mentioned the possibility of joint Austro-Italian action to his Italian counterpart. San Giuliano's initial response was lukewarm; he knew that the Italian prime minister and Italian public opinion opposed the idea of intervention.[84] After the fall of Scutari, Berchtold again approached San Giuliano, arguing that if Italy joined Austria, the danger of a European war could be averted and Italy would gain new prestige as an Adriatic power. If she did not, Vienna would act on her own.

San Giuliano clearly opposed any unilateral Austrian action, believing that it would violate Article 7 of the Triple Alliance and would force Italy to take an unspecified "parallel action" to maintain the balance of power in the Adriatic. Like the British officials, he held that Montenegro would back down in time and could see no reason for Austria or Italy to alienate Europe for the sake of expediting the inevitable.[85] The specter of San Giuliano invoking Article 7 disturbed Berchtold, who continued to apply pressure on the Italian government through Mérey, his ambassador in Rome.[86]

Berchtold's persistence irritated most Italian politicians, and on 28 April, San Giuliano told Hans von Flotow, the German ambassador, that common action with Austria was currently impossible, and that Italy also opposed a European mandate for separate Austrian action. He conveyed a similar opinion to Sir J. Rennell Rodd, the British ambassador, appealing for some kind of British or French participation that would "be sufficient to maintain the international character of action," and thus enable Italy to take part.[87] Despite his official policy to the contrary, San Giuliano privately considered that Italy might have a lot to gain by cooperation with Vienna. On 30 April, he secretly presented Austria with a list of conditions for Italian participation, stipulating that Austria must promise not to act while there was still hope that the London conference might achieve results or that Montenegro might surrender voluntarily, and that she must pledge not to violate Montenegrin territory. In addition, he required Vienna to agree beforehand on the strategy, size, and target of the planned operations, as well as on the territorial adjustments to be made following the intervention.

Berchtold bristled at these conditions, firmly believing that immediate Austrian action was justified by Montenegro's repeated refusal to acquiesce in the decisions of the Powers. He also felt that it would be impossible to conclude an agreement on a post-intervention situation before the action actually took place. San Giuliano was greatly disturbed by Berchtold's stubbornness, especially his refusal to limit his goals beforehand. This implied the potential of an Austro-Hungarian territorial acquisition in the Balkans—perhaps Lovćen—as a by-product of the contemplated action in Albania, an acquisition against which Italy could not claim reciprocal compensation.[88]

By 3 May, San Giuliano realized that he could not accept Berchtold's objections, and the chances for a joint campaign waned as rapidly as they had risen. On the other hand, San Giuliano did not rule out an independent Italian action in the south. In order to keep Austria "honest," he indicated that if Vienna occupied Lovćen or other Montenegrin territory, Rome would be obliged to occupy Vlorë and possibly other Albanian ports.[89] He backed this threat by initiating Italian military preparations.[90]

On 2 May, still uncertain about Italy's position, Berchtold presided over a critical meeting of the Dual Monarchy's joint ministerial council.[91] The fate of Scutari headed the agenda of what became a war council. Those present agreed with Berchtold that the prestige of Austria-Hungary had been challenged and must be defended. Indeed, many of the ministers were more bellicose than the foreign minister, who suggested a limited military response. After much discussion, especially over the domestic ramifications of mobilization, the council accepted Berchtold's plan and agreed to prepare for unilateral action against Montenegro, while holding the door open for possible Italian participation.[92]

Berchtold immediately advised the Austrian consul general in Scutari to prepare the families of Habsburg officials for evacuation and to anticipate a second siege. Similarly, on the night of 3 May, Giesl was directed to be ready for the worst; in the event of a break in diplomatic relations, he was told to entrust the protection of the legation and the defense of Austro-Hungarian nationals to Eckardt and the German embassy.[93] "The border was closed off, [and] traffic with the Montenegrin authorities had long since stopped," Hubka recounted. "In the kafanas of Cetinje a depressed mood reigned, and the braggarts had gotten meek again. The ecstasy of victory was followed by an awful headache, made worse by the reports from Belgrade, Sofia, and Athens that the allies had to take into consideration their people's great need for peace, and therefore were not in any position to support Montenegro in a conflict with Austria-Hungary."[94] Rumors of all kinds abounded during this uncertain period. Some held that the abdication or the overthrow of King Nicholas was imminent, others that the Austro-Hungarian army was poised on the border and ready to strike at any minute. The latter rumors proved closer to the truth.

Montenegro's Capitulation

Grey's warnings, Montenegro's isolation, and the apparent imminence of an Austro-Hungarian strike finally turned the tide of royal Montenegrin obduracy. In the face of his cabinet's bitter opposition, the king conceded that the Montenegrin falcon, deserted by all its friends, was no match for the Habsburg eagle in physical combat. Rather than risk losing his gains east of Podgorica and in the Sandžak, he chose to submit to the "will of Europe" and surrender Scutari unconditionally.

Nicholas first contemplated sending former foreign minister Dušan Gregović to the Hofburg with a personal letter to Francis Joseph, offering the city's surrender in return for minor frontier rectifications, but he soon realized that this might antagonize the Austrians. Afraid that Gregović would not be able to reach Vienna in time to halt an Austrian offensive, he considered dispatching a telegram to the Habsburg emperor instead. This met with the firm opposition of his advisers. At a stormy session at the palace on the night of 3 May, Nicholas, his ministers, sons, daughters, generals, leading politicians, and ordinary citizens, all argued over the proper course of action. They could not even agree upon which chief of state to approach with the news of their surrender. Not even the tsar pleased them, as most felt he had forfeited his ancestors' privileged place in Montenegro's affairs by failing to support her. In the end, Nicholas decided to notify Grey, the least controversial possibility. Prime Minister Martinović and his cabinet, far from attempting a palace coup as many had feared, resigned their offices, giving Nicholas much greater freedom in dealing with the Powers. He promised to announce a new government within a few days.[95]

On the morning of 4 May, Nicholas wired his decision to his representative in London. He initially contemplated having Popović withhold announcement of Montenegro's surrender until after the start of the ambassadors' conference the following morning.[96] Having second thoughts on the virtue of procrastination, he decided to have de Salis inform Grey immediately. He declared: "My dignity and that of my people not permitting me to submit to isolated demands, I leave the fate of the town of Scutari in the hands of the Powers."[97] Hubka later wrote that "the soap bubble of Montenegrin insolence and obstinacy was [thus] punctured and collapsed into nothingness."[98]

On the evening of 3 May, Giesl learned of the tempestuous meeting in the royal palace from Montenegro's unofficial liaison, the German minister. Eckardt presented his colleague with an urgent request from Nicholas for a forty-eight-hour delay in any Austrian action that might have been planned. "Recognizing the debacle in the palace," Giesl chose to apply even more pressure on the king before acceding to this request. He demanded "unreserved fulfillment" of Austria's demands in the Palić and Hubka affairs, and, in order to assure a speedy reply, asked Berchtold for permission to affix a twelve-hour time limit.[99]

Although Eckardt believed that Nicholas would submit to these new demands in short order, they rubbed salt into very fresh wounds. Sharp debate over the Austrian proposals took place the next day. In the end, the latest spurt of Montenegrin resentment was quelled, and on the afternoon of the fourth, Eckardt conveyed the king's acceptance of Giesl's stipulations.[100] Still not satisfied, the Austrian now demanded a formal Montenegrin note. One arrived the same evening.[101]

Buoyed by the news from Cetinje, the ambassadors began their conference on 5 May in unusually good spirits, believing that the Scutari crisis, which had occupied so much of their time during the previous few weeks, was now finally drawing to a close. Although Popović did not make his dramatic entrance as originally prescribed, Grey read Nicholas's telegraphic message, formally conveying his decision to evacuate Scutari. Mensdorff confidentially apprised his colleagues of Giesl's late-night message of 3 May to the same effect, as well as Berchtold's decision to refrain from issuing any ultimata with short time limits. He announced that Austria-Hungary would defer any military action in order to give the Montenegrins an opportunity to prove their good faith.[102]

The Powers quickly prepared a collective note acknowledging their satisfaction with Nicholas's decision. Grey stated in a separate dispatch his belief that the king's action was "a real contribution to general peace and is in the true interest of Montenegro."[103] Simultaneously, the admirals were instructed to prepare for the occupation of Scutari as soon as they could come to an agreement with the Montenegrins over the details of surrendering the city.[104]

On Tuesday, 6 May, the *Neue Freie Presse* reported that "the question of Scutari no longer stands as much in the foreground of European politics." In the days that followed, fewer and fewer columns in the papers were devoted to the northern Albanian problem, and the participants in the London conference looked forward to a fortnight's hiatus in their deliberations. Their satisfaction regarding Scutari was reinforced by Serbia's decision of 5 May to withdraw the last of her troops from Durrës.[105] At the end of the week, Sir Francis Cartwright wrote Nicolson and apologized for not having more to report: "the Montenegrin 'coup de théâtre' has practically put an end to the long crisis through which we have been passing, and what remains now to do is comparatively speaking simple work, as there are no questions left over which seem likely to put the European Powers by the ears."[106] Sazonov, in particular, was happy that he had not been placed in the embarrassing position of deciding how to react to an Austrian invasion of Montenegro.[107]

On 5 May, while the conference in London was congratulating itself on Montenegro's capitulation, Avarna, the Italian ambassador in Vienna, who had not been fully apprised of recent developments, visited Berchtold with an outline of Italy's "battle plan" for Albania. As was frequently the case with Italian foreign policy, it was too little too late. Berchtold took almost cruel pleasure in informing his ally that Montenegro's decision to surrender the city eliminated the need for immediate military intervention. Thus, he vetoed Rome's plans to exercise Italian authority in southern Albania while reserving for himself the opportunity to extend Austria's own influence over that region at some future date.[108] In Rome, San Giuliano tried to extricate himself from a potentially embarrassing situation, claiming that Italy's proposed course in Albania had actually been designed to make "Austria pause for serious reflection before taking any action calculated to have far-reaching consequences." San Giuliano only hoped that the other Powers appreciated Italy's "contribution" toward settlement of the Scutari crisis.[109]

In Montenegro, reaction to the king's decision was unexpectedly mild. Nicholas survived the immediate aftermath of surrender in remarkably good form. Gossip concerning the possibility of his abdication eventually receded into the background, and Montenegrins actually greeted their ruler with cheers. The skupština, which had been called into extraordinary session by Martinović at the height of the Scutari crisis, still met. The decision to capitulate had already been made, and the members had only to ratify it. Late in the afternoon of 8 May, the king, attended by his three sons, introduced his new cabinet to the national assembly and attempted to account for his performance during the last few days.[110]

Vienna could find little relief in Nicholas's choice of a successor to Martinović. The new prime minister was none other than General Janko Vukotić, "the man with the iron fist," a well-known and generally feared figure at the Ballhausplatz. At the time of the Bomb Affair in 1907, he had shown boundless energy as governor of Cetinje in cracking down on the prince's opponents. In 1908, as Montenegro's special envoy to Serbia, he had been unceremoniously detained by Austro-Hungarian authorities at the Zagreb train station, after which he declared that in the future he would only cross Habsburg territory with a sword in his hand. Vukotić's rabid Austrophobia was combined with his desire to strengthen relations with Serbia. Neither view augured well for the future of Austro-Montenegrin relations—nor did Vukotić's growing inclination to take a more independent stance than any other Montenegrin prime minister in recent memory. The Ballhausplatz was distressed as well by the fact that Vukotić, like his predecessor, also assumed the post of war minister.

The new foreign minister was Petar Plamenac, a relatively young man, educated in Western Europe, who had served his country for several years as consul general in Scutari, where he currently held the post of civil governor. In October 1912, he was Montenegro's chargé d'affaires in Constantinople, in which capacity he had delivered Montenegro's declaration of war to the Turkish government.[111]

The skupština listened dutifully as Nicholas explained his decision to surrender Scutari, listing as his principal reasons Montenegro's complete diplomatic isolation and the threat of Austro-Hungarian intervention. For the time being, the delegates accepted Nicholas's explanation at face value, but that did not mean that they or the Montenegrin people had completely reconciled themselves to the loss of Scutari. The king had failed to deliver what he had promised and what the country had long dreamed of. His position was thus weaker than ever before.[112] Sensing the popular mood, Nicholas reluctantly agreed to free most of the remaining prisoners from the 1907 Bomb Affair, many of whom had been clubbed and shackled under Vukotić's expert supervision. Vukotić had since become a popular war hero, and as prime minister he would reflect and represent in official circles the Serbophile aspirations of many of the Montenegrin people.

Despite his unconditional surrender, Nicholas still worked hard to secure the financial and territorial compensations that he had either been denied or had himself rejected. He was supported by various Great-Power spokesmen who appreciated the king's difficult internal situation, and hoped to ameliorate it. After the decision to evacuate Scutari had been made, for example, Avarna advised Berchtold to show generosity towards his would-have-been victim. Up to a point, the foreign minister was willing to comply with this recommendation. Still, before anything could be agreed to, he insisted upon Scutari's actual evacuation.[113]

San Giuliano shared his ambassador's beneficent views. He even took matters one step further, suggesting that some territorial award might now be in order. Grey recounted the argument of the Italian ambassador in London: "The object should be to assure to Montenegro a certain degree of welfare, to make her an element of order rather than a source of agitation. She should be given financial help, and the delimitation of the boundaries agreed upon by the Powers should be traced eventually with a benevolent disposition."[114]

The Russian press similarly called for generosity. *Novoe vremia* argued that because Montenegro had done Europe a "valuable service" by surrendering, the least Europe could do in return would be to recognize some of the country's minor territorial claims. The *Birzhevye vedomosti* was almost poetic in its appeal:

> The Scutari question has been settled according to the will of Europe. But this success obliges Europe. If during the Scutari crisis, the European Powers reckoned solely with the intentions of Austria-Hungary, so must they now reckon with the legitimate requests of Montenegro. Montenegro has surrendered to Europe not just Scutari, but also her destiny.[115]

Even the king of England suggested a territorial adjustment in Montenegro's favor.[116]

While the Powers discussed the possibility of territorial indemnification, Serbia took the first tentative steps in this direction. She let it be known that Cetinje could expect "special consideration" when the two countries sat down to negotiate their new common border in the Sandžak. But Serbian generosity aside, Montenegrin gains in the relatively infertile Sandžak were little more than a consolation prize.[117]

More than a week elapsed between Montenegro's decision to relinquish control of Scutari and her actual surrender of the city. In the interim, details concerning the transfer of power were worked out between Plamenac and Admiral Burney.[118] On 9 May, the two finally signed a protocol governing the formal surrender.[119] It divided Scutari into different sectors, one for each of the international detachments that would be occupying the city. Collectively the commanders would govern Scutari until the Powers could make other arrangements. In the spirit of cooperation, the Montenegrins permitted Austrian and Italian relief units to enter Scutari on 7 May with food and medication.[120]

This seemingly auspicious beginning was unexpectedly marred by fire. Scutari, which had miraculously withstood the ravages of a six-month siege and weeks of shelling, fell victim to a conflagration that ravaged its important bazaar district. Although the mercantile quarter was situated on the lake, no water pumps were at hand, and many shops with valuable merchandise burned to the ground. It was widely alleged that disgruntled and ill-disciplined Montenegrin troops had laid a torch to the town, as many remembered Gregović's earlier warning: if Montenegro were forced to leave Scutari, she would leave it in rubble.[121]

On Wednesday, 14 May, the international detachments entered the charred city and assumed control. In place of the Montenegrin tricolor, hundreds of Albanian flags now flew, the black eagle of Scanderbeg upon a blood-red field. Admiral Burney became the city's chief administrator.[122] Although the Montenegrins had agreed to leave the city's basic fortifications intact, some one thousand troops remained behind to oversee the transfer of Montenegrin war matériel out of the city. On the same day, the Great-Power blockade of the Montenegrin coast formally ended.[123]

In the weeks that followed, Montenegrin troops effected a step-by-step withdrawal from Scutari and the surrounding area. Although Berchtold periodically complained that the evacuation was too protracted, Burney and the international commission commended the speed with which the operation was carried out.[124]

The Crisis in Perspective

At one level, the resolution of the Scutari crisis represented a great victory for Austria-Hungary. She had saved Scutari for Albania, and in the process preserved her own prestige and that of the Concert of Europe. But, she had also deprived Montenegro of what many in that country honestly believed to be her historic due. Berchtold's harsh, unyielding policies dealt a severe blow to whatever hopes existed for an Austro-Montenegrin rapprochement. In the days ahead, Montenegrin politicians periodically wooed Vienna and called for better relations, but the hearts of many Montenegrin subjects were set on revenge for the ignominy suffered in May 1913. Like Conrad, they looked forward to an opportunity to settle old scores.

In terms of territory and population, Montenegro's gains in the First Balkan War were not insignificant, but the new land in the Sandžak and along Albania's northern frontier contributed little to the economic well-being of the kingdom. Despite extravagant claims to the contrary, it is very doubtful whether Scutari would have provided a panacea for Montenegro's numerous ailments. Yet the loss of the city came to symbolize the country's miserable economic condition as well as Austria's apparent determination to keep it impoverished.

The Scutari crisis further diminished the prestige and authority of King Nicholas and his dynasty. Ironically, Austria-Hungary's foreign policy suffered as a result. If Nicholas had been a perpetual thorn in the side of the Monarchy, at least he had been a tolerable one, whose interests and policies were designed to put Montenegro first. Now more and more Montenegrins were looking beyond the country's borders, to Serbia, for salvation. Before the war, Nicholas, the authoritarian patriarch, had run a tight ship at home, concentrating most of the powers of government in his own hands. In the wake of Scutari, however, he had to share some of this power with politicians such as the popular Serbophile Vukotić, who was determined to find some way to improve his country's fortunes.

In many respects, the Scutari crisis of 1913 was a dress rehearsal for the prelude to war the following summer. In both instances, Germany backed Austrian action against a small Balkan state. It is too much to say, as Albertini has done, that Berlin wrote Vienna a "blank check" in the spring of 1913; before ultimately supporting Austrian proposals for military action, the Wilhelmstrasse exercised considerable restraint, a fact that proponents of Fritz Fischer's theses on German war guilt should keep in mind.[125] Yet the denouement of the Scutari crisis indicated to Berchtold that he could have his way by threatening to use force against a lesser adversary. In the next fourteen months, he would twice issue similar ultimata to Serbia. In 1913 as in 1914, Italy shied away from rendering full-fledged support to her *Dreibund* ally. In both crises, Italy's fear of Austria's territorial aspirations in the Balkans frustrated potential understandings between the two countries and tested the solidarity of the Triple Alliance: it was becoming increasingly clear that the differences that separated the two rivals were more formidable than the ties that formally bound them together.

Despite these similarities, at least one thing was different in the two crises. For all its shortcomings, painfully slow negotiations, and innumerable démarches, the London conference, led by Sir Edward Grey, had played an important role in preserving the peace of Europe. In 1914, however, the Powers closest to the fires of war seemed unwilling to give the conference apparatus another opportunity to save the peace.[126]

CHAPTER NINE
From Scutari to Sarajevo: 1913–1914

In the wake of the Scutari crisis, Montenegro marked time. While Nicholas contemplated how to finance the costly enterprises of the past few months and to consolidate his territorial gains, his erstwhile Balkan allies—Serbia, Greece, and Bulgaria—bickered over the spoils of the First Balkan War. The result was a second conflict in which Nicholas became a reluctant participant.[1]

Serbia and Bulgaria were the two Balkan states most at odds in the late spring of 1913. Having enjoyed great success, while Bulgaria experienced unexpected difficulties in vanquishing the Turks, and having been deprived by the London conference of Albanian land and an outlet on the Adriatic, Serbia was dissatisfied with the tentative territorial agreement she had concluded with Sofia in March 1912 and pressed for its revision. Even before the Treaty of London ending the First Balkan War was signed on 30 May 1913, the Serbians joined the Greeks, who had numerous grievances of their own, in a new anti-Bulgar front.

Anxious to avert another conflict, Russia, the godmother of the Balkan alliance, invited the prime ministers of the victorious Balkan states to St. Petersburg to discuss their differences. But before they could meet, Bulgaria's Tsar Ferdinand on the night of 29 June ordered an attack on Serbian and Greek positions. Although the Bulgarians struck the first blow, the Serbians and Greeks, joined in the struggle by Rumania, Turkey, and Montenegro, soon gained the upper hand. Sofia's situation became untenable. Surrounded by hostile forces, its army collapsed, and its government was forced to sue for peace.

Neither the Serbo-Bulgarian nor the Greco-Bulgarian dispute directly concerned Montenegro, although Nicholas himself sympathized more with Ferdinand than with King Peter. During the First Balkan War, Sofia had extended more financial assistance to Cetinje than had Belgrade. Moreover, geographical considerations had meant that feuds with Bulgaria were virtually nonexistent, while the propinquity of Serbian troops and conflicting territorial aspirations often led to Serbo-Montenegrin friction. Nicholas, jealous of his son-in-law's popularity in Montenegro, hoped that Bulgaria could hold Serbia in check and, perhaps, tarnish Peter's otherwise sterling image. No doubt Nicholas would have preferred to remain a spectator in the Second Balkan War, but his country's intense Serbophilia and his ministers' realistic appraisal of political conditions dictated that he become a participant on the side of Belgrade.[2]

On the eve of the Second Balkan War, Nicholas dispatched forces to Peć; with the outbreak of fighting, some fourteen thousand Montenegrin troops advanced beyond Prizren. Anxious to avoid any unnecessary fighting, Nicholas warmly endorsed Russian proposals for the cessation of hostilities and Russian mediation, but these proposals came to nought. During the war, his troops fought side by side with Serbians, participating in the crucial battle of Bregalnica and in other engagements.

The Treaty of Bucharest, formally ending the Second Balkan War, was signed on 10 August 1913. Bulgaria paid bitterly for her indiscretion. Rumania was given the northern Dobrudja, and the Serbians and Greeks kept those parts of Macedonia they had occupied during the war. Thus, the struggle that had been waged largely over the partition of Macedonia resulted in Bulgaria's virtual expulsion from the region. She lost Ohrid and Bitola to Serbia, Salonica and Kavalla to Greece, and retained only a short segment of the Aegean coastline between the Mesta and Marica rivers. Despite the participation of her troops in the conflict, Montenegro played only a very small role at the peace conference. Having no direct claims on Bulgarian territory, her delegates concentrated on supporting the claims of her allies. What the country would gain from the war would be decided by direct, bilateral negotiations between Belgrade and Cetinje.

None of the Great Powers was pleased with the Treaty of Bucharest. A melancholy Berchtold, who had sided with Sofia, wrote that "the chimes of peace . . . have a hollow sound."[3] Grey observed that the treaty carried "the seeds of inevitable future trouble,"[4] while Sazonov, who had tilted toward Belgrade, termed the agreement nothing but "plaster" on the unhealed wounds of the Balkans.[5] For King Peter and Pašić, however, the Second Balkan War marked an important stage in the evolution of Greater Serbia. After five hundred years, the defeat on the plains of Kosovo had been avenged; all Serbs were now freed from Ottoman rule. The Serbs of Serbia and Montenegro had a common frontier, and their unification seemed more feasible than ever.

While negotiating that common frontier, Nicholas tried to achieve what had previously been denied him on the field of battle or by Great-Power politics. His territorial demands on Serbia were great, but few believed that any dispute between the two Serb states would lead to a third Balkan war. As Pašić had promised in May, Serbia was remarkably generous to Montenegro, yielding to most of her demands in the Sandžak, including Pljevlja, Bijelo Polje, Peć, and Djakovica.[6]

Some observers believed that Montenegro's diplomatic victory was actually a pyrrhic one—that the tiny kingdom had bitten off far more than it could chew, let alone digest.[7] It had expanded by 8,248 square kilometers, roughly doubling its population.[8] It was the opinion of Rudolf Weinzetl, the Austrian chargé d'affaires in Cetinje, that Serbia had deliberately ceded Djakovica, knowing that the city, considerably larger than Nicholas's capital, would be a substantial financial and administrative burden. Many Montenegrins perceived that their impoverished country had merely added to its woes. As one of Nicholas's countrymen lamented, "Djakov[ic]a will be our grave."[9]

Most of the residents of Djakovica and its hinterland were Muslim Albanians. They joined the already large number of Albanians, both Muslim and Catholic, that had recently come under Montenegro's jurisdiction. The Great Powers, particularly Austria-Hungary and Italy, were eager to ameliorate the implicit injustice done those Albanians compelled to live beyond the borders of the new Albanian state and took limited steps to safeguard their rights. In mid-August, they presented a collective démarche, which followed up a representation made the previous spring on behalf of the ethnic minorities living in Montenegro.[10] Cetinje promptly responded that its Muslim and Catholic population would "enjoy all the rights and have all the responsibilities" of its Orthodox citizens, adding that Montenegro "has always been one of the most tolerant countries in Europe in her treatment of minorities." This assertion tested the credulity of those familiar with Montenegro's brutal history and of those who heard numerous reports later in the year of bloody persecutions of Catholic Albanians.[11]

The Albanian question remained unsettled after the Treaty of Bucharest. By late September 1913, the two boundary commissions appointed by the London conference to demarcate borders for a new Albanian state had barely begun their task. Frontier clashes and insurrections inevitably broke out along the long, uncertain border. Belgrade eventually took matters into its own hands by reoccupying much of northern Albania. The extremist Serb press cried for the region's outright seizure, which would hand the Powers a *fait accompli* they could not reverse without recourse to war.[12]

Serbia's unilateral action provoked Vienna. Armed with Germany's moral support, on 18 October Berchtold presented Belgrade with an ultimatum that gave it until 26 October to evacuate Albania, or "Austria would be forced . . . to have recourse to the proper measures to secure the realization of her demands."[13] Berchtold's decisive action quickly achieved the desired result. This undoubtedly encouraged him to issue another ultimatum in a crisis with Serbia the following summer.[14]

Even before Austria demanded it, Montenegro declared she would withdraw any of her troops on Albanian soil. Ironically, Austria-Hungary's "dampening of Serbia's adventurism" in Albania was not entirely unwelcome in Montenegrin court circles. The removal of Serbian troops so close to the Montenegrin heartland provided Nicholas a measure of relief in his running battle with advocates of union with Serbia.[15]

Unfortunately for the Albanians, the Serbian withdrawal was accompanied by bloodshed and terror. The Austro-Hungarian consul general in Scutari reported that as many as six hundred Albanians had been killed by Serbian soldiers. Despite pleas for Austrian intervention, the Ballhausplatz let the evacuation run its grim course, after which the battered Albanians attempted to resume a normal existence.[16]

Montenegro after the Balkan Wars

While Montenegro negotiated with Serbia over the fate of the Sandžak, rumors abounded in Europe that the negotiations were just the first step toward an eventual union between the two Balkan countries. The question of union dominated Montenegro's domestic politics and foreign relations from the end of the Balkan wars through the summer of 1914.

During the Balkan wars, the movement for unification had swelled within Montenegro. Since the early years of the century, Montenegrin students and liberals had looked to Belgrade for support and guidance, but the new Serbophilia reached beyond the Montenegrin intelligentsia to the people at large. The events of the past few years, especially the failure to take Scutari, had shaken their faith in Nicholas and his sons. The acquisition of a large number of non-Serbs during the "wars of liberation" had diluted support for the dynasty even further. The most compelling argument for union, however, remained the country's crushing poverty.[17]

Like his predecessors, Aehrenthal and Agenor Goluchowski, Berchtold believed that the creation of a Greater Serbia, especially one that included Montenegro and her coastline, would threaten the very existence of Austria-Hungary. He and most Habsburg officials feared the "moral and material reinforcement of [their] traditionally hostile neighbor . . . [and] the pan-Serb idea," and supported long-standing policy to prevent unification.[18] By November 1913, however, he had perceived that the movement for Serbo-Montenegrin union was a strong and deeply rooted one, which forced on him for the first time some flexibility in his thinking. In a policy shift revealed only to his closest advisors, he did not rule out the possibility of using force to keep Serbia and Montenegro apart but admitted that Austria's efforts to stop unification might ultimately fail. Should this happen and Austria be presented with a *fait accompli*, he was prepared to demand, in return for Vienna's approval of the situation, the cession of the Montenegrin littoral, including the ports of Bar and Ulcinj, to Albania. This he described as "a solution with full justification in view of the region's previously belonging to Turkey and the extensive Albanian population of the area."[19] No matter what else resulted, this would prevent Serbia from gaining a beachhead on the Adriatic.[20] Berchtold knew that before completing this contingency plan, he had to secure Italian approval of any transfer of Balkan territory. He postponed approaching his cantankerous ally for a number of months, however, fearful that the Italians might raise the sensitive question of Lovćen.

Although the unification movement in Montenegro had its own domestic imperatives, Berchtold did not doubt for an instant that Russia was behind it. He could only hope that if relations between Cetinje and St. Petersburg improved, Russian support for unification would diminish. During the Balkan wars, Russo-Montenegrin ties had become increasingly strained. The king resented Russia's unwillingness to intervene on behalf of Montenegrin claims and her failure to help pay Cetinje's war costs. He was outraged when Russia suspended her all-important military subsidy.[21]

In May 1913, the king demonstrated his petulance by writing the Dowager Empress of Russia, requesting the closing of Cetinje's Russian Institute, a school for Montenegrin girls founded by Empress Marie in 1869. Only four years before, at the time of his jubilee, he had praised the institute as a center of Slavic culture.[22] The king's letter was not well-received in St. Petersburg. Alexander Giers, the Russian minister to Montenegro, remarked that its tenor caused his government to doubt the sanity of the king, especially when one considered that Nicholas and his son Danilo still received substantial monetary support each year from Russia to meet the costs of maintaining their households.[23]

Giers and most other Russian officials were so disgusted with Nicholas's behavior that, as one diplomat observed, they would have been glad if the king burned all his bridges to the Neva, catapulting Montenegro willy-nilly into the arms of Serbia. The British chargé in St. Petersburg pointed out that this was "undoubtedly a convenient attitude, which, while soothing to Russia's sense of dignity, relieve[d] her of the necessity of showing over-much energy in championing her former protégé."[24] Giers antagonized Nicholas so much that Plamenac, the Montenegrin foreign minister, sought to arrange the minister's recall.[25] Before Russo-Montenegrin relations suffered a permanent rupture, however, Giers left Cetinje on extended leave.

With Russo-Montenegrin ties at a nadir, Nicholas reluctantly turned to Austria for support. Giesl and Weinzetl, long accustomed to the fluctuations in the king's relations with the two Powers, had predicted this turn of events.[26] As early as 5 August, before the conclusion of the Second Balkan War, a newspaper correspondent and confidant of Prince Mirko had visited Weinzetl with a plan for preventing what he feared was the imminent union of Serbia and

Montenegro. He suggested that Austria-Hungary occupy part of the Montenegrin Sandžak and thus create a buffer between the two Serb states that would render their union virtually impossible. In return, he suggested compensation for Nicholas in Albania.[27] A few weeks later, former prime minister Gregović called on Giesl. Complaining about the "imminent Serbian danger" and Russia's defection, he asked about the possibility of Austro-Hungarian assistance in securing an international loan and in arranging border rectifications along the northern Albanian frontier and in the region south of Lake Scutari.[28]

The Austrian diplomats responded to these overtures in typically cool fashion. Weinzetl refused to endorse any plan that threatened to upset hard-won international agreements. Giesl warned Gregović that before Austria-Hungary bestowed favors on his troubled land, it would have to discontinue its provocative policies of the past and earn Vienna's trust. Neither envoy offered Montenegro any tangible rewards for her friendship, a course Berchtold wholeheartedly approved.[29] Austrian officials remained unmoved when early in September Nicholas himself offered the Ballhausplatz an opportunity to "right past wrongs." He was willing to have Berchtold send advisors to help reorganize Montenegro's army and bureaucracy if Vienna recognized the Bojana River as his kingdom's boundary with Albania.[30]

The king's indiscreet overtures raised the ire of France, Russia, and even his own government. In years past, he might have been able to dictate policy according to whim, but those days were coming to an end. A new governmental system was slowly emerging, one that included the principles of royal as well as ministerial responsibility. In this instance, Nicholas's ministers acted to curb their monarch's abrasive behavior. Plamenac presented Nicholas with a foreign policy memorandum that underscored the government's commitment to friendship with Russia, France, Britain, and Serbia and demanded the king's signature on the document. Nicholas resented this challenge to his authority, but signed the memorandum.[31]

Mention of France in Plamenac's memorandum reflected Paris's growing financial interest in Montenegro and her role as Russia's financial second. The French minister in Cetinje, P. H. Delaroche-Vernet, shared Giers's dislike of Nicholas, however, and his reports to the Quai d'Orsay about the king's Austro-

Hungarian "flirtation" exaggerated the nature of the relationship, almost costing Cetinje French support for an international loan.[32] Plamenac's timely memorandum convinced the French foreign ministry that Montenegro could be trusted and Pichon accordingly approved a six-million-franc, Franco-Italian advance. The money was badly needed, as Montenegro was on the verge of financial exhaustion.

Yet even a loan of six million francs would not keep the country afloat for very long, and the Great Powers continued to discuss a comprehensive loan of thirty to thirty-two million francs as originally envisioned by the London conference. By the spring, the figure under discussion had risen to forty million, each Power committed to supplying one-sixth of the final total. Even Austria-Hungary was willing "under certain conditions," to grant the loan.[33] To eliminate any Austrian reservations, Plamenac, who toured Europe to win support for the loan, warned that without it "there might be a collapse in Montenegro, leading to the disappearance of the King and to union with Servia."[34] Despite the urgency felt by Nicholas, the chancelleries of Europe did not resolve the loan question before the outbreak of the First World War.[35]

While awaiting funding of the loan, Nicholas tried to avoid antagonizing his potential benefactors. Yet he found it difficult to contain his fundamental animosity toward Habsburg policies and his personal dislike of the Habsburg representative in Cetinje. During the Scutari crisis, Giesl had become persona non grata in the Montenegrin capital. The king and his family did little to conceal their feelings and worked for the Austrian's recall.[36]

As it happened, the Austro-Hungarian government decided on its own to transfer him to another post. In the autumn of 1913, Berchtold named Giesl to succeed Count Johann Forgách as his minister in Belgrade. There, in less than a year's time, he would supervise Austria's total estrangement from Serbia and the severance of diplomatic relations. Though his last days in Cetinje were not as fateful for the peace of Europe, they were nonetheless unpleasant. Nicholas saw to that.[37]

To underscore his personal hostility to Giesl, while simultaneously smoothing the Habsburg eagle's ruffled feathers, Nicholas accorded Eduard Otto, Giesl's successor, a warm reception. He wanted to make a good impression on the former ambassador to Tehran, if for no other reason than to secure the international loan. Otto was not taken in by Nicholas's greeting, likening the king to Abdul Hamid, the ex-sultan, who had the ability to charm or cajole almost anyone when he had a mind to.[38]

Nicholas soon put Otto to the test. In late January 1914, Montenegrin troops occupied the district of Vermosh along the disputed Albanian border. A small basin named for a tributary of the Lim River and a traditional summer pasturage for the Klementi tribe, Vermosh formed a wedge between the Montenegrin towns of Podgorica and Gusinje. Both Albania and Montenegro laid claim to the region, and the Northern Albanian Border Commission, inactive during the winter months, had not rendered its final judgment. Otto recognized that the Montenegrins had a strong case and so reported to his government. Consequently, the Powers did not compel Nicholas to withdraw; they merely noted that he had acted "prematurely." On 29 January, the Triple Alliance reminded him that his occupation was provisional and denied him the right to raise taxes in the area until the boundary was officially fixed. In the spirit of collegiality, the British chargé made a similar representation.[39]

Only two weeks after the Vermosh operation, Montenegro undertook additional military measures relating to Albania. After a meeting of the country's leaders on the night of 16 February, purportedly to discuss improved Russo-Montenegrin relations, the army disrupted ordinary transportation throughout the country without warning and shifted men and matériel in the general direction of the Albanian border. Orders for the call up of additional troops were issued. The Montenegrins disclaimed any malevolent intentions, insisting that these measures were in keeping with a periodic rotation of troops in the border garrisons. But the secrecy and speed with which they operated were totally out of keeping with their usual performance, and the fact that 6,000 men were being called up to relieve 3,800 border troops indicated that something unusual was afoot. Hubka, the Austro-Hungarian military attaché, relayed rumors that trouble was brewing in neighboring Albania and that Montenegro was taking measures to bolster her defenses in the frontier region. King Nicholas went one step farther, informing the German minister that he would have patience with the neighboring Hoti and Grudi tribes, whose land he wanted for his own, "only until the end of the month."[40] Conrad, who, as ever, was prepared for the possibility of Austro-Hungarian military action in Albania, wondered whether Montenegrin intervention there would remain a localized "Balkan rumble" or provide the spark that would set off the long-awaited war with Russia.[41]

Actually, one and a half months passed before Nicholas made good his threats against the Hoti and Grudi. On 15 April, after the tribesmen rejected Montenegrin demands, General Martinović attacked Albanian positions east of Podgorica and Tuzi with a force of 6,000 men.[42] Days later he crossed into forbidden Kastrati territory.[43] Fearing a general uprising of Kastrati and Skreli tribesmen, Colonel G. F. Phillips, the commander of the British detachment at Scutari, recommended sending an international force to the troubled region. The Powers rejected this proposal, yet took a far harder line toward Cetinje than they had after Vermosh.[44] Sazonov instructed his representative in Montenegro to denounce the operations and call for their immediate termination.[45] The affair gave impetus to the border commission, which reconvened on 24 and 25 April, after a four-month recess.[46]

Another incident, this time on the Austro-Montenegrin frontier, proved to be even more serious and dealt a blow to relations between Cetinje and Vienna. At stake was the ownership of Sjenokos, a few square meters of rocky terrain with a burned-out Turkish blockhouse, situated near the newly acquired Montenegrin town of Metaljka. On 7 March, Austrian officers advised Lieutenant Vojin Mićanović, the commander of a Montenegrin border patrol, that his troops had crossed into Habsburg territory and instructed them to withdraw. The Montenegrins, who had occupied the blockhouse, refused. Early the next morning, Eduard Schreiber, the president of Bosnia's Čajniče district, visited the fortification in a futile effort to convince Mićanović that the salient unquestionably belonged to his jurisdiction. Shortly afterwards, while Mićanović was inspecting other sentry positions along the border, Austro-Hungarian troops launched an attack on Sjenokos. The opposing sides were ill-matched: several squads of Austro-Hungarian soldiers versus four Montenegrins. Within minutes, the Austrians seized the blockhouse and the road leading to it, killing at least two Montenegrin soldiers and a peasant. There were no Austrian casualties.[47]

Each side naturally accused the other of provoking the incident and firing the first shot. The Montenegrins claimed that they were guilty of nothing except refusing to evacuate their own property. Previous Turkish occupation of Sjenokos seems to lend credence to the Montenegrin argument. The Ottomans had held the site for many years before surrendering it to victorious Serbian troops in the First Balkan War. In turn, the Serbians had transferred the territory to Montenegro at the conclusion of the Serbo-Montenegrin territorial agreement. Reshid Bey, the director of political affairs at the Turkish foreign ministry and a former ambassador in Vienna, indicated that Sjenokos was but one spot on a long border that had given rise to frequent disagreements between the Porte and the Ballhausplatz, but that Turkish troops had held it without provoking an Austrian attack. The Austrians, of course, claimed that the Ottomans had occupied Sjenokos at their pleasure.[48] The evidence, however, suggests that General Oskar Potiorek, the governor of Bosnia, was ultimately responsible for the incident, as it was he who prompted Austrian border troops to "reclaim" Sjenokos, which they did without first consulting the Ballhausplatz.[49]

Nicholas responded sharply, but did not push matters to the breaking point. Some opponents accused him of going soft on Austria in order to secure his loan. Others accused him of selling documents to the Austrians proving Montenegro's ownership of Sjenokos. Otto feared the extent to which radical nationalist elements might use the incident to cause trouble for Nicholas and call for union with Serbia. Vukotić, in fact, claimed that the future of his cabinet was in jeopardy.[50] Despite the exhortations of the Serbian press, Belgrade cautiously refused to intervene on Cetinje's behalf; Pašić told Nicholas to make his peace with Austria-Hungary and avoid even more dangerous events.[51] Such peace, however, was never achieved, and border disputes continued to plague Austro-Montenegrin relations.

Russo-Montenegrin Relations

Despite numerous frontier incidents and the difficulty of reaching agreement on the delimitation of Montenegro's borders with the Dual Monarchy, especially the new border in the Sandžak, the major problem for Vienna remained the question of Montenegro's future as an independent state and the corollary issue of Serbo-Montenegrin union.[52] At the center of these questions stood the Russians.

In the absence of Minister Giers, Nikolai Obnorsky, the Russian chargé d'affaires, had made concerted efforts to improve relations with Cetinje, and also with Vienna. Obnorsky was a sincere and honest diplomat, one of few who earned Giesl's trust and respect.[53] In November, he apprised the Habsburg minister of his plans to replace Giers's policy of antagonism toward Cetinje and Vienna with one of reconciliation. He wanted to cool the Austro-Russian rivalry in the Balkans and believed that one way to accomplish this would be to work together to prevent Serbo-Montenegrin union. This would mean that St. Petersburg would once again provide Cetinje with financial and military assistance—a revitalization of Russia's traditional physical and moral presence in the country—but Obnorsky argued that this was not incompatible with Vienna's own interests. After all, Austria was already accustomed to a Russian-subsidized Montenegro, and she obviously wanted to avoid a Serbian-controlled one. To allay fears about a new Russian military presence in the Black Mountain, Obnorsky suggested that Russian advisors would be given purely technical responsibilities, and he promised they would be withdrawn in the event of conflict with the Habsburg Empire.[54]

Giesl did not commit himself one way or the other to Obnorsky's proposals. Although privately comforted that at least one Russian diplomat seemed determined to stop the rush toward Serbo-Montenegrin union, the prospect of a Russo-Montenegrin reconciliation left him uneasy. With a hint of bitterness, he predicted that Montenegro would once again wheedle her way into Russia's good graces:

> The status quo ante will establish itself, proof that Montenegro has "learned nothing and forgotten nothing" and that all the high-sounding statements about leaving Russian slavery and drawing close to Austria-Hungary were only empty and tendentious phrases, just as they were valued from the beginning.[55]

Giesl could really expect little else, however, as Vienna had done nothing to win Nicholas and his people to its side. As he well knew, Austria would be lucky to maintain her small commercial influence in Montenegro. The Austrians ultimately decided not to obstruct Obnorsky's plans, but both Giesl and Berchtold were agreed that should Russia prove unable to stop unification, Austria should act boldly to protect her interests and occupy the entire Montenegrin coast between Kotor and Albania.[56]

Obnorsky's arguments ran counter to the pan-Slav policies of Giers currently ascendant in St. Petersburg. Therefore, before the Russian chargé could convince the Austrians of his program's desirability, he had to convince his own government, which he did in short order. Sazonov commissioned him to approach the Montenegrin king with a peace offering, and at a reception at the Russian embassy on 19 December, Obnorsky told Nicholas that Russia would be willing to renew payments of the military subsidy under certain conditions. The impoverished king welcomed the news, although he was disappointed when St. Petersburg refused his request to open a Montenegrin mission in the Russian capital, a step that he had hoped would expedite the financial arrangements. As in the past, the Russians preferred to deal with their obstreperous ward through their emissaries in Cetinje and make payments according to their own schedule.[57] In another effort to accelerate the timetable of payments, the Montenegrin finance officer published a financial report the following month, which declared a budget deficit of some four million perpers.[58]

Though Otto, Giesl's successor, was not aware of the full extent of Obnorsky's success, he noted that a reconciliation with Russia was clearly under way. Rumors were afloat in the capital that a Montenegrin delegation would travel to Russia for the dedication of a statue of Grand Duke Nicholas Nikolaievich, the king's son-in-law, and that Danilo and his wife would also visit St. Petersburg.[59] The British representative reported that "thanks in particular to the efforts of the Russian Chargé d'Affaires—the relations between Cettigne and Petersburg have so much improved that, after having incurred the displeasure of her old protector and having been considered as a black sheep, Montenegro is now about to be restored to the fold."[60] The official restoration took place on 15 February, when the Russian emperor wrote a conciliatory letter to King Nicholas. Without specifying a timetable, he informed the king that Russia would resume her military payments and send him army instructors. Nicholas agreed to accept whatever conditions Russia chose to impose.[61]

Henceforth, Russian policy adhered closely to Obnorsky's program and strove to hold the line against the immediate union of Montenegro and Serbia. This did not mean that St. Petersburg opposed the *eventual* amalgamation of the two Serb states. When Pašić visited the Russian capital in February, both the tsar and Sazonov reaffirmed their support for unification as a long-term proposition.[62] They looked forward to the day when a larger Yugoslav state would provide them with an even more powerful chess piece in their matches with Austria. But they both agreed that unification should not imperil the present peace of Europe. They were willing to shelve the question as long as Nicholas lived—or maintained his throne. Unification was to be the result of a natural progression of events—so natural that when realized, it could not possibly be interpreted as a threat to any one nation.

At the end of February 1914, Sazonov tried to convey Russia's new position to Count Friedrich Szápáry von Szápár, since October the Habsburg ambassador in St. Petersburg. While conceding Austria's interests in keeping Serbia and Montenegro apart, he tried to convince Szápáry that union was inevitable in the long run and probably would not be as catastrophic as Vienna feared. Despite Sazonov's expression of such disconcerting sentiments, Szápáry concluded that the foreign minister was genuinely trying to control unionist fervor in the two Serb states, as indeed he was. In informing Pašić of his conversation with the ambassador, he reminded him to show the "utmost caution" and not to precipitate matters.[63] He did likewise on many subsequent occasions.

These admonitions reflected the fears of many observers that Serbia would try to settle the unification question on her own. Turkey and Bulgaria, for example, were convinced that Belgrade's recent military buildup was related to an impending move toward unification.[64] In the face of obvious international concern, Serbia's leaders tried to clarify their position. King Peter told a departing Italian military attaché that although the Montenegrins were Serbs, many of whom would gladly join the Serbian state, he did not want to force the issue as long as Nicholas lived.[65] Pašić echoed his sovereign, saying that although Serbia was prepared to work in close cooperation with Montenegro (especially in economic matters), what she needed now more than anything else was an extended period of peace.[66] He repeatedly assured Hartwig and Sazonov that he did not intend to rock Europe's boat, and he meant what he said.[67]

Despite the fanfare of reconciliation, one part of Obnorsky's program was never implemented. Although the tsar had pledged to renew Russia's military subsidy, no money or instructors reached Cetinje before the outbreak of the First World War. Tsarist officials spent much time in inconclusive discussions about the nature of their new commitment to Montenegro—the amount of money to be allocated, the conditions to be imposed, etc.—with little result. With an eye toward the kopek-conscious duma, and ever mindful of King Nicholas's past abuses of Russian generosity and his present activities in Albania, the sums under discussion were progressively pared. This dismayed certain military men such as Russia's General Yuri Danilov, who feared that any reduction in Russian assistance would undermine the building of a Montenegrin army strong enough to draw Austro-Hungarian troops from the Russian front in the event of war.[68] While limiting their own contribution, Russian officials contemplated having Serbia share expenses for Montenegro's border posts or having Nicholas use part of his projected international loan for military purposes. It was even suggested that Serbia could supply military instructors along with, or even in lieu of, Russian advisors. All of these proposals, except that concerning the maintenance of Montenegrin border garrisons, were dismissed by Obnorsky and Sazonov in view of anticipated Austrian opposition.[69]

In the meantime, Cetinje's financial picture worsened daily. In May, Obnorsky wrote that the situation was "not only critical, but directly [would] be hopeless."[70] Officers had not been paid for weeks, and protest demonstrations were reported in various parts of the country. Nicholas pleaded for an emergency payment of 200,000 rubles, without which, Obnorsky asserted, the existence of the dynasty and the maintenance of peace could be severely jeopardized. Still Russia did not act. Sazonov was busy trying to resolve the question of Montenegro's international loan and was not inclined to pay Montenegrin back salaries.[71]

Late in the month, French and Italian banks—not Russian ones—came to the rescue, providing a much-needed three-million-franc advance on the international loan. Instead of money, Russia sent a military delegation to Cetinje to celebrate Nicholas's twenty-fifth year as the honorary commander of the Fifteenth Rifle Regiment. Without Russian pecuniary assistance, however, there could be no guarantee there would ever be a twenty-sixth anniversary.[72]

Closer Serbo-Montenegrin Ties

Just as some feared that Serbia might force union on Montenegro, others suspected that Montenegro might provide the spark for unification. Unionist sentiment was strong among a large segment of the Montenegrin population, and this was reflected in the country's changing politics.[73] The liberal Narodna Stranka (the so-called *klubaši*) emerged from political limbo to dominate Montenegro's domestic stage; the conservative Prava Narodna Stranka (the *pravaši*) gradually saw its political star eclipsed. When Vukotić assumed the prime ministership in May, he had called for closer relations with Serbia. When new elections for the national assembly were finally held in January 1914, the liberals became the strongest political faction.[74] Vukotić interpreted the results as a show of support for his approach to Serbo-Montenegrin relations. Addressing the new skupština in February, he announced that "we stand for the unity of Serbs and Croats and, true to the traditions of Montenegro and her gospodars, we will work for Yugoslav solidarity and community . . . with special reliance on our powerful and centuries-old protectress, the great Russian Empire."[75] The Serbians had already confided to Vukotić that the time was ripe for the fusion of certain administrative functions—but that for the time being the independence and prestige of both dynasties and states would have to be maintained.[76]

In a speech on 11 February, Nicholas echoed this Serbian view. He affirmed the need for cooperation and closer relations with Belgrade and mentioned specifically the possibility of common diplomatic and military action "in all questions affecting both Serb kingdoms and the realization of legitimate national aspirations." But the cautious king did not go so far as to call for union. Indeed, although he indulged in characteristically flowery language to describe Montenegro's solidarity with all Yugoslav peoples, he did not once utter the word *union*.[77] He told the German minister that he was merely trying to pacify opposition sentiment and had no intention of letting unification take place.[78] In its response to the king's address, the skupština also avoided referring per se to union by name, but suggested that a formal arrangement be concluded to regulate interstate relations. Although the legislative body was not yet in a position to force its will on the king, many delegates felt that the advantages of union outweighed the disadvantages.[79]

Under pressure from his national assembly and advisors, Nicholas at least went through the motions of bowing to their wishes. On 15 March, he addressed what Albertini has called a "bombastic epistle" to King Peter, in which he sang the praises of both Serbia and Russia. He spoke of an agreement between their two kingdoms to preserve the "independence and equality of rights for our respective states and dynasties, and which shall lay down exactly the duties of each in the military, diplomatic, and financial sphere." But he avoided committing himself to anything more than "the hope of an approaching union" and was careful to mention that one of his aims was "to assure the succession of our thrones"—his own as well as Peter's.[80]

Sazonov crowed privately to Georges Maurice Paléologue, the new French ambassador in St. Petersburg, that he was largely responsible for the king's agreeing "almost with joy" to "dying by inches." This was idle boasting. Nicholas did not advocate rushing into formal dialogue with Serbia, but clung to his old dreams. Perhaps Russia's renewed subsidy and the international loan would keep his ship of state afloat and enable him to retain his throne and freedom of action. As if to underscore his residual independence, he took over a week to provide Obnorsky with a copy of his letter to Peter.[81]

One week later, Peter, aided by Hartwig, Pašić, and Mijušković (since November the Montenegrin minister in Belgrade), wrote a reply that echoed his father-in-law's high-sounding phrases. While mentioning union by name, he moderated his remarks by stating that a Serbo-Montenegrin agreement would "ensure our successors of a quiet and prosperous life." He envisioned a future Serbo-Montenegrin commonwealth along the lines of imperial Germany, with Serbia and the Karadjordjevići assuming the role and functions of Prussia and the Hohenzollerns, Montenegro and the Petrovići those of Bavaria and the Wittelsbachs. But the precise nature of the relationship lay open to the negotiations with Montenegro that Peter hoped would be forthcoming. He nominated Pašić and Mijušković to be the negotiators.[82]

Russia's tack of encouraging a gradual amalgamation thus appeared to bear results. Giesl seemed resigned to union: "It will be so; it must be so." No one, he added, "who has followed the developments in the two Serb states in the last few years can doubt that the union must come or at least will be attempted in the future."[83]

Gellinek, the Austro-Hungarian military attaché in Belgrade, shared Giesl's views, adding that all Montenegrin problems were now being thought of as Serbian ones. Despite the government's cautious attitude, many Serbians vocally protested Austria's occupation of Sjenokos and demanded an end to her designs on Lovćen.[84]

Austrian observers watched the activities of the Montenegrin ruling house with dismay, for a strong, popular dynasty might have served as a breakwater against the rising tide of unionism. The prestige of Nicholas's family, however, seemed to be sinking ever deeper, weighted down by new scandal and rumors of scandal. In the winter, stories circulated that Nicholas had mishandled state funds and pocketed huge sums of money earmarked by the Russians for the doweries of Montenegrin girls. At the same time, the palace confirmed the separation of Prince Mirko and his wife of eleven years, Princess Natalija. In many eyes, the country was left without a successor worthy of the name. Danilo, the nominal heir, was seen as weak, deceitful, and ambitious. His questionable behavior during the First Balkan War and his marked preference for living abroad had destroyed public sympathy for him. Although Mirko still enjoyed a modicum of goodwill, his controversial personal life now seemed to eliminate him as a possible successor. Giesl feared that the precipitous decline in the dynasty's prestige might accelerate the unwritten timetable for unification.[85] Sazonov had already indicated that he would do nothing to intervene if the Montenegrin people rose in revolt.[86] It soon appeared that they might do just that. In May, Obnorsky complained of uprisings and general discontent. Hubka subsequently reported that a group of *klubaši* had planned to depose Nicholas when he was out of the country. News of the plot reached the king in Munich, whereupon he immediately headed for home. The assassination of Archduke Francis Ferdinand soon turned everybody's attention to other matters.[87]

Sazonov's boasts notwithstanding, Serbo-Montenegrin negotiations proceeded fitfully in the months following Nicholas's exchange of letters with King Peter. A basis for talks was Pašić's program of a joint general staff, a merger of the two armies along German lines (each sovereign retaining nominal control of his own army in his own territory), and the fusion of the ministries of justice, finance, and communications.[88] As one scholar has observed, "in order to facilitate success, the plenipotentiaries aimed only at the achievement of minimum goals so as to parry the possibility of Austrian counteraction."[89] By the summer, negotiations had made some progress, and Serbia had announced that Montenegrin subjects could enter Serbian military schools for noncommissioned officers and could serve in her army on the same basis as Serbian subjects. But in the charged atmosphere of July 1914, Sazonov thought it best to suspend the talks. They were never resumed.[90]

The Question of Unification: Effects on the Triple Alliance

The unification question had disquieting effects on the Triple Alliance. For a long time, Germany misunderstood Berchtold's tentative policy regarding union and irritated Vienna with avuncular advice. Italy and Austria remained at arm's length, unable or unwilling to agree on a common approach to the problem. This lack of cooperation bothered Germany more than did the actual fate of the Black Mountain.

In late March and early April 1914, rumors about Montenegro once again circulated throughout Europe—this time claiming that Nicholas intended to sell his kingdom to Serbia for a handsome sum, thus effecting a Serbo-Montenegrin union through the back door. The version that reached the ears of the German emperor held that Hartwig, the godfather of the Balkan alliance, was behind a scheme to have Russia advance Serbia the purchase price, in return for "compensation" on the Adriatic coast. The transaction would take place secretly, so that Italy and especially Austria would be kept in the dark as long as possible. Should Vienna try to force Serbia to renounce her bargain purchase, then Russia stood ready to defend the honor and interests of her Balkan protégé. Kaiser William found the rumors plausible, and stated that if such a scenario did come true, "the world war would be at hand." In this regard, it was reported that the Russians were already arming themselves and had purchased some thirty thousand horses in the past four weeks.[91]

Albertini has bitterly condemned the German emperor's handling of this rumor as evidence of William's "utter irresponsibility."[92] But such was the Byzantine world of the Balkans that neither William, who termed the plan "oriental" and "strange," nor Chancellor Theobald von Bethmann Hollweg, who called it "fantastic," would dismiss out of hand any scheme, no matter how hairbrained, involving either Hartwig or Nicholas.

The chancellor requested Eckardt's evaluation of the rumors and advised the German representatives in Vienna and Rome to convey the information to the Austrian and Italian foreign ministries. Eckardt was quick to denounce the story as a "malevolent contrivance of intriguers who want to compromise the king."[93] It was, in fact, totally false.

The Germans worried incessantly about the Balkan entanglements of their allies. The fact that William mentioned Montenegro as a possible cause of world war is a measure of that concern. Yet because of their growing interest in Balkan affairs, they frequently became exasperated with Austrian policies, failing to understand them, and sometimes chiding the Ballhausplatz to the point of reprimanding. It was with a strong element of condemnation, for example, that Carl Georg von Treutler, the influential foreign office representative at the German court, commented on Vienna's presumed designation of the union of Montenegro and Serbia as totally "unacceptable." What exactly did "unacceptable" mean, he asked? To what extent was Austria determined to have her own way?[94]

It was Treutler's belief that "the union of Serbia and Montenegro cannot be prevented, and therefore Vienna should not say it is 'unacceptable.'" This position coincided with William's, as expressed in one of the emperor's marginalia: "The union is definitely not to be prevented, and if Vienna were to attempt this, she would be committing a great folly and conjuring up the danger of war with the Slavs, a proposition which would leave us quite cold." This and many subsequent statements relating to Montenegro by William and his subordinates indicate that contrary to the assertion of some historians, including Fritz Fischer and Imanuel Geiss, Germany was not always waiting for a suitable opportunity to make war. In no case, Treutler suggested, "should Germany permit Austria to lay her prestige on the line and designate as 'unacceptable' that which she would later give way on."[95] In a final assault on Vienna's *Balkanpolitik*, he stated that it would behoove the Dual Monarchy to reach a modus vivendi with Serbia for the sake of all concerned. Far more reasonable in German eyes was the "rational" approach they attributed to Count Stephen Tisza, the Hungarian prime minister, namely that Austria-Hungary could not hope to prevent the Serbo-Montenegrin *Anschluss* by force and should not try. Instead, she should attempt to work out an arrangement with Italy providing for the cession of Montenegro's coastal strip to Albania.

Perhaps the Germans had not paid attention to a report from Tschirschky on 15 February, in which he had apprised Berlin of Berchtold's earlier change of policy concerning the cession of the Montenegrin coast in the event of Serbo-Montenegrin union.[96] Perhaps William and his colleagues had simply drawn the wrong conclusions from their recent conversations with Francis Joseph and other leading Habsburg policymakers. In any case, Berchtold quickly pointed out that there was little difference between his position and what the Germans perceived Tisza's to be. The fate of Montenegro's coast would prove to be a stumbling block, not only for better Serbo-Habsburg relations, but, more importantly from the German viewpoint, also for Austro-Italian ties.[97]

By the spring of 1914, Berchtold had won German approval for the policy he had decided upon the preceding November. He encountered serious trouble, however, when he tried to win Italian acquiescence in the plan. The Italians feared that an Austrian acquisition of Montenegro's littoral would upset the maritime balance of power in the Adriatic to their detriment. They were particularly paranoid regarding Austrian designs on Lovćen.[98]

Between 14 and 18 April 1914, Berchtold and San Giuliano met at Opatija, a fashionable resort town in Istria, to discuss the future of Albania and to reconcile their differences. Berchtold presented a now familiar litany of Austrian worries about the Balkans, including the dangers inherent in a Serbo-Montenegrin union. The only way to lessen the negative effects, he argued, would be to prevent Serbia's expansion to the sea. He asked his colleague to approve his plan to give the coastal region to Albania. Though San Giuliano was more concerned with Austro-Hungarian aggrandizement than a Serbian presence on the Adriatic, he went one step further and called for a firm agreement concerning Albania; it was clear that he had Lovćen on his mind. Berchtold faltered when confronted by such boldness and was relieved when San Giuliano suggested that both countries needed more time to study the problem and its possible solutions before signing anything. To Tschirschky, the German ambassador, Berchtold later complained that

San Giuliano had undoubtedly wanted "to tie the hands of the Monarchy now and for all time."[99]

Neither foreign minister left Opatija completely satisfied with the result of the meeting. Nor was the Wilhelmstrasse happy with the differences that continued to separate its allies. With an eye toward maintaining the integrity of the Triple Alliance, Bethmann Hollweg instructed his ministers in Rome and Vienna to do what they could to facilitate an understanding.[100] Although Mérey still believed an agreement to be unattainable, Flotow asked him to keep trying to secure one, because Germany, too, had an interest in the outcome.[101] Bethmann, for his part, believed that the time had come for some German pressure to be applied to Vienna. He told Gottlieb von Jagow, the German state secretary for foreign affairs: "Vienna in its overall policy begins to emancipate itself rather too much from us and must, in my opinion, be reined in before it is too late."[102]

In early May, Mérey reported from Rome that he had heard new rumors that the Russians were now advising Serbia and Montenegro to effect an immediate union in case of the death of the aging Habsburg emperor, who had recently fallen ill with pneumonia. Their alleged rationale seemed plausible: that Francis Ferdinand would not want to inaugurate his reign with a war in the Balkans over something as insignificant (as far as most Habsburg subjects were concerned) as the fate of Montenegro or her coast. The rumors had no substance, and in any case, the emperor's recovery rendered the question moot.[103]

Yet the question of Serbo-Montenegrin union would not go away so easily. Even after the assassination of Archduke Francis Ferdinand on 28 June, while Europe inched toward war, the problem continued to occupy the attention of Europe's chancelleries. Indeed, some considered it to be as fraught with danger as the archduke's murder. On 1 July, for example, *Le Figaro* printed word of Serbia's imminent union with Montenegro. "This decision," the article claimed, "was supposed to have been announced on the anniversary of the battle of Kosovo, that is the day before yesterday, but because of the murder of Archduke Francis Ferdinand and his wife, the date of the announcement has been postponed—but it is only a delay." Specifically, the newspaper mentioned a customs union and the establishment of joint ministries of finance and foreign affairs. Despite a vigorous denial of the report by the Serbian embassy in Berlin, *Le Figaro* stood by its story, and other

European papers followed its lead in prematurely announcing the birth of a federal state system.[104] As Dayrell Crackanthorpe, the British legation secretary, pointed out, however, news of the archduke's assassination did not reach Belgrade until later in the afternoon of the twenty-eighth. There had been plenty of time for an announcement if one had been scheduled.[105]

Although Tschirschky also deemed the newspapers' stories "hardly believable," he nevertheless used the occasion of their publication to question Berchtold once more on the state of Austro-Italian negotiations over Montenegro. The German government clearly feared that Vienna and Rome would delay coming to an agreement until it was too late. At a time when Count Alex Hoyos was preparing to defend Austria-Hungary's case against Serbia before the highest circles in Berlin, it seemed expedient for the two allies to reach an accord. "They ought to make up their differences," Emperor William had written some time before. "It must be realized that in the long run, as Tisza says, Serbia and Montenegro will come together in any case."[106] But both Berchtold and Avarna admitted that little had been accomplished since Opatija. Although San Giuliano had expressed an interest in reaching an accord, Avarna had not talked to Berchtold about it. Negotiations concerning Albania proper had taken precedence. The Austrian foreign minister had similarly put matters off, not wishing to take a stand on Lovćen's future.[107]

In Rome, Flotow tried to prod San Giuliano by arguing that the transfer of Montenegro's coast to Albania and even the cession of Lovćen to Austria were not incompatible with long-range Italian interests. But the foreign minister parried such arguments with the threat of a Russo-Italian alliance.[108] He cited only one possible way that Italy might be persuaded to accept Austria's annexation of Lovćen: the cession to Italy of Austrian territory in the Trentino region—land that he considered *Italia irredenta*. On the eve of war, San Giuliano thus announced his price for Italy's cooperation in the days ahead, a price Austria was unwilling to pay.[109] Echoing his emperor's earlier words, Flotow wrote: "One cannot close one's eyes to the fact that this is a most serious question which may, to say the least, shatter the Triple Alliance, and perhaps even lead to a European war." Ironically, a fortnight after the events in Sarajevo, at a time when Austria's "blank check" was being arranged in Berlin, some German diplomats still feared that Montenegro might prove to be the catalyst of war.[110]

CHAPTER TEN

Into Armageddon— The Outbreak of War: 1914

On 28 June 1914, in the Bosnian capital of Sarajevo, a Serb nationalist shot and killed Archduke Francis Ferdinand, the heir to the thrones of Austria and Hungary, and his wife, the Duchess of Hohenberg. It was a Sunday, St. Vitus's Day (*Vidov dan*), the 525th anniversary of Serbia's tragic defeat on the plain of Kosovo. The assassin, Gavrilo Princip, an Austro-Hungarian citizen, had not acted alone. He and other members of the semisecret Young Bosnia (*Mlada Bosna*) movement, who had been nurtured on pan-Serb ideals and inspired and tutored by the Serbian terrorist sect known as the Black Hand (*Crna Ruka*), had long conspired to take dramatic action to promote their goal of joining their Bosnian homeland to Greater Serbia.[1]

Francis Ferdinand was a convenient and logical target. He was convenient because he had been attending army maneuvers in Bosnia at the time, against the advice of many familiar with the unsettled political situation in the empire's most recent territorial acquisitions. He was a logical choice not only because he was the heir presumptive, but because he was a man whose unusual programs for reforming Francis Joseph's empire threatened Serbia's preeminent position in the South Slav community and ran counter to the designs of the Black Hand and Young Bosnia. It was widely believed that Francis Ferdinand contemplated converting the Habsburg Empire into a tripartite monarchy, an act that would have given the Slavs of Austria-Hungary a greater political voice.[2] Such an arrangement might have conciliated the various disaffected Slav groups, especially those southern Slavs who habitually looked to Serbia as the Piedmont of a future great South Slav (Yugoslav) empire. Indeed, the archduke's scheme might have succeeded in transferring the torch of Slavic sovereignty from Serbia to the new tripartite monarchy, perhaps sealing the doom of the independent Serbian kingdom as well. *Mlada Bosna* would not countenance such possibilities, no matter how remote.

Austria-Hungary's official investigation of the crime quickly ascertained what almost everybody had suspected: that the roots of the conspiracy went all the way to Belgrade. The Serbian government had taken steps to warn Vienna about the possibility of an attack on the archduke's life, and Francis Ferdinand's sudden death was not deeply lamented in certain circles in the empire (especially in Budapest). Despite these two facts, Austro-Hungarian leaders, long embittered by what they took to be provocative Serbian effrontery, agreed in their determination to call Serbia to account. Precisely how this was to be achieved would not be so quickly or unanimously decided. Motivated by pride, outrage, and fear, the Habsburg decision-makers set out to redeem the Dual Monarchy's damaged reputation and to reassert its status as a Great Power. The path they eventually chose became the road to war.

Initial Responses

King Nicholas was out of the country on the day Francis Ferdinand was killed. Immediately upon hearing the news, he predicted to his personal physician that war would result. Later the same day in Trieste, Nicholas boarded a steamer, which docked at Bar the following evening. As soon as he arrived in his capital, he took steps to control the uncertain situation. He paid his respects to Chargé d'affaires Lothar Egger von Möllwald (Otto had not yet returned from vacation), and ordered a fifteen-day period of court mourning. As if to set an example, he attended a special service that was held in the court chapel.[3] Later he offered to send Crown Prince Danilo to represent Montenegro at Francis Ferdinand's funeral.[4] In Bar, however, where the Catholic archbishop conducted a mass in the archduke's memory, an old Montenegrin reflected reality more accurately than Nicholas's gestures: "The bloodshed in Sarajevo is the spark that will ignite flammable materials long smouldering in the Balkans. . . . We South Slavs are surely heading into difficult, but if God wills, happier times."[5]

On the morning of 30 June, Austro-Hungarian border troops reported that the tiny Montenegrin town of Metaljka, the site of a frontier skirmish only three months earlier, was adorned with flags and banners, as if in joyous celebration. As there had been no decorations in Metaljka the previous day and St. Vitus's Day had been celebrated on the twenty-eighth, the angry Austrians concluded that the town was engaging in a tasteless and reprehensible affront to the memory of the slain archduke. The war ministry, with its usual alacrity in such matters, hastened to share the reports with Berchtold, who lodged a protest at Cetinje and demanded an explanation.[6] The Montenegrin government denied any knowledge of the incident, but promised to make an immediate telegraphic inquiry. Prime Minister Vukotić and Foreign Minister Plamenac assured the Austro-Hungarian legation secretary that if the Austrian reports proved accurate, they would take action against those responsible, just as if the memory of the Montenegrin crown prince had been defamed.[7]

As it happened, the events at Metaljka did pertain to the crown prince, but in an entirely different fashion. The end of the month marked Danilo's forty-third birthday, and the authorities of the newly annexed town, eager to wave the Montenegrin flag and royal standard, had merely carried out orders sent them before the assassination. As soon as news of the archduke's death had reached Cetinje, the government had cancelled those orders in the capital, but the countermand had not reached Metaljka in time.[8] The matter was quickly cleared up and by 1 July all street decorations were taken down.[9]

Unlike the situation in 1908, there had been no immediate outbursts in Montenegro in the wake of the assassination. The archduke's death, unlike the annexation of Bosnia-Hercegovina, in no way threatened the integrity of the Serbian or Montenegrin people. Even in the king's absence, all public events scheduled in connection with St. Vitus's Day had been cancelled;[10] and the *Glas Crnogorca,* in its first issue after the assassination, reported that Francis Ferdinand had fallen victim to a gang of "horrible assassins."[11] Thus, official behavior seemed to bear out the appraisal of Hubka, the Austro-Hungarian military attaché in Cetinje, that the Montenegrins were "the only chivalrous, sympathetic people in the Balkans."[12] Even so, Austrian officials in Montenegro, including Hubka, worried about the large number of Montenegrins who seemed to view the assassins as national heroes.[13] Their fears were justified.

When grieving Habsburg patriots attacked Serbs in Sarajevo and other towns, Montenegrins finally gave vent to their own anti-Austrian sentiments. In Hubka's words, "the hatred against Austria-Hungary which had been simmering since the Scutari Crisis, began to boil anew." Protests were organized, largely by members of the growing opposition to Nicholas's rule, among them proponents of unification with Serbia, who decried the excesses perpetrated against their Serb brethren living in the Dual Monarchy.[14]

In part because of the dangerous domestic aspect of the anti-Austrian drive, Nicholas tried to curb his subjects' explosive temperament. On the evening of 4 July, for example, he symbolically rode in front of the Austro-Hungarian legation accompanied by his queen. Later he had an adjutant patrol the streets outside the legation.[15] But although the king and most of his ministers opposed the demonstrations, they were in no position to prevent them. Running the risk of alienating all patriotic Montenegrins, Nicholas played what the French minister called a "daring" game, seeking to control the demonstrations he knew would take place sooner or later.[16]

As it happened, Plamenac was having tea with Otto (just back from vacation) at the Austro-Hungarian legation when the storm finally broke. A crowd of four hundred marched outside the building and hooted insults at its occupants, including the horrified Montenegrin foreign minister. Once again, the king personally intervened, this time appearing in his car to control the demonstrators as best he could. Berchtold and Conrad took due note of Nicholas's personal intervention.[17] Before long, another incident contributed to deteriorating Austro-Montenegrin relations.

On 12 July, Montenegrin authorities apprehended twenty-seven-year-old Muhamed Mehmedbašić, a carpenter from Stolac in Bosnia, who was sought by the district court in Sarajevo for complicity in the archduke's assassination.[18] The Austro-Hungarian finance ministry, formally responsible for the provincial government of Bosnia-Hercegovina, hurriedly took steps to secure his extradition; but before arrangements could be made, the fugitive, the only Muslim among the Sarajevo conspirators, managed to escape from prison in Nikšić.[19] Count Berchtold and other Habsburg officials suspected Montenegro's connivance.

Plamenac assured Otto that the Montenegrin government had nothing to do with the escape and would do its utmost to punish those responsible for the "mistakes of Nikšić."[20] Vukotić dispatched the interior minister to Nikšić to investigate the matter personally and supervise efforts at reapprehending Mehmedbašić. The police searched houses in the area, including, much to the outrage of certain parliamentarians, the homes of three skupština delegates.[21] As Plamenac had promised, the gendarmes responsible for guarding Mehmedbašić were arrested, but the assassin himself remained at large.[22]

This series of events rankled in Vienna. In the first place, Austria-Hungary had informed Cetinje of Mehmedbašić's whereabouts as early as 7 July, but the Montenegrins, on the pretext of observing the suspect, had not apprehended him until the twelfth, only to have him escape two days later.[23] To make matters worse, during his brief captivity, Mehmedbašić had freely admitted (indeed he had boasted of) his complicity in the Sarajevo conspiracy.[24]

The Bosnian's escape embarrassed the Montenegrin government, but it surely saved it even more trouble. If Nicholas had permitted Mehmedbašić's extradition to Austria-Hungary to stand trial, he would have been branded a traitor by a majority of his subjects. If he had refused Vienna's request for extradition, he would have been in an equally uncomfortable position.[25] Some have suggested that Montenegro's protests of innocence in the affair notwithstanding, Mehmedbašić's escape was an ingenious solution to Nicholas's dilemma. Indeed, the French minister reported to the Quai d'Orsay: "I do not think that the guilty [i.e. responsible] official will have his future advancement retarded by the initiative he has taken in this affair."[26] Otto, on the other hand, believed that Plamenac's dismay and the government's efforts to recapture the fugitive were genuine.[27]

Efforts at Accommodation

Despite the festooning of Metaljka, the anti-Austrian demonstrations in Cetinje, and Mehmedbašić's untimely escape from Nikšić, the Austro-Hungarian and Montenegrin governments spent the greater part of the five weeks following the Sarajevo murders trying to reach a peaceful accommodation. Despite his belief that Montenegro would sooner or later cast her lot with Belgrade, even Field Marshal Conrad acknowledged the feasibility of trying to pry Nicholas and his four army divisions away from Serbia, at least until Serbia had been disposed of.[28] The king's personal intervention in the Cetinje demonstrations had made a "very good impression" in Vienna and opened the way for Berchtold to approach Nicholas.[29] Thus began a strange period of official courting and reciprocal obeisances.

The Austrian foreign minister's initial step was to inform Nicholas that, although the official inquiry into the archduke's murder had not yet been completed, investigators had determined beyond any doubt that Belgrade was behind the Sarajevo conspiracy. More importantly for Austro-Montenegrin relations, he could say that Montenegro was "in no way implicated in this or any other plot" against the Monarchy. Taking aim at an object of their mutual hostility, Berchtold instructed Otto to remind Nicholas that he, like the Habsburgs, had been a victim of the Belgrade "system" on more than one occasion. As a final example of his friendship for Montenegro, he pointed to his efforts to secure an advance on an international loan at rates that would not burden the small country's treasury.[30]

As Otto had been received at the palace twice since his return to Cetinje less than two weeks before, he was reluctant to visit the royal residence again, even to communicate Berchtold's message. He knew that any unseemly political familiarity with Nicholas might prejudice the king's standing with the Montenegrin people. On the other hand, he had little time to lose.[31] As it happened, another Balkan rumor made a visit to the palace not only justifiable, but perhaps necessary. On 19 July, various European newspapers, including *Le Temps* and *Corriere della Sera*, reported that Austria-Hungary was planning a surprise attack on Lovćen.[32] Although the *Fremdenblatt* carried the Austrian government's official denial two days later, Otto requested an audience with the king to repudiate the rumors in person.[33] He also used the occasion to convey Berchtold's message of goodwill. Nicholas thanked Otto and voiced the hope that the "era of misunderstandings" between their two countries was over and that they could look forward to better days. At the same time, he requested that Berchtold's denial of Montenegrin culpability in the Sarajevo affair be tendered in the form of an official declaration, which he could use in resisting the rising tide of pro-Belgrade sentiment in Montenegro.[34]

Otto surmised what Nicholas wanted in return for his nonparticipation in the Austro-Serbian conflict: nothing less than Scutari and northern Albania. The king seemed to feel that Vienna now might be willing to arrange the cession of Scutari to Montenegro. Giving a unique interpretation of Austro-Montenegrin relations over the past six years, Nicholas and his foreign minister cited numerous instances of Montenegrin loyalty to the Habsburg Empire, an allegiance which in their estimation deserved a better reward than the treatment accorded the tiny kingdom in 1913. They argued that Montenegrin expansion in the direction of Albania was actually in Austria-Hungary's own interest, reasoning that if Montenegro received the Bojana or the Drin as a border, the danger of her absorption by Serbia would be put aside. The additional territory would buttress the economy and give the Petrović dynasty a new lease on life. The choice for Austria-Hungary, then, was a simple one: a greater Montenegro now (albeit at Albania's expense) or a greater Serbia on the Adriatic later. In this spirit, Nicholas asked Otto, whom he found somewhat more sympathetic than Giesl, to travel to Vienna to represent Montenegro's case and secure the means with which to show the Montenegrin people the benefits of an Austrophile policy.[35]

The argument that territorial cession might prevent Montenegro's annexation was a reminder that the new crisis had not entirely eclipsed old problems. They were and remained connected. The Austro-Hungarian legation consul in Belgrade, for example, confident that war with Serbia was just a question of time, suggested using the persistent rumors about Serbo-Montenegrin unification as a pretext for "settling accounts." Yet even he conceded that there was little real danger of an imminent union.[36] Talks continued, but the union itself seemed distant.

Interest in Albania was not confined to Montenegro. Italy, too, glanced covetously at the land across the Strait of Otranto. In the wake of the Sarajevo assassination, San Giuliano intimated that Italy *might* require a quid pro quo in southern Albania to pursue a pro-Austrian policy in the face of overwhelming public sentiment favoring the Serbian underdog. Because of this ambiguous attitude, Vienna feared the possibility of an Italo-Montenegrin understanding regarding Albania.[37]

Reports from Bar indicated that Montenegro might be planning to invade her neighbor—perhaps to cover Serbia's rear in the event of an Albanian attack, perhaps for her own aggrandizement.[38] As early as mid-July, Conrad received reports that Nicholas's soldiers had violated Albanian territory at Zumbi and Bastriku.[39] Hubka, on the other hand, maintained that the army's movements were probably in keeping with the regular rotation of frontier troops.[40]

Just as Conrad feared that a Montenegrin attack on Albania was in preparation, the Montenegrins had good reason to believe and act on the numerous rumors concerning Austria-Hungary's own involvement in Albania. Following Aehrenthal's dubious example in 1908, Berchtold and August Ritter von Kral, the Austro-Hungarian consul general in Durrës, offered financial and military assistance to pro-Habsburg tribesmen, including the Malissori, in return for their support in the event of war with Serbia.[41] Berchtold thus gave substance to the rumors and prompted the very reaction from Montenegro he was trying to prevent.

The Ultimatum

On Thursday, 23 July, almost four weeks after the archduke's assassination, Baron Giesl delivered his government's famous ultimatum to Serbia, giving her until 6 P.M. on Saturday, the twenty-fifth, to reply. The ultimatum demanded that Belgrade eradicate all anti-Habsburg activity on Serbian soil. This included suppressing the anti-Austrian press; disbanding anti-Austrian clubs and organizations, including the *Narodna Odbrana* (but not the *Crna Ruka* band, of which Vienna knew little or nothing); dismissing military and civil personnel guilty of propagating or pursuing an anti-Austrian line; and arresting two particular Serbian officials. In order to prevent the recurrence of what Vienna perceived as repeated Serbian violations of agreements, especially her promises of 31 March 1909, Berchtold also called for the participation of Austro-Hungarian officials in the suppression and prosecution of anti-Austrian organizations and personalities in Serbian territory.[42]

In a lengthy note to the Powers on 25 July, Berchtold sought to justify the ultimatum.[43] Two days before, he had exonerated

Montenegro of any wrongdoing, stating "happily" that his demands had nothing to do with the mountain kingdom.[44] The news of the ultimatum, however, cast a pall over prospects for an immediate improvement in Austro-Montenegrin relations. Although Nicholas was relieved that Berchtold had emphasized Montenegro's innocence in the Sarajevo tragedy, he was still worried that he might be drawn into war "on the strength of public opinion."[45] As in 1908, his options were limited by the will of his subjects.

While Nicholas privately told Otto he hoped Belgrade would concede all points of the ultimatum, Plamenac correctly anticipated that the Serbians would have a hard time agreeing to the points that demanded an Austro-Hungarian presence on their territory. Unlike the government, the Montenegrin press was vociferous in its condemnation of the ultimatum. The *Dnevne Novosti*, a paper that first appeared after the archduke's death, made no pretense at seeking peace with Austria. One banner headline read: "Little Mother Russia is with us," a posture that presumed a great deal, but set the stage for the events that would follow.[46]

Despite the ultimatum's poor reception in the Montenegrin capital, Hubka believed that official Montenegrin neutrality could still be procured for the right price. He urged Berchtold to compromise with Nicholas, something the Ballhausplatz had shown itself singularly unwilling to do in the past. On this occasion Conrad agreed with Hubka's assessment. In the margin of the attaché's report of 24 July, he scribbled: "Don't spare the money."[47] On 25 July, he suggested that Berchtold promise the Montenegrin king anything within reason—to insure his throne, to support Montenegrin economic development, or to provide certain "pecuniary inducements"—in order to secure his neutrality.[48]

Plamenac's doubts concerning Serbia's response to the Habsburg ultimatum proved to be more accurate than the king's hopes for a peaceful submission. On 25 July, just minutes before the expiration of the forty-eight-hour deadline, Pašić delivered his government's response to Giesl at the Austro-Hungarian legation in Belgrade. The reply was basically conciliatory, perhaps even sycophantic.[49] Pašić agreed to most of the Austrian demands, hedged on others, and rejected only one, point six, which provided for the participation of Austro-Hungarian officials in judicial proceedings.[50] Still, this was not the response Vienna had demanded.

Into Armageddon—The Outbreak of War: 1914

Plamenac urged Berchtold to extend the ultimatum's deadline, arguing that Serbia's response had been positive and conciliatory, and that the points that the Serbians did not concede should not be regarded as outright refusals. He asserted that letting the matter come to *ultima ratio*, in the face of Serbia's unexpectedly sweeping concessions, would only serve to create the impression that Austria-Hungary had wanted war all along, and provoked it by insisting on intentionally unfulfillable demands.[51] He was neither the first nor the last who urged Vienna to meet its adversary halfway. But in the hot summer of 1914, pride, compounded by the genuine and halfhearted bellicosity of a handful of men, ultimately decreed that the Habsburg Monarchy, guaranteed by the might of imperial Germany, would stand firm.[52] Baron Giesl rejected Serbia's note and broke relations, an act traditionally the prelude to war.[53] Still, Vienna's official preparations gave evidence of a firm hope, if not full confidence, that the struggle with Serbia would remain localized and limited in scope.[54] At noon on 28 July, Austria-Hungary declared war on Serbia.

Even before the declaration of war, Nicholas, in the show of patriotism expected of him, exchanged telegrams with Alexander, the prince regent of Serbia, assuring his grandson that Montenegro would act in concert with Serbia "for the defense of the Serb race." More ominously, as far as Austria-Hungary was concerned, he told Alexander that "my Montenegrins are on the frontier [presumably the one with Austria], prepared to fall in defense of our independence."[55]

Now more than ever Berchtold wanted to prevent Montenegro from making common cause with Serbia. In trying to justify Austria's declaration of war, he told Nicholas that he had had no alternative but to defend Austria-Hungary's "vital interests." Recognizing that the king was caught in the middle between his own professed desire for peace and his people's apparent lust for war, the Austrian foreign minister sought to sweeten the pill he hoped Nicholas would swallow.[56] The previous day he had wired Nicholas that, although Montenegro's request for a six-million-crown advance was in trouble with some of the other Great Powers, he would take it upon himself to try to secure a new, equally favorable loan guaranteed by Austria-Hungary and Italy.[57] In addition, he assured Nicholas that he had no intention of pursuing a policy of conquest vis-à-vis Serbia and that the Austrian campaign would observe and support the integrity of the Serbian state.[58] Finally, amid reports of Montenegrin mobilization and solidarity with Serbia, he empowered Otto to do "anything reasonable" to keep Montenegro out of the war.[59] Precisely what was and was not "reasonable" was not clear.

In anticipation of the outbreak of hostilities between Austria-Hungary and Serbia, Montenegro on 29 July ordered a general mobilization of her army. The government gave two reasons for its decision: the uncertainty of the situation and the unwarranted concentration of Austro-Hungarian troops on the Montenegrin frontier. On the same day, Prime Minister Vukotić returned from a trip to Italy, and the Montenegrin skupština was called to meet on 1 August.[60] The Russian minister told Otto that he had not yet received specific instructions from his government. In the meantime, he was counselling Montenegro to keep the peace.[61]

Rumor followed rumor. On 29 July, the British press announced Austria's decision to launch an attack on Lovćen in the next few days. On the thirtieth, the *Times* reported that Montenegro had decided not to defend Lovćen and, in consequence, the Montenegrin court had withdrawn from Cetinje.[62] Both stories were false.

Edging toward War

Late in July, Austro-Hungarian civil and military authorities in Dalmatia, acting sometimes without instructions from the Ballhausplatz, took measures along the Montenegrin frontier that exacerbated the already troubled relations between Vienna and Cetinje. On 26 July, Plamenac voiced his government's alarm at reports of Montenegrin peasants on their way to Kotor being turned back at the border because they did not have new special passes. Incoming reports of a buildup of Austrian naval forces in the Bay of Kotor and army maneuvers along the Montenegrin border between Bileća and Bijela Gora made matters worse.[63]

Berchtold explained that the new border regulations had been enacted for Dalmatia as a whole, especially for the exposed coastal region, but there was no doubt that they were aimed against Montenegro. On the other hand, he stated that special provisions were being arranged for border dwellers such as those Montenegrins who depended on the Austrian market to sell their goods and produce. As far as the reports of increased military activity were concerned, he admitted that the army was conducting maneuvers, but pointed out that they were being held in the usual training area near Bileća.[64] He later asserted that the naval maneuvers were of a defensive nature and did not extend to the Montenegrin coast.[65] Whatever the reasons behind these various measures, they antagonized the sensitive Montenegrins and cost Otto much goodwill. Unfortunately, more Austro-Hungarian steps contributed to a spiral of misunderstanding.

When Habsburg authorities ordered all Montenegrins living in Kotor to depart at once, Cetinje promptly retaliated by ordering the expulsion of all Austro-Hungarian citizens, save diplomats.[66] To make matters worse, Habsburg postal officials, acting without Berchtold's knowledge, chose this moment to terminate all telegraphic service between the two countries.[67]

Initially, Franz Colombani, the Austro-Hungarian legation secretary, led Otto to believe that the disruption in telegraphic communication was the result of sabotage. Having just returned from Kotor, he told the minister that he had heard that rewards were being offered for information leading to the capture of the party responsible. It soon became evident that the party responsible was none other than the Austro-Hungarian Post and Telegraph Administration, not a group of Serb renegades.[68] While Otto was relating to Plamenac Colombani's version of what had transpired, the Montenegrin foreign minister was handed a fresh telegram from the Austro-Hungarian ministry of commerce, stating very abruptly that service between the two countries would not be possible until further notice. Plamenac, understandably furious, swore at Otto and demanded that the Austrian set matters right at once. This was not an easy assignment, as Otto's communications had also been cut. He could not cable Vienna unless he travelled to Kotor.[69]

The comedy of errors continued. As Otto prepared to send Colombani to Kotor with messages for the Ballhausplatz, the secretary's rented automobile, the legation's only link with the outside world, was impounded by the Cetinje police. Plamenac apologized for the seizure but did not act quickly to return the car. Instead he explained that the police had only reciprocated the seizure of a Montenegrin car by officials in Kotor. His patience running short, Otto demanded absolute freedom of movement for himself and his staff and threatened to close his legation in Montenegro if the situation did not improve. The car was put at the disposal of the legation once again, but not until 28 July.[70]

The harried Austrian minister initiated his courier service with Kotor, whence his messages could be telegraphed to Vienna. Yet driving to and from the port city took a lot of time, and in the prevailing circumstances, time was precious. Otto rightly called the disruption in normal communications "a real calamity," not only for himself, but also for the other diplomats in Cetinje. He pleaded with Berchtold to do what he could to have the onerous measures rescinded.[71] By the time he received Otto's plaintive message, Berchtold had been informed that the lines between Vienna and Cetinje had been restored.[72] Such, unfortunately, was not the case, and crucially important messages to and from Otto still had to go by way of Colombani's car.[73]

In some other respects, Berchtold achieved more immediate success. After his initial justification of the measures along the Montenegrin border and in Kotor, he had invited Montenegro to take some conciliatory step that would permit Vienna to return to the status quo ante.[74] He soon took such a step himself, informing Cetinje that, although he could not have the Kotor measures rescinded in their entirety, he had succeeded in having them changed to apply to men only. Thus, women and children could remain in or return to Kotor. Berchtold made it clear that he expected the Montenegrin government to act in similar fashion regarding its expulsion of certain Austro-Hungarian subjects.[75]

Despite deteriorating relations, Otto still believed that Nicholas wanted to follow a neutral course in Austria's Serbian conflict. The military party, on the other hand, demanded solidarity with Belgrade; and measures such as those taken by Austro-Hungarian authorities in Kotor and elsewhere only fanned the flames of Montenegrin hatred.[76] When news was received that Austrian bullets had actually drawn Serbian blood, Nicholas's delicate position became even more precarious, but in a long interview on 29 July, Plamenac assured Otto that his government would continue to observe strict neutrality as long as possible. At the same time, he requested something tangible on the part of Austria-Hungary, ideally a guarantee of Montenegro's "continued existence," which in the king's parlance meant Berchtold's acceptance of an enlarged Montenegrin state.[77] A short time later, apparently not content with Berchtold's earlier assurances, he made formal inquiry as to the nature of Austria's war aims.[78]

Hubka, convinced that this was a now-or-never situation, once again urged the Habsburg foreign minister to come to terms with Nicholas by making the following assurances: (1) no territorial acquisition by Austria-Hungary at Serbia's expense, (2) the maintenance of the integrity of the Montenegrin state, and (3) financial support (along with territorial expansion) for Montenegro. Berchtold's reply, late as it was, signalled an important departure in Austrian policy vis-à-vis Montenegro.[79]

In a desperate message to Otto, Berchtold once again declared that Austria-Hungary had no territorial designs on Serbia and did not intend to occupy Serbian territory for a long period; he again pledged the Monarchy's present and future support and added his belief that Italy could be counted on to do the same. Up to this point, Berchtold's assurances did not differ substantially from his previous statements. When it came to Hubka's third point, however, the Austrian foreign minister took a bold, unprecedented step: he not only promised to give Montenegro generous financial support at the end of the war with Serbia, but, for the first time, he gave official sanction for Montenegro's territorial growth in the direction of the Sandžak and, eventually within the framework of a necessary agreement with Italy, in the direction of northern Albania.[80] Thus, at the eleventh hour, Berchtold seemed willing to concede Scutari to Montenegro in exchange for a pledge of neutrality in the war with Serbia—a virtual "diplomatic revolution" in Austria's dealings with her neighbor.

The theoretical ramifications of Berchtold's proposal are striking. In the fury of the moment, he appeared ready to promote a disruption of the Balkan status quo in return for a free hand in punishing Serbia allegedly for the same offense. Austria would thus be violating what had been a fundamental tenet of her own foreign policy ever since Aehrenthal's annexation of Bosnia-Hercegovina in 1908. From the Montenegrin side, the possibilities were even more paradoxical. Additional expansion into the Sandžak, for example, implied territorial aggrandizement at Serbia's expense. Nicholas would be guilty of doing precisely what he demanded Austria-Hungary not do as a condition for his neutrality. Indeed, the king would be put in the unaccustomed position of secretly hoping for an Austrian victory over Serbia, because only a Serbian defeat would gain him the pound of flesh that, according to his own propaganda, was necessary for Montenegro's material well-being. A Serbian victory, on the other hand, would surely signal the end of the Petrović-Njegoš dynasty and Montenegrin independence.

If Berchtold's Sandžak proposition was barely plausible, his Albanian suggestion was virtually unthinkable. Italy would never consent to the award of bits and pieces of Albanian territory to a third country that promised to fall into Vienna's orbit—that is, unless Berchtold were also willing to compensate Italy satisfactorily, not only in the Trentino, but also in Albania. Of course, such compensation would be detrimental to Vienna's conception of a suitable balance of power in the Balkans. In essence, then, the foreign minister's quixotic overture was merely a desperate play for Montenegrin neutrality, designed to give Nicholas what he wanted, at least on paper, and simultaneously to placate the Montenegrin people, the majority of whom, Berchtold hoped, would still follow the lead of their king.

Notwithstanding the unique opportunity to regain Scutari and realize an old dream, the Montenegrin king could not ride roughshod over the wishes of his people. Even if Nicholas and his conception of the Montenegrin state stood to benefit materially from a policy of neutrality, this meant little to most of his subjects. In the crisis at hand, they were Serbs first, an attitude that played increasingly into the hands of Montenegrin unionists. The territorial possibilities of Berchtold's diplomatic initiative simply did not touch the heart and soul of the average Montenegrin. For him, it was enough to know that Austria was the traditional foe, Russia the traditional friend, and Serbia the threatened kinsman. To sacrifice Serbia for some parochial gain would have been an act of treachery. By the time Berchtold's proposals reached Nicholas, it was already too late. The Montenegrin people, through their skupština delegates, had declared themselves for war.

Montenegro's Declaration of War

In the wake of Montenegro's mobilization order of 28 July, Otto reported that four Montenegrin battalions had been assigned to the Austro-Hungarian border and that war and Red Cross supplies of all kinds were being transported out of Bar and Ulcinj, the two principal coastal towns vulnerable to Austro-Hungarian naval attack.[81] In Scutari, the Montenegrin consul provocatively informed the resident British commander-in-chief that Montenegro was ready for all contingencies: if attacked in the back by Berchtold's hired Malissori bands, she was ready to occupy and lay waste most of northern Albania.[82] To add to the general confusion concerning Nicholas's intentions, Berchtold received a batch of military reports that indicated that Montenegro did not plan to deploy her troops along the long Austro-Hungarian border, as reported by Otto, but intended instead to put them at the disposal of Serbia by way of the Sandžak.[83] Ominously, American newspaper accounts had the two countries already at war, with Austrian forces supposedly occupying Lovćen and Montenegrin troops in Kotor, which, given the geographical possibilities of the terrain, would have been an extraordinary feat indeed.[84]

Montenegrin officials naturally tried to play down their military activities. On the same day that Nicholas ordered mobilization, Prime Minister Vukotić told Italian journalists that his country was simply not ready for war.[85] To Hubka he said: "We have, to be sure, several million rounds, but only a couple thousand rusted guns; the material is unusable, the munitions unreliable and in short supply; we have no victuals, no money, and no credit. How are we supposed to be able to wage another war?"[86] Three days later, Plamenac echoed Vukotić: Montenegro had no money, no guns, and no ammunition; therefore, Austria had no reason to continue her elaborate military preparations along the Montenegrin frontier.[87]

Yet despite this disclaimer, Plamenac added his realistic appraisal of the situation: Montenegro could remain neutral if and only if Russia stayed out of the conflict, limiting her protests to diplomatic channels.[88] Russia's attitude was thus crucial to the denouement of the "Montenegrin question," as well as the summer crisis as a whole.[89]

On Thursday, 30 July 1914, Russia ordered a partial mobilization of thirteen army corps along the Austro-Hungarian frontier. Berchtold, still hoping to come to terms with Sazonov, was forced in turn to approve Austria-Hungary's mobilization. Amid growing pessimism as to the chances for peace, Russia, responding more to Germany's preparations than to Austria's, gave a new order on 31

July for the general mobilization of her forces. Thus, four million Russians were called to arms. The following day, Germany formally declared war on Russia. The dominoes were starting to fall, but Austria-Hungary had not yet declared war on Russia, or vice versa.[90]

On 1 August, the Montenegrin skupština met in extraordinary session, stimulated by the news that Russia had ordered general mobilization and the rumor that she had already invaded Austrian Galicia. War fever was high. Every member of the skupština was present, every seat in the gallery was taken. Speaker after speaker denounced Austria-Hungary and called for war. "Our centuries-old enemy, the other Asian, is Austria," exclaimed Janko Tošković. "She wants to prepare another Kosovo for us. . . . I therefore demand that the royal government declare war on Austria immediately."[91] Not surprisingly, the assembly unanimously passed a motion calling for war, or in its words, "to extend a helping hand" to its "Serb brothers."[92] The skupština gave the Vukotić government a vote of confidence and extended it a free hand to take any and all necessary measures.

The same afternoon, the king received the members of the parliament, thanking them for their patriotism, but urging them to remain calm and leave the affairs of state in his capable hands.[93] He still would not take a firm stance. Perhaps he was waiting for the arrival of three of his children, due any hour in Kotor.[94] Perhaps he was waiting for a miracle that would permit him to take advantage of Berchtold's striking proposals, which he had received only after the skupština's session. While Montenegro continued her military preparations (supposedly against Trebinje and Dubrovnik), Plamenac indicated to the French and Russian ministers that he was only waiting until the appropriate moment to hand Otto his passport.[95]

On 3 and 4 August, Montenegrin authorities toyed with the Austro-Hungarian legation in Cetinje, stopping its mail service, interdicting its courier service with Kotor, and cutting off its electricity. Austro-Hungarian subjects of military age were apprehended. Still the king would not declare war; he waited instead for some sign from St. Petersburg. Every day he visited his troops posted in mountain passes and urged them not to fire until he gave the word. Finally, at 6 P.M. on 5 August, Plamenac informed Otto that his mission in Montenegro was over. The following day, the

Into Armageddon—The Outbreak of War: 1914

Austro-Hungarian legation staff left Montenegro while Russia and Austria-Hungary exchanged declarations of war.[96]

King Nicholas did not want to go to war, but the times and the security of his throne and dynasty demanded it. In a final audience with Hubka, he movingly insisted: "God is my witness that I never willed the war, for I know what is at stake. Destiny fulfills itself; it is stronger than the human will."[97] Thus, Montenegro joined the march into Armageddon.

Conclusion

In the decade before World War I, Montenegro exercised political influence far out of proportion to her small size and meager resources. This stemmed, in part, from the ambitions of her sovereign; from her location in the volatile Balkans, a region of conflicting nationalist aspirations and Great-Power rivalries; and from her threatening position at Austria's back door. Cetinje, her unimposing mountain capital, was the site of constant diplomatic activity. Nicholas, her prince and later king, used his country's critical position to great advantage and became an important figure in European politics. The monarchs of Europe vied with one another to court his favor and to conclude matrimonial alliances with his numerous offspring. Nicholas's policies alternately helped and harmed his country, and ultimately affected all the European Powers. His country was often a bone of contention between Austria-Hungary and Russia, a source of discomfort for the Triple Entente, and a wedge that threatened to split the Triple Alliance. On more than one occasion, especially during the Scutari crisis, he led Europe to the brink of war in the Balkans. On the eve of the First World War, some diplomats believed that Montenegro would provide the spark to set Europe ablaze.

At the heart of Montenegro's foreign policy was a burning desire, some said a compelling need, for more money and land. A proud but impoverished country, she did not have the means to support herself. Her rulers had long relied on external financial assistance to make ends meet. To alleviate this embarrassing plight, they sought salvation in territorial growth, hoping that physical expansion would provide the economic wherewithal to sustain political independence. This economic imperative was but one component of an age-old Serbo-Montenegrin aspiration: to resurrect the medieval Serbian empire of Stephen Dušan. Ambitious for his dynasty as well as his country and incited by the nationalism of his people, Nicholas dreamed of uniting all Serbs under his aegis and of sitting upon Dušan's throne in Prizren.

The European Power most responsible for impeding the realization of Montenegrin aspirations was Austria-Hungary. A multinational empire with a large South Slav population, she looked with apprehension upon the growth of a Serb state along her borders. Although she occasionally tolerated and even fostered Montenegrin growth when her own interests seemed to dictate it, she always sought to direct Cetinje's expansionism and subordinate it to her own imperial designs. The divergent policies of Vienna and Cetinje—their respective quests for gold, glory, influence, and *Lebensraum*—caused a succession of diplomatic crises and skirmishes in the years before World War I.

One of the most serious crises erupted in the fall of 1908 when Austria-Hungary annexed Bosnia and Hercegovina. Although in return Vienna agreed to withdraw her troops from the Sandžak of Novi Pazar and surrender her rights under the Treaty of Berlin to patrol Montenegrin waters, Montenegro felt threatened by the formal extension of Habsburg sovereignty over her neighboring provinces. Nicholas regarded this land as his patrimony; his countrymen felt it was part of their greater Serb homeland. They rose in protest, along with their Serbian cousins, but were unable to reverse the *fait accompli*. Austria firmly rejected all demands for territorial compensation.

The annexation brought Austro-Montenegrin relations close to the breaking point and clouded efforts at reconciliation in years to come. It confirmed that any future Montenegrin expansion would have to be in the direction of the Sandžak or Albania—in either case against the wobbly Ottoman Empire. Yet here, too, the Austrians and their allies interposed themselves. That Serbia and Montenegro should not establish a common frontier in the Sandžak long remained a basic tenet of Habsburg policy. In northern Albania, Austria sought to preserve a sphere of influence whose foundation was a centuries-old cultural protectorate over Albanian Catholics.

Despite Austria's influence, Nicholas made an unsuccessful bid to extend his own authority in northern Albania in 1910 and 1911. By supporting the neighboring Catholic tribesmen in one of their periodic struggles against their Turkish overlord, he hoped to undermine Vienna's moral presence, present himself as their friend, and offer his rule as an attractive alternative to the sultan's. Austria and Russia, however, opposed any disruption of the status quo and forced the rebels to come to terms with Constantinople and Nicholas to withdraw his support for Albanian refugees. Despite this Great-Power chastisement, Nicholas soon took advantage of the opportunity presented by the Turco-Italian War to renew his campaign to have himself crowned king of northern Albania—once more to no avail. His public concern for the Malissori tribesmen was a façade; his military campaign in northern Albania during the First Balkan War the following year treated the Albanians as brutally as it did the Turkish enemy.

The First Balkan War was brought about by the Balkan Alliance of 1912, a compact whose principal *raison d'être* was territorial expansion at Turkey's expense. This alliance with Serbia, Greece, and Bulgaria gave Nicholas additional strength and a unique opportunity to shake off the constraints that Austria-Hungary sought to impose on him. Within weeks after firing the first shot, Montenegro's troops joined Serbia's in dividing the Sandžak between them, effectively terminating Vienna's policy of keeping the two Serb states physically apart. Although Conrad and others urged Berchtold to turn the clock back, the foreign minister reconciled himself to the corridor's loss and the necessity of redefining Balkan frontiers. On the other hand, he was determined to limit the sphere of Serbo-Montenegrin territorial aggrandizement, regardless of the war aims of the various belligerents—hence his program to create an autonomous Albania and prevent either Belgrade or Cetinje from expanding along the Albanian coast.

One of Montenegro's principal war aims was the annexation of Scutari. The fate of the largely Albanian city sparked one of the most important crises faced by pre-1914 Europe. In the early stages of the First Balkan War, when Montenegro's conquest of Scutari was taken for granted, Berchtold seemed open-minded about its future. But when the Montenegrin war machine stalled, and Nicholas turned a deaf ear to Habsburg plans for an Austro-Montenegrin customs union and resolutely declined to cede any part of Mount Lovćen to Austria in return for Vienna's blessings, the foreign minister resolved that Albania—not Montenegro—should have the city. At the Conference of Ambassadors in London, the Austrians labored long and hard to win the agreement of the other Powers. Nicholas, by refusing to obey the conference's decision regarding Scutari, came dangerously close to provoking unilateral Austrian intervention. Only his last-minute capitulation staved off a military strike that might have led to a wider conflict.

Despite the resolution of this crisis in Austria's favor, and the conference's decision to create an independent Albania, Austria and Montenegro continued to argue over the future Albanian-Montenegrin border until the outbreak of world war. While the Northern Albanian Border Commission slowly demarcated the official frontier, Montenegrin troops frequently crossed into disputed territory. In October 1913, when Austria almost resorted to military action to compel the evacuation of Serbian troops from the region, Montenegro took the hint and withdrew her own lingering forces. Yet only months later, Nicholas began to peck away at bits of neighboring land. In some instances, Austria accepted his claims and provisional occupation; in others, she did not. As in the past, the Austro-Montenegrin frontier was also the scene of serious disputes, including the one at Sjenokos in March 1914.

Although such border incidents had a debilitating effect on Austro-Montenegrin relations, they were overshadowed by a far more important territorial question: that of a political union of Serbia and Montenegro, a possibility engendered by the creation of their common border during the Balkan wars. Many Austrians, and even some independence-minded Montenegrins, suggested that Austria should extinguish any thought of union by reoccupying all or part of the Sandžak, but Berchtold rejected such extreme measures. He eventually even accepted the idea of an amalgamation, but for a price: the cession of Montenegro's Adriatic coast to Albania and other border rectifications. The latter included the possibility of securing Lovćen for Austria. Nicholas was tempted to reach an agreement with the Dual Monarchy, especially one that proscribed union, as he feared a merger with Serbia would mean an end to his crown and dynasty, but a rapprochement was never achieved. Austria remained suspicious of Nicholas and could not forget his past hostility. Nicholas, for his part, could do little against the Serbophile sentiments of his subjects. Only when it was too late did Austria move to grant the king what he had long asserted would preserve his independence—northern Albania. Even then the new policy was motivated less by a desire to buttress Nicholas than to secure his neutrality in an approaching war with Serbia.

Austro-Montenegrin relations before the First World War were not exclusively antagonistic or estranged. Austria periodically extended loans to Montenegro; signed postal, coinage, and commercial conventions with her; and constructed roads on her rocky terrain. During Nicholas's jubilee celebration in 1910, Aehrenthal and the Austrian press saluted the new king, and Francis Joseph sent a warm congratulatory letter. In 1912, the emperor went one step further, formally receiving Nicholas at the Hofburg and naming him honorary commander of an Austrian regiment. But such short-lived manifestations of goodwill did not translate into long-term friendship. There was more form than substance to Austria's overtures. Her numerous schemes for closer commercial relations, designed primarily to lure Montenegro away from Russia, offered the tiny kingdom little more than economic vassalage. Austria rarely did anything gratis; every Austrian quid had a Montenegrin quo. The Ballhausplatz even viewed such an inconsequential undertaking as the repair of Nicholas's yacht in utilitarian terms.

One scholar has argued that Austria-Hungary was "blind to the advantages of a little kindness and courtesy in dealing with the Balkan peoples."[1] It is true that Austro-Hungarian officials generally looked upon the residents of the peninsula as inferiors. Aehrenthal was frequently curt with the Montenegrins, holding their sovereign in low esteem, and Berchtold did little to show himself their friend. The conduct of Austria's ministers in Cetinje and their personal relations with Nicholas also had an adverse effect. They inevitably lost patience and tact in their dealings with Montenegrin officials. Giesl, in particular, often exchanged harsh, undiplomatic words with the king and boasted of his brusqueness in his dispatches and memoirs.

Officials outside the diplomatic service also contributed to poor relations. At one time or another, the Zagreb police, local authorities in Kotor, Austro-Hungarian postal officials, and, most especially, the military created headaches for the Ballhausplatz. Conrad's frequent threats to unleash war on the Monarchy's neighbors kept the Balkans on edge. Although Aehrenthal and Berchtold sought to muzzle the field marshal and tone down his remarks, the Montenegrins realized that many other Austrians shared his sentiments and wanted to snuff out their liberty. The bellicose feelings of Austria-Hungary's ministers at the height of the Scutari crisis bear this out.

It can be argued that Austria-Hungary could have been more conciliatory toward Montenegro, more amenable to questions of territorial compensation and border rectifications, more inclined to join the other Powers in extending international loans. Perhaps she should have been less abrasive in rejecting some of Nicholas's claims, less reluctant to accept certain *faits accomplis,* less eager to seek military solutions to diplomatic deadlocks. To be generous with her small neighbor might have enhanced Austria's international reputation and allayed Montenegrin fears about her hegemonic intentions. Yet it would be unfair to place the whole blame for the unfortunate course of Austro-Montenegrin relations on Vienna. After all, the Dual Monarchy could not have been expected to endorse all of Montenegro's expansionist claims. Nicholas was frequently provocative, tactless, and petty. When relations with Austria were strained, he would frequently refuse to see the Habsburg minister for weeks on end or ostentatiously ignore his representations. During the Scutari crisis, he cut off telegraphic communications with the outside world. On this occasion and again the following summer, when Vienna interdicted communications, he tried to frustrate the Austrian legation's efforts to reestablish contact with its government. When he did talk to a minister, there was no guarantee that the conversation would remain confidential. All too often, Kuhn, Giesl, or Otto would confide something to Nicholas, only to be queried about it the following day by the Italian, German, or Russian minister.

Yet when Nicholas wanted to keep a secret, he could. His surprise visit to Vienna in 1912 was a masterpiece of concealment. Only later did the Austrians discover that they had been bamboozled and the visit's purpose was not to talk to them about peace, but to arrange an alliance with Bulgaria for war. It was difficult for Austro-Hungarian ministers to penetrate the decision-making process of the Montenegrin government. Often, this simply meant fathoming Nicholas's own thoughts, but the king's words usually hid as much as they revealed; and the reports of confidants, other ministers, or even his own sons rarely told the Ballhausplatz everything it wished to know. Matters became even more confused when Nicholas was compelled to share power with civilian ministers, military leaders, and others.

Given the deeply rooted Russophilia and pan-Serbism of the Montenegrin people, it is doubtful whether Austria could have done much to win their affection. They always would have retained the suspicion that characterizes a small country's relationship with a large, imposing neighbor, especially one as unsettled in its internal affairs and international objectives as Austria-Hungary. It is even more doubtful whether Aehrenthal or Berchtold could have done anything to earn Nicholas's long-term trust and friendship short of granting his every entreaty. Nicholas was a manipulator, quick to pounce upon what he perceived to be a weakness. For every inch that was granted him, he coveted another mile. His gratitude was notoriously short-lived, as his dealings with his Russian benefactor showed. In the end, only catering to him would have kept him reasonably close to the Monarchy—but this was incompatible with Austria's imperial interests, sense of prestige, and status as a Great Power.

Before World War I, Russia, like Austria, confronted a host of problems caused by or related to Montenegro, a country whose political and financial interests she had tended off and on for over two hundred years. The ethnic, religious, and dynastic ties that bound the two Slavic countries could not induce Nicholas to be the tsar's dutiful ward. While Russia tried to subordinate Montenegro to her larger imperial interests, Nicholas tried to play off St. Petersburg against Vienna in his own efforts at expansion. Fortunately for the Ballhausplatz, Russo-Montenegrin feuding generally had a salutary effect on Austro-Montenegrin relations. One of the best Montenegrin scholars of recent times has remarked that during the reign of Vladika Njegoš, "Montenegro was dragging [Russia] into embarrassing situations and constantly confronting [her] with aggravations."[2] Seventy years later, little had changed. Nicholas, like Njegoš, was "caught between two fires: he was driven by duty and the highest obligation to an evil thing—to be insincere toward those he least wished to offend, the Russians. An extremely delicate diplomacy and an underhanded struggle on all sides was inevitable."[3] With shocking regularity, Montenegro bit the hand of her benefactor, providing a lesson for all great powers hoping to purchase a small, underdeveloped country's abiding loyalty with money or military assistance.

In the years before the First World War, Russia subsidized the Montenegrin ruling house and in 1910 concluded a military convention to provide the Montenegrin army with money, matériel, and instructors. When Nicholas thumbed his nose at Russia two years later, however, she retaliated by cutting off the military assistance that had been largely responsible for the king's reckless independence. Although Russia continued to support Nicholas's territorial claims, relations between the two countries approached the breaking point; some Russian officials desired to finish with their unruly client once and for all and have Serbia absorb his kingdom. Only the influence of the Russian chargé in Cetinje and fear of Austria's reaction moderated Russian policy. St. Petersburg reluctantly decided to prop up Nicholas for the time being, while cautiously promoting Russia's ultimate goal of the gradual unification of the two Serb states. One consideration in the minds of the tsar's strategists was that Montenegro—like Serbia—could draw Habsburg troops away from the Russian border in the event of an Austro-Russian war.

Though her political interests in Montenegro and the Balkans were circumscribed, France came to play an increasingly important role as Russia's financial and diplomatic second, keeping pace with St. Petersburg's lead in the various Balkan crises before the First World War. In 1913 and 1914, her minister in Cetinje wrote scathing criticisms of Nicholas and his rule, but the Quai d'Orsay remained at the forefront of the movement to arrange an international loan for the king. Great Britain was much less inclined than France to involve herself unnecessarily in Balkan affairs, and when she did, it was generally in an effort to keep the peace. As chairman of the London Conference of Ambassadors, one of Sir Edward Grey's most significant accomplishments was the preservation of peace between Austria and Montenegro during the Scutari crisis.

Just as Montenegro caused problems for members of the Triple Entente, she also disturbed the Triple Alliance, raising issues that exposed its weaknesses—in particular its unstable Austro-Italian component. Italy and Austria were just as much rivals as allies, vying with each other for preeminence in the Balkan peninsula, especially along the Adriatic coast. Italy, the newest of the Great Powers, sought to expand her influence in the area and check any hint of Austrian expansionism with calls for compensation under Article 7 of their alliance treaty. Her relations with Montenegro were facilitated by her large capital investments, especially in railroads, port facilities, and various monopolies, and by Nicholas's ties to the Italian royal house.

For the most part, official Italy kept stride with Austrian policy in Montenegro, or fell only a step or two behind. Austria did little to earn Italy's trust by peremptorily annexing Bosnia and Herzegovina in 1908, but Italy returned the favor by declaring war on Turkey in 1911. In 1912, the two allies joined as midwives of the new Albanian state, which both believed offered fertile field for their influence peddling.

Unofficial Italy was often at odds with the Consulta; the Italian press frequently damned the Triple Alliance and called on Rome to oppose rather than assist Austrian policies in the Balkans. During the Malissori crisis, unauthorized Italian volunteers appeared on the opposite side of the Adriatic to aid Nicholas and his Albanian friends; and during the Scutari crisis, many demanded that Italy not take part in any Austrian-inspired attack on Montenegro. When it came to the future of Mount Lovćen, however, the Italian government and public opinion were generally of one mind, agreeing that Vienna should be prevented from annexing the mountain and tilting the balance of power in the Adriatic even more in Austria's favor. San Giuliano warned Berlin that Rome might have to look elsewhere for succor; the rabid Italian press warned that Lovćen's acquisition would constitute a *casus belli*. European newspapers kept Lovćen before the public eye, eagerly seizing upon rumors (some of them true) concerning Austrian plans to acquire the mountain. The Ballhausplatz consistently denied these rumors, but lent credence to them by refusing to sign away future claims. Austrian inflexibility impeded efforts to formulate a joint Austro-Italian approach to the question of Serbo-Montenegrin union and the fate of the Montenegrin coast. Italy was ill-prepared to have Austria annex the latter or Mount Lovćen.

The inability of Vienna and Rome to come to terms greatly distressed Berlin. German leaders, including William II, Bethmann Hollweg, and Jagow, warned each other and their allies of the possible dire consequences of uninterrupted bickering. Italy's demands for Austria's cession of the Trentino was too high a price for Vienna to pay. Austro-Italian differences remained unsolved, and Italy eventually went her own way.

Just as Montenegro figured prominently in Berlin's efforts to have Austria and Italy close ranks, she was also a factor in direct Austro-German relations. Germany was generally willing to concede to Vienna a measure of independence in formulating Balkan policy. Sometimes, as in 1908, Habsburg ministers took advantage of this freedom. In the three years following the annexation crisis, however, Vienna steered a more conservative course, which met with Berlin's approval.

Montenegro's attack on Turkey in 1912 came as a shock to Germany, but she, like Austria, soon resigned herself to the end of Turkish power in Europe. At the London conference in 1912 and

1913, she backed Austria's positions on the creation of an Albanian state, the expulsion of Serbian forces from the Adriatic, and the disposition of various Albanian cities, including Scutari. Yet it would be wrong to conclude, as Albertini has done, that Germany's support was tantamount to warmongering. Even Fritz Fischer concedes, almost apologetically, that the Wilhelmstrasse exercised restraint on the Dual Monarchy in the spring of 1913.[4] Still, he does not examine in detail the Scutari crisis, during which Germany alternated calls for action with pleas for reserve. Before signing a prototype of the famous blank check, Germany worked hard to secure arrangements that would uphold the decisions of the conference, maintain the unity of its members, and preclude the necessity of unilateral Austrian military action, which she feared might lead to general war. Then and subsequently, Bethmann Hollweg and other leading Germans noted that Austria had to be reined in before it was too late. This attitude lends little support to the theories put forth by Fischer and others that Berlin could barely contain its aggressive impulses in the days before the outbreak of the First World War.

As we have seen, Montenegro's relations with Serbia, especially the question of their political union, were important factors in Balkan politics before the world war. Though many observers tended to view Montenegro as Serbia's lackey, she was anything but that. Nicholas envied his son-in-law, King Peter, and did not get along with him. Only when vital pan-Serb interests were at stake were they able to close ranks—and sometimes not even then. The dynastic rivalry between the Petrovići and the Karadjordjevići poisoned interstate relations. As the ruler of a country whose claims to independence antedated Serbia's and whose international reputation rested on a glorious history of fighting Serbdom's Turkish oppressor, Nicholas had long been a focal point of Serb political aspirations and was understandably reluctant to yield his primacy to Peter. The Cetinje and Kolašin bomb affairs exacerbated matters, and for several years, it was almost unpatriotic for a Montenegrin to espouse the cause of Karadjordjević Serbia. The tense state of relations and the lack of a common frontier made the question of union largely an academic one before 1912. The Balkan wars changed all that.

It can be argued that the drive for territorial expansion that had long motivated Nicholas and his princely predecessors was in the long run self-defeating for the maintenance of an independent Montenegrin state. The territorial acquisitions of the Balkan wars did little to alleviate the country's economic misery. Ironically, the more it expanded, the less "Montenegrin" it became, absorbing thousands of new subjects not wedded to Montenegrin tradition. If most of Nicholas's "old" subjects considered themselves Montenegrins first and Serbs second, many of his new ones were Serbs first and last. Gradually, even old-line Montenegrins grew disenchanted with Nicholas's autocratic rule. Liberals, many of whom still nursed wounds inflicted in the bomb affairs of 1907 and 1909, were dissatisfied by the slow pace of movement toward Serbia, considering the Serbophile government of Janko Vukotić to be only a partial palliative. Belgrade-educated youth felt especially hamstrung by Montenegro's political system, and the small but growing labor movement created anomalous difficulties for a ruler with one foot in a medieval past. The government tried to move with the tide of public opinion, but it did not move fast enough. The prince, deemed progressive by many in the nineteenth century, appeared to be out of place in the twentieth.

A roll call of Cetinje's foreign legations testifies to Nicholas's march into diplomatic and political oblivion. In 1908, the Montenegrin capital hosted ten formal diplomatic representations and an occasional American minister sent from Athens. In 1912 and 1913, the Turkish and Bulgarian ministers took leave of Cetinje for the last time; in August 1914, the Austrian and German legations closed their doors. One and a half years later, with Austro-Hungarian troops at the gate of the city, the representatives of the Triple Entente and Italy fled, never to return. The lone Greek diplomat who remained behind soon closed up shop. Cetinje's career as a diplomatic capital, and Nicholas's as a king, were over. His exodus in January 1916, signalled the end of old Montenegro—the Montenegro that had confounded and vexed friend and foe alike for many years, the same Montenegro that had a centuries-old history of independence and resistance to foreign invaders. Instead of following King Peter's heroic example in retreating over snow-capped mountains to fight another day, Nicholas fled into exile with his court camarilla and empty dreams of a postwar restoration. Peter shared the privations of his troops on Corfu and in Salonica, while Nicholas languished in Italy and on the French Riviera, where he eventually died at Cap d'Antibes in 1921.

Conclusion

Austria-Hungary shared Montenegro's fate as a casualty of war. Her lackluster army hastened Montenegro's demise, but could not stave off her own. Ironically, Conrad, who had vigorously rattled his saber at Montenegro for many years, proved incapable of storming her bastions by himself. As in so many other instances, Vienna had to rely on Berlin's assistance—but all for nought. The postwar settlements saw the dissolution of the Habsburg Empire as well as the extinction of the Montenegrin kingdom, though the latter was a nominal victor. Much of Austria-Hungary and all of Montenegro became part of the new Kingdom of Serbs, Croats, and Slovenes under the Karadjordjević standard, as Yugoslavism and Greater Serbism joined forces. The war that Berchtold and Nicholas had hoped would preserve their respective countries and systems of government marked the end of both.

Notes

Abbreviations

AMD	*Aus meiner Dienstzeit*
APS	*Die auswärtige Politik Serbiens*
BD	*British Documents on the Origins of the War*
CV	*Cetinjski Vjesnik*
DAC MUD	*Državni Arhiv Cetinje, Ministarstvo unutrašnjih djela*
DDF	*Documents diplomatiques français*
DDI	*I Documenti diplomatici italiani*
DMC	*Državni Muzej Cetinje*
GC	*Glas Crnogorca*
GP	*Die grosse Politik der europäischen Kabinette*
HHStA, PA	*Haus-, Hof- und Staatsarchiv, Politisches Archiv*
IB	*Die internationalen Beziehungen im Zeitalter des Imperialismus*
IZ	*Istorijski Zapisi*
LT	The *Times*
MO	*Mezhdunarodnie otnosheniia v epokhu imperializma*
NA	National Archives
NFP	*Neue Freie Presse*
NYT	*New York Times*
OUA	*Österreich-Ungarns Aussenpolitik*
PRO, FO	Public Record Office, Foreign Office
SSIP	Savezni Sekretarijat za inostrane poslove
Z	*Zapisi*

Also:

m.e.	morning edition
a.e.	afternoon edition
e.e.	evening edition
O.S.	Old Style

Preface

1. Whitney Warren, *Montenegro: The Crime of the Peace Conference* (New York: Brentano's, 1922), p. 60.
2. L. S. Stavrianos, *The Balkans since 1453* (New York: Rinehart, 1958), p. 237.
3. Sidney Bradshaw Fay, *The Origins of the World War*, 2d ed. rev., 2 vols. (New York: Macmillan, 1939), I: 433–34.
4. Franz Conrad von Hötzendorf, *Private Aufzeichnungen: Erste Veröffentlichungen aus den Papieren des k.u.k. Generalstabs-Chefs* (Vienna and Munich: Amalthea-Verlag, 1977), p. 217.
5. Fritz Fischer rekindled interest in the war guilt question and stimulated historical argument with the publication of *Germany's Aims in the First World War* (New York: W. W. Norton, 1967). In *War of Illusions: German Politics from 1911 to 1914*, trans. Marian Jackson (London: Chatto and Windus, 1975), he examined Germany's belligerent tendencies in the years immediately before the outbreak of the First World War.
6. Edward C. Thaden, "Montenegro: Russia's Troublesome Ally, 1910–1912," *Journal of Central European Affairs*, XVIII (July 1958): 111–33; Hans Heilbronner, "The Merger Attempts of Serbia and Montenegro, 1913–1914," *Journal of Central European Affairs*, XVIII (October 1958): 281–91; Ernst C. Helmreich, "The Serbian-Montenegrin Alliance of September 23/October 6, 1912," *Journal of Central European Affairs*, XIX (January 1960): 411–15; Richard D. Challener, "Montenegro and the United States: A Balkan Fantasy," *Journal of Central European Affairs*, XVII (October 1957): 236–42.
7. Mihailo Vojvodić, *Skadarska kriza 1913. godine* (Belgrade: Zavod za izdavanje udžbenika Socijalističke Republike Srbije, 1970); Dimitrije-Dimo Vujović, *Crna Gora i Francuska 1860–1914* (Cetinje: Obod, 1971).
8. Milosch Boghitschewitsch [Miloš Bogićević], *Die auswärtige Politik Serbiens, 1903–1914*, 3 vols. (Berlin: Brückenverlag, 1928–31) (hereafter cited as *APS*).
9. Austria-Hungary, Ministerium des Äussern, *Österreich-Ungarns Aussenpolitik von der bosnischen Krise 1908 bis zum Kriegsausbruch 1914. Diplomatische Aktenstücke des österreichisch-ungarischen Ministeriums des Äussern*, edited by Ludwig Bittner and Hans Uebersberger, 8 vols. and index (Vienna: Österreichischer Bundesverlag für Unterricht, Wissenschaft und Kunst, 1930) (hereafter cited as *OUA*).
10. Russia, Komissiia po izdanii dokumentov epokhi imperializma, *Mezhdunarodnie otnosheniia v epokhu imperializma: Dokumenti iz arkhivov tsarskogo i vremennogo pravitel'stv 1878–1917 gg.* (hereafter cited as *MO*), ed. A. P. Bol'shemennikov, A. S. Erusalemskii, A. A. Mogilevich, and F. A. Rotshtein, 2d series: 1900–1913, vols. XVIII-XX (Moscow: Gospolizdat, 1938–40); 3d series: 1914–1917, vols. I-X (Moscow: Gosudarstvennoe Sotsial 'no-Ekonomicheskoe Izdatel'stvo, 1931–38). German edition: *Die internationalen Beziehungen im Zeitalter des Imperialismus: Dokumente aus den Archiven der zarischen und der provisorischen Regierung, 1878–1917* (hereafter cited as *IB*), ed. Otto Hoetzsch (Berlin, 1931–).

Notes for pages xiii–4 215

11. Wladimir Giesl, *Zwei Jahrzehnte im Nahen Orient*, ed. Eduard Ritter von Steinitz (Berlin: Verlag für Kulturpolitik, 1927); Gustav von Hubka, "Diplomatum in Montenegro," *Berliner Monatshefte*, XIV (August 1936): 657–62; Hubka, "König Nikolaus von Montenegro," *Deutsche Revue*, XLVI (April; June 1921): 23–32, 174–84; Hubka, "Kritische Tage in Montenegro," *Berliner Monatshefte*, IX (January 1931): 27–45. Two of Durham's best works are *The Struggle for Scutari (Turk, Slav, and Albanian)* (London: E. Arnold, 1914) and *Twenty Years of Balkan Tangle* (London: G. Allen and Unwin, 1920). These and many of her other books and articles are cited throughout this study.

CHAPTER ONE

1. H. C. Darby, "Montenegro," *A Short History of Yugoslavia*, ed. Stephen Clissold (Cambridge: Cambridge University Press, 1968), p. 73. The old Montenegrin legend that begins Darby's paragraph is a familiar tale with many variants. Novelist Joyce Cary recalled this version: "When God was putting the earth together, he began with clay. It was of course easier to his thumb. When he had finished this first model, he poured the water into the holes he had made for the seas. Lastly he took a sack of stones, and started putting them in here and there wherever he thought they looked best. But the sack was not very strong, and as he was passing over Montenegro, he gave it an accidental jolt and the bottom fell out. God, who was perhaps losing his first enthusiasm as a practical geographer, did not pick up the stones again but exclaimed, 'Damn—it's a son-of-a-bitch country anyway.'" Joyce Cary, *Memoir of the Bobotes* (Austin: University of Texas Press, 1960), p. 42.
2. These and subsequent population figures are based primarily on statistics in J. D. Bourchier, "Montenegro," *Encyclopaedia Britannica*, 11th ed., XVIII: 766–73, and *Almanach de Gotha; annuaire généalogique, diplomatique et statistique* (Gotha: J. Perthes, 1908–1914). See also Henryk Batowski, "Teritorialni razvoj Crne Gore," *Zapisi* (hereafter cited as Z), X, Knj. XVIII, No. 2 (1937): 74–78.
3. Jovan Erdeljanović, *Stara Crna Gora: etnička prošlost i formiranje Crnogorskih plemena* (Belgrade, 1925).
4. Dragoljub Šaranović, *Montenegro—Yesterday and Today* (Belgrade: Medjunarodna Politika, 1971), p. 3.
5. Žarko Bulajić, *Agrarni odnosi u Crnoj Gori (1878–1912)* (Titograd, 1959).
6. Stavrianos, *The Balkans since 1453*, p. 237. For general economic data, see Great Britain, Foreign Office, Historical Section, *Montenegro* (London: H.M.S. Stationery Office, 1920); Bourchier, "Montenegro;" N. I. Khitrova, "Sotsial 'no-ekonomicheskoe razvitie Chernogorii v kontse XIX-nachale XX v. i konstitutsiia 1905 g.," *Kratkie Soobshcheniia Instituta Slavi-*

anovedeniia, XX (1956): 85–94. For financial information, see Mirčeta Djurović, *Crnogorske finansije, 1860–1915* (Titograd, 1960); Djurović, *Trgovački kapital u Crnoj Gori u drugoj polovini XIX i početkom XX vijeka* (Cetinje: Obod, 1958); Djurović, "Formiranje akcionarskih društava u Crnoj Gori početkom XX vijeka u pojedinim privrednim granama," *Istorijski Zapisi* (hereafter cited as *IZ*), XII, Knj. XVI, Nos. 3–4 (1959): 79–111.

7. D. Franetović, *Historija pomorstva i ribarstva Crne Gore do 1918. godine* (Titograd, 1960).

8. Niko S. Martinović, "Počeci radničkog pokreta u Crnoj Gori," *IZ*, XII, Knj. XV, No. 1 (1959): 7–30; J. Bojović, "Radnička klasa i njeno organizovanje u Crnoj Gori do 1914," *Prvo radničko društvo u Jugoslavenskim zemljama*, Material of the Osijek Assembly (Slavonski Brod, 1969), pp. 317–39.

9. For an excellent study of the problem of Montenegrin emigration, see Djordjije D. Pejović, *Iseljavanja Crnogoraca u XIX vijeku* (Titograd: Obod, 1962), and his "Uzroci masovnog iseljavanja stanovništva iz Crne Gore (1878–1916)," *IZ*, XV, Knj. XIX, No. 2 (1962): 209–53.

10. Mirčeta Djurović, *Novčani zavodi u Crnoj Gori* (Cetinje: Narodna Knjiga, 1959).

11. For overviews of Montenegrin history in English, see Darby, "Montenegro"; Bourchier, "Montenegro"; Vladimir Dedijer, et al., *History of Yugoslavia*, trans. Kordija Kveder (New York: McGraw-Hill, 1974); Great Britain, Foreign Office, *Montenegro*, especially pp. 9–41. See also Francis Seymour Stevenson, *A History of Montenegro* (London: Jarrold & Sons, 1912); William Denton, *Montenegro: Its People and Their History* (London: Daldy, Isbister & Co., 1877); Sir John Wilkinson, *Dalmatia and Montenegro with a Journey to Mostar in Herzegovina and Remarks on the Slavonic Nations* (London: John Murray, 1848); Reginald Wyon and Gerald Prance, *The Land of the Black Mountain* (London: Methuen and Co., 1903). In German: Hugo Grottie, *Durch Albanien und Montenegro* (Munich, 1913); Spiridon Gopčević, *Geschichte von Montenegro und Albanien* (Gotha: F. A. Perthes, 1914), and his earlier study, *Montenegro und die Montenegriner* (Leipzig: H. Fries, 1877). In Serbo-Croatian, the place to begin is the projected 8-vol. history of Montenegro, *Istorija Crne Gore*, published by the Istorijski Institut and the Historical Commission of the Central Committee of the League of Communists of Yugoslavia (1967–). See also Jagoš Jovanović, *Stvaranje Crnogorske države i razvoj Crnogorske nacionalnosti: Istorija Crne Gore od početka VIII vijeka do 1918. godine* (Cetinje: Obod, 1947); Djordje Lazarević, *Istorija Crne Gore* (Belgrade: Privrednik, 1935); Djordje Popović, *Istorija Crne Gore* (Belgrade: P. Burčica, 1896); Savo Brković, *O postanku i razvoju Crnogorske nacije* (Titograd: Grafički Zavod, 1974). For political developments in the nineteenth century, see Tomica Nikčević, *Političke struje u Crnoj Gori u procesu stvaranja države u XIX vijeku* (Cetinje: Narodna Knjiga, 1958). On cultural developments, see Djoko Pejović's unsurpassed *Razvitak prosvjete i kulture u Crnoj Gori, 1852–1916* (Cetinje: Obod, 1971). On Montenegro in the early twentieth century, see Nikola P. Škerović, *Crna Gora na osvitku XX vijeka*, Srpska Akademija Nauka i Umetnosti, Posebna Izdanja, Vol. CCCLXIX (Belgrade, 1964), and Jovan Djonović, *Ustavne i političke borbe u Crnoj Gori, 1905–1910* (Belgrade: K. J. Mihailović, 1939).

12. Denton, *Montenegro*, p. 231. See also Gligor Stanojević, *Crna Gora u doba vladike Danila* (Cetinje, 1955).

13. No full-length study of Nicholas exists. See Nikola I Petrović Njegoš, *Cjelokupna djela Nikole I Petrovića Njegoša* (Cetinje: Obod, 1969); Henry Baerlein, "The First and Last King of Montenegro," *Contemporary Review*, CLXXXVII (August 1955): 170–74; Hubka, "König Nikolaus von Montenegro." Wadham Peacock, "Nicholas of Montenegro and the Czardom of the Serbs," *Nineteenth Century and After*, LXXII (November 1912): 879–88; René Pinon, "Le Monténégro et son prince," *Revue des deux mondes*, 5th période, LVI (March-April 1910): 76–111; J. D. Bourchier, "Nicholas," *Encyclopaedia Britannica*, 11th ed., XIX: 651. The best general survey of Nicholas's reign is P. Popović et al., *Spoljašnja i unutrašnja politika Crne Gore od 1851 do 1918*, 2 vols. (Belgrade, 1937).

14. Montenegrin marriages: Crown Prince *Danilo* and Augusta Charlotte (Milica), daughter of the grand duke of Mecklenburg-Strelitz, in 1899; *Zorka* and Peter Karadjordjević (later Peter I of Serbia), 1883; *Milica* and Grand Duke Peter Nikolaievich of Russia, 1889; *Anastasia* (Stana) and (1) Prince Romanovsky, 1889, (2) Grand Duke Nicholas Nikolaievich of Russia, 1907; *Jelena* (Elena) and the Prince of Naples (later King Victor Emmanuel of Italy), 1896; *Anna* and Prince Francis Joseph of Battenberg, 1897; Prince *Mirko* and Natalija Konstantinović, 1902; and Prince *Peter* and Violet Emily Wagner, 1924. Unmarried Montenegrin princesses: *Marija* (Marica), *Sophia*, *Ksenija* (Xenia), and *Vjera* (Vera).

15. Mary Edith Durham, "King Nikola of Montenegro," *Contemporary Review*, CXIX (April 1921): 475.

16. Studies on the Habsburg Empire and its foreign policy are numerous. Perhaps the best place to begin is Hugo Hantsch, *Die Geschichte Österreichs*, 2 vols. (Graz: Styria Verlag, 1962). For foreign affairs in the nineteenth and twentieth centuries, see Barbara Jelavich, *The Habsburg Empire in European Affairs, 1914–1918* (Chicago: Rand McNally, 1969); F. R. Bridge, *From Sadowa to Sarajevo: The Foreign Policy of Austria-Hungary, 1866–1914* (London and Boston: Routledge and Kegan Paul, 1972); Friedrich Engel-Jánosi, *Geschichte auf dem Ballhausplatz: Essays zur österreichischen Aussenpolitik, 1830–1945* (Graz: Verlag Styria, 1963); Fritz Klein, ed., *Österreich-Ungarn in der Weltpolitik, 1900 bis 1918* (Berlin: Akademie-Verlag, 1965); Alfred Francis Pribram, *Austrian Foreign Policy, 1908–1918* (London: George Allen and Unwin, 1923); and Pribram, *The Secret Treaties of Austria-Hungary, 1879–1914*, trans. Denys P. Myers and J. G. D'Arcy Paul, 2 vols. (Cambridge, Mass.: Harvard University Press, 1920–21). See also Adolf Beer, *Die orientalische Politik Österreichs seit 1774* (Prague: F. Tempsky, 1883); the classic but outdated work by Theodor von Sosnosky, *Die Balkanpolitik Österreich-Ungarns seit 1866*, 2 vols. (Stuttgart and Berlin: Deutsche Verlagsanstalt, 1913); and two works by Richard Charmatz, *Geschichte der auswärtigen Politik Österreichs im 19. Jahrhundert*, 2 vols. (Leipzig: B. G. Teubner, 1912–14), and *Österreichs äussere und innere Politik von 1895 bis 1914* (Leipzig and Berlin: B. G. Teubner, 1918). For Austro-Montenegrin relations, see Vladan Djordjević, *Crna Gora i Austrija 1814–1894*, Srpska Kraljevska Akademija Nauka i Umetnosti, Posebna Izdanja, Vol. CLIX, Društveni Istorijski Spisi, Vol. XIX (Belgrade: Radoljub, 1924).

17. Dušan Vuksan, *Petar I Petrović Njegoš i njegovo doba* (Cetinje: Narodna Knjiga, 1951); Dušan Lekić, *La Politique extérieure de Pierre Ier Petrovich, Métropolite du Monténégro (1784–1830)* (Paris: Librairie L. Rotstein, 1940).

18. For a discussion of Montenegro's status in international law, see Ilija Radosavović, *Medjunarodni položaj Crne Gore u XIX vijeku* (Belgrade, 1960). Russia had long regarded Montenegro as an independent state, but Britain, more given to legal propriety, had never recognized the de jure independence of the land. A measure of success in avoiding Turkish rule is the country's noninclusion in Peter F. Sugar's study of *Southeastern Europe under Ottoman Rule, 1354–1804* (Seattle and London: University of Washington Press, 1977). On the other hand, Sugar examines Dubrovnik as a tribute-paying state.

19. Gligor Stanojević, "Prilozi za diplomatsku istoriju Crne Gore od Berlinskog kongresa do kraja XIX veka," *Istorijski časopis*, II (1960): 149–73; Novak Ražnatović, *Crna Gora i Berlinski kongres* (Cetinje: Obod, 1979); Ražnatović, "Sprovodjenje XXIX Čg. Berlinskog ugovora o Crnogorskim primorju i ingerenciji Austro-Ugarske u luci Bar," *IZ*, XXV, Knj. XXIX, Nos. 3–4 (1972): 383–413. See also William N. Medlicott, *The Congress of Berlin and After: A Diplomatic History of the Near Eastern Settlement, 1878–1880* (London: Methuen, 1938); Spiridon Gopčević, *Der turco-montenegrinische Krieg*, 3 vols. (Vienna: L. W. Seidel & Sohn, 1879; Milo Vukčević, *Crna Gora i Hercegovina uoći rata 1874–1876* (Cetinje: Narodna Knjiga, 1950); Mihailo D. Stojanović, *The Great Powers and the Balkans, 1875–1878* (Cambridge: Cambridge University Press, 1939); David Harris, *A Diplomatic History of the Balkan Crisis of 1875–1878* (Stanford, 1936); G. H. Rupp, *A Wavering Friendship: Russia and Austria, 1876–1878* (Cambridge, Mass.: Harvard University Press, 1941). Despite the provision of the Treaty of Berlin recognizing Montenegro's sovereignty, David MacKenzie asked an interesting question in an excellent study of the Near Eastern crisis: "Can one, however, regard as truly independent a country prohibited by treaty from fortifying its most exposed frontier and whose naval police would be under foreign (Austrian) control?" *The Serbs and Russian Pan-Slavism, 1875–1878* (Ithaca: Cornell University Press, 1967), p. 318, n. 70.

20. Radoman Jovanović, "Pokušaj Austro-Ugarske da dobije koncesiju za izgradnju željeznice u Crnogorskom primorju," *IZ*, XVI, Knj. XX, No. 2 (1963): 311–15.

21. Kennedy memorandum, 11 June 1900, Public Record Office, Foreign Office correspondence (hereafter cited as PRO, FO) 103/50.

22. An astute British observer summed up Austro-Montenegrin relations this way: "It is difficult for anyone who has not resided in Montenegro to realize the deep but judiciously suppressed detestation of Austria which rankles in the hearts of all Montenegrins, from the Prince down to the humblest of his subjects. . . . Montenegro feels that she has been abandoned to the tender mercies of Austria, who exercises a pressure on her, both military and commercial, which not only compromises her future expansion, but even threatens to destroy her very existence. . . . I can best describe this country's feelings and attitude toward Austria by comparing

Montenegro to a wild animal which is being gradually entangled in the toils of the hunter, but continues lying low fearing the disastrous consequences which would follow if a desperate attempt were made to break through them." Kennedy to Lansdowne, 27 May 1904, PRO, FO 103/54/19.

23. Jagoš Jovanović, "Veze Crne Gore sa Rusijom od druge polovine XVI veka do danas," *IZ*, I, Knj. II, Nos. 3–4 (1948): 139–60; Nos. 5–6: 248–58; Knj. III, Nos. 3–4: 120–33; Knj. IV, Nos. 1–3: 30–36. See also Jovan Jovanović, "Rusija i Crna Gora," *Z*, VII, Knj. XII, No. 2 (1933): 109–13; Radovan Lalić, "O tradicionalnim vezama izmedju Crne Gore i Rusije," *IZ*, IV, Knj. VII, Nos. 7–9 (1951): 273–93; and Vladan Djordjević, *Crna Gora i Rusija 1784–1814* (Belgrade, 1914).

24. Durham, *Twenty Years of Balkan Tangle*, p. 20.

25. In addition to MacKenzie, *The Serbs and Russian Pan-Slavism*, see Edward C. Thaden, *Conservative Nationalism in Nineteenth Century Russia* (Seattle: University of Washington Press, 1964), especially chapters 6 and 10; Hans Kohn, *Pan-Slavism: Its History and Ideology*, 2d ed. (New York: Vintage Books, 1960); Charles Jelavich, *Tsarist Russia and Balkan Nationalism: Russian Influence in the Internal Affairs of Bulgaria and Serbia, 1879–1886* (Berkeley: University of California Press, 1958); B. H. Sumner, *Russia and the Balkans, 1870–1880* (Oxford: Clarendon Press, 1937); Michael B. Petrovich, *The Emergence of Russian Panslavism, 1856–1870* (New York: Columbia, 1956).

26. Dušan Vuksan, *Pregled štampe u Crnoj Gori, 1834–1934* (Cetinje: Obod, 1934), pp. 31–35.

27. Arthur J. May, *The Habsburg Monarchy, 1867–1914* (Cambridge, Mass.: Harvard University Press, 1965), p. 392.

28. De Salis, "Montenegro: Annual Report, 1911," PRO, FO 371/1398/424, p. 4.

29. Kennedy to Lansdowne, 2 February 1901, PRO, FO 103/51/5.

30. For an overview of Italian foreign policy, see R. J. B. Bosworth, *Italy, the Least of the Great Powers: Italian Foreign Policy before the First World War* (Cambridge: Cambridge University Press, 1979); and Gaetano Salvemini, *La Politica estera dell'Italia dal 1871 al 1915*, 2d ed. rev. (Florence, 1950). Also useful are Leonida Bissolati, *La Politica estera dell'Italia dal 1897 al 1920* (Milan: Fratelli Treves, 1923); Claude Alexandre Cailler, *La Politique balkanique de l'Italie entre 1875 et 1914* (La Tour de Peilz: Stalder-Vodoz, 1951); Francesco Cataluccio, *Antonio di San Giuliano e la Politica estera italiana dal 1910 al 1914* (Florence: F. le Mounier, 1935); and R. W. Seton-Watson, *The Balkans, Italy and the Adriatic* (London: Nisbet & Co., 1912).

31. The literature on the various Balkan railroad projects is enormous. See, for example, Dragomir Arnaoutovitch [Arnautović], *Histoire des Chemins de fer yugoslaves, 1825–1937* (Paris: Dunod, 1937); Stanley H. Beaver, "Railways in the Balkan Peninsula," *Geographical Journal*, XCVII (May 1941): 273–94; Jovan Jireček, *Projekat željeznice Dunav-Niš-Jadransko More* (Belgrade, 1908); Arthur J. May, "Trans-Balkan Railway Schemes," *Journal of Modern History*, XXIV (December 1952): 352–67; May, "The

Novibazar Railroad Project," *Journal of Modern History,* X (December 1938): 496–527; Walther Rechberger, "Zur Geschichte der Orientbahnen: Österreichische Eisenbahnpolitik auf dem Balkan," *Österreichische Osthefte,* II, No. 5 (1960): 348–59; III, No. 2 (1961): 102–12; Oscar Remy, "Sandschakbahn und Donau-Adriabahn: Ein Kapitel aus der Vorgeschichte des Weltkrieges," *Archiv für Eisenbahnwesen,* L, No. 5 (1927): 1189; Wilhelm Reuning, "The Sanjak Railroad: A Reply to Italian Economic Penetration," *Susquehanna University Studies,* IX (June 1973): 149–76; Soloman Wank, "Aehrenthal and the Sanjak of Novibazar Railway Project: A Reappraisal," *Slavonic and East European Review,* XLII (June 1964): 353–69. See also chapter 8 of Wayne S. Vucinich, *Serbia between East and West: The Events of 1903–1908* (Stanford: Stanford University Press, 1954).

32. Walter Schinner, *Der österreichisch-italienische Gegensatz auf dem Balkan und an der Adria von seinen Anfängen bis zur Dreibundkrise, 1875–1896* (Stuttgart: W. Kohlhammer, 1936); William C. Askew, "The Austro-Italian Antagonism, 1896–1914," *Power, Public Opinion and Diplomacy: Essays in Honor of Eber Malcolm Carroll by His Former Students,* edited by Lillian Parker Wallace and William C. Askew (Durham, N.C.: Duke University Press, 1959), pp. 172–221.

33. The best study of Franco-Montenegrin relations is Vujovic's *Crna Gora i Francuska.*

34. The latest and best study of Serbia in the nineteenth and twentieth centuries is Michael B. Petrovich's *History of Modern Serbia, 1804–1918,* 2 vols. (New York and London: Harcourt Brace Jovanovich, 1976). For an overview of Serbian political history, see Živan Živanović, *Politička istorija Srbije u drugoj polovini devetnaestog veka,* 4 vols. (Belgrade, 1923–25). On the Austro-Serbian antagonism, see Vucinich, *Serbia between East and West;* Vladimir Ćorović, *Odnosi izmedju Srbije i Austro-Ugarske u XX veku* (Belgrade: Državna Štamparija, 1936); Hans Uebersberger, *Österreich zwischen Russland und Serbien: Zur südslawischen Frage und der Entstehung des Ersten Weltkrieges* (Cologne and Graz: Verlag Hermann Böhlaus Nachf., 1958); and R. W. Seton-Watson, *The Southern Slav Question and the Habsburg Monarchy* (London: Constable, 1911). On the Pig War, see Dimitrije Djordjević, *Carinski rat Austro-Ugarske i Srbije, 1906–1911,* Jugoslovenske zemlje u XX veku, Vol. I (Belgrade: Istorijski Institut, 1962). On Serbo-Montenegrin relations, see Bogumil Hrabak, "Crna Gora i Srbija na početku nove ere u južnoslovenskoj povesti (1903–1904)," *Istorijski Časopis,* XX (1973): 319–58; Novak Ražnatović, "Crnogorsko-srpski odnosi i pitanje prestolonasljedja u Srbiji 1900–1903 godine," *IZ,* XXX, Knj. XXXIV, Nos. 3–4 (1977): 655–706; Raznatović, "Rusko posredovanje u crnogorsko-srpskim odnosima od bombaškog procesa do aneksione krize," *IZ,* XV, Knj. XIX, Nos. 3–4 (1962): 540–62.

35. William Miller, *The Balkans: Roumania, Bulgaria, Servia, and Montenegro* (London: T. Fisher Unwin, 1923), p. 517.

36. Ibid., pp. 517–18.

37. The best introductions to the annexation crisis are Bernadotte Schmitt, *The Annexation of Bosnia, 1908–1909* (Cambridge: Cambridge

University Press, 1937); Momtchilo Nintchitch [Momčilo Ninčić], *La Crise bosniaque (1908–1909) et les Puissances européennes*, 2 vols., (Paris: A. Costes, 1937); and Wilhelm Mauritz Carlgren, *Isvolsky und Aehrenthal vor der bosnischen Annexionskrise: Russische und österreich-ungarische Balkanpolitik 1906–1908* (Uppsala: Almqvist & Wiksells, 1955).

38. In 1905 Croat and Serb delegates—in the Fiume and Zara (Rijeka and Zadar) resolutions—expressed their desire for a restored kingdom of Croatia, Dalmatia, and Slavonia under the Habsburg eagle.

39. Josef M. Baernreither, *Fragmente eines politischen Tagebuches: Die südslawische Frage und Österreich-Ungarn vor dem Weltkrieg*, ed. Joseph Redlich (Berlin: Verlag für Kulturpolitik, 1928), p. 36; quoted in Albertini, *Origins of the War*, I:191. See Soloman Wank, "Aehrenthal's Programme for the Constitutional Transformation of the Habsburg Monarchy: Three Secret *Mémoires*," *Slavonic and East European Review*, XLI (June 1963): 513–36.

CHAPTER TWO

1. Charykov to Stein, 22 September/5 October 1908, cited in Radoman Jovanović, "Stav Crne Gore prema aneksiji Bosne i Hercegovine," *IZ*, XVI, Knj. XX, No. 1 (1963): 91; Jovanović, "Crna Gora i istočna Hercegovina za vrijeme aneksione krize 1908–1909," *Jugoslovenski narodi pred Prvi svetski rat*, ed. Vasa Čubrilović (Belgrade: Naučno Delo, 1967), p. 289.

2. Aehrenthal to Kuhn, Kuhn to Aehrenthal, 7 October 1908, *OUA*, I, Nos. 170–71. Cf. Ražnatović, "Sprovodjenje XXIX Čg. Berlinskog ugovora."

3. *Cetinjski Vjesnik* (hereafter cited as *CV*), 24 September 1908, Old Style (hereafter given as O.S.); *Glas Crnogorca* (hereafter cited as *GC*), 24 September 1908 O.S.; Kuhn to Aehrenthal, 9 October 1908, *OUA*, I, No. 187; *Neue Freie Presse* (hereafter cited as *NFP*), 9 October 1908, m.e., p. 7.

4. Note of the Montenegrin foreign ministry to foreign legations in Cetinje, 24 September/7 October 1908, supplement to a report from Cetinje, 8 October 1908, *OUA*, I, No. 190; *NFP*, 8 October 1908, m.e., p. 6; *CV*, 24 September 1908, O.S.

5. Aehrenthal to Kuhn, 14 October 1908, *OUA*, I, No. 274; Kuhn to Aehrenthal, 15 October 1908, No. 284.

6. Note of the Montenegrin foreign ministry to German minister, 10 October 1908, supplement to a report from Cetinje, 12 October 1908, *OUA*, I, No. 252.

7. *NFP*, 27 October 1908, m.e., p. 5; *New York Times* (hereafter cited as *NYT*), 11 October 1908, p. 2. See Luka Vukčević, "Diplomatska aktivnost Crne Gore na dobijanju Spiča za vrijeme aneksione krize (1908–1909)," *IZ*, XXV, Knj. XXX, Nos. 3–4 (1972): 463–73.

8. Crown Prince Danilo also represented the Montenegrin cause in Paris. *NFP*, 29 October 1908, m.e., p. 6.

9. Jovanović, "Stav Crne Gore prema aneksiji," pp. 97–99. For an overview of British policy, see M. B. Cooper, "British Policy in the Balkans, 1908–9," *Historical Journal*, VII, No. 2 (1964): 258–79.

10. *CV*, 27 September 1908 O.S.; Niko S. Martinović, "Otpor naroda u Crnoj Gori protiv aneksije Bosne i Hercegovine," *Jugoslovenski narodi pred Prvi svetski rat*, pp. 503, 507; Kuhn to Aehrenthal, 8 October 1908, *OUA*, I, No. 186; The *Times* (hereafter cited as *LT*), 10 October 1908, p. 7.

11. Kuhn to Aehrenthal, 9 October 1908, *OUA*, I, No. 207. At the time of the riot in Cetinje, the French minister addressed a crowd of Montenegrins in noncommittal fashion, stating that France had always been a friend of Montenegro and would remain one now. For the most part, however, the French government's posture was one of reciprocity toward Austria-Hungary for the latter's conciliatory attitude during the Moroccan crisis. Still, France did not go so far as to repudiate her Russian ally. Vujović, *Crna Gora i Francuska*, pp. 329–32. See also *NFP*, 9 October 1908, m.e., p. 7; 10 October 1908, m.e., p. 5, e.e., p. 5.

12. Kuhn to Aehrenthal, 8 October 1908, *OUA*, I, No. 188.

13. Državni Arhiv Cetinje, Ministarstvo Unutrašnjih Djela (hereafter cited as DAC MUD), 27 September 1908 O.S., No. 5611; 29 September 1908 O.S., No. 5583; *CV*, 4 October 1908 O.S.

14. *GC*, 1 October 1908, O.S.; *CV*, 4 and 11 October 1908 O.S.

15. *NFP*, 24 October 1908, m.e., p. 5; *GC*, 11 October 1908 O.S.

16. DAC MUD, 27 September 1908 O.S., Nos. 5607, 5610. See also *NFP*, 21 October 1908, m.e., p. 3.

17. *CV*, 1 October 1908 O.S.; *GC*, 4 October 1908 O.S.

18. *CV*, 11, 15, and 25 October 1908 O.S.

19. Austria successfully exploited the fears of the Muslim population and reinforced the age-old division between the Christians and the Muslims of the Sandžak. Martinović, "Otpor naroda u Crnoj Gori," p. 508. Aehrenthal had no intention of letting Serbia and Montenegro carve up the Sandžak. See memorandum, 9 August 1908, *OUA*, I, No. 32.

20. Martinović, "Otpor naroda u Crnoj Gori," p. 508; *GC*, 4 October 1908 O.S.

21. Montenegrin propaganda efforts in Hercegovina and preparations for armed conflict were quite extensive. See Jovanović, "Stav Crne Gore prema aneksiji," pp. 107–10.

22. Ibid., pp. 112–15; Martinović, "Otpor naroda u Crnoj Gori," pp. 505–6, Djurović, *Trgovački kapital u Crnoj Gori*, pp. 247–48; Djurović, *Crnogorske finansije*, pp. 146–51. Serbia's *Odjek* demanded that Belgrade follow Cetinje's example in boycotting the Austrians, but the Serbian government did little, a fact that vexed the Montenegrins. *NFP*, 6 January 1909, m.e., p. 7; 22 January 1909, m.e., p. 6. There were, of course, two sides to the boycott question. For all practical purposes the usual markets of Budva, Petrovac, and Sutomore in Austrian territory were cut off. On the one hand the Montenegrins lost their monetary income; on the other the Austrian population in Budva had to pay three times as much for a piece of

meat. The same was true for other imported items. To alleviate food shortages, Habsburg authorities contemplated purchasing beef in Bosnia or Hungary. In this war of attrition, it was unclear which side would hold out longer. The Austrian press reported that deprivations resulting from the boycott had led to anti-government demonstrations in Montenegro. In a transparently propagandistic article, the *Neue Freie Presse* published an imaginary conversation between an Austrian and a Montenegrin on either side of the frontier: "You have it good," says the Montenegrin. "You have something to eat and have warm clothing while we freeze and our wives and children starve at home." *NFP*, 1 January 1909, m.e., p. 8; 2 January 1909, m.e., p. 9. See also *GC*, 8, 13, and 20 December 1908 O.S.

23. Kuhn to Aehrenthal, 8 October 1908, *OUA*, I, Nos. 185, 190.
24. Kuhn to Aehrenthal, 8 October 1908, *OUA*, I, No. 186.
25. Kuhn to Aehrenthal, 8 October 1908, *OUA*, I, No. 189.
26. Aehrenthal to Kuhn, 8 and 10 October 1908, *OUA*, I, Nos. 188, 223.
27. Kuhn to Aehrenthal, 13 October 1908, *OUA*, I, No. 267.
28. *NFP*, 11 October 1908, m.e., p. 7.
29. Kuhn to Aehrenthal, 15 October 1908, *OUA*, I, No. 283.
30. Aehrenthal to Kuhn, 17 October 1908, *OUA*, I, No. 308.
31. Telegram to St. Petersburg and Rome, 17 October 1908, *OUA*, I, No. 317.
32. Aehrenthal to Kuhn, 17 October 1908, *OUA*, I, No. 308.
33. Kuhn to Aehrenthal, 18 October 1908, *OUA*, I, No. 322.
34. Jovanović, "Stav Crne Gore prema aneksiji," p. 95; Škerović, *Crna Gora na osvitku XX vijeka*, p. 465.
35. Milovanović to Montenegrin government, 26 September 1908 O.S., Državni Muzej Cetinje, Papers of Nikola I (hereafter cited as DMC-N I), No. 74; "Nekoliko dokumenata iz aneksije Bosne i Hercegovine," *Z*, X, Knj. XVII, No. 4 (1937), No. 1, pp. 239–40. Cetinje thought the proposal regarding the Sandžak might lead to trouble with Turkey. Montenegrin government to Serbian government, undated, No. 2, pp. 241–42.
36. See also "Montenegrinische Dokumente zur Annexionskrise," *Berliner Monatshefte*, XV (August 1937), p. 702. Prince Peter, the youngest son of Nicholas, and his cousin, Crown Prince George of Serbia, followed their elders' example by exchanging telegrams. Showing that he was his father's son, Peter indulged in typical Petrović bravado, calling on God to "grant that we may soon greet each other on the field of battle." *NFP*, 15 October 1908, m.e., p. 4.
37. *NFP*, 21 October 1908, m.e., p. 3; *GC*, 4 October 1908 O.S.
38. Note of the Chief of the General Staff, 20 October 1908, *OUA*, I, No. 347b. One of the so-called agitators, Ilija Jovanović-Bjeloš, was detained somewhat longer than Vukotić. In Zemun, across the Sava River from Belgrade, Vukotić's retainer and baggage were again detained. For Vukotić's account of the incident, see *NFP*, 21 October 1908, m.e., p. 3. For an extensive rendering of Montenegrin sources relating to the "Vukotić affair," see Jovanović, "Stav Crne Gore prema aneksiji," p. 96, n. 26.
39. Vukotić was hailed by an exceptionally large crowd at the Hotel

Moskva. Only hours after his arrival he was received by the king. At 7 P.M. another demonstration—this time by students—took place outside the hotel. A short time later thousands marched in a torchlight procession in his honor. *NFP*, 21 October 1908, m.e., p. 3; 23 October 1908, m.e., p. 4. Ironically, as the *Neue Freie Presse* was quick to point out, until the annexation crisis and his difficulties in Zagreb, Vukotić, one of the principals in the suppression of the Cetinje Bomb Affair, had been one of the most despised Montenegrins in all of Serbia, a favorite target of the Serbian press. Now even the progressive *Pravda* wanted to avenge the dishonor done Vukotić in Zagreb by having the Austrian representative in Cetinje bound and taken to the Austro-Montenegrin frontier. *NFP*, 22 October 1908, e.e., p. 5.

40. Aehrenthal to Kuhn, 20 October 1908, *OUA*, I, No. 342.

41. For the text of the treaty, see Nintchitch, *La Crise bosniaque*, II: 83–84. See also *LT*, 31 October 1908, p. 7; *NFP*, 27 October 1908, m.e., p. 4; 28 October 1908, m.e., p. 6; Martinović, "Otpor naroda u Crnoj Gori," p. 504; confidential report of Serbian confidant, 30 October 1908, *OUA*, I, No. 450.

42. For the course of the negotiations with the Porte, see Ernst C. Helmreich, *The Diplomacy of the Balkan Wars, 1912–1913* (Cambridge, Mass.: Harvard University Press, 1938), pp. 16–21. For documents relating to negotiations, see "Nekoliko dokumenata iz aneksije." At Vukotić's suggestion the Montenegrin government decorated a number of Turkish officers, and several friendly meetings took place between Montenegrin and Turkish military officials. *GC*, 25 October and 7 November 1908 O.S.; Martinović, "Otpor naroda u Crnoj Gori," p. 504; *NFP*, 23 November 1908, a.e., p. 6. The *Neue Freie Presse* offers extensive coverage of the Montenegrin and Serbian missions to Constantinople.

43. Forgách to Aehrenthal, 25 October 1908, *OUA*, I, No. 389. Underscoring the fact that the Serbo-Montenegrin rapprochement was directed against Vienna and not Constantinople, only the Ottoman minister was invited to attend the state dinner. Forgách to Aehrenthal, 27 October 1908, No. 421.

44. *Samouprava*, 26 October 1908, addendum to report from Belgrade, 27 October 1908, *OUA*, I, No. 421; *NFP*, 25 October 1908, m.e., p. 6. Pašić also made a point of traveling to St. Petersburg via Rumania rather than Austria-Hungary. *NFP*, 22 October 1908, e.e., p. 5.

45. Forgách to Aehrenthal, 27 October 1908, *OUA*, I, No. 421.

46. O'Reilly to Grey, 31 December 1908, PRO, FO 371/694/3991; *NFP*, 28 October 1908, m.e., p. 6; *GC*, 17 October 1908 O.S.

47. The claim to Spič was included in the list of demands handed Izvolsky by Mijušković in October. Pašić also supported Montenegrin claims to Spič when he visited St. Petersburg. See instructions to Pašić, undated, "Nekoliko dokumenata iz aneksije," Pt. 1, pp. 243–45.

48. Jovanović to Velimirović, 6 October 1908, Savezni sekretarijat za inostrane poslove (hereafter cited as SSIP), No. 2456.

49. Kuhn to Aehrenthal, 11 November 1908, *OUA*, I, No. 548.

50. Kuhn to Aehrenthal, 13 November 1908, *OUA*, I, No. 562. Re-

garding Montenegrin hopes for an international conference, see *GC*, 25 October, 7 and 15 November, and 8 December 1908 O.S.

51. Aehrenthal to Kuhn, 21 November 1908, *OUA*, I, No. 619. The German minister in Cetinje expressed similar sentiments. Much to his dismay, reports of his private conversation with Prince Nicholas concerning a possible Austro-Montenegrin agreement were published by the *Glas Crnogorca*. *GC*, 30 October 1908 O.S.

52. Kuhn suspected Izvolsky's hand in the Spič matter and the Russian government's hand in the Montenegrin note. Kuhn to Aehrenthal, 25 November 1908, *OUA*, I, No. 640; supplement to report from Cetinje 27 November 1908, No. 658; *pro memoria*, 12/23 November 1908, "Nekoliko dokumenata iz aneksije," Pt. 2, No. 13, pp. 310–15.

53. Aehrenthal to Kuhn, 26 November 1908, *OUA*, I, No. 651.

54. Kuhn to Aehrenthal, 27 November 1908, *OUA*, I, No. 658.

55. The *Neue Freie Presse* soon suggested that Nicholas had contemplated storming Spič on 17 December, his birthday. *NFP*, 2 January 1909, m.e., p. 9.

56. Kuhn to Aehrenthal, 15 December 1908, *OUA*, I, No. 748.

57. Kuhn to Aehrenthal, 25 December 1908, *OUA*, I, No. 795.

58. Aehrenthal to Kuhn, 4 January 1909, *OUA*, I, No. 841.

59. Foreign Office notation on report from O'Reilly to Grey, 31 December 1908, PRO, FO 371/694/3991.

60. O'Reilly, acting in the absence of the regular minister, was normally councillor at the British embassy in Rome. Perhaps his relative unfamiliarity with the political terrain in Montenegro explains his unusual sympathy for the prince and his politics.

61. O'Reilly to Grey, 31 December 1908, PRO, FO 371/694/3991.

62. Kuhn to Aehrenthal, 7 January 1909, *OUA*, I, No. 858.

63. Kuhn to Aehrenthal, 6 January 1909, *OUA*, I, No. 849.

64. Kuhn to Aehrenthal, 7 January 1909, *OUA*, I, No. 858. Russia hedged on provoking Aehrenthal unnecessarily. In mid-December, Mijušković returned from an extended visit to St. Petersburg, where he had championed Montenegrin claims in official and unofficial circles. Izvolsky would not stick his neck out for Spič or any other Montenegrin territorial demands. He was supposed to have told Mijušković that the prospects for an international conference were in fact not very good. Later, the Montenegrin told a Dutch diplomat that Montenegro had to improve her "living conditions," i.e., win territorial compensation, or else fight a "war of honor" with Austria, a war that could only end in defeat for the principality. Mijušković mused aloud that the country would at least have a better economic future as an Austrian province. Kuhn to Aehrenthal, 9 December 1908, No. 707.

65. See, for example, Kuhn to Aehrenthal, 15, 21, and 25 October 1908, *OUA*, I, Nos. 282, 353, 395; Aehrenthal to Kuhn, 23 October 1908, No. 372.

66. *GC*, 11 October 1908 O.S.; Zavičajni Muzej Nikšić, Arhiv Kapetana Djorka Visnjića, Knj. 9, 7 October 1908, cited in Martinović, "Otpor naroda u Crnoj Gori," p. 504.

67. Fearful of the martial inclinations of the principality, the Powers urged Montenegro to pursue a moderate and nonbelligerent course. Italy, for example, refused to sell artillery to Montenegro. More surprisingly, even Russia recalled a ship, the *Heron*, which was already en route to Bar at the time of the annexation, carrying arms and munitions. Nicholas was furious with Russia's act, but managed to restrain his anger toward the Russian minister. Jovanović, "Stav Crne Gore prema aneksiji," pp. 106–7.

68. Kuhn to Aehrenthal, 15 October 1908, *OUA*, I, No. 282.

69. Franz Conrad von Hötzendorf, *Aus meiner Dienstzeit, 1906–1918* (hereafter cited as *AMD*), 5 vols. (Vienna: Rikola Verlag, 1921–25), I:119.

70. Aehrenthal to St. Petersburg and Rome, 17 October 1908, *OUA*, I, No. 317.

71. Conrad, *AMD*, I:120.

72. Conrad to Aehrenthal, 18 October 1908, ibid., p. 122.

73. Aehrenthal to consuls general in Scutari and Salonica, 21 October 1908, *OUA*, I, No. 361. As time went on, even more elaborate plans were made for smuggling arms into Albania. Tel. to Rappaport, 30 January 1909, No. 944; Aehrenthal to Kral, 18 February 1909, No. 1011. See especially Haus-, Hof- und Staatsarchiv, Politisches Archiv (hereafter cited as HHStA, PA), Geheimakten, Liasse XXIX/g. karton rot 486. Italy, rightly mistrustful of Austro-Hungarian intentions in northern Albania, "worked to have Turkey insist that Austria renounce her protection of the Albanian Catholics." Askew, "Austro-Italian Antagonism," p. 204.

74. Aehrenthal to Conrad, 20 October 1908, *AMD*, I:124.

75. Like Aehrenthal, Francis Ferdinand was unwilling to concede anything to either Serbia or Montenegro, especially territorial compensation: "One must remain firm!" Private letter from Francis Ferdinand to Aehrenthal, 20 October 1908, *OUA*, I, No. 347a.

76. On 24 October, Conrad had informed Aehrenthal that the plan for a partial Brown Mobilization would require seventeen days to complete. The chief of staff explained that the process would take so long because he wanted to try to maintain normal appearances on the railroads on which the troops would be transported. On the other hand, he assured Aehrenthal that the mobilization could be accelerated if the need arose. Conrad to Aehrenthal, 24 October 1908, *AMD*, I:125.

77. Aehrenthal was basing his statement on cold facts. According to Montenegrin documents, a Bosnian named Leontije Ninković had petitioned the Montenegrin government, in the name of the Bosnian diet, for permission to unleash a full-fledged rebellion in Bosnia and Hercegovina as soon as hostilities broke out. Ninković to the *kapetan* of Grahovo, 2 October 1908 O.S., "Nekoliko dokumenata iz aneksije," Pt. 2, No. 12, p. 309 ("Montenegrinische Dokumente," p. 703). Anti-Austrian guerrillas (*komitadje*) were active—and destructive—in the two provinces.

78. Aehrenthal to Great-Power and Balkan capitals, 16 November 1908, *OUA*, I, No. 588.

79. "Foundations for Concrete Preparations for War for the Year 1909," *AMD*, I:608.

80. Ibid., p. 612. Conrad estimated that Montenegro could count on

40,000 troops, including 10,000 men expected to return from abroad. Indeed, Montenegrins living around the world rallied to the cause of their fatherland. In the United States, Montenegrin emigrés and workers attended meetings protesting the annexation. In Canada, they set up the "Brotherhood of Prince Ivan Crnojević," named after the medieval Montenegrin ruler. As the threat of war grew, Montenegrins began to return home from the United States, Canada, Russia, Turkey (especially Constantinople), and elsewhere. Jovanović, "Stav Crne Gore prema aneksiji," pp. 93–94, n. 13.

81. Joseph Redlich, *Schicksalsjahre Österreich, 1908–1919: Das politische Tagebuch Josef Redlichs*, ed. Fritz Fellner, 2 vols. (Graz and Cologne: Hermann Böhlaus Nachf., 1953), I: 8 December 1908, p. 2.

82. Conrad, *AMD*, I:121.

CHAPTER THREE

1. Redlich, *Das politische Tagebuch*, I, 9 December 1908, p. 3.
2. For a detailed discussion of the negotiations leading up to the Austro-Turkish agreement, see Schmitt, *Annexation of Bosnia*, pp. 100–24.
3. Though jealous and fearful of Austria's presence in the Balkans, Tittoni initially believed that Vienna's renunciation of its rights in the Sandžak was a bigger gain for Rome than the annexation of Bosnia was for Austria. Askew, "Austro-Italian Antagonism," pp. 211–12.
4. Forgách to Aehrenthal, 3 January 1909, *OUA*, I, No. 833; Aehrenthal to Forgách, 3 January 1909, No. 832.
5. Forgách to Aehrenthal, 4 January 1909, *OUA*, I, No. 837.
6. Aehrenthal to Forgách, 5 January 1909, *OUA*, I, No. 843; Forgách to Aehrenthal, 7 January 1909, Nos. 853–54. Aehrenthal informed the British ambassador in Vienna that despite all that had happened "he had a very high regard for [Milovanović] personally, and that he considered him to be one of the most moderate and reasonable of Serbian politicians." He argued further that the "outburst of virulence" in Belgrade was a sign of "demoralisation." Cartwright to Grey, 6 January 1909, *British Documents on the Origins of the War, 1898–1914* (hereafter cited as *BD*), ed. G. P. Gooch and Harold Temperley, 11 vols. (London: H. M. Stationery Office, 1926–38), V, No. 504.
7. Quotations from Albertini, *Origins of the War*, I:264–65.
8. O'Reilly to Grey, 31 January 1909, PRO, FO 371/694/5874.
9. Gregović vigorously protested the Austro-Turkish accord and for days the press speculated on what he might have had to say to the grand vizier or the Turkish foreign minister. In the end, he denied rumors, tendered especially by the Slavophile *Turquie*, that he had claimed Turkey's "capitulation" meant that Montenegro had regained her "freedom of action." After all, Montenegro had not concluded a formal treaty with the

Porte. The Austrian government and press took exception to his allegation that the Austro-Turkish agreement included some kind of promise of compensation for Montenegro. *NFP*, 20 January 1909, m.e., p. 5; 24 January 1909, m.e., p. 7; 26 January 1909, m.e., p. 7; 27 January 1909, m.e., p. 6.

10. About the time of Turkey's agreement with Austria, it was reported that the sixty-eight-year-old Nicholas had abdicated. It was also alleged that he was planning a mission to St. Petersburg. *NFP*, 16 January 1909, e.e., p. 2; 17 January 1909, m.e., pp. 4–5.

11. The Montenegrin skupština unanimously approved the government's actions and encouraged an even more energetic policy. Tomanović's fiery speech seemed to make no special impression in Serbia. Those papers that printed it did so without commentary. *Politika* and *Pravda* did not print it at all. The Austrian press concluded that the Serbians were too involved with their own domestic problems to give special attention to Tomanović's "generalities." Moreover, there was some talk in Belgrade about a possible Austro-Montenegrin rapprochement. If Tomanović was given short shrift in Belgrade, such was not the case in Russia, where the speech caused a new outburst of pan-Slav mania. *Novoe vremia* called it a "last warning to [European] diplomacy." Only a few days later the *Berliner Tageblatt* reported a new pan-Slav collection for "Montenegro's defense against Austria." The aim: to purchase two airplanes "of the Wright brothers' type" for the purpose of tossing dynamite bombs onto Austrian territory. *NFP*, 23 January 1909, m.e., p. 6; 24 January 1909, m.e., p. 7; 25 January 1909, a.e., p. 7; 28 January 1909, e.e., p. 3.

12. O'Reilly to Grey, 31 January 1909, PRO, FO 371/694/5874. See also *NFP*, 2 February 1909, m.e., p. 4, for another account of Tomanović's comments on Serbo-Montenegrin relations.

13. Redlich, *Das politische Tagebuch*, I, 20 February 1909, p. 7.

14. Ibid., 22 February 1909, p. 7. About this time the French government informed Izvolsky that it did not consider the question of Bosnia-Hercegovina vital to Russian interests and that it did not want war. Pichon's frank statements left a painful impression in St. Petersburg. For a good study of this period, see Vujović, *Crna Gora i Francuska*, p. 335.

15. Many expected Russia to come to the aid of Serbia. Moltke, the German chief of staff, wrote to his Austrian counterpart: "The moment Russia mobilizes, Germany will also mobilize, and will unquestionably mobilize her whole army." Moltke to Conrad, 21 January 1909, *AMD*, I: 379.

16. Minute, Bertie to Grey, 7 January 1909, *BD*, V, No. 506.

17. See Schmitt, *Annexation of Bosnia*, pp. 144–207.

18. As late as March, Nicholas was still citing Grey's tentative approval for the cession of Spič. *NFP*, 2 March 1909, e.e., p. 2.

19. Schmitt, *Annexation of Bosnia*, p. 164. See also Grey to Bertie, 2 March 1909, *BD*, V, No. 638; Nicolson to Grey, 27 February 1909, No. 619.

20. Izvolsky to Sergeiev, 27 February 1909, cited in Schmitt, *Annexation of Bosnia*, p. 164; Albertini, *Origins of the War*, I:277.

21. Cartwright to Grey, 5 March 1909, *BD*, V, No. 649.

22. See, for example, Milovanović's draft note, Sergeiev to Izvolsky, 2 and 3 March 1909, cited in Schmitt, *Annexation of Bosnia*, p. 168; Grujić to Grey, 10 March 1909, *BD*, V, No. 662; Forgách to Aehrenthal, 10 March 1909, *OUA*, II, No. 1160.
23. Cartwright to Grey, 2 March 1909, *BD*, V, No. 636.
24. Telegram to Great-Power and Balkan capitals, 1 March 1909, *OUA*, II, No. 1080.
25. Kuhn to Aehrenthal, 5 March 1909, *OUA*, II, No. 1114; *NFP*, 9 March 1909, m.e., p. 5, citing Montenegrin official gazette. See also *NFP*, 6 March 1909, m.e., p. 4; 7 March 1909, m.e., p. 6.
26. Kuhn to Aehrenthal, 5 March 1909, *OUA*, II, No. 1115.
27. Aehrenthal to Kuhn, 7 March 1909, *OUA*, II, No. 1137.
28. See Schmitt, *Annexation of Bosnia*, p. 168.
29. Kuhn to Aehrenthal, 8 and 10 March 1909, *OUA*, II, Nos. 1142, 1167.
30. Kuhn to Aehrenthal, 8 March 1909, *OUA*, II, No. 1143.
31. Kuhn to Aehrenthal, 8 March 1909, *OUA*, II, No. 1142.
32. Aehrenthal to Kuhn, 9 March 1909, *OUA*, II, No. 1153.
33. Kuhn to Aehrenthal, 10 March 1909, *OUA*, II, No. 1166. Cf. Stein's secret telegram, 26 February 1909 O.S., Državni Muzej Cetinje, Prinovljeni spisi (rukopisi) (hereafter cited as DMC-PR), No. 20a.
34. Grujić to Grey, 10 March 1909, *BD*, V, No. 622; Forgách to Aehrenthal, 10 March 1909, *OUA*, II, No. 1160; Aehrenthal's circular note, 16 March 1909, No. 1235.
35. Conrad, *AMD*, I:138–57.
36. Kuhn to Aehrenthal, 17 March 1909, cited in Kuhn to Aehrenthal, 22 March 1909, *OUA*, II, No. 1310.
37. Aehrenthal to Kuhn, 20 March 1909, cited in Kuhn to Aehrenthal, 22 March 1909, *OUA*, II, No. 1310.
38. Kuhn to Aehrenthal, 22 March 1909, *OUA*, II, No. 1310. The size of the Montenegrin force mobilized was variously reported as a battalion, a brigade, half a division, and a full division. *NFP*, 18 March 1909, m.e., p. 5; 19 March 1909, m.e., p. 5; 23 March 1909, m.e., p. 7. The Austrians did not dismiss the mini-mobilization out of hand. The *Neue Freie Presse* printed a long article on Montenegro's military capability and the difficulty of waging a conventional war in her mountains. *NFP*, 24 March 1909, m.e., pp. 4–5.
39. Redlich, *Das politische Tagebuch*, I, 15 March 1909, p. 9.
40. Jovanović, "Stav Crne Gore prema aneksiji," p. 116.
41. Conrad, *AMD*, I:162.
42. Fay, *Origins of the World War*, I:392.
43. Schmitt, *Annexation of Bosnia*, p. 225.
44. Historians are at odds as to whether Germany's intervention was motivated by altruism, spite, or a simple desire to end the crisis once and for all. Fay has suggested that Bülow "let Izvolski easily out of the embarrassing blind alley into which he had strayed." Fay, *Origins of the World War*, I:389. A. J. P. Taylor, on the other hand, believes that Bülow and Kiderlen Waechter, the German state secretary, wanted "to press M. Izvolski to the

wall." Taylor, *The Struggle for Mastery in Europe, 1848–1918* (Oxford: Clarendon Press, 1954), p. 455. Albertini leans more toward Taylor than Fay: "An ultimatum in the literal sense it hardly was, but in substance it was one. . . ." In part he defends his conclusion by citing Kiderlen's purported explanation: "I knew the Russians were not ready for war, that they could not in any case go to war, and I wanted to make what capital I could of this knowledge. I wanted to show that Germany which had been in Russia's leading strings since 1815, was now free of them." Albertini, *Origins of the War*, I:286. In a recent study Dwight Lee does not come down on either side: "Certainly, whether or not the note of 21 March was an ultimatum, Russia, whose ministers unanimously agreed to give assent to the annexation, was in no position to say no. . . ." Lee, *Europe's Crucial Years: The Diplomatic Background of World War I, 1902–1914* (Hanover, N.H.: University Press of New England, 1974), p. 204. See also Heinz Günther Sasse, *War das deutsche Eingreifen in die bosnische Krise im März 1909 ein Ultimatum?* (Stuttgart: W. Kohlhammer, 1936), and, more recently, Heinz Gerhardt, *War in der bosnischen Annexionskrise die deutsche Demarche vom 22. März 1909 ein Ultimatum?* (Berlin: E.-Reuter Gesellschaft, 1965).

45. Bülow to Pourtàles, 21 March 1909, *Die Grosse Politik der europäischen Kabinette, 1871–1914* (hereafter cited as *GP*), ed. Johannes Lepsius, Albrecht Mendelssohn Bartholdy, and Friedrich Thimme, 40 vols. (Berlin: Deutsche Verlagsgesellschaft für Politik und Geschichte, 1922–27), XXVI/2, No. 9460. Actually, it was Kiderlen who composed the note to the Russian foreign minister. Interestingly, Sir Edward Grey used almost the same phraseology in communicating with Count Paul Metternich, the German ambassador in London. Metternich to foreign ministry, 22 March 1909, No. 9466. Initially, at least, the tsar considered the German step a commendable attempt "to find a peaceful way out of the present difficulties." In one of the famous Nicky-Willy exchanges, he endorsed the German proposal and informed William that he had instructed Izvolsky "to show every disposition ot meet him halfway." Nicholas II to William II, 22 March 1909, No. 9465. Later, however, he wrote his mother that "the form and the method of Germany's action—I mean towards us—has simply been rude and we won't forget it." Cited in Lee, *Europe's Crucial Years*, pp. 203–4.

46. Report of Košutić, 3 March 1909, cited in Fay, *Origins of the World War*, I:384–85.

47. René Albrecht-Carrié, *A Diplomatic History of Europe since the Congress of Vienna* (New York: Harper, 1958), p. 267. For an Austrian analysis of "peace," see *NFP*, 30 March 1909.

48. Verbal note of the Serbian legation in Vienna, 31 March 1909, *OUA*, II, No. 1425. Translation of text in Albertini, *Origins of the War*, I:291.

49. Telegram to Great-Power and Balkan capitals, 31 March 1909, *OUA*, II, No. 1428.

50. Conrad, *AMD*, I:163.

51. Kuhn to Aehrenthal, 28 March 1909, *OUA*, II, No. 1391.

52. Grey to Goschen, 31 March 1909, *BD*, V, No. 816; Grey to Cartwright, 1 April 1909, No. 819. The Serbians were rightly disturbed by

Montenegro's recalcitrance, suspecting that Nicholas wanted to engage in some last-minute bravado to discredit the Karadjordjević dynasty, which in addition to its surrender to the demands of the Powers was troubled by the recent abdication of Prince George as heir to the throne. *NFP,* 2 April 1909, m.e., p. 4; 3 April 1909, m.e., p. 3.

53. Lützow to Aehrenthal, 25 March 1909, *OUA,* II, No. 1357. As a result of his "cooperation," Tittoni had already begun to lose favor with his countrymen, who distrusted Austria's, especially Conrad's, machinations. Lützow to Aehrenthal, 16 February 1909, No. 1001. Despite the fact that he had recently survived a vote of confidence in the chamber of deputies, Tittoni's *Dreibundpolitik,* tentative though it seemed to most Austrians, antagonized most Italians. Lützow wrote Aehrenthal that he knew Tittoni's days were numbered when he saw a popular Italian cartoon depicting the foreign minister polishing the boots of the Habsburg emperor. Lützow to Aehrenthal, 2 March 1909, No. 1089. In point of fact, Tittoni did not finish the year in office.

54. Lützow to Aehrenthal, 26 March 1909, *OUA,* II, No. 1375. The Russians subsequently tried to throw a monkey wrench into the negotiations by insisting on the abrogation of all the significant paragraphs of Article 29, including No. 6. As Grey had already accepted the Italian proposals, he tried to mollify Izvolsky by stating that the British government "had no intention of deviating a hair's breadth from their policy of supporting Russia in the Near East." Pichon followed Grey's lead. Schmitt, *Annexation of Bosnia,* pp 238–39; Appendix II, "The Montenegrin Negotiations, April-May 1909," *BD,* V, p. 822; Vujović, *Crna Gora i Francuska,* p. 336.

55. Aehrenthal to Lützow, 28 March 1909, *OUA,* II, No. 1400. The Germans advised Aehrenthal to be conciliatory toward Montenegro, to consider economic aid, and not to exclude the possibility of frontier rectifications. *Vossische Zeitung,* 1 April 1909.

56. Aehrenthal to Lützow, 29 March 1909, *OUA,* II, No. 1412. It was at this juncture that Aehrenthal, confident of Montenegro's imminent capitulation, advised Kral in Scutari to stop his agitation among the Albanians. Aehrenthal to Kral, 1 April 1909, No. 1439. (See Chapter 2, n. 73).

57. Lützow to Aehrenthal, 29 March 1909, *OUA,* II, No. 1413.

58. Kuhn to Aehrenthal, 2 April 1909, *OUA,* II, No. 1441, translation of note in Schmitt, *Annexation of Bosnia,* p. 238. See also *NFP,* 5 April 1909, m.e., p. 3.

59. Aehrenthal to Lützow, 2 April 1909, *OUA,* II, Nos. 1444–45.

60. Lützow to Aehrenthal, 3 April 1909, *OUA,* II, No. 1256.

61. Kuhn to Aehrenthal, 5 April 1909, *OUA,* II, No. 1471.

62. Aehrenthal to Lützow, 2 April 1909, *OUA,* II, No. 1444.

63. Kuhn to Aehrenthal, 5 April 1909, *OUA,* II, No. 1471. Perhaps to firm up his southern flank, Nicholas used this time to award the vali of Scutari the Order of Danilo. Other Turkish officers were also decorated and feted. Gregović in Constantinople indicated that Montenegro had little choice but to follow Serbia's reluctant example. *NFP,* 3 April 1909, e.e., pp. 2–3.

64. Izvolsky to Stein, 20 March 1909 O.S., DMC-PR, No. 49; *NFP,* 7 April 1909, m.e., p. 3; e.e., p. 2. The same day the *Neue Freie Presse* ran its initial coverage of Montenegro's capitulation, it also printed a story about a two-week-old incident on the Austro-Montenegrin frontier in which two Austrian soldiers were captured and taken to Cetinje. Each side blamed the other for the affair, but neither let it impinge on the more important matters at hand.

65. Kuhn to Aehrenthal, 6 April 1909, *OUA,* II, No. 1478; *NFP,* 8 April 1909, e.e., p. 2.

66. Kuhn to Aehrenthal, 7 April 1909, *OUA,* II, No. 1487.

67. Kuhn to Aehrenthal, 7 April 1909, *OUA,* II, No. 1486.

68. Aehrenthal to Francis Joseph, 7 April 1909, *OUA,* II, No. 1493.

69. For the text of Aehrenthal's note to the Montenegrin government, see Aehrenthal to Kuhn, 7 April 1909, *OUA,* II, No. 1485.

70. In a querulous telegram to Lützow in Rome, Aehrenthal flailed Tittoni for his unsanctioned independence in dealing with Nicholas, unfavorably comparing Tittoni's handling of Montenegro with the British cabinet's success in bringing Serbia to terms. Aehrenthal to Lützow, 8 April 1909, *OUA,* II, No. 1496. Tittoni, on the other hand, told the British ambassador in Rome that he believed that "the intractable attitude [Aehrenthal] had adopted was not altogether willingly assumed by him." Despite all that had transpired, he had found Aehrenthal generally "conciliatory." In his eyes, Francis Ferdinand was the real villain. Rodd to Grey, 6 April 1909, *BD,* V, No. 827.

71. Kuhn to Aehrenthal, 7 and 9 April 1909, *OUA,* II, Nos. 1487, 1499; *NFP,* 8 April 1909, e.e., p. 2.

72. Nicholas specified four points of assistance: (1) drainage of part of Lake Scutari, (2) obtaining capital to buy out the Italian rail and tobacco monopolies, (3) rail and road construction, and (4) a commercial treaty. O'Reilly to Grey, 15 April 1909, PRO, FO 371/694/15935.

73. Memorandum of the Chief of the General Staff, 2 July 1909, *OUA,* II, No. 1666.

CHAPTER FOUR

1. Dušan Vuksan, "Što je prethodilo tituli knjaza Nikole 'Kraljevsko visočanstvo,'" *Z,* VIII, Knj. XIII, No. 1 (1935):14–16.

2. Jovanović, *Stvaranje Crnogorske države,* pp. 383–88. Jovanović's account of the abortive conspiracy, published shortly after the end of the Second World War, exhibits a distinct political orientation: Jovanović is sympathetic to the conspirators and unfailingly critical of Nicholas and his persecution of the *klubaši.*

3. The Podgorica organization had a central committee composed of its ten founding members. The organization's rules obligated each mem-

ber of the committee to enlist ten new members in the conspiracy. In turn, each new member was responsible for recruiting three additional members, and each of these for two more. The lower echelon of the organization was so devised that any individual member knew only two or three fellow conspirators, usually those he worked with on a regular basis. Each member had to take an oath to guard the secrecy of the organization and carry out all executive orders without question. Ibid., pp. 384–85.

4. The British representative reported, that with the failure of the conspiracy, some fifteen persons, one retired major and relatives of individuals imprisoned in connection with the 1907 Bomb Affair, had fled into Albania to be condemned in absentia. Beaumont to Grey, 25 October 1909, PRO, FO 371/694/39863.

5. Ibid.

6. Vujović, *Crna Gora i Francuska*, p. 339.

7. Jovanović, *Stvaranje Crnogorske države*, p. 386; *CV*, 21 and 25 November 1909 O.S. See also Novica Rakočević, " 'Radničke novine' i Crna Gora 1903–1914," *Počeci socijalističke štampe na Balkanu*, ed. by Milo Popović et al. (Belgrade, 1974): pp. 481–83.

8. Beaumont to Grey, 10 December 1909, PRO, FO 371/694/45854; *CV*, 2, 9 and 11 December 1909 O.S. Belgrade blamed socialists for the demonstrations Milovanović claimed he did not have the power to stop. *CV*, 25 November and 30 December 1909 O.S.

9. Jovanović, *Stvaranje Crnogorske države*, p. 386.

10. Ibid., pp. 386–87.

11. Vujović, *Crna Gora i Francuska*, p. 340.

12. Beaumont to Grey, 4 October 1909, PRO, FO 371/694/37371.

13. Beaumont to Grey, 11 October 1909, PRO, FO 371/694/38482.

14. Beaumont to Grey, 22 October 1909, PRO, FO 371/694/39628.

15. *LT*, 4 January 1910. Apparently French and Russian intervention stopped Nicholas from expelling Petković. Vujović, *Crna Gora i Francuska*, pp. 340–42. For Montenegrin commentary on the visit of the French fleet, see *CV*, 28 November, 16, 19, 23 and 30 December 1909 O.S.

16. Giesl to Aehrenthal, 21 February 1910, *OUA*, II, No. 2009. Giesl had served previously as military attaché in Constantinople, 1893–1909.

17. Giesl reported that upon his arrival in Cetinje, he had noticed that Petković had had his bags packed on the pretext of going to Dubrovnik for a few weeks. As time went on and Petković remained in Cetinje, Giesl concluded that the minister actually wanted to be ready for a quick escape. Ibid.

18. Ibid. In his memoirs, Constantin Dumba, a former Austro-Hungarian minister to Serbia, wrote that he had repeatedly petitioned the Ballhausplatz for oral or written instructions as to what the aims of Austria-Hungary's Balkan policy really were. The only "constructive remark" he received from Vienna was that "in no circumstances can we permit a union of the Kingdom of Serbia and the Principality of Montenegro; we shall prevent it even if it means going to war to do so." Constantin Dumba, *Memoirs of a Diplomat*, trans. Ian F. D. Morrow (Boston: Little, Brown and Co., 1932), pp. 91–92.

19. Giesl to Aehrenthal, 9 February 1910, HHStA, PA XVII/Montenegro, Liasse IX, No. 11.
20. Giesl to Aehrenthal, 1, 2, and 3 March 1910, HHStA, PA XVII/Montenegro, Liasse IX, Nos. 7473, 7143, 7766, 9030; Aehrenthal to Giesl, 3 March 1910, No. 21; *CV,* 13, 17 and 20 February 1910 O.S.
21. Giesl to Aehrenthal, 6 March 1910, *OUA,* II, No. 2025.
22. Giesl to Aehrenthal, 17 March 1910. See directive to Cetinje, 27 April 1910, *OUA,* II, No. 2137.
23. On Montenegrin plans to elevate the principality to the rank of kingdom, see HHStA, PA XVII/Montenegro, Liasse X; *CV,* 21 April 1910 O.S. and Novica Rakočević, "Politička osnova proglašenja Crne Gore za Kraljevina 1910. godine," *Balcanica,* VIII (1977): 455–60.
24. Giesl to Aehrenthal, 7 April 1910, *OUA,* II, No. 2100.
25. Giesl to Aehrenthal, 13 April 1910, *OUA,* II, No. 2110.
26. Aehrenthal to Giesl, 18 April 1910, *OUA,* II, No. 2121.
27. Giesl to Aehrenthal, 19 April 1910, *OUA,* II, No. 2122.
28. Private letter from Aehrenthal to Giesl, 25 April 1910, *OUA,* II, No. 2130.
29. Nicholas was undoubtedly buoyed by the news of King Peter's unsuccessful journey to Constantinople. Both Peter and King Ferdinand of Bulgaria had travelled to the Porte to make personal pleas for permission to build the projected Danube-Adriatic railroad across Turkish territory. Nicholas was opposed to the scheme because he wanted the railroad to have its terminus at Bar in Montenegro, rather than in Turkish Albania. Giesl to Aehrenthal, 13 April 1910, *OUA,* II, No. 2110.
30. Initially Lazar Mijušković, Filip Jergović, and Miloje Jovanović conducted discussions with Giesl alone. In time the Austrian minister was assisted by Richard Riedl and Gustav Koloman, officials of the Austrian and Hungarian trade ministries, respectively. The two sides signed an agreement on 6 February 1911. The Montenegrin skupština approved the treaty on trade and shipping pending conclusion of a monetary convention between the two countries. On 1 March 1912, the Montenegrins eventually ratified the trade treaty, which was scheduled to remain in force until 31 December 1917. *CV,* 26 June, 10 July 1910; 29 January, 22 June, 2 July, 24 September 1911; *GC,* 30 January 1911 and 25 February 1912 (all O.S.); *Reichsgesetzblatt für die im Reichsrate vertretenen Königreiche und Länder,* Vienna, 10 March 1912. Novica Rakočević, unpublished manuscript on relations between Austria-Hungary and Montenegro, 1904–1914, pp. 110–11.
31. Little was accomplished as the two sides could not agree on the division of land atop Mount Dvrsnik. *CV,* 31 July 1910 O.S.
32. Giesl to Aehrenthal, 7 April 1910, *OUA,* II, No. 2100.
33. Giesl to Aehrenthal, 13 April 1910, *OUA,* II, No. 2110.
34. Giesl to Aehrenthal, 19 April 1910, *OUA,* II, No. 2122.
35. Telegram from Aehrenthal To Cetinje, Rome, and Berlin, 18 April 1910, *OUA,* II, No. 2121.
36. Giesl to Aehrenthal, 19 April 1910, *OUA,* II, No. 2122.
37. Report from Giesl to Aehrenthal, 20 April 1910, *OUA,* II, No. 2123.

38. Reference to unpublished telegram of 17 March 1910 in directive to Cetinje, 27 April 1910, *OUA*, II, No. 2137.
39. Directive to Cetinje, 27 April 1910, *OUA*, II, No. 2137.
40. The Italian government has not yet published documents for this period.
41. Directive to Cetinje, 27 April 1910, *OUA*, II, No. 2137.
42. Beaumont to Grey, 16 May 1910, PRO, FO 371/929/17997.
43. Vujović, *Crna Gora i Francuska*, p. 342.
44. Cartwright to Grey, 17 June 1910, PRO, FO 371/929/21619.
45. Beaumont to Grey, 5 July 1910, PRO, FO 371/929/24721.
46. Whitehead to Grey, 4 July 1910, PRO, FO 371/929/24924.
47. Beaumont to Grey, 1 August 1910, PRO, FO 371/929/28432. For Montenegrin coverage of this question, see *CV*, 27 January, 8 and 15 May, 21 July, 4 and 15 August 1910 O.S.
48. Aside from the gifts, deputations, special messages, and, of course, the international significance of the occasion, the jubilee celebration was noteworthy because it cost an estimated one hundred fifty thousand crowns, a sum roughly equivalent to the country's entire annual school budget. One highly-touted accomplishment was the installation of electric lighting in Cetinje by an Austrian company. Unfortunately, an explosion severely damaged the electric power plant only one month after it was put into operation. The principality-turned-kingdom also purchased an English roller to improve its notoriously poor roads. Beaumont to Grey, 1 August 1910, PRO, FO 371/929/28432. The king issued a partial pardon—not an amnesty—for certain political prisoners involved in the 1907 and 1909 conspiracies. Many remained imprisoned, though, including the former minister, Radović. The measure did little to placate the estranged adherents of the People's Party. Beaumont to Grey, 8 September 1910, PRO, FO 371/929/33116; *LT*, 26 August and 7 September 1910; *CV*, 15 August 1910 O.S.
49. *CV*, 27 January, 8 August 1910 O.S. See, *inter alia*, Dimitrije Vujović, "Francuski dokumenti o crnogorsko-bugarskim odnosima, 1879–1912," *IZ*, XVIII, Knj. XXII, No. 2 (1965): 330–60, esp. pp. 357–58.
50. Beaumont to Grey, 1 August 1910, PRO, FO 371/929/28432; Vujović, *Crna Gora i Francuska*, p. 342; *LT*, 23, 25, 31 August, 1 September 1910; President Taft's autograph letter, 12 July 1910 (delivered 30 August 1910), National Archives (hereafter cited as NA), M 349–1.
51. "Ruski car Nikola II imenuje kralja Nikolu za feldmaršala," *Z*, XII, Knj. XXII, No. 5 (1939): 294. In addition to naming Nicholas a field marshal (only the second foreigner after the Duke of Wellington to receive the honor, the tsar also named Crown Prince Danilo a major general and Prince Mirko a lieutenant general in the Russian army. *LT*, 29 and 30 August 1910. Despite Russia's effusive display of affection, the British ambassador in St. Petersburg reported that official Russian circles looked on Montenegro's undertaking with "good-humored astonishment." O'Beirne reported that the tsar himself looked at the event "chiefly from the humorous point of view." Beaumont to Grey, 12 September 1910, PRO, FO 371/929/33887; O'Beirne to Grey, 6 September 1910, PRO, FO 371/929/32993; *LT*, 31 August 1910; *CV*, 25 August 1910 O.S.

52. *LT,* 30 August 1910; *CV,* 5 May 1910 O.S.
53. Barclay to Grey, 1 September 1910, PRO, FO 371/929/32185; Vujović, *Crna Gora i Francuska,* p. 343.
54. Beaumont to Grey, 12 September 1910, PRO, FO 371/929/33887; *CV,* 15 September 1910 O.S.
55. Beaumont to Grey, 6 September 1910, PRO, FO 371/929/33114; *LT,* 25 and 27 August 1910; *CV,* 15 August 1910 O.S.
56. Cartwright to Grey, 27 August 1910, PRO, FO 371/929/31424.
57. Schönaich to Aehrenthal, 3 January 1909 HHStA, PA XVII/Montenegro, Liasse VIII, Karton 47, No. 11946; Aehrenthal to Schönaich, 15 October 1909, No. 3235.
58. Aehrenthal to Giesl, 19 January 1910, HHStA, PA XVII/Montenegro, Liasse VIII, Karton 47, No. 138; Giesl to Aehrenthal, 20 June 1910, No. 40.
59. The two officers, Capt. Leo Wiesinger of the 16th Infantry Regiment and cadet officer (Fännrich) Walter Köller of the 95th Infantry Regiment (Sutomore/Spič), said that they had been well treated, but complained about poor food and quarters. Giesl contended that they should have been released immediately in Bar, rather than interned overnight and taken to Cetinje. Giesl to Aehrenthal, 17 July 1910, HHStA, PA XVII/Montenegro, Liasse VIII, Karton 47, No. 65.
60. Schönaich to Aehrenthal, 25 August 1910, HHStA, PA XVII/ Montenegro, Liasse VIII, Karton 47, No. 9491; Aehrenthal to Schönaich, 12 September 1910, No. 2524.
61. Because of pecuniary exigencies, the Russian military administration found it necessary to reduce the original 1,300,000 ruble outlay to 900,000 rubles. The kopek-conscious prime minister, Stolypin, reduced it even further—to 600,000 rubles. See Nikola P. Škerović, "Iz odnosa Crne Gore i Rusije: Vojna konvencija iz 1910.," *IZ,* XII, Knj. XVI, Nos. 3–4 (1959): 113–23. See also the report on negotiations concerning renewal of the military treaty between Russia and Montenegro, 3 February/21 January 1914, *IB,* I/1, No. 165.

CHAPTER FIVE

1. Durham, *Struggle for Scutari,* p. 17; Durham, *Twenty Years of Balkan Tangle,* pp. 212–13.
2. Conrad, *AMD,* II:157.
3. Ibid., p. 158. Nor was this a new idea. See memorandum of the Austro-Hungarian consul in Scutari, 20 June 1877, HHStA, PA XII/ Türkei I-V, Karton 256.
4. Conrad, *AMD,* II:158. Vlorë was also the Adriatic terminus of a traditional trade route between the western Balkans and Constantinople via Bitola (Monastir) and Salonica.

5. As quoted in Stavro Skendi, *The Albanian National Awakening, 1878–1912* (Princeton: Princeton University Press, 1967), p. 249. In 1904, Tittoni told the Italian Chamber of Deputies that "the proper value of Albania resides in her ports and in her seacoast, the possession of which would mean, for either Italy or Austria, the incontestable supremacy over the Adriatic Sea." As quoted in Constantine A. Chekrezi, *Albania: Past and Present* (New York: Macmillan, 1919), p. 81.

6. Perhaps both sides were interested in a greater prize: " 'Constantinople is the key of the Near East; Albania is the key of Constantinople,' say the Albanians. . . . Those within the empire knew that, so far as Turkey in Europe is concerned, the side that could enlist the Albanians, solid, must 'come out on top.' " Mary Edith Durham, *High Albania* (London: E. Arnold, 1909), p. 299. In 1896, following the marriage of Victor Emmanuel and Princess Jelena, Nicholas proposed that Montenegro should take northern Albania, Italy southern Albania. Nothing came of the suggestion. Austria hurried up plans of her own to establish a protectorate over Albania in the event that the Ottoman Empire disintegrated. Askew, "Austro-Italian Antagonism," pp. 199–200. See also Hans Dieter Schanderl, *Die Albanienpolitik Österreich-Ungarns und Italiens, 1877–1908,* Albanische Forschungen, Vol. IX (Wiesbaden: Otto Harrassowitz, 1971). For an excellent discussion of Italian economic interests in Albania, see Bosworth, *Italy,* passim.

7. See Th. A. Ippen, "Das religiöse Protectorat Österreich-Ungarns in der Türkei," *Kultur,* III (1902): 298–316; Anna H. Benna, "Studien zum Kultusprotektorat Österreich-Ungarns in Albanien im Zeitalter des Imperialismus (1888–1918)," *Mitteilungen des Österreichischen Staatsarchivs,* LXXIII, No. 7 (1954): 13–47. For a better view of the racial/tribal/religious mix in northern Albania, see Carleton S. Coon, *The Mountain of Giants: A Racial and Cultural Study of the North Albanian Mountain Ghegs* (Cambridge, Mass.: Harvard University Press, 1950); and Yu. B. Ivanova, *Severnaia Albaniia v XIX-nachale XX v. Obshchestvennaia zhizn'* (Moscow: Nauka, 1973). For an older report, see *LT,* 11 October 1912, p. 5.

8. Skendi, *Albanian Awakening,* p. 131.

9. Ibid., pp. 252–53. In renewing the Triple Alliance in 1887, Italy and Austria-Hungary had signed a separate treaty "whereby the two parties pledged themselves to preserve the *status quo* in the Balkans, the coasts, and the Turkish islands in the Adriatic and the Aegean. If this were not possible, they would consult each other and agree as to the steps to be taken, according to the principle of 'reciprocal compensation' for every territorial or other advantage." Ibid., p. 241. See also Fritz Fellner, *Der Dreibund: Europäische Diplomatie vor dem Ersten Weltkrieg* (Vienna: Verlag für Geschichte und Politik, 1960), pp. 29–32.

10. Durham, *Struggle for Scutari,* p. 12; *LT,* 12 April 1910, p. 5.

11. Durham, *Struggle for Scutari,* p. 159; Skendi, *Albanian Awakening,* p. 61. Battles between the opposing sides gave rise to an Albanian folk epic, "The Lute of the Mountains."

12. Durham, *High Albania,* pp. 81–82; Skendi, *Albanian Awakening,* p. 201. In 1901, the Albanians occupied the Montenegrin town of Kolašin,

killing a large number of the Orthodox population. See also Milovan Djilas's moving saga, *Land Without Justice* (New York: Harcourt, Brace and Co., 1958).

13. Durham, *Struggle for Scutari*, p. 133.
14. Ibid., p. 17.
15. Skendi, *Albanian Awakening*, p. 200.
16. "To the Christians, especially," Durham recounted, "the moment was supreme. 'We are free! We are free!' cried an old man. 'All my life I have waited for this moment. Now thank God, I shall die happy!' " Durham, *High Albania*, p. 223.
17. See E. V. [Iora], *Die Wahrheit über das Vorgehen der Jungtürken in Albanien* (Vienna and Leipzig, 1911); L. von Chlumecky, "Die Jungtürken und Albanien," *Österreichische Rundschau*, XXVI (January-March 1911): 268–74; I. G. Senkevich, "Mladoturetskaia revoliutsiia 1908 goda i albanskoe national'noe dvizhenie," *Sovetskoe vostokovedenie*, I (1958): 31–41.
18. In one celebrated instance, Ahmed Riza, the president of the Turkish parliament, interrupted a speaker to declare that "there are no Albanians; there are only Ottomans." The Albanian deputies protested indignantly. Joseph Swire, *Albania: The Rise of a Kingdom* (London: William & Norgate, 1929), p. 92; Skendi, *Albanian Awakening*, pp. 362–63. Subsequently the Turks even barred the printing of the words "Albania" and "Albanian."
19. Durham, *High Albania*, p. 224. In another book, Durham said the same thing a different way: " 'You can pass a law, if you like,' said I, 'that all cats are dogs; but they will remain cats.' " Durham, *Struggle for Scutari*, p. 8.
20. Swire, *Albania*, p. 89.
21. Skendi, *Albanian Awakening*, p. 341.
22. Ibid., p. 392; Swire, *Albania*, pp. 92–94; *LT,* 4 November 1909.
23. Swire, *Albania*, pp. 94–95; Skendi, *Albanian Awakening*, p. 405.
24. In the vicinity of Priština, Turkish troops fought a contingent of insurgents estimated by some at ten thousand. Forgách to Aehrenthal, 6 April 1910, *OUA*, II, No. 2096; *LT,* 6 April 1910, p. 5; 7 April 1910, p. 5; 8 April 1910, p. 5; *CV,* 27 and 31 March, 3 and 6 April 1910 O.S.
25. Pallavicini to Aehrenthal, 13 April 1910, *OUA*, II, No. 2111; *LT,* 11 April 1910, p. 5. Durham: "Never to this day have I been able to understand those enthusiasts at home and abroad who believed that the Young Turk could possibly succeed, overwhelmed the new Government with praise, before it had had time to display the smallest capacity for governing, and started its representatives upon their career, surfeited with the most fulsome flattery and with their heads more than sufficiently turned." Durham, *Struggle for Scutari*, p. 4.
26. Aehrenthal to Pallavicini, 21 April 1910, *OUA*, II, No. 2126.
27. Pallavicini to Aehrenthal, 9 April 1910, *OUA*, II, No. 2106; *LT,* 8 April 1910, p. 5.
28. Barclay to Grey, 16 December 1910, *BD*, IX/1, No. 201.
29. Aehrenthal to Pallavicini, 7 April 1910, *OUA*, II, No. 2101.

30. Ibid.; Aehrenthal to Great-Power capitals, 6 May 1910, *OUA*, II, No. 2153.
31. Aehrenthal to Pallavicini, 25 April 1910, *OUA*, II, No. 2131.
32. Pallavicini to Aehrenthal, 28 April 1910, *OUA*, II, No. 2143.
33. Mérey to Aehrenthal, 26 April 1910, *OUA*, II, No. 2135.
34. Mahmud Shevket Pasha, the Ottoman war minister, took leave of the capital to observe operations first hand. Pallavicini to Aehrenthal, 6 and 7 May, 5 June 1910, *OUA*, II, Nos. 2152, 2155, 2156, 2188; Skendi, *Albanian Awakening*, pp. 405–6; Swire, *Albania*, p. 95; *LT*, 16 May 1910, p. 5; 3 June 1910, p. 5; 8 June 1910, p. 7.
35. Pallavicini to Aehrenthal, 5 June 1910, *OUA*, II, No. 2188.
36. Pallavicini to Aehrenthal, 29 May 1910; Aehrenthal to Pallavicini, 17 June 1910, *OUA*, II, Nos. 2187, 2199.
37. Aehrenthal to Pallavicini, 10 June 1910, *OUA*, II, No. 2190; Swire, *Albania*, p. 99; Skendi, *Albanian Awakening*, pp. 406–8.
38. Pallavicini to Aehrenthal, 25 June 1910, *OUA*, II, No. 2204. To use a British turn of phrase, disarmament was carried out "in the usual Turkish style." Findlay to Grey, 2 August 1910, *BD*, IX/1, No. 163. For British reports on disarmament efforts in Albania and elsewhere, see *BD*, IX/1, Nos. 159–76; *LT*, 18 and 27 May 1910. Cf. Durham, *Struggle for Scutari*, pp. 15–16.
39. Conrad, *AMD*, II:160.
40. The plan assigned Montenegro Peć and Berane. Giesl to Aehrenthal, 20 April 1910, *OUA*, II, No. 2123.
41. Giesl to Aehrenthal, 17 May 1910, *OUA*, II, No. 2175.
42. Aehrenthal to Pallavicini, 25 May 1910, *OUA*, II, No. 2183.
43. Giesl to Aehrenthal, 16 June 1910, *OUA*, II, No. 2197. For numbers, see Durham, *High Albania*, passim. See also Branko Perović (ed.), *Prvi balkanski rat, 1912–1913 (Operacije srpske vojske)* (Belgrade: Vojno-istorijski institut, 1959), pp. 77–84.
44. Giesl to Aehrenthal, 16 June 1910, *OUA*, II, No. 2197. On Boletin, see Bogumil Hrabak, "Arbanaški prvak Isa Boletinac i Crna Gora 1910–1912. godine," *IZ*, XXX, Knj. XXXIV, No. 1 (1977):177–92.
45. Aehrenthal to Pallavicini, 30 June 1910, *OUA*, II, No. 2210.
46. On the other hand, the Russian whetted his host's territorial appetite by indicating that sooner or later, because of the Ottoman Empire's internal collapse, Montenegro would get her due. Giesl to Aehrenthal, 14 November 1910, HHStA, PA XII/Albanien, Liasse XXXIV, Karton 33, No. 100-B.
47. *LT*, 30 November 1910, p. 5. The Albanians also received arms and support from a Garibaldi association in Italy. See *Daily Chronicle*, 11 May 1911; Barclay to Grey, 30 March 1911, *BD*, IX/1, No. 469. Durham also frequently mentioned a Garibaldi connection—e.g., Durham, *Struggle for Scutari*, pp. 18–19. The exact nature and value of the Italian contribution is open to question, although a British reporter concluded that Ricciotti Garibaldi's promises were "voluble but unfulfilled." *LT*, 17 August 1911; also 11, 13, and 15 May, 7 and 20 June, and 14 August 1911.

48. Skendi, *Albanian Awakening*, pp. 408–9.
49. Ibid., p. 410.
50. Ibid., p. 411; *LT*, 24 January 1910, p. 5; 28 February 1910, p. 5. Moses to Secretary of State, 6 April 1911, NA, RG 59, State Decimal File 1910–1929, No. 867.00/335.
51. The American minister to Greece and Montenegro noted that "this year's rebellion is some six weeks later, according to the Albanian revolutionary calendar—which calls for a revolt to begin regularly in the month of February." Moses to Secretary of State, 6 April 1911, NA, RG 59, State Decimal File 1910–1929, Nos. 867.00/335 and 336. See also Parà to Aehrenthal, 27 March 1911, HHStA, PA XII/Albanien, Liasse XXXIV, Karton 33, No. 27; *LT*, 30 March 1911, p. 8; 31 March 1911, p. 5; 25 April 1911, p. 3. According to Durham, the Catholics should not have acted unilaterally: "This sudden commencement before due preparations was a fatal error, engineered possibly by folk who meant the revolt to fail. It had been intended that Moslems and Christians should rise together. But the Christians having begun, Bedri Pasha . . . proclaimed a Holy War, and called on the Moslems of Scutari and the environs to rise and protect the Faith. It is a cry that perhaps never fails. The Moslems flocked to receive arms, and started out." Durham, *Struggle for Scutari*, p. 19.
52. Szögyény to Aehrenthal, 25 April 1911, *OUA*, III, No. 2518.
53. Danilo left little doubt that his own personal sympathies were on the side of the Albanians. For Durham, who viewed all Montenegrin intentions with jaundiced eyes, Danilo's professions of peace, "when his stout cousin, Yanko, was actively engaged in supplying arms, keeping up the revolt, and preparing for war, and when a Montenegrin officer and several men had been wounded, were so impudent as to border on the sublime." Durham, *Struggle for Scutari*, p. 66.
54. Swire, *Albania*, p. 102; Durham, *Twenty Years of Balkan Tangle*, p. 217.
55. *LT*, 30 March 1911.
56. Barclay to Grey, 30 March 1911, *BD*, IX/1, No. 469.
57. Lucas-Shadwell to Grey, 31 March 1911, PRO, FO 371/1151/12660.
58. Moses to Secretary of State, 4 May 1911, NA, RG 59, State Decimal File 1910–1929, No. 867.00/336.
59. Szögyény to Aehrenthal, 25 April 1911, *OUA*, III, No. 2518.
60. Cartwright to Nicolson, 13 April 1911, *BD*, IX/1, No. 471. For an excellent summary of Montenegro's activities, see Risto J. Dragićević, "Malisorske bune 1910. i 1911. godine," *Z*, XIII, Knj. XXIV, No. 3 (1940):144–59; No. 4: 202–22; No. 5: 274–89. See also Dragan R. Živojinović, "Ustanak Malisora 1911. godine i američka pomoć Crnoj Gori," *IZ*, XX, Knj. XXIV, No. 2 (1967): 323–38.
61. Durham, *Twenty Years of Balkan Tangle*, p. 217.
62. Durham, *High Albania*, pp. 268–69.
63. Goschen to Grey, 8 September 1911, *BD*, IX/1, Nos. 520.
64. Cartwright to Nicolson, 13 April 1911, *BD*, IX/1, No. 471.
65. Italian text in HHStA, PA XIV/Albanien, Liasse XXXIV, Karton 35.

66. Swire, *Albania,* p. 104; Edward Thaden, *Russia and the Balkan Alliance of 1912* (University Park, Pa.: Pennsylvania State University Press, 1965), p. 30; Durham, *Struggle for Scutari,* p. 24.

67. Italian translation in appendix to a report from Scutari, 27 May 1911, HHStA, PA XIV/Albanien, Liasse XXXIV, Karton 35, No. 52.

68. Durham, *Struggle for Scutari,* p. 26; Swire, *Albania,* p. 104.

69. The Mirdites, the strongest of the Catholic Albanian tribes, could put as many as 10,000 men in the field in early June. They proclaimed their independence, established a provisional government, and attacked Turkish troops at Lezhë. *LT,* 5 and 6 June 1910; Durham, *Struggle for Scutari,* p. 43.

70. Skendi, *Albanian Awakening,* pp. 415–16.

71. *LT,* 14 June 1911.

72. Tewfik Pasha to Nicolson, 14 June 1911, *BD,* IX/1, No. 480; Conrad, *AMD,* II:162; Skendi, *Albanian Awakening,* p. 416; *LT,* 24 June 1911. Indeed, the Turkish minister in Cetinje said that if the rebels did not accept the terms of peace, they would be swept into Montenegro and prevented from returning to Albania. Moses to Secretary of State, 22 June 1911, NA, RG 59, State Decimal File, 1910–1929, No. 867.00/341. A report reached Conrad that simultaneously with their proclamation of amnesty, the Turks gave orders for an attack on the region of Pulati and Shala. Nopcsa to Conrad, 22 June 1911, *AMD,* II:163; *CV,* 8 June 1911 O.S.

73. *CV,* 16 June 1911 O.S. The motives behind Ismail Kemal Bey's trip are unclear. See Skendi, *Albanian Awakening,* pp. 416–17; Swire, *Albania,* pp. 105–6; Thaden, *Russia and the Balkan Alliance,* p. 36; *LT,* 26 June 1911.

74. Durham, *Struggle for Scutari,* pp. 54–57.

75. Skendi, *Albanian Awakening,* p. 419.

76. Ibid.; Thaden, *Russia and the Balkan Alliance,* p. 36; Swire, *Albania,* p. 109; *LT,* 17 and 18 July 1911.

77. Durham, *Struggle for Scutari,* pp. 63–64.

78. Swire, *Albania,* p. 107; *LT,* 31 March 1911. Cf. Moses to Secretary of State, 11 June 1911, NA, RG 59, State Decimal File 1910–1929, No. 867.00/339.

79. Skendi, *Albanian Awakening,* pp. 414–15; *NYT,* 25 May 1911, p. 6; Rifaat Pasha, the Turkish foreign minister, emphatically declared that Turkey had no intention whatsoever of attacking Montenegro. Lowther to Grey, 30 May 1911, *BD,* IX/1, No. 473; *NYT,* 30 May 1911, p. 3.

80. See Bax-Ironside to Grey, 1 June 1911, *BD,* IX/1, No. 474.

81. Skendi, *Albanian Awakening,* pp. 414–15; Neratov to Charykov, 23/10 May 1911, *MO,* XVIII/1, No. 27; Buchanan to Grey, 26 May 1911, *BD,* IX/1, No. 472; Moses to Secretary of State, 4 May 1911, NA, RG 59, State Decimal File 1910–1929, No. 867.00/336; Durham, *Struggle for Scutari,* p. 38. *CV,* 11, 18, 25 and 28 May, 1 June 1911 O.S.

82. Lucas-Shadwell to Grey, 23 February 1911, PRO, FO 371/1151/7475. In April, Nicholas announced his intention to postpone his projected visits "to sundry European capitals," notably Vienna and St. Petersburg. *LT,* 17 and 18 February, 20 April 1911.

83. Aehrenthal to Sofia and Cetinje, 26 April 1911, n. C., *OUA*, III, No. 2522. According to Durham, Montenegrin preparations continued unabated. In her diary she wrote: "Rifles are being distributed to all over eighteen, and everyone is agog. We are on complete war footing. Every man has orders to hold himself in readiness, with five days provisions and two pairs of opanke (raw-hide sandals), to start at any moment. Chetas are being raised from 100 to 150 men. Eight to ten chetas make a battalion. All work is at a standstill. Extraordinary state of nervous tension. Place crammed with staff officers." Durham, *Struggle for Scutari*, pp. 38–39.

84. Aehrenthal, caught between his responsibilities to the Albanians and Turks, deeply lamented the second Malissori uprising, yet he knew that Turkey's difficulties were largely of her own making. In 1910, he had repeatedly advised the Ottomans to be more conciliatory toward their Albanian subjects, but the Young Turks seemed determined to settle the delicate problem with a blunt sword. Aehrenthal to Müller, 10 March 1911, *OUA*, III, No. 2479.

85. Cartwright to Grey, 8 June 1911, *BD*, IX/1, No. 476. The article in the *Fremdenblatt* caused quite a stir in Berlin, where German officials, mindful of 1908, feared that Aehrenthal was once again asserting his independence to the detriment of German interests in Turkey. Cartwright cynically observed that "Germany is annoyed whenever she discovers that Count von Aehrenthal holds the opinion that the Balkan question touches Austria more closely than Germany and that therefore Balkan policy should be shaped in Vienna rather than in Berlin." Cartwright to Grey, 12 June 1911, No. 477. Aehrenthal himself summed up the situation this way: "Germany has her own policy in the Balkans and in Asia Minor. She pursues her economic interests and supports every Turkish government. Naturally since the annexation we have gone with Germany through thick and thin: in Constantinople and in Algeciras. But—it is clear that there is a certain limit. We cannot pursue a Turcophile policy at all cost—e.g., not in the Albanian question." Redlich, *Das politische Tagebuch*, I, 20 July 1911, p. 92; *LT*, 9, 10, and 12 June 1911.

86. Akers-Douglas to Grey, 17 June 1911, *BD*, IX/1, No. 482.

87. Cartwright to Grey, 14 June 1911, *BD*, IX/1, No. 478.

88. De Salis to Grey, 17 June 1911; Foreign Office notation, Akers-Douglas to Grey, 17 June 1911; O'Beirne to Grey, 18 June 1911; Akers-Douglas to Grey, 20 June 1911, *BD*, IX/1, Nos. 481, 482, 484, 488.

89. Grey to Russell, 21 June 1911, *BD*, IX/1, No. 489; Grey to de Salis, 26 June 1911, No. 498.

90. Grey to O'Beirne, 24 June 1911, *BD*, IX/1, No. 496.

91. O'Beirne to Grey, 23 June 1911, *BD*, IX/1, No. 493.

92. O'Beirne to Grey, 26 June 1911, *BD*, IX/1, No. 499.

93. Grey to de Salis, 26 June 1911, *BD*, IX/1, No. 489.

94. De Salis to Grey, 28 June 1911, *BD*, IX/1, No. 501.

95. Durham ridiculed the notion of Montenegrin relief: "But for the fund I raised the wretched refugees would have suffered yet more bitterly. Montenegro cared nothing for them. All she wanted was territory." Durham, *Twenty Years of Balkan Tangle*, pp. 218–19. A Montenegrin scholar, on

the other hand, contends that the Montenegrin people sincerely greeted the Albanian struggle, making voluntary contributions approximating four hundred thousand perpers to Albanian relief. Jovanović, *Stvaranje Crnogorske države*, p. 391. One of Durham's countrymen reported that "each Albanian is supposed to receive 20 kilos of maize a month from the Montenegrin Government, and though I am told that the distribution is not perfectly organized, there is no doubt that it suffices to keep all the refugees who apply for it from starvation." *LT*, 1 August 1911. The American minister, George Moses, corroborated this evaluation: "The Montenegrin peasants have displayed a remarkable generosity to their self-invited guests, sharing with them their scanty food and giving them shelter in the cabins. The Montenegrin Government, too, has organized relief work through a daily distribution of maize at Podgoritza at an expense of some 50,000 crowns per month—which amounts to nearly twenty per cent of the total revenue of the country in normal times. . . ." Even so, he suggested that conditions among the Albanians merited the "sympathy and assistance" of the American Red Cross. Moses to Secretary of State, 1 July 1911, NA, Reel 349-2, No. 873.48.

96. Giesl to Aehrenthal, 17 August 1911, *OUA*, III, No. 2592; Neratov to Nicholas II, 30/17 June 1911, *MO*, XVIII/1, No. 142.

97. Potapov to Zhilinsky, 16/3 June 1911, *MO*, XVIII/1, No. 108.

98. Neratov to Arseniev, 29/16 June 1911, in Neratov to Nicholas II, 30/17 June 1911, *MO*, XVIII/1, No. 142, pp. 156–57, n. 1. Arseniev to Neratov, 26/13 June 1911, No. 131. The Bank of Montenegro was certainly not in the same league with the Old Lady of Threadneedle Street. A British minister once described it as consisting of "a half empty safe in a one storied cottage." Beaumont to Grey, 16 November 1909, PRO, FO 371/694/42754.

99. Potapov to Zhilinsky, 2 July/19 June 1911, *MO*, XVIII/1, No. 150.

100. Durham, *Twenty Years of Balkan Tangle*, p. 218; Durham, *Struggle for Scutari*, p. 67. Turgut Pasha echoed Vukotić's confidence, claiming that his troops could capture Cetinje without difficulty. *LT*, 5 July 1911.

101. Paget to Grey, 2 August 1911, *BD*, IX/1, No. 514.

102. Charykov to Neratov, 14/1 July 1911, *MO*, XVIII/1, No. 198.

103. Charykov to Neratov, 21/8 July 1911, *MO*, XVIII/1, No. 234; Thurn to Aehrenthal, 4 August 1911, *OUA*, III, No. 2581.

104. Arseniev to Neratov, 26/13 July 1911, *MO*, XVIII/1, No. 251.

105. Giesl to Aehrenthal, 4 August 1911, *OUA*, III, No. 2580.

106. Arseniev to Neratov, 26/13 July 1911, *MO*, XVIII/1, No. 251; *LT*, 4 August 1911. For a list of concessions, see *LT*, 3 August 1911.

107. Durham: "Only last night weapons had been given out, and now—peace. . . . It was incredible, impossible. . . . Had a Turkish shell landed suddenly in the town, it could not have caused such astonishment." Durham, *Struggle for Scutari*, p. 72.

108. Durham, *Twenty Years of Balkan Tangle*, p. 219.

109. Swire, *Albania*, pp. 109–10; Durham, *Struggle for Scutari*, pp. 76–83.

110. Durham *Struggle for Scutari*, p. 82; Thaden, *Russia and the Balkan*

Alliance, p. 37; *NYT*, 4 August 1911, p. 4; *CV*, 23 and 27 July, 3 August 1911 O.S. Many of the Malissori tribesmen were reluctant to make peace. Initially only the Kastrati and the Shreti accepted the Turkish terms, while the Grudi and the Hoti refused them and the Klementi wavered. *LT*, 5 August 1911. In order to facilitate a positive decision on the part of some hesitant chiefs, the Montenegrin government withdrew all means of subsistence. *LT*, 12 August 1911. See also Moses to Secretary of State, 11 August 1911, NA, RG 59, State Decimal File 1910–1929, No. 767.00/346. The Mirdites, for their part, continued to demand the same concessions granted the Malissori. *LT*, 20 and 28 September 1911.

111. Note of the Chief of the General Staff, 18 July 1911, *OUA*, III, No. 2567. Cf. Conrad to Aehrenthal, 11 May 1911, *AMD*, II:160, and Aehrenthal to Conrad, 31 May 1911, *AMD*, II:161.

112. Note of Conrad, 17 March 1911, *OUA*, III, No. 2487.

113. Note of Conrad, 18 July 1911, *OUA*, III, No. 2567. Cf. Cartwright to Nicolson, 13 April 1911, *BD*, IX/1, No. 471.

114. Aehrenthal to Conrad, 21 July 1911, *OUA*, III, No. 2568.

115. Note of Conrad, 24 July 1911, *OUA*, III, No. 2571.

116. Aehrenthal to Conrad, 30 July 1911, *OUA*, III, No. 2574.

117. Aehrenthal to Thurn, 16 June 1911, *OUA*, III, No. 2545.

118. Redlich, *Das politische Tagebuch*, I, 20 July 1911, p. 92. See also Cartwright to Nicolson, 7 June 1911, *BD*, IX/1, No. 475; and "Die Wiederanknüpfung 'normaler' Beziehungen zwischen Russland und Österreich-Ungarn," *GP*, XXVII/2, CCXC, pp. 433–517.

119. Thaden, *Russia and the Balkan Alliance*, p. 37.

120. Giesl to Aehrenthal, 24 July 1911, *OUA*, II, No. 2569. While Danilo was in London representing Montenegro at the coronation of the new British king-emperor, Jovan Jovanović, a Montenegrin subject not a member of Danilo's official retinue, made a startling proposal to the British foreign office. In the name of the Montenegrin government, he proposed ceding the port town of Ulcinj and the Bay of Noce to Great Britain without compensation. Letter from Jovanović, 24 July 1911, PRO, FO 371/1151/35234. The foreign office apparently did not connect the Montenegrin offer with the summer crisis but conjectured that "the principal idea underlying the suggestion is that H. M. Gov[ernmen]t would develop the harbour of Noce and Dulcigno and would insist that one of those places or Antivari should become the Adriatic terminus of the proposed Trans-Balkanic or Trans-Servian railway." Foreign Office draft, 7 July 1911, 371/1151/35234. On 3 August, Sir Edward Grey formally declined the Montenegrin offer as "not one which H. M. Gov[ernmen]t could entertain." Langley to Jovanović, 3 August 1911, 371/1151/35234. Two weeks later, the Austro-Hungarian embassy in London learned of the Montenegrin proposal through the Rumanian minister. The legation counsel surmised that Grey had turned down the offer out of deference to Austria-Hungary. Trauttmansdorff to Aehrenthal, 17 August 1911, *OUA*, III, No. 2594. Apparently one of the last to hear about the Ulcinj/Noce deal was Count de Salis, the British minister in Cetinje, who caught wind of the project only in September—from the Bulgarian minister! De Salis to Grey, 2 Sep-

tember 1911, PRO, FO 371/1151/35234. There was a curious precedent for Montenegro's atypical territorial largesse. In May 1909, shortly after the end of the annexation crisis, Prime Minister Tomanović offered to give the United States the Bay of Noce and fifteen to twenty square miles of adjacent territory for use as a naval station. Then in June 1911, even before the Montenegrin representations in London, Nicholas made a similar offer to George Moses, the American minister to Greece and Montenegro, urging the United States to accept Ulcinj as a naval station. See Challener, "Montenegro and the United States," and Bogdan Popović, "Jedna ponuda Kralja Nikole Amerikancima," *Prilozi za književnost, jezik, istoriju i folklor,* I/2 (1960): 110–18. Obviously, Nicholas was seeking to have relatively disinterested countries (the more disinterested the better) occupy a portion of the Montenegrin littoral in order to deter more predatory Powers from intervening in Montenegrin affairs. Needless to say, Austria was not offered a piece of Montenegrin real estate.

121. In February, the long-awaited Austro-Montenegrin trade treaty had been signed. At the height of the Malissori crisis in July, the Montenegrin press noted with considerable interest the submission of the agreement to the Hungarian parliament for approval. *CV,* 22 June and 2 July 1911 O.S.

122. Giesl to Aehrenthal, 4 August 1911, *OUA,* III, No. 2580. In mentioning the year 1702, the king was referring to the so-called Montenegrin Vespers discussed in chapter 1.

123. Ibid.

124. Giesl to Aehrenthal, 17 August 1911, *OUA,* III, No. 2592.

125. De Salis to Grey, 24 August 1911, PRO, FO 371/1151/33996.

126. Gregović, like his predecessor, accused Austria-Hungary of building fortifications on contested territory (see chapter 4).

127. Notes on a conversation with Gregović on 18 September 1911, undated, *OUA,* III, No. 2635. Aehrenthal was a conscious participant in the Montenegrin double game and even tried to make Nicholas a pawn in a game of his own. The foreign minister told Redlich: "King Nicholas takes money from both Russia and Turkey. We've only repaired his yacht for him—but he's useful to us." Redlich, *Das politische Tagebuch,* I, 7 August 1911, p. 97.

CHAPTER SIX

1. The best specialized treatment of the Turco-Italian War is William C. Askew's *Europe and Italy's Acquisition of Libya, 1911–1912* (Durham, N.C.: Duke University Press, 1942). The best general treatment is in Albertini, *Origins of the War.* For an excellent account of the diplomatic negotiations and agreements by which Italy secured recognition of her rights in Tripoli before the war, see Fellner, *Dreibund.* See also John D. Treadway, "Tem-

perate Coercion: Aehrenthal's Balkan Diplomacy at the Outbreak of the Turco-Italian War," *Essays in History,* XVIII (1974): 5–32; Dimitrije Djordjević, "Italijansko-turski rat 1911–1912. godine i njegov uticaj na Balkanu," *Istoriski Pregled,* I, No. 4 (1954): 46–54.

2. Directive from Aehrenthal to Constantinople, Rome, and Berlin, 31 July 1911, *OUA,* III, No. 2576.

3. Giolitti, on the other hand, listed the "Austrian" rather than the "Balkan" problem among his reasons for moving against Tripoli. In his memoirs, the Italian prime minister stated that when he learned that Aehrenthal had expressed displeasure concerning Italy's position in Tripoli (sometime after the onset of the Morocco Crisis of 1911), he decided to force the question. Giovanni Giolitti, *Memoirs of My Life,* trans. Edward Storer (London: Chapman and Dodd, 1923), p. 275.

4. Aehrenthal to Flotow, 27 September 1911, *OUA,* III, No. 2655. Before the outbreak of hostilities, Italy had requested an early renewal of the Triple Alliance with Germany and Austria-Hungary. Renewal negotiations continued off and on for the duration of the Turco-Italian war. Fellner, *Dreibund,* pp. 74–83.

5. Morley was referring to the German gunboat, *Panther,* whose anchorage at Agadir, Morocco, provoked a major diplomatic crisis in the summer of 1911. See, for example, Albertini, *Origins of the War,* pp. 327–40; Oswald Henry Wedel, *Austro-German Diplomatic Relations, 1908–1914* (Stanford: Stanford University Press, 1932), pp. 125–35.

6. Foreword to Vol. IX, *BD,* p. vii.

7. Ugron to Aehrenthal, 21 and 26 September 1911, *OUA,* II, Nos. 2641, 2650; Szilassy to Aehrenthal, 26 September 1911, No. 2649.

8. Some remarks of the Serbian prime minister indicate the tenuous nature of peace in the Balkans and the land hunger of the Balkan states: "We are prepared to fight either at the side of Austria and others to get Turkish territory or by the side of Turkey and others against Austria." Paget to Grey, 28 September 1911, *BD,* IX/1, No. 249.

9. Telegram from Aehrenthal to London, Berlin, St. Petersburg, Paris, Rome, Constantinople, and Bucharest, 29 September 1911, *OUA,* III, No. 2666.

10. Telegram from Aehrenthal to Balkan capitals, 29 September 1911, *OUA,* III, No. 2673.

11. Ugron to Aehrenthal, 28 September 1911, *OUA,* III, No. 2661. Milovanović made similar remarks to the British and Russian envoys, but at the same time insisted that Austria intended to foment trouble in the Balkans. Paget to Grey, 28 September 1911, *BD,* IX/1, No. 249; Hartwig to Neratov, 1 October 1911, *IB,* I/2, No. 506.

12. Ugron to Aehrenthal, 28 September 1911, *OUA,* III, No. 2661.

13. Telegram from Aehrenthal to Constantinople and Bucharest, 15 October 1911, *OUA,* III, No. 2763; Askew, *Europe and Libya,* pp. 74–75.

14. Aehrenthal to Ugron, 15 October 1911, *OUA,* III, No. 2759.

15. Ibid.

16. Telegram from Aehrenthal to Constantinople and Bucharest, 15 October 1911, *OUA,* III, No. 2763.

17. Like Conrad, who also wrote about Serbia in disparaging terms, Gellinek was no friend of Serbia.

18. Gellinek to Conrad, 6 November 1911, *OUA*, III, No. 2849. Serbia voiced fears regarding a possible reoccupation of the Sandžak immediately after the Italian declaration of war. See Hartwig to Neratov, 2 October 1911, *IB*, I/2, No. 514.

19. Paget to Grey, 19 October 1911, *BD*, IX/1, No. 522; Cartwright to Grey, 13 October 1911, PRO, FO 371/1048/163.

20. Aehrenthal wrote Ugron that the rumors contained "not a single true word." Directive from Aehrenthal to Cetinje, 25 October 1911, *OUA*, III, No. 2823. In reference to the Serbian "phantasy," Gellinek observed that "Serbian desires reflect themselves in Serbian fears." Gellinek to Conrad, 6 November 1911, No. 2849.

21. Ugron to Aehrenthal, 12 and 14 November 1911, *OUA*, III, Nos. 2911, 2921; Gellinek to Conrad, 15 and 22 November 1911, Nos. 2928, 2929, 2966.

22. Giesl to Aehrenthal, 1 November 1911, *OUA*, III, Nos. 2857; Ugron to Aehrenthal, 4 October 1911, No. 2701; Neratov to Obnorski, 2 October 1911, *IB*, I/2, No. 508; Giolitti, *Memoirs*, p. 282.

23. Ugron to Aehrenthal, 4 October 1911, *OUA*, III, No. 2701; Giesl to Aehrenthal, 5 October 1911, No. 2707.

24. Giesl to Aehrenthal, 17 October 1911, *OUA*, III, No. 2774. Unknown to either Giesl or Aehrenthal was the fact that only a few days before, Nicholas had informed the Russian chargé that Montenegro would march into the Sandžak within a week, a step certainly not in keeping with Aehrenthal's wishes. Needless to say, Nicholas did not follow through with his threat. Obnorsky to Neratov, 14 October 1911, *IB*, I/2, No. 626.

25. See, for example, Hartwig to Neratov, 8 and 22 October 1911, *IB*, I/2, Nos. 562, 697.

26. Giesl to Aehrenthal, 17 October 1911, *OUA*, III, No. 2774. In mid-October, Nicholas made a tiring trip through parts of western Montenegro near the Austrian border. In the vicinity of Krivošije he spoke of Emperor Francis Joseph in unusually warm terms, fueling speculation about a new pro-Austrian tack. About the same time, the king pursued a question he had raised earlier with Giesl concerning the possibility of Serb judges from the Dual Monarchy assisting in the reform of Montenegrin judicial institutions. Though Aehrenthal approved the idea and went so far as to name three judges, the Montenegrin prime minister intervened with Nicholas, arguing that Montenegro should have some say in the naming of the jurists. Much to Giesl's chagrin, the project was temporarily shelved, only to be dusted off the following year. Rakočević, unpublished manuscript on relations between Austria-Hungary and Montenegro, 1904–1914, pp. 123–24; *CV*, 8 October 1911 O.S.

27. Directive from Aehrenthal to Cetinje, 25 October 1911, *OUA*, III, No. 2823.

28. Giesl to Aehrenthal, 1 November 1911, *OUA*, III, No. 2857.

29. Emphasis mine. Giesl to Aehrenthal, 1 November 1911, *OUA*, III, No. 2857.

30. Ibid.

31. Aehrenthal to Giesl, 11 November 1911, *OUA*, III, No. 2903; Thaden, "Montenegro," pp. 119–20.

32. De Salis to Grey, 10 December 1911, PRO, FO 371/1151/50560; HHStA, PA XVII/Montenegro, Liasse XI-Montenegrinische Anleihe, 1911–1920, Karton 48, esp. Giesl to Aehrenthal, 9 November 1911, No. 58, and Rudolf Sieghart to Aehrenthal, 11 November 1911. The agreement was signed 8/9 December 1911.

33. See also Pallavicini to Aehrenthal, 21 November 1911, *OUA*, III, No. 2961; Aehrenthal to Weinzetl, 25 November 1911, No. 2984. While discounting official Italian involvement in any disruption of the status quo, San Giuliano explained that he could not be held responsible for the actions of all Italian journalists, priests, teachers, businessmen, workers, etc., in the Balkans, some of whom were driven by "political fanaticism." Mérey to Aehrenthal, 9 December 1911, No. 3082.

34. Aehrenthal to Weinzetl, 25 November 1911, *OUA*, III, No. 2984.

35. Actually, Nicholas's project did not require much original thinking. Its main elements had been the subject of earlier negotiations between the Montenegrins and the Turks. The Velika region, whose *S*-shaped frontier had been demarcated at the time of the Congress of Berlin, had long been a source of "endless frontier incidents and commissions." Of particular importance were the heights of Čakor and Jezerski Vrh. At the time of the annexation crisis, a brief rapprochement between the two countries resulted in a mixed boundary commission formulating a settlement based on an exchange of territory. The Montenegrins ratified the agreement, but the Turks did not. In 1911, in the wake of the Malissori "settlement," the two sides tried again. The result was that the boundary commission was dissolved. For a short history of the Turco-Montenegrin border disputes, see de Salis, "Montenegro: Annual Report, 1911," PRO, FO 371/1398/424. For a longer discussion, especially on conditions after the annexation crisis, see Novica Rakočević, "Stanje na crnogorsko-turskoj granici uoči balkanskog rata (1908–1912)," *IZ*, XV, Knj. XIX, Nos. 3–4 (1962): 485–515.

36. Aehrenthal to Berlin, 22 December 1911, *OUA*, III, No. 3154; Pallavicini to Aehrenthal, 20 December 1911, No. 3145.

37. Aehrenthal to Weinzetl, 20 December 1911, *OUA*, III, No. 3143.

38. Szögyény to Aehrenthal, 22 December 1911, *OUA*, III, No. 3155.

39. Aehrenthal to Berlin, 22 December 1911, *OUA*, III, No. 3157; Lucas-Shadwell to Grey, 16 January 1912, PRO, FO 371/1398/2973.

40. Aehrenthal to Pallavicini, 22 December 1911, *OUA*, III, No. 3157; Directive to Berlin, 27 December 1911, No. 3166.

41. Weinzetl to Aehrenthal, 29 December 1911, *OUA*, III, No. 3176.

42. Lucas-Shadwell to Grey, 16 January 1912, PRO, FO 371/1398/3973.

43. See de Salis to Grey, 15 November 1911, PRO, FO 371/1151/46323.

44. In January, Montenegro scored an additional ecclesiastical triumph, ending a long dispute with Rome. The Holy See agreed to appoint a

Montenegrin, Nikola Dobrečić, parish priest of Cetinje, as the new archbishop of Bar, traditionally a post filled by an Austrian Croat. Indeed, upon the death of the last archbishop, the Vatican, in accordance with the concordat of 1886, had appointed another Austrian subject. The Montenegrin government, however, refused to recognize either him or his interim surrogate, an Italian Franciscan monk, Giovanni di Salvo. After a two-year deadlock, the Vatican agreed to appoint Dobrečić archbishop, while Cetinje agreed in turn to accept the Italian as ecclesiastical administrator. Founded by Pope Alexander III in the twelfth century, the archbishopric of Bar was revived when the town of Bar was transferred to Montenegrin sovereignty following the Congress of Berlin. The archbishop of Bar still nominally was Primate of Serbia (Primas Serbiae), a point that irritated Belgrade. Lucas-Shadwell to Grey, 20 January 1912, PRO, FO 371/1398/3304; *CV*, 4 and 8 February 1912 O.S. For an excellent discussion of Montenegro's relations with the Vatican, see de Salis, "Montenegro: Annual Report, 1911," PRO, FO 371/1398/424, pp. 6–7, and "Montenegro: Annual Report, 1912," 371/1681/424, p. 11. See also Dragoje Živković, "Konflikt izmedju Crne Gore i Vatikana oko ustoličenja privremenog nasljednika barskog biskupa Milinovića," *Glasnik Cetinjskih Muzeja*, II (1969): 183–97. Durham reported that Nicephor had been dismissed for "drunkenness and other inappropriate conduct." Durham, *Twenty Years of Balkan Tangle*, p. 221.

45. The foreign office rightly noted that this represented an "exaggerated view of the state of popular feeling in Montenegro towards Servia." "One has the impression that more animosity is felt in official and Court circles than among the populace." Lucas-Shadwell to Grey, 6 January 1912, PRO, FO 371/1398/1; de Salis to Grey, 23 December 1911, 371/1398/20; Lucas-Shadwell to Grey, 6 January 1912, 371/1398/1796; Weinzetl to Aehrenthal, 26 December 1911, *OUA*, III, No. 3164.

46. Lucas-Shadwell to Grey, 9 January 1912, PRO, FO 371/1296/1852.

47. See, for example, Albertini, "Conrad's Plans for War against Italy and His Dismissal," *Origins of the War*, I:349–52; Conrad, *AMD*, II: 15, 282, 448–50; Foreign Office minutes for Eardley-Russell to Russell, 27 December 1911, PRO, FO 371/1048/51616.

48. Eardley-Russell to Cartwright, 3 December 1911, PRO, FO 371/1048/48615.

49. Giesl to Aehrenthal, 25 January 1912, *OUA*, III, No. 3247.

50. Thurn to Aehrenthal, 1 February 1912, *OUA*, III, No. 3263; Mensdorff to Aehrenthal, 2 February 1912, No. 3265.

51. The original timetable was disrupted by an Adriatic storm. Lucas-Shadwell to Grey, 28 January 1912, PRO, FO 371/1398/4039; *CV*, 21 January 1912 O.S.

52. Giesl feared that Nicholas had other reasons in mind. The king had told him that he believed Bulgaria would be a hotbed of trouble come spring. Of course the monarch wanted to be back in his own capital by the time the winter snows began to melt. Giesl to Aehrenthal, 25 January 1912, *OUA*, III, No. 3247; *CV*, 21 January 1912 O.S.

53. Ibid.

54. Lucas-Shadwell to Grey, 30 January 1912, PRO, FO 371/1398/5102.
55. Ibid.
56. Lucas-Shadwell to Grey, 3 February 1912, PRO, FO 371/1398/4943. Upon reaching Kotor, the king sent a warm telegram to Francis Joseph. *LT,* 31 January 1912, p. 5.
57. Report from Berlin, 22 February 1912, *OUA,* IV, No. 3312. Cf. *CV,* 1, 4 and 8 February 1912 O.S. St. Petersburg promised Nicholas financial assistance in constructing a rail line between Virpazar and Cetinje.
58. *LT,* 13 February 1912, p. 5.
59. De Salis to Grey, 29 February 1912, PRO, FO 371/1398/10992. On the other hand, it was reported that the Russians offered to help construct a railway from Bar to Cetinje. De Salis, "Montenegro: Annual Report, 1912," 371/1681/424, pp. 1–2; Buchanan to Grey, 24 February 1912, *BD,* IX/1, No. 553.
60. De Salis, "Montenegro: Annual Report, 1912," PRO, FO 371/1681/424.
61. Miller to Sazonov, 15/2 February 1912, *MO,* XIX/2, No. 477; Sazonov to Miller, 20/7 February 1912, No. 500.
62. Miller to Sazonov, 1 March/17 February 1912, *MO,* XIX/2, No. 574, p. 222, n. 1; *GC,* 25 February 1912 O.S. Cf. *Reichsgesetzblatt für die im Reichsrate vertretenen Königreiche und Länder,* Vienna, 10 March 1912.
63. *CV,* 8 February 1912 O.S. Nicholas told Giesl that he did not want to impose himself on Vienna at the time of Aehrenthal's death and therefore did not stop in the city on his return from Russia.
64. Solomon Wank, "The Appointment of Count Berchtold as Austro-Hungarian Foreign Minister," *Journal of Central European Affairs,* XXIII (July 1962): 143–51; Buchanan to Grey, 24 January 1912, PRO, FO 371/1296/3887.
65. Alexander von Musulin, *Das Haus am Ballplatz: Erinnerungen eines österreichisch-ungarischen Diplomaten* (Munich: Verlag für Kulturpolitik, 1924), pp. 177–78; Hugo Hantsch, *Leopold Graf Berchtold: Grandseigneur und Staatsmann,* 2 vols. (Graz and Cologne: Styria Verlag, 1963).
66. Heinrich Kanner, *Kaiserliche Katastrophenpolitik* (Vienna: 1922), p. 89.
67. See Robert A. Kann, "Erzherzog Franz Ferdinand und Graf Berchtold als Aussenminister, 1912–1914," *Mitteilungen des österreichischen Staatsarchivs,* XXII (1969): 246–78.
68. Pallavicini to Berchtold, 12 March 1912, *OUA,* IV, No. 3369.
69. Report on Berchtold's conversations with Emperor William held on 23 March, 24 March 1912, *OUA,* IV, No. 3394.
70. Berlin to Berchtold, 1 April 1912, *OUA,* IV, No. 3407.
71. Durham, *Twenty Years of Balkan Tangle,* p. 225.
72. Ibid., p. 227.
73. De Salis to Grey, 26 March 1912, PRO, FO 371/1398/13758; *CV,* 7, 10 and 14 March 1912 O.S.
74. De Salis, "Montenegro: Annual Report, 1912," PRO, FO 371/

1681/424, p. 10; Warren, *Montenegro*, p. 19. The alleged treaty was again printed by Serbian newspapers during the First World War.

75. Berchtold to Belgrade, 15 May 1912, *OUA*, IV, No. 3522; Giesl, *Zwei Jahrzehnte*, p. 227.

76. Fürstenberg to Berchtold, 21 May 1912, *OUA*, IV, No. 3531.

77. Originally the king had insisted on taking a number of Montenegrin officials who were either former Austrian subjects or personae non gratae, Tomanović among them. In the end, the Austrians and the Montenegrins agreed upon the following entourage: Foreign Minister Gregović, War Minister Martinović, Court Marshal Ramadanović, and the king's physician and his adjutant. Of these, only Martinović and the adjutant qualified as "genuine" Montenegrins, but the Austro-Hungarian government voiced no objections to the inclusion of the others. Giesl, *Zwei Jahrzehnte*, p. 228; *CV*, 23 and 26 May 1912 O.S.

78. Giesl, *Zwei Jahrzehnte*, p. 228; *CV*, 30 May 1912 O.S.

79. Cartwright to Grey, 12 June 1912, PRO, FO 371/1398/25124; Second report on a visit by the Italian ambassador, 11 June 1912, *OUA*, IV, No. 3563.

80. De Salis to Grey, 20 June 1912, PRO, FO 371/1398/27085. See also *CV*, 2 and 6 June 1912, O.S. In the summer of 1912, a travelling wares museum organized by the Hungarian commerce ministry visited Cetinje. Though the organizers were unhappy with the commercial results of the visit, the exhibit was well attended. De Salis, "Montenegro: Annual Report, 1912," PRO, FO 371/1681/424, p. 18.

81. Giesl, *Zwei Jahrzehnte*, p. 227.

82. De Salis to Grey, 20 June 1912, PRO, FO 371/1398/27085. See also *CV*, 6 and 9 June 1912 O.S.

83. Actually, it appeared that the Turks were trying not to antagonize the Albanians. Giers to Sazonov, 8 July/25 June 1912, *MO*, XX/1, No. 279; Marling to Grey, 8 August 1912, PRO, FO 371/1398/34844. Indeed, Ali Riz Bey, the Muslim Albanian head of the boundary commission, who had just finished a tour of the region trying to win approval for the protocol, reported that the Albanians of Kosovo had concluded a *besa* that not an inch of Albanian soil should be forfeited, especially to Montenegro. Giesl to Berchtold, 1 October 1912, *OUA*, IV, No. 3895.

84. Obnorsky to Neratov, 18/5 July 1912, *MO*, XX/1, No. 328; De Salis to Grey, 18 July 1912, PRO, FO 371/1398/31327; Pallavicini to Berchtold, 25 July 1912, *OUA*, IV, No. 3649; *NYT*, 19 July 1912, p. 1.

85. Potapov to Zhilinsky, 28/15 June 1912, cited in 14/1 May 1912, *MO*, XX/1, No. 3, p.3, n. 1.

86. Weinzetl to Berchtold, 3 August 1912, *OUA*, IV, No. 3666.

87. Whitehall noted in a minute: "It is fortunate that Rustem Bey was disavowed, and the notes he wrote lend colour to Miss Durham's assertion that he suffers from morphinomania." De Salis to Grey, 9 August 1912, *BD*, IX/1, No. 604. See also Obnorsky to Neratov, 3 August/21 July 1912, *MO*, XX/1, No. 406; *LT*, 8 August 1912, p. 5; 9 August 1912, p. 3; *CV*, 25 and 28/July 1912 O.S.

88. Weinzetl to Berchtold, 10 August 1912, *OUA*, IV, No. 3677.

89. See *LT* for month of August; *CV,* 1 and 4 August 1912 O.S.
90. Marling to Grey, 19 August 1912, *BD,* IX/1, No. 631.
91. Grey to de Salis, 20 August 1912, *BD,* IX/1, No. 637; Grey to Marling, 20 August 1912, No. 638.
92. Goschen to Grey, 23 August 1912, *BD,* IX/1, No. 650.
93. De Salis to Grey, 24 August 1912, *BD,* IX/1, No. 651; *NYT,* 27 August 1912, p. 3.
94. *LT,* 28 August 1912, p. 3.
95. Marling to Grey, 26 August 1912, *BD,* IX/1, No. 653.
96. *CV,* 18 and 22 August 1912 O.S. See de Salis, "Montenegro: Annual Report, 1912," PRO, FO 371/1681/424, p. 9.
97. Ibid., p. 3; Tarnowski to Berchtold, 29 August 1912, *OUA,* IV, No. 3745; Eckardt to foreign office, *GP,* XXXIII, No. 12107. For details concerning Kolushev's journey, see Andrew Rossos, *Russia and the Balkans: Inter-Balkan Rivalries and Russian Foreign Policy, 1908–1914* (Toronto: University of Toronto Press, 1981), p. 58.
98. Giesl, *Zwei Jahrzehnte,* p. 229; *CV,* 14 August 1912 O.S.
99. Durham, *Twenty Years of Balkan Tangle,* p. 223.
100. For a full discussion of the origins of the Balkan alliance, see Helmreich, *Diplomacy of the Balkan Wars;* Thaden, *Russia and the Balkan Alliance;* and Otto Bickel, *Russland und die Entstehung des Balkanbundes 1912: Ein Beitrag zur Vorgeschichte des Weltkrieges* (Königsberg and Berlin: Osteuropa-Verlag, 1933); Branko Perović, et al., *Prvi balkanski rat, 1912-1913* (Belgrade: Vojnoistorijski institut, 1959–75), Vol. 1, Branko Perović, et al., *Operacije Srpske vojske,* pp. 84–132; and Rossos, *Russia and the Balkans,* pp. 8–69.
101. De Salis to Grey, 15 November 1911, PRO, FO 371/1151/46323; *CV,* 25 October 1911 O.S.
102. Cleanthes Nicolaides, *Griechenlands Anteil an den Balkankriegen, 1912–13* (Vienna, 1914), p. 260; Helmreich, *Diplomacy of the Balkan Wars,* p. 83. On the evolution of the Bulgaro-Montenegrin agreement, see Mihailo Vojvodić, "Bugarsko-Crnogorski pregovori i sporazum 1912. godine," Belgrade University *Zbornik filozofskog fakulteta,* VIII (1964): 741–51; Rossos, *Russia and the Balkans,* pp. 56–59.
103. De Salis, "Montenegro: Annual Report, 1911," PRO, FO 371/1398/424, p. 6.
104. Durham, *Twenty Years of Balkan Tangle,* pp. 222–23.
105. Sazonov to Nekliudov, 23/10 May 1912, *MO,* XX/1, No. 64.
106. Thaden, *Russia and the Balkan Alliance,* p. 103. See also Vujović, "Francuski dokumenti o Crnogorsko-bugarskim odnosima," pp. 358–60.
107. One Bulgarian source puts the subsidy at 35,000 leva daily, another at 750,000 leva monthly over a four month period. Tarnowski reported to Berchtold that Montenegro was receiving 30,000 francs daily from Sofia. Thaden gave the figure as 700,000 francs for the duration of the war. Potapov wrote St. Petersburg that Bulgaria pledged to pay 70,000 (crowns?) every month of the war. A. Toshev, *Balkanskite voini,* 2 vols. (Sofia, 1929–31), I:361; B. D. Kesiakov, *Prinos kŭm diplomaticheskata istoriia na Bŭlgariia,* 4 vols. (Sofia, 1925–35), I:45; Tarnowski to Berchtold, 1 Oc-

tober 1912, *OUA*, IV, No. 3906; Thaden, *Russia and the Balkan Alliance*, p. 106; Helmreich, *Diplomacy of the Balkan Wars*, p. 87.

108. Helmreich, *Diplomacy of the Balkan Wars*, p. 89.

109. Perović, *Prvi balkanski rat (Operacije Srpske vojske)*, pp. 128–31; Rossos, *Russia and the Balkans*, pp. 62–63; Ernst C. Helmreich, "The Serbian-Montenegrin Alliance of September 23/October 6, 1912," *Journal of Central European Affairs*, XIX (January 1960):411–15.

110. Poincaré to Paul Cambon, 15 October 1912, *Documents diplomatiques français, 1871–1914* (hereafter cited as *DDF*), ed. Commission de publication des documents relatifs aux origines de la guerre de 1914, 2d and 3d series (Paris: Alfred Costes, 1929–59), 3d. series, IV, No. 170; quoted in Helmreich, *Diplomacy of the Balkan Wars*, p. 147.

111. Giesl, *Zwei Jahrzehnte*, p. 230.

112. Italy was merely a stopover on the way to France. Giesl speculated that Danilo had traveled to Paris to plead with Grand Duke Nicholas, who was there as a military observer, for at least the moral support of the tsar. Rumors abounded that the visit also had a pecuniary significance. Giesl to Berchtold, 17 September and 2 October 1912, *OUA*, IV, Nos. 3798, 3915. In October, Izvolsky recounted a story that Danilo had attempted to secure a loan of ten million crowns from a Paris banking house. Having failed in his attempt to raise the money through conventional channels, he approached the bank again, this time informing its officials that a Balkan war was inevitable and that he was prepared to tell them the exact date set for Montenegro's declaration of war fully three days before the outbreak of hostilities. Szécsen to Berchtold, 12 October 1912, No. 4058. Izvolsky could not vouch for the validity of this account, but a story in the *Libre Parole* of 9 November lent credence to it, naming the Viennese bank of Reitzes as the principal institution of payment via its branch in Paris. Szécsen to Berchtold, 9 November 1912, No. 4340. Sazonov, who did not hold a particularly high opinion of Danilo's moral character, told Thurn, the Austro-Hungarian ambassador, that he had heard that the crown prince had deposited upwards of twelve million crowns in foreign banks—which, he concluded, obviously must have been taken from the coffers of his impoverished land. Thurn to Berchtold, 12 December 1912, V, No. 4889. See also Giesl, *Zwei Jahrzehnte*, p. 230. In Helmreich's words, "There is some proof of having the pudding in eating it, and there never were any evidences of superfluous wealth in Cetinje." Moreover, Helmreich's attempts to ascertain irregular Montenegrin dealings with the firm of Reitzes proved fruitless. Helmreich, *Diplomacy of the Balkan Wars*, pp. 141–45.

113. Berchtold's circular note, 13 August 1912, *OUA*, IV, No. 3687; "Count Berchtold's Initiative, August-October 1912," *BD*, IX/1, Ch. LXXVII; Skendi, *Albanian Awakening*, pp. 434–37, 447; Swire, *Albania*, pp. 119–25.

114. Skendi, *Albanian Awakening*, pp. 449–50.

115. See Durham, *Twenty Years of Balkan Tangle*, pp. 225–27.

116. Pallavicini to Berchtold, 23 September 1912, *OUA*, IV, No. 3832.

117. Circular telegrams, 28 and 30 September 1912, *OUA*, IV, Nos. 3868, 3882.

118. Giesl to Berchtold, 1 October 1912, *OUA*, IV, No. 3894; circular telegram, 30 September 1912, No. 3882; *CV*, 19 September 1912 O.S. As many preparations had already been made, Giesl estimated that the army would be ready for action within a period of forty-eight hours. Giesl, *Zwei Jahrzehnte*, p. 230. Durham held slightly different opinions: "Montenegro had been preparing over a year, and could have begun in July." Durham, *Twenty Years of Balkan Tangle*, p. 228. The *Times* had this to say: "Mobilization in Montenegro consists of doling out cartridges from the magazines, for every man has always with him his rifle and equipment. It has always been supposed that the whole available fighting strength of the country could be collected in six days. . . ." *LT*, 9 October 1912, p. 6.

119. It is interesting to note that when mobilization was ordered on 1 October, the Montenegrins had not yet concluded their military convention with Serbia, or Bulgaria hers with Greece. The countries acted on instinct. The Serbo-Montenegrin agreement was signed only on 6 October, two days before Montenegro's declaration of war. See Helmreich, "Serbian-Montenegrin Alliance;" Rossos, *Russia and the Balkans*, pp. 68–69.

120. Schemua to Francis Joseph, 28 September 1912, *OUA*, IV, No. 3869.

121. Circular telegram, 30 September 1912, *OUA*, IV, No. 3875. Regrettably, the Russians used precisely this time to conduct a trial mobilization of their own (order issued 26 August) in several military districts, including some along Austria-Hungary's border. The Russian government assured the other Powers that the maneuvers had nothing to do with the crisis in the Balkans. Szilassy to Berchtold, 1 October 1912, Nos. 3901–2.

122. Pallavicini to Berchtold, 1 October 1912, *OUA*, IV, No. 3897.

123. Report on a visit by the Russian ambassador, 1 October 1912, *OUA*, IV, No. 3900.

124. Ambrózy to Berchtold, 1 and 2 October 1912, *OUA*, IV, Nos. 3899, 3924. Durham seems to have shared San Giuliano's estimate. Durham, *Twenty Years of Balkan Tangle*, p. 231.

125. Berchtold to Flotow, 2 October 1912, *OUA*, IV, No. 3912.

126. Giesl to Berchtold, 1 October 1912, *OUA*, IV, No. 3895.

127. Giesl, *Zwei Jahrzehnte*, p. 230.

128. Durham, *Twenty Years of Balkan Tangle*, p. 230.

129. In Durham's caustic words, "though [Russia] was no longer supporting Nikola, [she] was actively training young Montenegrins as cannon-fodder." Durham, ibid., p. 229.

130. Ibid.

131. Telegram to Balkan capitals, 7 October 1912, *OUA*, IV, No. 3990; Circular telegram, 7 October 1912, No. 3973; Giesl to Berchtold, 8 October 1912, No. 3997; Giers to Neratov, 8 October/25 September 1912, *MO*, XX/2, No. 951, p. 400, n. 3; *CV*, 26 September 1912 O.S.

132. Lowther to Grey, 8 October 1912, *BD*, IX/2, No. 1.

133. *LT*, 9 October 1912, p. 6; *CV*, 26 September 1912 O.S.

134. Giesl, *Zwei Jahrzehnte*, p. 230. Durham, on the other hand, thought Montenegro's unilateral action to be a manifestation of illusions of grandeur: "They began purposely before their allies, and, I believe, without

informing them; for they believed themselves invincible, and meant to sweep up all Kosovo vilayet before the Serbs were ready. Of the Serbs they had no opinion at all. When I asked, 'What is the Servian army worth?' 'They are a lot of swineherds,' was the invariable reply." It augured ill for Serbo-Montenegrin cooperation in the days ahead. Durham, *Struggle for Scutari*, p. 183. See also de Salis to Grey, 9 October 1912, PRO, FO 42392/ 33672/12/44, cited in Lowther to Grey, 8 October 1912, *BD*, IX/2, No. 1.
    135. *CV*, 28 September 1912 O.S.

CHAPTER SEVEN

1. For overviews of Montenegro's military operations during the Balkan wars, see Perović et al, *Prvi balkanski rat, 1912–1913;* Vol. 1, Perović, *Operacije srpske vojske;* Vol. 2, Borislav Ratković, *Operacije Srpske vojske;* and esp. Vol. 3, Mitar Djurišić, *Operacije Crnogorske vojske*. See also Božidar-Božo S. Vuković, *Rat Crne Gore protiv Turske i Bugarske 1912–1913 i rad Crne Gore na uniji i saradnji sa Srbijom* (Cetinje: Obod, 1971); Pavle Milošević, "Operacije Istočnog odreda crnogorske vojske u Sandžaku, Gornjem Polimlju i Metohiji 1912. godine," *IZ*, XXV, Knj. XXX, Nos. 3–4 (1972):279–382. For particulars concerning the siege of Scutari, see Živko Pavlović's classic study, *Opsada Skadra 1912–1913* (Belgrade, 1926), and Jovan Ćetković's *Borbe oko Skadra 1912–1913* (Belgrade: Prosveta, 1954). For a Serbian viewpoint, see Vojin Maksimović, *Rat Srbije sa Turskom* 1912–1913 (Belgrade, 1922).

2. "The Montenegrins showed once and for all that their idea of fighting was that of their medieval ballads: Let us charge! They rushed like a pack of wolves, howling war-cries, and had no notion of how to take cover or spread. It was this which brought about Montenegro's high death-roll." Durham, *Struggle for Scutari*, p. 193. See also *LT*, 12 October 1912, p. 6; 17 October 1912, p. 6; De Salis, "Montenegro: Annual Report, 1912," PRO, FO 371/2041/424, p. 20. Hospital wards were set up in the building of the cadet corps and in the main barracks, the Vojni Stan. *CV*, 12 and 24 October 1912 O.S.

3. *LT*, 28 October 1912; *Fremdenblatt*, 15 November 1912; Memorandum on the conference in the Austro-Hungarian foreign ministry, undated (between 25 and 30 October 1912), *OUA*, IV, No. 4170; Berchtold to Mérey, 17 November 1912, No. 4469. See also the reference to Helmreich's 1930 conversation with Rappaport, the Albanian expert at the Ballhausplatz. Helmreich, *Diplomacy of the Balkan Wars*, p. 196, n. 12.

4. Durham, *Struggle for Scutari*, p. 228.

5. In the early stages of the campaign, it was reported that Montenegrin women were abusing Albanians. Durham recorded that "one Catholic woman, [a] sister of a man I knew well, told that, when in her house alone, a party of Montenegrin women rushed in on her. Three held her down and by the throat while the others plundered her clothes-chest of everything." Elsewhere she recounted the words of a Bosnian: "A Montenegrin

woman will march 100 kilos to steal one shirt!" Durham, ibid., pp. 225–26. Then again, it was a Balkan custom for men to dress up as women when committing foul deeds. Cf. Berchtold to Thurn, 8 August 1912, *OUA*, IV, No. 3675.

6. Albertini, *Origins of the War*, I:386.

7. Protocol of conference in the Austro-Hungarian foreign ministry, 16 October 1912, *OUA*, IV, No. 4118. See Albertini, *Origins of the War*, I:385–391; Rossos, *Russia and the Balkans*, pp. 91–93; and Ćorović, *Odnosi izmedju Srbije i Austro-Ugarske*, pp. 376–77.

8. Protocol of conference in the Austro-Hungarian foreign ministry, 19 October 1912, *OUA*, IV, No. 4140.

9. One recalls Aehrenthal's words of the previous autumn concerning Austria's Sandžak policy: "The more these states believe in the possibility of the intervention of our troops in the Sandžak, the greater will be their fear to exploit complications in the Balkans..." Directive from Aehrenthal to Cetinje, 25 October 1911, *OUA*, III, No. 2823.

10. Giesl to Berchtold, 12, 17, and 19 October 1912, *OUA*, IV, Nos. 4054, 4123, 4138.

11. Giesl to Berchtold, 3 October 1912, *OUA*, IV, No. 3934.

12. Giesl to Berchtold, 12 October 1912, *OUA*, IV, No. 4045.

13. Berchtold to Giesl, 13 October 1912, *OUA*, IV, No. 4071.

14. Giesl to Berchtold, 19 and 21 October 1912, *OUA*, IV, Nos. 4138, 4149.

15. Giesl to Berchtold, 26 October 1912, *OUA*, IV, No. 4176. Prof. Stanojević told Helmreich that the question of Austria's response did not enter into Serbia's decision to invade the Sandžak. Helmreich, *Diplomacy of the Balkan Wars*, p. 195, n. 8.

16. Giesl to Berchtold, 29 and 31 October 1912, *OUA*, IV, Nos. 4198, 4213.

17. Giesl, *Zwei Jahrzehnte*, 29 October 1912, p. 231; Novica Rakočević, "Oslobodjenje Plevalja i Kamene Gore u Balkanskom ratu 1912. godine," *Simpozijum "Seoski dani Sretena Vukosavljevića" VII* (Prijepolje, 1979):137–47.

18. Initially, the Montenegrins did not admit any foreign help or doctors into their hospitals. Durham said it was because they were too embarrassed to let foreigners "see the shocking mess they were in." Durham, *Struggle for Scutari*, p. 191. Before long, Italian and Austrian Red Cross units set up hospitals of their own.

19. Giesl to Berchtold, 28 October 1912, *OUA*, IV, No. 4191. Nose-cutting was a Balkan custom somewhat akin to scalping in the American West. Before fighting had begun in earnest, a Professor Kovačević, a teacher of French and German at the Podgorica gymnasium, told Durham that before long Turkish noses would be coming in: " 'We shall not leave many a Turk with a nose.' 'If you do any such swinery' said I, 'you will rightly lose all European sympathy.' He was very angry. 'It is our old national custom,' he declared; 'how can a soldier prove his heroism to his commander if he does not bring in noses? Of course we shall cut noses; we always have!' " Durham, *Struggle for Scutari*, p. 185. Joyce Cary, who was serving in the British Red Cross at the time, argued, like King Nicholas,

that whatever nose-cutting was done was the work of Albanian irregulars. Cary, *Memoir of the Bobotes*, p. 33.

20. For Tschirschky's analysis of the war's effect on Austro-Russian relations, see Tschirschky to Bethmann Hollweg, 11 October 1912, *GP*, XXXIII, No. 12261. See also *LT*, 10 October 1912, p. 5.

21. The *Times* noted that one of the first effects of the Montenegrin offensive "is to cast doubt on Russian sincerity. Since Montenegro is generally believed to act in obedience to the will of St. Petersburg, it is assumed, perhaps erroneously, that King Nicholas must have received from some Russian quarter a hint to celebrate his 71st birthday in the manner most agreeable to his subjects." *LT*, 9 October 1912, p. 5. The German ambassador in St. Petersburg reported that pan-Slav agitation, while considerable, was not as great as one might have expected. Pourtalès to Bethmann Hollweg, 9 October 1912, *GP*, XXXIII, No. 12258.

22. Giesl to Berchtold, 15 October 1912, *OUA*, IV, No. 4096.

23. As late as 27 October, Nicholas denied that Potapov was assisting the Montenegrin war effort. Giesl to Berchtold, 28 October 1912, *OUA*, IV, No. 4191.

24. Szécsen to Berchtold, 12 October 1912, *OUA*, IV, No. 4058. Cf. Izvolsky to Sazonov, 23/10 October 1912, *Der diplomatischer Schriftwechsel Iswolskis, 1911–1914. Aus den Geheimakten der russischen Staatsarchive* (hereafter cited as *DSI*), ed. Friedrich Stieve, 4 vols. (Berlin: Deutsche Verlagsgesellschaft für Politik und Geschichte, 1925), II, No. 526.

25. Hantsch, *Berchtold*, I:327–30; Cartwright to Grey, 26 October 1912, *BD*, IX/2, No. 64.

26. Alfred Francis Pribram, *Austria-Hungary and Great Britain, 1908–1914*, trans. Ian F. D. Morrow (Oxford: Oxford University Press, 1951), p. 164. Cf. note on the conference in the Austro-Hungarian foreign ministry, undated (between 25 and 30 October 1912), *OUA*, IV, No. 4170.

27. Helmreich, *Diplomacy of the Balkan Wars*, pp. 52–53. In a directive sent to Berlin on 30 October, Berchtold outlined his program in seven points. Berchtold to Szögyény, 30 October 1912, *OUA*, IV, No. 4205. He renounced all territorial claims in the Balkans with the exception of Ada Kaleh, a small island in the Danube, which had first been fortified by Austria in 1717. See chapter 8, n. 115.

28. *LT*, 5 November 1912, p. 8; Kiderlen to Tschirschky, 31 October 1912, *GP*, XXXIII, No. 12307; Tschirschky to Kiderlen, 31 October and 1 November 1912, Nos. 12310–11; Grey to Bertie, 30 October 1912, *BD*, IX/2, No. 83; Bertie to Grey, 1 November 1913, No. 84.

29. Hantsch, *Berchtold*, I:333–34.

30. *LT*, 6 November 1912, p. 7; 7 November 1912, p. 5; Hantsch, *Berchtold*, I:338–40.

31. Helmreich, *Diplomacy of the Balkan Wars*, p. 209 n. 58; *NFP*, 18 December 1912; Baernreither, *Fragmente eines politischen Tagebuches*, pp. 171–84; Thomas Masaryk, *The Making of a State: Memoirs and Observations* (New York: H. Fertig, 1969), pp. 2–3. Czechs were very interested in the South Slav question and occasionally caused problems for the Ballhausplatz.

32. Berchtold to Giesl, 10 November 1912, *OUA*, IV, No. 4355; de Salis to Grey, 13 November 1912, *BD*, IX/2, No. 189.
33. Berchtold to Mérey, 10 November 1912, *OUA*, IV, No. 4360.
34. Giesl to Berchtold, 12 November 1912, *OUA*, IV, No. 4386; Giesl, *Zwei Jahrzehnte*, 12 November 1912, pp. 231–32; *LT*, 14 November 1912, p. 5.
35. Giesl to Berchtold, 13 November 1912, *OUA*, IV, Nos. 4401–2; Mérey to Berchtold, 12 November 1912, No. 4388; Giesl, *Zwei Jahrzehnte*, 13 November 1912, p. 232; de Salis to Grey, 13 November 1912, *BD*, IX/2, No. 189; Note of Kiderlen, 13 November 1912, *GP*, XXXIII, No. 12367; *LT*, 15 November 1912, p. 5. The Stefani news agency later mistakenly denied that the Austro-Hungarian and Italian representations had been made. *LT*, 20 November 1912, p. 7.
36. *CV*, 2 November 1912 O.S.; Giesl to Berchtold, 13 and 16 November 1912, *OUA*, IV, Nos. 4402, 4454; *LT*, 16 November 1912, p. 7. De Salis told Nicholas that he "deprecated the raising of any controversy at [the] present moment on separate points which might suitably be dealt with later as part of a general settlement." De Salis to Grey, 18 November 1912, *BD*, IX/2, No. 223.
37. Berchtold to Giesl, 15 November 1912, *OUA*, IV, No. 4443. At least one Balkan leader, Lambros Coromilas of Greece, heartily endorsed Nicholas's refusal to accept Giesl's note. The Greek foreign minister spoke sharply about Austria-Hungary and said he would even go to war with her to support the claims of his ally. Braun to Berchtold, 15 November 1912, No. 4431.
38. On 12 November, the day Giesl had first tendered his message to the king, he reported that Nicholas, who had been complaining of foot pains, had to be carried from his car into a house. Giesl to Berchtold, 12 November 1912, *OUA*, IV, No. 4386.
39. Giesl to Berchtold, 16 November 1912, *OUA*, IV, No. 4454.
40. It was noted that the German minister had not delivered a note of his own. To stifle any talk about a split in the Triple Alliance, Berchtold turned to Kiderlen Waechter. On 30 November, Eckardt, whom Giesl frequently characterized as a Serbophile entirely under Nicholas's influence, delivered his government's note, which read exactly as Giesl's. Giesl to Berchtold, 16, 22, and 30 November 1912, *OUA*, IV, Nos. 4454, 4564, 4720; 1 December 1912, V, No. 4734; Berchtold to Szögyény, 27 November 1912, IV, No. 4648; Berchtold to Giesl, 29 November 1912, No. 4703; Kiderlen to Eckardt, 28 November 1912, *GP*, XXXIII, No. 12449.
41. The *Times* reported that the Serbians believed "they will the more easily gain the sanction of the Great Powers for annexing . . . a port if they have previously occupied it with an army." *LT*, 13 November 1912, p. 9. See also *LT*, 18 November 1912, p. 5; Giesl, *Zwei Jahrzehnte*, p. 232; Durham, *Struggle for Scutari*, p. 232. A British reporter noted that the ragged Montenegrin army on one side of the river looked like little more than a national militia, while the Serbians on the other side looked like a "real army." *LT*, 22 November 1912, p. 6.
42. Dimitrije Popović, *Borba za narodno ujedinjenje 1908–1914* (Bel-

grade: G. Kohn, 1936), pp. 106–8; Ludwig Schargl, "Die Affäre des österreichisch-ungarischen Konsuls Prohaska im ersten Balkankriege, 1912," *Berliner Monatshefte,* VII (April 1929): 345–54; Helmreich, *Diplomacy of the Balkan Wars,* pp. 213–15, 227–30; Robert A. Kann, "Die Prochaska Affäre vom Herbst 1912: zwischen kaltem und heissem Krieg," *Österreichische Akademie der Wissenschaften. Philosophisch-Historische Klasse,* Sitzungsbericht No. 319, Vienna 1977.

43. Helmreich, *Diplomacy of the Balkan Wars,* pp. 215–20, 461–62.

44. Ibid., pp. 221–25.

45. Note on the conference in the Austro-Hungarian foreign ministry, undated (between 25 and 30 October 1912), *OUA,* IV, No. 4170; Memorandum on the Sandžak question, 25 (?) October 1912, No. 4171, translated in Albertini, *Origins of the War,* I:391.

46. Paget to Grey, 11 November 1912, *BD,* IX/2, No. 176; Kiderlen to Griesinger, 15 November 1912, *GP,* XXXIII, No. 12371. Overtures were also made to Bulgaria. Bax-Ironside to Grey, 12 November 1912, *BD,* IX/2, No. 181.

47. Albertini, *Origins of the War,* I:394.

48. *LT,* 25 November 1912, p. 8. Pašić claimed that Wickham Steed had used his name without authorization. Cf. Benckendorff to Sazonov, 26/13 November 1912, *Graf Benckendorffs diplomatischer Schriftwechsel* (hereafter cited as *BDS*), ed. Benno von Siebert, 3 vols. (Berlin and Leipzig: Verlag von Walter de Gruyter & Co., 1928), II, No. 736; Sazonov to Benckendorff, 27/14 November 1912, No. 737; Paget to Grey, 17 November 1912, *BD,* IX/2, No. 220, n. 3; Grey to Buchanan, 25 November 1912, No. 272; Buchanan to Grey, 29 November 1912, No. 309. Cf. Griesinger to Bethmann Hollweg, 18 November 1912, *GP,* XXXIII, No. 12408. For a detailed study of Serbia's efforts to gain a foothold on the Adriatic, see Richard Giesche, *Der serbische Zugang zum Meer und die europäische Krise, 1912* (Stuttgart: W. Kohlhammer, 1932), and Dimitrije Djordjević, *Izlazak Srbije na Jadransko more i konferencija ambasadora u Londonu 1912.* (Belgrade: Slobodan Jović, 1956). Sir Ralph Paget, the British minister in Belgrade, sympathized with the Austrian point of view. He wrote Grey: "I am afraid the Servians are utterly obstinate and unreasonable. If one tells them they will provoke an European war they shrug their shoulders and say that Austria not they will be responsible if there is war, that Austria is merely trying to oppress them and prevent their economic deve[lopmen]t, and that although they may suffer considerably in a war with Austria and may lose all they have gained, they will 'die fighting.' This phrase has become a sort of mania with them. . . . [T]hey have visions of blue seas and Servian ships in the offing bringing home the wealth of the Indies etc. In plain words, they are quite off their heads. . . ." Paget to Grey, 30 November 1912, Grey Papers, PRO, FO 800/76/23. Grey, however, was still searching for a middle way, a solution "which will dispel the apprehensions of Austria-Hungary and secure to Servia the substance of what she desires." Note of the English embassy in Berlin, 8 November 1912, *GP,* XXXIII, No. 12340.

49. Helmreich, *Diplomacy of the Balkan Wars,* pp. 130–31; Ćorović,

Odnosi izmedju Srbije i Austro-Ugarske, pp. 388–389; Djordjević, *Izlazak Srbije*, p. 34.

50. Helmreich, *Diplomacy of the Balkan Wars*, p. 226; Tschirschky to Bethmann Hollweg, 13 November 1912, *GP*, XXXIII, No. 12377.

51. See Mihailo Vojvodić, "Jedan neuspeli pokušaj Austro-Ugarske da sklopi carinsku uniju sa Crnom Gorom," *Jugoslovenski narodi pred Prvi svetski rat*, pp. 117–25; Vojvodić, *Skadarska kriza*, pp. 25–29.

52. Berchtold to Giesl, 17 November 1912, *OUA*, IV, Nos. 4467–68. Interestingly, the same day Berchtold wired his Montenegrin program to Giesl, he also discussed the outline of his Albanian program with San Giuliano. Although expressing his desire that as many Albanians as possible should belong to the future Albanian entity, he also said that Montenegrin claims had "a certain legitimacy," and that he was prepared to accept Montenegro's annexation of Scutari following its occupation, provided that the Montenegrins acceded to certain conditions, namely to promise to refrain from indulging in any future border incidents and agree to certain border rectifications in the neighborhood of Kotor. Thus, without mentioning his specific intentions, he sought to prepare the Italian foreign minister for the Lovćen exchange. Berchtold to Mérey, 17 November 1912, No. 4469.

53. Giesl to Berchtold, 21 November 1912, *OUA*, IV, No. 4539.

54. Giesl to Berchtold, 18 November 1912, *OUA*, IV, No. 4482.

55. Berchtold to Giesl, 21 November 1912, *OUA*, IV, No. 4537.

56. Giesl to Berchtold, 23 and 25 November 1912, *OUA*, IV, Nos. 4576, 4577, 4609. Nicholas said later that the Triple Entente—and "perhaps some others"—had already decided on the side of the Balkan states, which were prepared in any case to defend every disputed point with 650,000 bayonets.

57. In his memoirs, Giesl turned things around, perhaps deliberately. Without explaining the background of his meeting with Nicholas, he wrote: "The king said to me: in the event that we get together with him on the question of Scutari and the Albanian coast, he would perhaps be prepared for a border regulation east of Kotor. He clearly thinks of Lovćen." Giesl, *Zwei Jahrzehnte*, 23 November 1912, p. 232.

58. N. Kolushev, the Bulgarian minister in Cetinje, told Giesl that whereas a customs union between Serbia and Bulgaria was a possibility, one between Serbia and Montenegro, owing to their long rivalry, was not. He believed that if such a union came to pass, it would reduce Montenegro to a political and cultural province of the more advanced Serbian state. Giesl to Berchtold, 26 November 1912, *OUA*, IV, No. 4628.

59. Giesl to Berchtold, 25 November 1912, *OUA*, IV, No. 4609; Giesl, *Zwei Jahrzehnte*, 24 November 1912, p. 232.

60. Report to Pašić, 25/12 November 1912, SSIP, Političko odeljenje, Fas. VIII, Dos. 9, No. 19. See also de Salis to Grey, 25 November 1912, *BD*, IX/2, No. 269.

61. Giesl to Berchtold, 27 and 28 November 1912, *OUA*, IV, Nos. 4653, 4678; Giesl, *Zwei Jahrzehnte*, 28 November 1912, pp. 232–33.

62. Giesl noted that the general opinion of outside observers was that

the prince's illness was merely a pretext for not returning to the field of battle. If Danilo was temporarily disenchanted with the soldier's life, he soon found himself back on the front lines. It was he who accepted the surrender of Scutari the following April. Giesl, *Zwei Jahrzehnte*, 26 November 1912, p. 232.

63. The new French minister, Joseph Raymond Aynàrd, reported the general malaise in Montenegro and the danger to the king and his house. Vujović, *Crna Gora i Francuska*, p. 370.

64. Giesl to Berchtold, 1 December 1912, *OUA*, V, No. 4733.

65. Francis Joseph remarked that the situation was "more serious than in 1866." Albertini, *Origins of the War*, I:410; Helmreich, *Diplomacy of the Balkan Wars*, pp. 227–30. On the general situation and the Austro-Russian antagonism, see August Bach, "Die November und Dezemberkrise 1912: Ein Vorspiel zum Weltkrieg," *Berliner Monatshefte*, XIII (February 1935): 101–22, and Rudolf Kiszling, "Russlands Kriegsvorbereitungen im Herbst 1912 und ihre Rückwirkungen auf Österreich-Ungarn," *Berliner Monatshefte*, XIII (March 1935): 181–92. On Conrad's reappointment, see Mérey to Berchtold, 11 and 18 December 1912, *OUA*, V, Nos. 5871, 4965; Conrad, *AMD*, II:373–5; Rodd to Grey, 15 December 1912, *BD*, IX/2, No. 384. On the renewal of the Triple Alliance, see Alfred F. Pribram, *The Secret Treaties of Austria-Hungary, 1879–1914*, trans. Denys P. Myers and J. G. D'Arcy Paul, 2 vols. (Cambridge, Mass.: Harvard University Press, 1920–21), I:244–59; II:143–73; Carlo Avarna, *L'ultimo Rinnovo della Triplice, 5 dicembre 1912* (Milan: Alpes, 1924); Bernadotte E. Schmitt, *Triple Alliance and Triple Entente* (New York: H. Holt and Co., 1934); Willy Kalbskopf, *Die Aussenpolitik der Mittelmächte im Tripoliskrieg und die letzte Dreibunderneuerung: Eine Studie zur Bündnispolitik der europäischen Grossmächte vor dem Weltkrieg* (Erlangen: K. Döres, 1932); Luigi Salvatorelli, *La Triplice Alleanza, Storia diplomatica, 1877–1912* (Milan: Instituto per gli studi di politica internazionale, 1939).

66. For a short time Giesl appeared at the London conference as a Balkan expert. Reasons of health forced him to leave London for the Continent. For an excellent discussion of Anglo-German relations at the conference, see R. J. Crampton, *The Hollow Detente: Anglo-German Relations in the Balkans, 1911–1914* (Atlantic Highlands, N.J.: Humanities Press, 1980), especially chapters 5 and 6.

67. Berchtold to Mérey, 29 December 1912, *OUA*, V, No. 5110; N. Giers to Sazonov, 20 December/2 January 1913, *BDS*, III, No. 796; Benckendorff to Sazonov, 21 December/3 January 1913, No. 797; *CV*, 1 January 1912 O.S.

68. Berchtold to Mérey, 29 December 1912, *OUA*, V, No. 5110; Mérey to Berchtold, 1 January 1913, No. 5156; Grey to Rodd, 4 January 1913, *BD*, IX/2, No. 452. San Giuliano threatened to make agreements with other Powers if Italy's interests were not safeguarded. Askew, "Austro-Italian Antagonism," pp. 206–7, n. 138–41. As Askew noted, "Italy insisted that Article 7 of the Triple Alliance covered the whole Balkan peninsula and pledged Austria not to move without prior agreement with Italy based on suitable compensation. This interpretation would have given Italy a

kind of veto on Austrian moves. Austria-Hungary insisted that Article 7 applied to the nonindependent parts of the Balkan peninsula but not to the independent states." Ibid., p. 211.

69. Mérey to Berchtold, 1 January 1913, *OUA*, V, No. 5156; Vojvodić, *Skadarska kriza*, p. 44.

70. Report from St. Petersburg to Pašić, 2 January 1913, SSIP, Političko odeljenje, Fas. III, Dos. 13, No. 4, and 3 January 1913, Fas. I, Dos. 32, No. 41. See also Berchtold to Berlin, Rome, and London, 6 January 1913, *OUA*, V, No. 5216; Zimmermann to Tschirschky, 4 January 1913, *GP*, XXXIV/1, No. 12610.

71. Berchtold to Mérey, 29 and 30 December 1912, *OUA*, V, Nos. 5110, 5124.

72. Mérey to Berchtold, 1 January 1913, *OUA*, V, No. 5156. Giolitti recalled that both San Giuliano and he were often tempted to show Mérey the door. Giolitti, *Memoirs*, pp. 359–60.

73. Szögyény to Berchtold, 8 January 1913, *OUA*, VI, No. 5258; Mérey to Berchtold, 8 January 1913, V, No. 5272; Weinzetl to Berchtold, 14 January 1913, No. 5383. On the development of Italian support for Austria during the First Balkan War, see Albertini, *Origins of the War*, I: 418–22.

74. Report from Cetinje to Pašić, 21 December 1912 O.S., SSIP, Fas. I, Dos. 9, No. 4856. See also Popović, *Borba za narodno ujedinjenje*, pp. 120–21.

75. Grey to de Salis, 28 January 1913, *BD*, IX/2, No. 565.

76. In fact, Austria was prepared to sacrifice Prizren and Peć from the start. Although provided by the Ballhausplatz with a map showing these two cities outside Austria's proposed boundaries for Albania, Mensdorff, the Austrian ambassador, chose not to introduce it in the early meetings, so as to have greater bargaining power. See Helmreich, *Diplomacy of the Balkan Wars*, 255–57; 286–94; Rossos, *Russia and the Balkans*, pp. 112–17.

77. This concession was later recounted with pleasure by Grey: "Mensdorff entered briskly, even a little breathless with haste, delighted with the good news he brought and exclaiming, 'We give up Djakova!'" Sir Edward Grey, *Twenty-five Years, 1892–1916*, 2 vols. (New York: Frederick A. Stokes, 1925), I:259.

78. Rossos, *Russia and the Balkans*, pp. 122–25.

79. The Montenegrin rebuked the captain of the *Skodra*, a Hungarian-Croat steamer at Shëngjin, for refusing to continue rescuing Serbian troops from a Greek transport for fear of drawing the fire of the Turkish cruiser *Hamidie*, which had broken through the Greek naval blockade. Conrad, *AMD*, III:171 ff.; de Salis, "Montenegro: Annual Report, 1913," PRO, FO 371/2041/424, p. 8; Vojvodić, *Skadarska kriza*, pp. 75–76.

80. After meeting with Conrad on 18 March, Berchtold decided to take more forceful action and demand that Montenegro halt the bombardment of Scutari until the civil population had been given an opportunity to evacuate the city. The following day an Austro-Hungarian naval force steamed out of the huge naval base at Pula bound for the Bay of Kotor.

Vojvodić, *Skadarska kriza*, pp. 84–85. Invited to join the Austrians in forcing Nicholas's hand, the Italians demurred. Still, San Giuliano disliked the prospect of separate Austrian action and soon approached Berlin concerning a possible Austro-Italian mandate. If Berlin approved of the scheme, Grey did not. He wanted a unified response to the Montenegrin problem. He knew that Russia would be unhappy with two members of the Triple Alliance trying to enforce the will of Europe. Flotow to Jagow, 23 March 1913, *GP*, XXXIV/2, No. 13011; Jagow to Lichnowsky, 25 March 1913, No. 13015; Lichnowsky to Jagow, 26 March 1913, No. 13021; Pribram, *Austria-Hungary and Great Britain*, pp. 190–91; Mensdorff to Berchtold, 24 March 1913, *ÖUA*, V, No. 6287; Helmreich, *Diplomacy of the Balkan Wars*, pp. 295–98.

81. Mensdorff to Berchtold, 26 March 1913, *ÖUA*, V, No. 6313; Grey to Cartwright, 24 March 1913, *BD*, IX/2, No. 751.

82. *NFP*, 1 April 1913, p. 1.

CHAPTER EIGHT

1. Grey to de Salis, 1 April 1913, *BD*, IX/2, No. 785.

2. Berchtold to Mensdorff, 1 April 1913, *ÖUA*, VI, No. 6404; Berchtold to Francis Ferdinand, 1 April 1913, No. 6411; Berchtold to Francis Joseph, 1 April 1913, No. 6413. Cf. telegram of Austro-Hungarian war ministry, naval section, 27 March 1913, HHStA, PA XII/Türkei, Karton 426, Liasse XLV/11, No. 1315, p. 19; Pula to war ministry, No. 1314, p. 20; Tschirschky to Jagow, 2 April 1913, *GP*, XXXIV/2, No. 13065; Jagow to William II, 3 April 1913, No. 13078; *NFP*, 2 April 1913, m.e., p. 2.

3. Although both the *Breslau* and the *Goeben* were anchored near Athens, William ordered the former to Bar because she had a younger commander. He did not want the additional responsibility of the leadership of the naval demonstration, which fell automatically to the most senior naval commander present. Lichnowsky to Jagow, 1 April 1913, *GP*, XXXIV/2, No. 13059; Jagow to William II, 1 April 1913, No. 13060; Jagow to Lichnowsky, 1 April 1913, No. 13061. Germany originally wanted only four Powers, two from each alliance, to participate in the demonstration, so as not to call attention to Russia's absence. Jagow to Schoen, 2 April 1913, No. 13064; Mérey to Berchtold, 1 April 1913, *ÖUA*, VI, No. 6410; HHStA, PA/Türkei, Karton 426, Liasse XLV/11, No. 186.

4. Thurn to Berchtold, 7 and 12 April 1913, *ÖUA*, VI, Nos. 6503, 6596; Szécsen to Berchtold, 3 April 1913, No. 6437. For a discussion of pan-Slav activity, see Uebersberger, *Österreich zwischen Russland und Serbien*, pp. 127–29. Cf. Berchtold to Szögyény, 6 April 1913, *GP*, XXXIV/2, No. 13119; Buchanan to Grey, 3 April 1913, *BD*, IX/2, No. 798.

5. Buchanan to Grey, 31 March 1913, *BD*, IX/2, No. 770; Grey to Bertie, 2 April 1913, Nos. 789, 795. See communiqué, Buchanan to Grey,

3 April 1913, No. 796. Cf. Izvolsky to Sazonov, 4 April/22 March 1913, *DSI*, III, No. 817; Thurn to Berchtold, 3 and 7 April 1913, *OUA*, VI, Nos. 6440, 6501; Giesl to Berchtold, 5 April 1913, No. 6460; Jagow to William II, 4 and 6 April 1913, *GP*, XXXIV/2, Nos. 13081, 13092; Pourtalès to Bethmann Hollweg, 8 April 1913, No. 13125; *NFP*, 4 April 1913, m.e., p. 3. For a discussion of Anglo-German relations during the Scutari crisis, see Crampton, *The Hollow Detente*, pp. 83–93.

6. For a detailed description of some of the ships involved in the naval demonstration, see *NFP*, 2 April 1913, m.e., pp. 4–5.

7. Admiralty telegram, 5 April 1913, PRO, FO 16049/15076/13/44; Admiralty to Foreign Office, 5 April 1913, *BD*, IX/2, No. 809, n. 2; Giesl to Berchtold, 5 April 1913, *OUA*, VI, No. 6460; Mensdorff to Berchtold, 6 April 1913, No. 6482; Njegovan to war ministry, naval section, 6 April 1913, HHStA, PA XII/Türkei, Karton 426, Liasse XLV/11, No. 1458; Izvolsky to Sazonov, 7 April/25 March 1913, *DSI*, III, No. 825.

8. Mensdorff to Berchtold, 6 April 1913, *OUA*, VI, No. 6482. Still, Austria sent her light cruiser *Aspern* on a reconnaissance mission along the Albanian coast as far as Durrës. Rudnay to Berchtold, 7 April 1913, HHStA, PA XII/Türkei, Karton 426, Liasse XLV/11, No. 120.

9. Circular telegram from Berchtold to Great-Power capitals, 8 April 1913, *OUA*, VI, No. 6522.

10. Admiralty to foreign office, 8 April, 1913, *BD*, IX/2, No. 817. As early as 2 April, Berchtold proposed the landing of troops as the next logical step. Berchtold to London, Rome, and Berlin, 2 April 1913, *OUA*, VI, No. 6418. Germany generally supported this option, although Jagow doubted the ability of Britain or France to join. Szögyény to Berchtold, 7 April 1913, No. 6494. In fact, Britain and France left the door open for such a possibility, as well as separate Austro-Italian action. In Grey's words: "If the demonstration fails I do not see how any of us can in the last resort object to action by Italy and Austria to make Montenegro respect the decision of the Powers. . . ." Grey to Bertie, 1 April 1913, *BD*, IX/2, No. 772; Mérey to Berchtold, 8 April 1913, *OUA*, VI, No. 6520; Berchtold to Mérey, 10 April 1913, No. 6552; Szécsen to Berchtold, 20 April 1913, No. 6686; Tschirschky to Jagow, 9 April 1913, *GP*, XXXIV/2, No. 13120; Schoen to Jagow, 9 April 1913, No. 13126; Jagow to Lichnowsky, 14 April 1913, No. 13150.

11. Mensdorff to Berchtold, 9 April 1913, *OUA*, VI, No. 6536. Venizelos had intimated earlier that he would welcome such a blockade so as to relieve Greece from having to meet her treaty obligations to her allies in the face of Great-Power disapproval. Elliot to Grey, 6 April 1913, *BD*, IX/2, No. 810; Mensdorff to Berchtold, 10 April 1913, *OUA*, VI, No. 6549. Cf. Pourtalès to Bethmann Hollweg, 8 April 1913, *GP*, XXXIV/2, No. 13125, n.**; Eckardt to Jagow, 9 April 1913, No. 13128; Cartwright to Nicolson, 11 April 1913, *BD*, IX/2, No. 837. War matériel taken off the ships was transported overland to Macedonia and Albania. Kral to Berchtold, 9 April 1913, HHStA, PA XII/Türkei, Karton 426, Liasse XLV/11, No. 1426; Braun to Berchtold, 10 April 1913, No. 214 (1582).

12. Giesl to Berchtold, 1, 2, and 6 April 1913, *OUA*, VI, Nos. 6402, 6416, 6479; Hubka to Conrad, 3 April 1913, HHStA, PA XII/Türkei, Karton 426, Liasse XLV/11, No. 156; Telegram of Austro-Hungarian general staff headquarters, 6 April 1913, No. 1697; Treutler to Jagow, 7 April 1913, *GP*, XXXIV/2, No. 13107; de Salis to Grey, 6 April 1913, *BD*, IX/2, No. 811; *CV*, 27 March 1913 O.S.

13. Tschirschky to Bethmann Hollweg, 1 April 1913, *GP*, XXXIV/2, No. 13077; Jagow to William II, 6 April 1913, No. 13092; Treutler to Jagow, 7 April 1913, No. 13100; Jagow to Treutler, 7 April 1913, No. 13101; Giesl, *Zwei Jahrzehnte*, p. 242, esp. entries for 3 and 11 April. Giesl believed that Nicholas was still in command despite his "revolutionary ministers and other demonic advisors such as Count Lujo Vojnović." Giesl to Berchtold, 4 April 1913, HHStA, PA XII/Türkei, Karton 426, Liasse XLV/11, No. 32 A-B.

14. Berchtold to London, Berlin, and Rome, 1 April 1913, *OUA*, VI, No. 6403; Hubka to Conrad, 31 March 1913, HHStA, PA XII/Türkei, Karton 426, Liasse XLV/11, No. 1569; 4 April 1913, No. 1200/9.

15. The Austrians condemned as "most inopportune" the unloading of Russian war matériel at a time St. Petersburg had sanctioned the blockade of the Montenegrin coast. Sazonov explained that his government was not responsible for the shipments, the latest of which was supposed to have been ordered before the Turco-Italian War. Giesl to Berchtold, 2 April 1913, *OUA*, VI, No. 6416; Thurn to Berchtold, 7 April 1913, No. 6502; Berchtold to Thurn, 8 April 1913, No. 6523; Hubka to Conrad, 2 and 3 April 1913, HHStA, PA XII/Türkei, Karton 426, Liasse XLV/11, No. 153 and Evb. No. 1657; *NFP*, 4 April 1913, m.e., p. 1. The Germans estimated that the ships carried twenty-seven million rounds, seven thousand grenades, and ten thousand army coats. Report of Kageneck, 5 April 1913, *GP*, XXXIV/2, No. 13095.

16. Ugron to Berchtold, 7 April 1913, *OUA*, VI, No. 6492. See Djordjević, *Izlazak Srbije*. Giesl called the military actions of Montenegro and Serbia nothing less than a "uns allein ins Gesicht treffenden Peitschenschlag...." Giesl to Berchtold, 8 April 1913, HHStA, PA XII/Türkei, Karton 426, Liasse XLV/11, No. 34 A-C; 4 April 1913, No. 32 A-B. Serbian forces consisted of two infantry and one heavy artillery divisions.

17. Ugron to Berchtold, 11 and 12 April 1913, *OUA*, VI, Nos. 6560, 6576. Paget was notified a day earlier. Paget to Grey, 10 April 1913, *BD*, IX/2, No. 825; Jagow to Wangenheim, 12 April 1913, *GP*, XXXIV/2, No. 13141; Izvolsky to Sazonov, 12 April/30 March 1913, *DSI*, III, No. 837. Berchtold suggested that in view of Montenegro's recent refusal to forward messages to the Turkish garrison, a message should be sent through Serbian lines. In Constantinople, he advised the Porte to order Essad Pasha to hold his fire if and when Serbian troops left their positions. The Turkish government decided to transmit this order through the German legation in Cetinje. Circular telegram from Berchtold, 12 April 1913, *OUA*, VI, No. 6580; Pallavicini to Berchtold, 5 and 13 April 1913, Nos. 6461, 6602. Cf. Berchtold to Pallavicini, 3 April 1913, No. 6435; Szécsen to Berchtold, 4

April 1913, No. 6452; Circular note of the Montenegrin government, 26/13 March 1913, "Gradja iz borbe oko Skadra 1913. godine," *IZ*, III, Knj. V, Nos. 1–3 (1950), No. 5, p. 111.

18. Giesl to Berchtold, 18 April 1913, *OUA*, VI, No. 6667; Eckardt to Jagow, 16 April 1913, *GP*, XXXIV/2, No. 13168.

19. Giesl, *Zwei Jahrzehnte*, p. 243. Cf. Mérey to Berchtold, 14 April 1913, HHStA, PA XII/Türkei, Karton 427, Liasse XLV/11, No. 213 (2284).

20. Ugron to Berchtold, 14 April 1913, *OUA*, VI, No. 6611.

21. Some Serbian troops stayed behind in Albania. The Italian consul general in Durrës reported that Serbian military and civilian officials were signing one-year leases on houses, apparently counting on staying quite a while. Before withdrawing completely, they wanted some guarantees that the Powers would honor their decision of 17 December 1912 to provide them with an economic outlet on the Adriatic. Report on a visit by the Serbian minister, 12 April 1913, *OUA*, VI, No. 6575; Circular telegram from Berchtold to London, Rome, and Belgrade, 18 April 1913, No. 6669; Mérey to Berchtold, 19 April 1913, No. 6679; Berchtold to Mensdorff, 21 April 1913, No. 6693. Sazonov argued that the complete evacuation of Serbian troops would remove the only force capable of keeping order. Sazonov to Izvolsky, 18/5 April 1913, *DSI*, III, No. 841.

22. For Russian interest in monetary compensation, see inter alia, Sazonov to Benckendorff, 30/17 March 1913, *DSI*, III, No. 802; Izvolsky to Sazonov, 31/18 March and 15/2 April 1913, Nos. 804, 839. Popović actually raised the question of compensation with the Italian ambassador in London, and Eckardt wired Berlin that he had reason to believe that Nicholas would be interested in such a deal. Flotow to Jagow, 2 April 1913, *GP*, XXXIV/2, No. 13068; Eckardt to Jagow, 2 April 1913, No. 13073. See also Jagow to Tschirschky, 6 April 1913, No. 13091; and Jagow to Flotow, 6 April 1913, No. 13094.

23. Circular telegram from Berchtold, 5 April 1913, *OUA*, VI, No. 6466.

24. Giesl also mentioned the possibility of Austria-Hungary lending military support to the Petrović-Njegoš dynasty and the cession to the Monarchy of part of the Montenegrin-occupied Sandžak in exchange for "a material separation from Serbia." Giesl to Berchtold, 6 April 1913, *OUA*, VI, No. 6479; Szögyény to Berchtold, 9 April 1913, HHStA, PA XII/Türkei, Karton 426, Liasse XLV/11, No. 186 (1386). Mensdorff also recommended guaranteeing an international loan in conjunction with Russia and Italy. Mensdorff to Berchtold, 9 April 1913, No. 294 (1347). Cf. Jagow to William II, 6 April 1913, *GP*, XXXIV/2, No. 13093; Treutler to Jagow, 7 April 1913, No. 13104.

25. Jagow to Flotow, 8 April 1913, *GP*, XXXIV/2, No. 13106; Tschirschky to Jagow, 8 April 1913, No. 13117. For Giolitti's confusion on Italy's role, see Giolitti, *Memoirs*, p. 367, and Albertini, *Origins of the War*, I:442.

26. Circular telegram from Berchtold to Rome, Berlin, and Cetinje, 8 April 1913, *OUA*, VI, No. 6519; Berchtold to Mérey, 10 and 12 April 1913, Nos. 6552, 6586; Mérey to Berchtold, 11 April 1913, No. 6571; Report on a visit by the Italian ambassador, 15 April 1913, No. 6639. While

France energetically seconded Italy's initiative, Grey demurred, suggesting that those governments interested in the project should contact Montenegro directly. Having done what he could diplomatically to bring Nicholas around, he saw no reason why he should have to give the king money. Mensdorff to Berchtold, 4 April 1913, No. 6449; Grey to Buchanan, 1 April 1913, *BD*, IX/2, No. 779. In time, however, the British government decided to go along with the others. Even so, Asquith anticipated difficulties in getting Parliament's approval. Mensdorff to Berchtold, 15 April 1913, *OUA*, VI, Nos. 6637. Jagow shared Asquith's misgivings. Jagow to Flotow, 10 and 15 April 1913, *GP*, XXXIV/2, Nos. 13131, 13161; Flotow to Jagow, 17 April 1913, No. 13174; Tschirschky to Jagow, 12 April 1913, No. 13147.

27. Grey to Bertie, 17 April 1913, *BD*, IX/2, No. 860; Grey to de Salis, 18 and 24 April 1913, Nos. 861, 884; Lichnowsky to Jagow, 17 April 1913, *GP*, XXXIV/2, No. 13177; Mensdorff to Berchtold, 17 April 1913, *OUA*, VI, Nos. 6659–60. The press soon raised the figure to 50 million francs. Mérey to Berchtold, 24 April 1913, No. 6752.

28. The Montenegrins had in mind an indemnity in the neighborhood of 144,225,000 francs. Eckardt to Jagow, 9 April 1913, *GP*, XXXIV/2, No. 13128.

29. De Salis to Grey, 20 April 1913, *BD*, IX/2, No. 865.

30. Giesl to Berchtold, 18 April 1913, *OUA*, VI, No. 6667. Cf. Berchtold to Szögyény, 24 April 1913, No. 6737.

31. Giesl to Berchtold, 18 April 1913, *OUA*, VI, No. 6666.

32. Circular telegram from Berchtold, 18 April 1913, *OUA*, VI, No. 6664; Berchtold to Mensdorff, 21 April 1913, No. 6693; Jagow to Treutler, 20 April 1913, *GP*, XXXIV/2, No. 13179.

33. Circular telegram from Berchtold, 20 April 1913, *OUA*, VI, No. 6685.

34. Berchtold to Mensdorff, 21 April 1913, *OUA*, VI, No. 6692.

35. Many feared that Grey's temporary absence from the conference reflected divisions among British policymakers. See Lichnowsky to Jagow, 23 April 1913, *GP*, XXXIV/2, No. 13191.

36. Grey to Bertie, 21 April 1913, *BD*, IX/2, No. 869; Cartwright to Grey, 22 April 1913, No. 870; Izvolsky to Sazonov, 8 April/26 March and 10 April/28 March 1913, *DSI*, III, Nos. 827, 835; Mensdorff to Berchtold, 21 April 1913, *OUA*, VI, No. 6695. Cf. Grey to Bertie, 10 April 1913, *BD*, IX/2, No. 832; Berchtold to Great-Power capitals and Cetinje, 22 April 1913, Nos. 6703–4; Report on a visit by the Italian ambassador, 12 April 1913, No. 6587; Berchtold to Mensdorff, 22 April 1913, No. 6707; Lichnowsky to Jagow, 21 April 1913, *GP*, XXXIV/2, No. 13182. Jagow approved the formula. Jagow to Lichnowsky, 23 April 1913, No. 13183; Benckendorff to Sazonov, 19/6, 20/7, and 21/8 April 1913, *BDS*, III, Nos. 942–44.

37. *NFP*, 19 March 1913; Redlich, *Das politische Tagebuch*, I, 21 March 1913, p. 192.

38. Pözel to Berchtold, 14 April 1913, *OUA*, VI, No. 6617. For a Montenegrin analysis of Austro-Montenegrin incompatibility on the com-

mission, see Vukotić to Giesl, 9 April/26 March 1913, "Gradja iz borbe oko Skadra," No. 12, p. 117; No. 13, pp. 117–18; 10 April/27 March 1913, No. 14, pp. 118–19. See also *NFP*, 7 May 1913, m.e., p. 3; Durham, *Struggle for Scutari*, pp. 268–69.

39. The Austrians demanded that Cetinje build a monument to the martyred Palić, facilitate the construction of a Catholic church in Djakovica by Austria-Hungary, permit the transfer of Palić's remains, and have Montenegrin officials of ministerial or general rank present at the consecration of the church and the removal of Palić's body. Berchtold to Giesl, 27 April 1913, *OUA*, VI, No. 6786; *NFP*, 3 May 1913, e.e., p. 3. The Italians thought that these demands were excessive and might jeopardize a general settlement of the Scutari question. Mérey to Berchtold, 3 May 1913, *OUA*, VI, No. 6879.

40. A similar incident disrupted telegraphic communications in July, 1914, forcing Giesl's successor to set up an ad hoc shuttle service between Cetinje and Kotor. See chapter 10.

41. Giesl to Berchtold, 21 April 1913, HHStA, PA XII/Türkei, Karton 427, Liasse XLV/11, Nos. 3300, 3283, and 3288 (133), pp. 336, 338, 361. See also Hubka to Conrad, 21 and 23 April 1913, Nos. 3316 and 3784 (139), pp. 332 and 440; Hubka's report in supplement to Giesl's dispatch to Berchtold, 23 April 1913, No. 31, pp. 447–48. For Montenegro's protest concerning Hubka's activities, see preceding, pp. 444–46, and the verbal note of the Montenegrin government, 22/9 April 1913, "Gradja iz borbe oko Skadra," No. 2, p. 108.

42. Berchtold to Great-Power capitals and Cetinje, 28 April 1913, *OUA*, VI, No. 6798; Kageneck's report, 24 April 1913, *GP*, XXXIV/2, No. 13202. For text of Giesl's protest note, see Giesl to Vukotić, 29 April 1913, "Gradja iz borbe oko Skadra," No. 3, p. 109.

43. Cary, *Memoir of the Bobotes*, p. 144.

44. Giesl, *Zwei Jahrzehnte*, p. 243.

45. Giesl to Berchtold, 1 May 1913, *OUA*, VI, No. 6846; Vukotić to Giesl, 30/17 April 1913, "Gradja iz borbe oko Skadra," No. 4, p. 110. Giesl again blamed Eckardt for the Montenegrin attitude. See Giesl, *Zwei Jahrzehnte*, p. 245.

46. On 6 March, the same Essad Pasha had surrendered the Turkish garrison at Ioánnina to the Greeks. For one brief moment before Scutari's fall, Nicholas toyed with the Powers about his readiness to give up the siege. Izvolsky to Sazonov, 19/6 April 1913, *DSI*, III, No. 842. Cf. Giesl to Berchtold, 21 April 1913, HHStA, PA XII/Türkei, Karton 427, Liasse XLV/11, No. 3314 (132), p. 339.

47. Jagow to Tschirschky, 23 April 1913, *GP*, XXXIV/2, No. 13188, n.*. Cf. Giesl to Berchtold, 21 and 22 April 1913, HHStA, PA XII/Türkei, Karton 427, Liasse XLV/11, Nos. 3357 (135), 3555 (136), pp. 335, 401.

48. *NFP*, 8 May 1913, m.e., p. 1.

49. Many saw the hand of Russian pan-Slavists in negotiations leading to the agreement. Conrad accused Izvolsky of being involved. Conrad, *AMD*, III:309. Cf. Izvolsky to Sazonov, 24/11 April 1913, *DSI*, III, No.

847; Uebersberger, *Österreich zwischen Russland und Serbien*, p. 130, n. 1; Jagow to Tschirschky, 23 April 1913, *GP*, XXXIV/2, No. 13188. Durham, on the other hand, accused the Italians. Durham, "The Story of Essad Pasha," *Contemporary Review*, CXVIII (August 1920): 212.

50. Essad Pasha to Turkish war minister, 23/10 April 1913, "Gradja iz borbe oko Skadra," No. 18, p. 121. For the text of the agreement, see Vuković, *Rat Crne Gore*, pp. 112–13, or Pavlović, *Opsada Skadra*, p. 101. See also supplement to report from Zambaur to Berchtold, 24 April 1913, HHStA, PA XII/Türkei, Karton 427, Liasse XLV/11, No. 2540 (13), pp. 518–19. Essad's army was made up of some twelve thousand Albanians and eight thousand Turkish redifs and soldiers. On 9 May provisions were made for the repatriation of the latter, whose presence on Albanian soil worried the Powers. See editorial note, Grey to Cartwright, 29 April 1913, *BD*, IX/2, no. 904. Cf. Izvolsky to Sazonov, 1 May/18 April 1913, *DSI*, III, No. 863.

51. On 8 April, Popović intimated to Nicolson that Essad was ready to surrender Scutari if someone could find his "lost valise" with 80,000 pounds in it. Nicolson memorandum, 8 April 1913, PRO, FO 371/1770.

52. For the kaiser's assessment, see Griesinger to Jagow, 27 April 1913, *GP*, XXXIV/2, No. 13215, n. 1. Cf. Giesl to Berchtold, 25 April 1913, HHStA, PA XII/Türkei, Karton 427, Liasse XLV/11, No. 42, pp. 552–55.

53. Hubka wrote that "it can be taken as a miracle that no human life fell victim to this uncivilized demonstration of joy. Accidentally hit were street lights, conducting wires, store signs, and the like, while approximately a dozen bullet marks on the front of my house may not have been entirely accidental." Hubka, "Kritische Tage," pp. 34–35. Giesl to Berchtold, 24 April 1913, in Giesl, *Zwei Jahrzehnte*, pp. 243–44; Giesl to Berchtold, 23 April 1913, HHStA, XII/Türkei, Karton 427, Liasse XLV/11, Nos. 3834 (140) and 3798 (X), pp. 439, 441; 24 April 1913, No. 4009 (143), p. 488; *CV*, 10 and 11 April 1913 O.S. While Hubka wrote that the placard's inscription read "Vienna's Diplomacy," Durham recalled that it read "The Neue Freie Presse." Durham, *Struggle for Scutari*, p. 277.

54. Ugron to Berchtold, 23 April 1913, *OUA*, VI, No. 6715. Anti-Austrian demonstrations took place elsewhere, notably in Djakovica and Prizren. Pözel to Berchtold, 24 and 27 April, 5 May 1913, Nos. 6742, 6789, 6914; Berchtold to Ugron, 28 April 1913, No. 6976; Ugron to Berchtold, 30 April and 2 May 1913, Nos. 6830, 6861.

55. Gellinek to Conrad, 26 April 1913, *OUA*, VI, No. 6773.

56. Ugron to Berchtold, 24 April 1913, *OUA*, VI, No. 6735. Cf. 30 April 1913, No. 6831; Paget to Grey, 25 April 1913, *BD*, IX/2, No. 890; *CV*, 19 April 1913 O.S.

57. Tschirschky to Jagow, 24 April 1913, *GP*, XXXIV/2, No. 13203, translated in Albertini, *Origins of the War*, I:443.

58. Cartwright to Nicolson, 25 April 1913, *BD*, IX/2, No. 891.

59. Grey to de Salis, 23 April 1913, *BD*, IX/2, No. 875; de Salis to Vukotić, 23 April 1913, "Gradja iz borbe oko Skadra," No. 19, p. 122; Mensdorff to Berchtold, 23 April 1913, *OUA*, VI, No. 6721; Berchtold to

Great-Power capitals and Cetinje, 24 April 1913, No. 6741; Schoen to Jagow, 24 April 1913, *GP,* XXXIV/2, No. 13194; Benckendorff to Sazonov, 23 April 1913, *BDS,* III, No. 945.

60. Mensdorff to Berchtold, 23 and 24 April 1913, *OUA,* VI, Nos. 6722, 6748; Berchtold to Great-Power capitals and Cetinje, 23 April 1913, No. 6716; Berchtold to Mensdorff and Szögyény, 24 April 1913, No. 6746; Jagow to Treutler, 24 April 1913, *GP,* XXXIV/2, No. 13193; Communication from Mensdorff, 23 April 1913, *BD,* IX/2, No. 877; Benckendorff to Sazonov, 23 April 1913, *BDS,* III, No. 946.

61. Szögyény to Berchtold, 24 and 25 April 1913, *OUA,* VI, Nos. 6739, 6757; Treutler to Jagow, 23 and 25 April 1913, *GP,* XXXIV/2, Nos. 13190, 13205; Jagow to Lichnowsky, 25 April 1913, No. 13197. William wrote: "I surmise that if Grey does not decide on milit[ary] measures, the ambassadors' conference will be at an end. Then great words won't help anymore." Jagow to William II, 24 April 1913, No. 13195, marginalia.

62. Mensdorff to Berchtold, 24 April 1913, *OUA,* VI, No. 6747; Berchtold to Great-Power capitals and Cetinje, 23 April 1913, No. 6720; Jagow to Pourtalès, 25 April 1913, *GP,* XXXIV/2, No. 13199; Lichnowsky to Jagow, 24 April 1913, No. 13196; Izvolsky to Sazonov, 24/11 April 1913, *DSI,* III, No. 846.

63. Giesl to Berchtold, 27 April 1913, *OUA,* VI, Nos. 6787-88; de Salis to Grey, 28 April 1913, *BD,* IX/2, No. 896.

64. Eckardt to Jagow, 27 April 1913, *GP,* XXXIV/2, No. 13221; Giesl to Berchtold, 28 April 1913, *OUA,* VI, No. 6799. Writing years later, Giesl turned the story around, stating that in early May a "most" surprising dispatch" came from the Ballhausplatz, permitting him to negotiate with Nicholas in the sense of the king's proposal for a Lovćen-Scutari exchange as well as certain economic settlements. Giesl stated that he approached the king unofficially so as to spare the Austro-Hungarian government embarrassment, telling Nicholas that he enjoyed a "certain influence" with Francis Ferdinand, Berchtold, and Conrad, and might be able to persuade them to make a deal. According to this account, the following day Mijušković gave Giesl the king's negative reply: if he agreed to such a proposal, he would be chased out of the country. Although all of this was supposed to be done in the utmost secrecy, only two hours later, Giesl recorded that Squitti asked him: "Is it true that after all our démarches, you want to negotiate Lovćen for Scutari?" Giesl, *Zwei Jahrzehnte,* p. 246. The story, for which there is no corroborating evidence in the Austrian documents, would seem to follow the events of November 1912.

65. A second meeting Giesl had with Nicholas ended on an acrimonious note. As the Austrian was preparing to leave, the king inquired about his health: "Several weeks ago you underwent a difficult operation. How are you feeling now?" As Nicholas had ignored him for a long time, this sudden interest in his well-being provoked a very undiplomatic outburst: "Your Majesty, I urgently request that you no longer concern yourself with my health. When I came to your country with a serious operation wound, [both] doctor and druggist denied me any kind of assistance, which even wild peoples would not have withheld from an enemy." With that he took his leave. Giesl, *Zwei Jahrzehnte,* pp. 244-45. In February, Giesl had been

operated on a second time in Berlin for a kidney ailment. On his return to Cetinje, it was widely rumored that certain Montenegrins were planning to assassinate him. Ibid., pp. 236–37.

66. Zambaur to Berchtold, 28 April 1913, *OUA*, VI, No. 6813. See also *NFP*, 3 May 1913, m.e., p. 5.

67. Report on a visit by the German ambassador, 27 April 1913, *OUA*, VI, No. 6784; Mensdorff to Berchtold, 28 April 1913, No. 6806; Jagow to Lichnowsky, 26 April 1913, *GP*, XXXIV/2, No. 13207; Lichnowsky to Jagow, 28 April 1913, No. 13232; Grey to Goschen, 28 April 1913, *BD*, IX/2, No. 898; Grey to Cartwright, 28 April 1913, No. 899. R. J. Crampton argues that because Grey had met with the French and Russian ambassadors before the *réunion* on the twenty-eighth to coordinate policy, "in the last analysis, [he] considered the unity of the Entente even more important than the unity of the Concert." To be sure, in the long run Crampton's conclusion is probably correct, but at the time, Grey's policies were designed just as much to achieve something for Austria as to appease Russia. R. J. Crampton, "The Balkans, 1909–1914," *British Foreign Policy under Sir Edward Grey*, ed. F. H. Hinsley (New York, London, and Cambridge: Cambridge University Press, 1977), p. 264. As Grey himself recounted, "Britain's one paramount interest in the whole affair was that peace should be preserved. If this was done British interest was served. We did indeed wish to preserve also the Entente with France and Russia; but France did not want trouble to come upon her from a Balkan dispute in which French interests were not concerned; and Russia, though she would not stand a second humiliation like that of the Bosnia-Herzegovina dispute, was conciliatory and anxious only to maintain her position in the Balkans without striving to increase it at the expense of Austria." Grey, *Twenty-five Years*, I:263.

68. Regarding Italian "intimations," on 25 April, Imperiali had seconded Mensdorff's efforts to approve coercive measures in the event of an unsatisfactory Montenegrin response. The following day, Imperiali told Mensdorff that the Italian government was prepared to join in an Austro-Italian mandate, provided that the English participated in some fashion. Mensdorff to Berchtold, 28 April 1913, *OUA*, VI, No. 6803. On the other hand, Lichnowsky told Mensdorff of another statement made by the Italian ambassador to the effect that Italy could not agree to a mandate being given to Austria alone. Mensdorff to Berchtold, 27 April 1913, No. 6791. Moreover, the Italians told Flotow that joint Austro-Italian action without the participation of the other Powers was very unlikely. Flotow to Jagow, 26 April 1913, *GP*, XXXIV/2, No. 13210; Jagow to Lichnowsky, 27 April 1913, No. 13212.

69. Thurn to Berchtold, 29 April 1913, *OUA*, VI, No. 6828.

70. Report of Kageneck, 28 April 1913, *GP*, XXXIV/2, No. 13234.

71. Lichnowsky to Jagow, 30 April 1913, *GP*, XXXIV/2, No. 13243; Grey to Cartwright, 29 April 1913, *BD*, IX/2, No. 904.

72. Grey to Goschen, 30 April 1913, *BD*, IX/2, No. 909. Cf. paraphrase, aide-mémoire, 1 May 1913, *GP*, XXXIV/2, No. 13251.

73. Hantsch, *Berchtold*, I:411–12.

74. De Salis to Grey, 30 April 1913, *BD*, IX/2, No. 914; Note of

Montenegrin government, 30 April 1913, "Gradja iz borbe oko Skadra," No. 21, pp. 122–24.

75. Giesl reported a late night Montenegrin council on 29–30 April, which examined the possbility of inviting an international detachment to Scutari as Montenegro's guests, presumably to negotiate an agreement. Giesl concluded that this plan was the brainchild of Eckardt. The German minister's activities in this regard are not mentioned in the published German documents. Giesl to Berchtold, 30 April 1913, *OUA*, VI, No. 6834.

76. Grey to Goschen, 1 May 1913, *BD*, IX/2, No. 922; Mensdorff to Berchtold, 1 May 1913, *OUA*, VI, No. 6847; Lichnowsky to Jagow, 1 May 1913, *GP*, XXXIV/2, No. 13252.

77. Mensdorff to Berchtold, 1 May 1913, *OUA*, VI, No. 6847.

78. Mensdorff to Berchtold, 3 May 1913, *OUA*, VI, No. 6876; Thurn to Berchtold, 4 May 1913, No. 6898.

79. Grey to de Salis, 1 May 1913, *BD*, IX/2, No. 923; Mensdorff to Berchtold, 1 May 1913, *OUA*, VI, No. 6850. Cf. Grey to Buchanan, 2 May 1913, *BD*, IX/2, No. 934; de Salis's communication to Nicholas, "Gradja iz borbe oko Skadra," No. 23, p. 125.

80. Circular telegram from Berchtold to Great-Power capitals and Cetinje, 2 May 1913, *OUA*, VI, No. 6866; Tschirschky to Jagow, 2 May 1913, *GP*, XXXIV/2, No. 13259; Lichnowsky to Jagow, 3 May 1913, No. 13264; Pourtalès to Jagow, 4 May 1913, No. 13269. Cf. Grey to Cartwright, 3 May 1913, *BD*, IX/2, No. 942.

81. Buchanan to Grey, 1 and 2 May 1913, *BD*, IX/2, Nos. 925, 936, esp. enclosure. Cf. Grey to Bertie, 10 April 1913, No. 831.

82. Thurn to Berchtold, 2 May 1913, *OUA*, VI, No. 6869; Lichnowsky to Jagow, 1 May 1913, *GP*, XXXIV/2, No. 13252; Circular telegram from Sazonov to Great-Power capitals, 2 May/19 April 1913, *DSI*, III, No. 865. Paris agreed to work in Vienna in the sense of the Russian government's position, but doubted whether it would do any good. Izvolsky to Sazonov, 3 May/20 April 1913, No. 866.

83. Buchanan to Nicolson, 1 May 1913, *BD*, IX/2, No. 928.

84. Giolitti, *Memoirs*, p. 366; Bosworth, *Italy*, pp. 224–27.

85. Mérey to Berchtold, 27 April 1913, *OUA*, VI, Nos. 6794–95.

86. Jagow: "Italy would paralyze the Triple Alliance, if not make it bankrupt. I ask myself whether the widespread rumor that Italy undertook obligations vis-à-vis Russia at Racconigi, which contradict the Triple Alliance treaty, are not without foundation." Jagow to Flotow, 28 April 1913, *GP*, XXXIV/2, No. 13224. See also Jagow to Flotow, 28 April 1913, No. 13223; Flotow to Jagow, 26 and 28 April 1913, Nos. 13210, 13222; Jagow to Lichnowsky, 27 April 1913, No. 13212; Lichnowsky to Jagow, 27 April 1913, No. 13216; Flotow to Bethmann Hollweg, 28 April 1913, No. 13255; Grey to Rodd, 28 April 1913, *BD*, IX/2, No. 897; Berchtold to Rome, 28 April 1913, *OUA*, VI, No. 6807.

87. Flotow to Jagow, 28 April 1913, *GP*, XXXIV/2, No. 13228; Rodd to Grey, 28 and 30 April 1913, *BD*, IX/2, Nos. 895, 907.

88. Mérey to Berchtold, 28, 29, and 30 April 1913, *OUA*, VI, Nos.

6808, 6824, 6839–40; Flotow to Jagow, 29 and 30 April 1913, *GP,* XXXIV/2, Nos. 13235, 13240, 13244; Tschirschky to Jagow, 2 May 1913, No. 13257; Izvolsky to Sazonov, 30/17 April and 1 May/18 April 1913, *DSI,* III, Nos. 860, 864.

89. Bertie to Grey, 30 April 1913, *BD,* IX/2, No. 910; Askew, "Austro-Italian Antagonism," p. 208.

90. Mérey to Berchtold, 3 May 1913, *OUA,* VI, Nos. 6881–82; Flotow to Jagow, 3 May 1913, *GP,* XXXIV/2, No. 13265; Rodd to Grey, 3 May 1913, *BD,* IX/2, No. 940; Goschen to Grey, 4 May 1913, No. 943.

91. In attendance were Count Karl Stürgkh, the Austrian prime minister; Dr. Ladislaus Lukács, the Hungarian prime minister; Ritter Leon von Biliński, the common finance minister; Feldzeugmeister Alexander von Krobatin, the common war minister; Ritter Wenzel von Zalesky, the Austrian finance minister; Dr. Johann Teleszky, the Hungarian finance minister; and Court and Ministerial Counsel Ritter Alexander von Günther, who was in charge of protocol. Protocol of a meeting of the Council of Ministers for Joint Affairs, 2 May 1913, *OUA,* VI, No. 6870.

92. Helmreich, *Diplomacy of the Balkan Wars,* pp. 320–22. Cf. Redlich, *Das politische Tagebuch,* I, 1 May 1913, p. 198.

93. Berchtold to Zambaur and Mérey, 1 May 1913, *OUA,* VI, No. 6856.

94. Hubka, "Kritische Tage," pp. 35–36; Giesl, *Zwei Jahrzehnte,* p. 247. Regarding the border closing, see *NFP,* 2 May 1913, a.e., p. 5.

95. Hubka wrote: "The king may have breathed a sigh of relief that he was free of this government of the most brutal terror." Hubka, "Kritische Tage," p. 36. Eckardt reported that Nicholas had said he had "dismissed" his cabinet. Eckardt to Jagow, 3 May 1913, *GP,* XXXIV/2, No. 13266; Giesl to Berchtold, 6 May 1913, *OUA,* VI, No. 6932; *NFP,* 6 May 1913, m.e., p. 2; Vuković, *Rat Crne Gore,* pp. 117–18.

96. Giesl to Berchtold, 4 May 1913, *OUA,* VI, No. 6889; Berchtold to Mensdorff, 5 May 1913, No. 6907; Tschirschky to Jagow, 5 May 1913, *GP,* XXXIV/2, No. 13272.

97. De Salis to Grey, 4 May 1913, *BD,* IX/2, No. 948; Giesl to Berchtold, 5 and 6 May 1913, *OUA,* VI, Nos. 6905, 6932; Eckardt to Jagow, 4 May 1913, *GP,* XXXIV/2, No. 13267; *NFP,* 5 May 1913, a.e., pp. 1–2; 6 May 1913, m.e., p. 2; *GC,* 25 April 1913 O.S.; *CV,* 27 April 1913 O.S.

98. Hubka, "Kritische Tage," p. 37.

99. Berchtold to Giesl, 5 May 1913, *OUA,* VI, No. 6904; Giesl to Berchtold, 3 and 6 May 1913, Nos. 6873, 6932; Eckardt to Jagow, 3 May 1913, *GP,* XXXIV/2, No. 13266.

100. Unhappy with Eckardt's close relationship with the Montenegrin court, Giesl told the German minister that his conduct since the outbreak of the war was more befitting a Montenegrin politician than a representative of the Triple Alliance. According to Giesl's memoirs, "Herr v. Eckardt sank into his chair as though he were broken and buried his head in his hands. Without a word of parting, I left the room." Giesl, *Zwei Jahrzehnte,* p. 247. Giesl surmised that the German envoy's subsequent energetic representations with the king resulted from this scolding and the fear of being

held responsible in the event that renewed Montenegrin recalcitrance led to war. Giesl to Berchtold, 6 May 1913, *OUA,* VI, No. 6932. This Austro-German *Auseinandersetzung* is not mentioned in the published German documents.

101. Giesl to Berchtold, 4 May 1913, *OUA,* VI, Nos. 6890–1. On 13 May, the Montenegrin government formally apologized for the Hubka incident. Giesl to Berchtold, 13 May 1913, No. 7007. On 5 May, Eckardt, once again acting at the behest of Crown Prince Danilo, visited Giesl to communicate some Montenegrin views and requests concerning the post-surrender situation. Mindful of his colleague's sharp disapproval of his relationship with the royal family, Eckardt immediately informed Giesl that he was uncomfortable with the role of unofficial Montenegrin liaison with the Austrians, and had told the crown prince so himself. Conscious of Eckardt's predicament, Danilo apologized for the inconvenience he was causing, but explained that ever since the decision to evacuate Scutari had been made, he had suffered from a "great moral depression." Giesl was one of the last people he wanted to talk to. Protests and apologies thus lodged, Eckardt reported Danilo's appeals to Giesl, specifically that the Monarchy (1) stop operating torpedo boats in Montenegrin waters, (2) work to soften the Austrian press's harsh tones regarding Montenegro, (3) resume normal commercial traffic between Kotor and Cetinje, and (4) interdict Austro-Hungarian maneuvers along the Montenegrin border. Giesl rejected each request, arguing first that the operation of torpedo boats was the affair of Admiral Burney and, moreover, that Austro-Hungarian boats were the only ones available; second, that "preventive censorship" was not called for and the tone of the press would moderate itself in the course of normalization of relations; third, that the de facto restrictions hampering commercial relations would disappear shortly. Giesl's response to the fourth point was blunt and accusatory: "The sensitivity of the nerves of [Montenegrin] warriors who in two days had dropped 3,000 bombs on the peaceful Christian population of Scutari would not be affected in the same way by Austro-Hungarian operations." Giesl to Berchtold, 6 May 1913, No. 6933.

102. Grey to Cartwright, 5 May 1913, *BD,* IX/2, No. 954; Berchtold to Mensdorff, 4 May 1913, *OUA,* VI, No. 6894; Mensdorff to Berchtold, 5 May 1913, Nos. 6908, 6911; Lichnowsky to Jagow, 5 May 1913, *GP,* XXXIV/2, Nos. 13273–74.

103. Grey to de Salis, 5 May 1913, *BD,* IX/2, No. 952; de Salis to Montenegrin foreign minister, "Gradja iz borbe oko Skadra," No. 25, pp. 126–27; Mensdorff to Berchtold, 5 May 1913, *OUA,* VI, Nos. 6909, 6910, 6912; Circular telegram from Berchtold to Rome, Berlin, Paris, St. Petersburg, and Cetinje, 6 May 1913, No. 6939; *NFP,* 6 May 1913, m.e., p. 2.

104. Grey to Cartwright, 5 May 1913, *BD,* IX/2, No. 954; Grey to Bertie, 5 May 1913, No. 953; Mensdorff to Berchtold, 5 May 1913, *OUA,* VI, No. 6910; Berchtold to Rome, Berlin, Paris, St. Petersburg, and Cetinje, 6 May 1913, No. 6939; Izvolsky to Sazonov, 23 April/6 May 1913, *DSI,* III, No. 875.

105. *NFP,* 6 May 1913, e.e., p. 1; 7 May 1913, m.e., p. 3.

106. Cartwright to Nicolson, 9 May 1913, *BD*, IX/2, No. 968.
107. Thurn to Berchtold, 5 May 1913, *OUA*, VI, No. 6919; Pourtalès to Bethmann Hollweg, 6 May 1913, *GP*, XXXIV/2, No. 13282. Ironically, just as the crisis peaked, Sazonov seemed on the verge of sanctioning an international effort in Albania, if only to thwart unilateral Austrian action. Buchanan to Grey, 6 May 1913, *BD*, IX/2, No. 956; Mensdorff to Berchtold, 8 May 1913, *OUA*, VI, No. 6953. If Sazonov was relieved, Conrad was depressed by the turn of events. The one consolation of "the poor General von Conrad," as the German military attaché called him, was that he now did not have to cooperate with Italy in a joint operation. Report from Kageneck, 4 May 1913, *GP*, XXXIV/2, No. 13276. Berchtold seemed to share this viewpoint. He told Redlich that if it was uncomfortable to work with four other powers in the occupation of Scutari, it would have been much more painful to have had to work with Italy alone. Redlich, *Das politische Tagebuch*, I, 19 May 1913, p. 199.
108. Berchtold to Mérey and Szögyény, 6 May 1913, *OUA*, VI, No. 6915; Tschirschky to Jagow, 5 May 1913, *GP*, XXXIV/2, Nos. 13272, 13281; *NFP*, 6 May 1913, m.e., p. 5. Grey asserted that if any intervention became necessary in the future, it should be international in scope. Grey to Bertie, 5 May 1913, *BD*, IX/2, No. 953.
109. Rodd to Grey, 8 May 1913, *BD*, IX/2, No. 966; Bosworth, *Italy*, pp. 228–30.
110. *NFP*, 9 May 1913, e.e., pp. 1–2.
111. De Salis to Grey, 9 and 13 May 1913, PRO, FO 371/1681/2146 and 24367; *NFP*, 9 May 1913, e.e., p. 2; Giesl to Berchtold, 8 and 9 May 1913, HHStA, PA XVII/Montenegro, Karton 30, Nos. 187 and 51 A-F, pp. 29, 30–32.
112. *NFP*, 2 May 1913, a.e., p. 3; 6 May 1913, m.e., p. 3, e.e., p. 3; 8 May 1913, e.e., p. 1; 9 May 1913, m.e., pp. 1–2; Eckardt to Jagow, 8 May 1913, *GP*, XXXIV/2, No. 13286. The Powers in fact applied considerable pressure on Belgrade to try to convince Cetinje to surrender. Griesinger to Jagow, 3 May 1913, No. 13263; Bertie to Grey, 30 April 1913, *BD*, IX/2, No. 910; Izvolsky to Sazonov, 30/17 April 1913, *DSI*, III, No. 861. See also Hubka, "Kritische Tage," p. 35, and Popović, *Borba za narodno ujedinjenje*, p. 127.
113. Whereas, after the fall of Scutari on April 23 he had called the decisions of the conference concerning Djakovica's ownership null and void and had withdrawn his intention to participate in an international loan for Montenegro, he now conceded that he probably would drop the Djakovica matter and also join the loan project. Berchtold to Mérey, 7 May 1913, *OUA*, VI, No. 6945.
114. Berchtold understood the reasons for San Giuliano's generosity. In exchange for compromise and flexibility on the part of the Triple Alliance in the north of Albania, the Italian foreign minister was hoping to win the same consideration for Italian claims in the south. Mérey to Berchtold, 9 May 1913, *OUA*, VI, Nos. 6973–75; Flotow to Jagow, 6 May 1913, *GP*, XXXIV/2, No. 13277; Grey to Rodd, 7 May 1913, *BD*, IX/2, No. 963.
115. *NFP*, 10 May 1913, m.e., p. 3. Cf. Buchanan to Grey, 15 May

1913, *BD*, IX/2, No. 975. The Russians made some effort to achieve territorial concessions for Montenegro, especially after Austria-Hungary annexed the tiny (1¼-kilometer long) island of Ada Kaleh in the Danube. Telegram of the Hungarian interior minister, 13 May 1913, *OUA*, VI, No. 7013; Pallavicini to Berchtold, 15 and 22 May, Nos. 7020, 7107; Berchtold to Pallavicini, 22 May 1913, No. 7104; Mérey to Berchtold, 18 May 1913, No. 7051; Berchtold to Mensdorff, 19 May 1913, No. 7065; Thurn to Berchtold, 25 May/7 June 1913, No. 7299; Report on visit of Italian ambassador, 6 June 1913, No. 7294; Sazonov to Benckendorff, 3/16 May 1913, *DSI*, III, No. 884; Izvolsky to Sazonov, 5/18 May 1913, No. 886; *CV*, 8 May 1913 O.S. The Russian ambassador to Italy raised the possibility of reassigning to Montenegrin sovereignty the fertile coastal strip on the eastern shore of Lake Scutari betweenЛичeni Hotit and Vraka. Berchtold held his ground, and nothing came of the proposal. Berchtold to Rome, London, and St. Petersburg, 3 June 1913, *OUA*, VI, No. 7264; Mensdorff to Berchtold, 4 June 1913, No. 7274; Mérey to Berchtold, 6 June 1913, No. 7295; Mensdorff to Berchtold, 6 June 1913, No. 7293; Sazonov to Izvolsky, 20 May/2 June 1913, *DSI*, III, No. 904; Izvolsky to Sazonov, 22 May/4 June 1913, No. 906.

116. Because of reports that Nicholas had manipulated the Scutari crisis to his own advantage on the Paris, London, Vienna, and Frankfurt exchanges, King George believed that what Nicholas actually needed to pacify his subjects was land, not money. According to the stories, Nicholas had purchased various stocks that had fallen in value when war seemed imminent. When Montenegro capitulated, the value of the stocks rose dramatically, and Nicholas was supposed to have cashiered a "coup de bourse." Kageneck report, 4 May 1913, *GP*, XXXIV/2, No. 13276; Jagow to Tschirschky, 28 May 1913, No. 13340. Certainly Nicholas was not the only one who speculated. Redlich recounted: "Monday the peace 'broke out' officially. An enormous stock boom the result! Here the whole world plays! High officers and officials at the head! It's as bad as 1873." Redlich, *Das politische Tagebuch*, I, 10 May 1913, p. 199. Cf. Cartwright to Nicolson, 9 May 1913, *BD*, IX/2, No. 968. The reports of Nicholas's stock gains cooled British sympathy for Montenegro. See Uebersberger, *Österreich zwischen Russland und Serbien*, p. 126; Durham, *Struggle for Scutari*, p. 272.

117. *NFP*, 6 May 1913, e.e., p. 3.

118. De Salis to Grey, 7 May 1913, PRO, FO 21038/20810/13/44.

119. Admiralty to foreign office, 17 May 1913, PRO, FO 23100/20810/13/44; "Gradja iz borbe oko Skadra," No. 27, pp. 127–28. Cf. Plamenac's original bargaining position, No. 26, p. 127.

120. *NFP*, 9 May 1913, e.e., p. 2. Even before the takeover of the city, Catholic Scutarenes who still looked upon Austria as their trusted benefactor began to complain about the predominantly British character of the expedition. Berchtold, however, was quick to sanction this "leading role of England," because it preserved the international character of the operation and negated allegations that the occupation was merely part of Vienna's own plans concerning Albania. Zambaur to Berchtold, 11 May 1913, *OUA*, VI, No. 6996; Berchtold to Zambaur, 12 May 1913, No. 7003.

121. *NFP*, 9 May 1913, e.e., p. 2; 10 May 1913, m.e., p. 2; Berchtold to Zambaur and Mérey, 1 May 1913, *OUA*, VI, No. 6856.
122. *NFP*, 14 May 1913, m.e., p. 7; *CV*, 1 and 3 May 1913 O.S.
123. De Salis to Grey, 15 May 1913 PRO, FO 22388/20810/13/44, cited in *BD*, IX/2, No. 968, editorial note. See also Giesl to Berchtold, 8 and 10 May 1913, *OUA*, VI, Nos. 6952, 6980; Eckardt to Jagow, 8 May 1913, *GP*, XXXIV/2, No. 13286; Heeringen to Jagow, 10 May 1913, No. 13288; de Salis to Plamenac, 14 May 1913, "Gradja iz borbe oko Skadra," No. 28, p. 129. For an interesting description of the commission in Scutari, see Durham's letters to Grey, Grey Papers, PRO, FO 800/76/11. See also *NFP*, 15 May 1913, m.e., pp. 5–6.
124. Lichnowsky to Bethmann Hollweg, 31 May 1913, *GP*, XXXIV/2, No. 13354. Cf. Grey to Cartwright, 26 May 1913, *BD*, IX/2, No. 1002.
125. In his monumental study of the origins of the First World War, Albertini soundly condemned the German attitude during the Scutari crisis, accusing Jagow's instructions to Lichnowsky and Tschirschky of being nothing short of an "incitement to take action." "Here be it noted that those historians who have searched the German documents for proofs that in the course of the Balkan War Germany continually restrained Austria from provoking an outbreak, have not discovered a single word uttered by Berlin at this juncture to restrain Vienna from taking separate action (and thus running the risk of letting loose a European war), or asking Vienna at least to wait until after the failure of joint action by the Powers." Albertini, *Origins of the War*, I:444. In his overall assessment of the situation, Albertini is largely correct. The Germans were as impatient as the Austrians for a resolution of the Scutari crisis and repeatedly called for a quick stroke to cut the Gordian knot. William II criticized the reluctance of the Powers to contemplate strong measures in the event of an unsatisfactory Montenegrin response to the Great-Power démarches: ". . . no one has the courage to envision this eventuality and to grab for powder! They like pretty words, but to defend their honor and standpoint with arms—no!" Tschirschky to Jagow, 28 April 1913, *GP*, XXXIV/2, No. 13230, marginalia. On the evening of Austria's "war council"—2 May—William wrote that "I believe that the limit for Austrian temporizing has been reached, and a quick decisive hit is the only solution. . . . The more Austria temporizes and gives in and puts off, the more untenable the situation becomes. . . ." Lichnowsky to Jagow, 1 May 1913, No. 13252, marginalia. The same day, Jagow wrote the German ambassador in London: "We have no cause to advocate in Vienna either adhesion to [the latest] démarche or postponement of military action, because we do not want to urge on our allies a policy of weakness." Jagow to Lichnowsky, 2 May 1913, No. 13254. Yet despite this seemingly unlimited support for Austrian demands, the Germans, including the emperor, wanted Austria to act only within certain prescribed bounds. Less than one week before the council meeting, when the German military attaché reported Krobatin's suggestion that Austria and Italy should divide Albania between them, William exhibited exasperation: "The poor Greeks! And for this an autonomous Albania has been agreed to. Then Nicholas can keep Scutari, too!

Then we don't need any more action." Kageneck report, 26 April 1913, No. 13214. Similarly, when Berchtold suggested that it might prove difficult not to move against Serbia, too, Jagow wired that he would consider it "desirable" for Austria to restrict her activities to Montenegro. To be sure, this did not constitute a harsh slap on the wrists, but it indicates that Germany was not looking for all-out war. Tschirschky to Jagow, 27 April 1913, No. 13225; Jagow to Tschirschky, 28 April 1913, No. 13226. Nor should it be forgotten that before sanctioning isolated Austrian action, the Germans endeavored to have Italy participate in a multinational intervention.

126. See R. J. Crampton, "The Decline of the Concert of Europe in the Balkans, 1913–1914," *Slavonic and East European Review*, LII (July 1974): 393–419. In Grey's retrospective words: "The members of the Ambassadors' Conference of 1912–13 were all alive, available, and at their posts in 1914; but no one in Berlin or Vienna seems to have remembered the past or found in the recollection of 1912–13 any hope for the future. So, when the crisis came in 1914, although the suggestion of settling by the same machinery as in 1912 was made, it was dismissed peremptorily by Germany and Austria. Had there been two men, one in Vienna and one in St. Petersburg, wise enough to foresee their perils, one great enough to propose and the other great anough to accept the suggestion of making the London Conference, or something like it, a permanent machine, future Balkan disputes might have been settled with increasing ease. But there were no such statesmen in St. Petersburg or Vienna. . . ." Grey, *Twenty-five Years*, I:266–67. Fay skillfully summarized some of the reasons for Austria's reluctance to return to the conference table in July, 1914: "The decisions of the London Conference had brought her little or nothing, in her own opinion, except disappointments and illusions. Its delays and ineffectiveness in protecting Albanian interests, when defied by the Montenegrins at Scutari and the Serbians at Dibra, explain to some why Austria was absolutely unwilling, after the murder of Archduke Franz Ferdinand at Sarajevo, to submit her latest grounds of complaint against Serbia to another Conference of the Powers. . . . On the other hand, when Austria had acted quickly and energetically on her own account, by sending a peremptory ultimatum, Serbia had heeded her demands immediately, Russia had not interfered, and the Vienna Foreign Office had accomplished its immediate purpose." Fay, *Origins of the World War*, I:474–75. The ultimatum in question is discussed in the following chapter.

CHAPTER NINE

1. Albertini, *Origins of the War*, I: 448–60; Helmreich, *Diplomacy of the Balkan Wars*, pp. 341–406; Hantsch, *Berchtold*, II:419–70; Rossos, *Russia*

and the Balkans, pp. 153–206. For a contemporary account, see Spencer Campbell, "The Dissolution of the Balkan Allies," *Fortnightly Review*, n.s., XCIII (June 1913): 1963–1970.

   2. See Giesl to Berchtold, 10 and 24 June 1913, *OUA*, VI, Nos. 7320, 7478; Fürstenberg to Berchtold, 12 June 1913, No. 7343; Hubka to Conrad, 24 June 1913, No. 7479; *CV*, 28 June 1913, O.S. For a contemporary account of Cetinje's involvement, see V. B. Božović, *Krvavi Kamen: Crna Gora u drugom balkanskom ratu sa Bugarskom* (Belgrade, 1913).

   3. Hantsch, *Berchtold*, II:471. In addition, see Eduard Ritter von Steinitz's earlier study, "Berchtolds Politik während des Zweiten Balkankrieges: Das Endergebnis der Krise 1912/13," *Berliner Monatshefte*, X (July 1932): 660–74. During the war, Germany restrained Austria from embarking on projects which might have led to a more widespread conflict.

   4. Grey, *Twenty-five Years*, I:253.

   5. Sergei Sazonov, *Sechs schwere Jahre*, 2d ed. (Berlin: Verlag für Kulturpolitik, 1927), p. 120.

   6. Giesl to Berchtold, 25 and 30 August 1913, *OUA*, VII, Nos. 8468, 8512. See HHStA, PA XII/Türkei, Karton 440, Liasse XLV/221: Grenzverhandlungen zwischen Bulgarien, Serbien, Montenegro und Griechenland 1913–1914; Akers-Douglas to Grey, 19 November 1913, PRO, FO 371/1681/53210. The Serbo-Montenegrin agreement was not reached without some difficulty, and many members of the Serbian skupština objected to the treaty of 12 November.

   7. Czernin to Berchtold, 19/6 June 1914, *OUA*, VIII, No. 9890.

   8. Giesl to Berchtold, 1 September 1913, *OUA*, VII, No. 8524.

   9. Weinzetl to Berchtold, 2 December 1913, *OUA*, VII, No. 9045. Cf. Akers-Douglas to Grey, 18 November 1913, PRO, FO 371/1681/53210.

   10. Weinzetl to Berchtold, 10 August 1913, *OUA*, VII, No. 8321; Tel. No. 255, 17 August 1913, cited in report from Cetinje, 22 August 1913, No. 8447.

   11. Giesl to Berchtold, 22 August 1913, *OUA*, VII, No. 8447. See HHStA, PA XII/Albanien, Karton 45, Liasse IL/I: Feststellung der albanesischen Grenze zu Montenegro. For Austro-Montenegrin negotiations and concordat talks between Cetinje and the Vatican, see HHStA, PA XVII/Montenegro, Liasse XIII.

   12. For an excellent summary of this crisis, see Albertini, *Origins of the War*, I:471–87; and Hantsch, *Berchtold*, II:489–506. See also *CV*, 18 September 1913 O.S.

   13. Circular telegram, 19 October 1913, *OUA*, VII, No. 8871; Conrad, *AMD*, III:473; *GP*, XXXVI/1, pp. 394–402.

   14. Like the ultimatum of July 1914, this one was called a *befriste Note*. In October 1913 and July 1914, San Giuliano was away from Rome when Austria acted. On both occasions, Italian Secretary General de Martino learned of Vienna's intentions only hours in advance. In Albertini's words, "already in 1913 Austria took a step which might have led to a European war and in which she expected Italy to make common cause with her, without previous intimation to the Italian Government and without obtaining its consent." Albertini, *Origins of the War*, I:481.

15. Giesl to Berchtold, 21 October 1913, *OUA*, VII, No. 8896; *CV*, 16 October 1913 O.S.
16. Telegram to Cetinje, 17 October 1913, *OUA*, VII, No. 8855.
17. For an excellent review of Montenegro's woes, see Giesl to Berchtold, 25 August 1913, *OUA*, VII, No. 8468. On the subject of unification, see also Delaroche-Vernet to Doumergue, 26 May 1914, *DDF*, 3, X, No. 286.
18. Berchtold to Szögyény and Mérey, 4 July 1913, *OUA*, VI, No. 7612.
19. Berchtold to Ambrózy, 10 November 1913, *OUA*, VII, No. 8976.
20. Vienna had commercial as well as geopolitical reasons for opposing Serbian access to the sea, namely to keep Serbian goods travelling on the Dual Monarchy's railroads to her Adriatic ports. Some Austrians argued that Serbia's annexation of Montenegro would enhance her prestige only nominally and not significantly alter the balance of power in the Balkans. They reasoned that Montenegro's primitive harbors were incapable of handling the large volume of Serbian trade that paranoid Habsburg officials envisioned being rerouted to the south. In 1913 these arguments had little effect on Berchtold. Cf. de Bunsen to Nicolson, 24 April 1914, *BD*, X/1, No. 358.
21. Hans Heilbronner writes that "in September, 1912, Russia had abrogated the program of military assistance owing to the Tsar's displeasure over Montenegro's unapproved attack upon Scutari." If Heilbronner is using the Gregorian calendar, he is mistaken about the dates, as war did not break out until October. Heilbronner, "Merger Attempts," p. 282.
22. O'Beirne to Grey, 1 October 1913, *BD*, X/1, No. 310; Risto J. Dragićević, "Djevojački institut na Cetinju," *IZ*, Pt. 1: II, Knj. IV, Nos. 4–6 (1949): 130–51; Pt. 2: III, Knj. V, Nos. 1–3 (1950): 40–61; Pejović, *Razvitak prosvjete i kulture u Crnoj Gori*, pp. 126–32.
23. Nicholas received an annual gift of 250,000 crowns, Danilo 60,000. The Russians responded to Nicholas's request by first abolishing the Nikolai cadet corps, then in September by closing the institute. Giesl to Berchtold, 25 August 1913, *OUA*, VII, No. 8468. For particulars, see Dragićević, "Djevojački institut," Pt. 2, esp. pp. 55–61.
24. O'Beirne to Grey, 1 October 1913, *BD*, X/1, No. 310.
25. Vujović, *Crna Gora i Francuska*, p. 369.
26. Giesl queried Berchtold as to the kind of assistance Austria-Hungary might be prepared to offer; the foreign minister remained silent. Giesl to Berchtold, 25 August 1913, *OUA*, VII, No. 8468.
27. Weinzetl to Berchtold, 5 August 1913, *OUA*, VII, No. 8228. For a detailed study of Montenegrin approaches to Austria-Hungary during the late summer and early fall of 1912, see Novica Rakočević, "Odnosi izmedju Crne Gore i Austro-Ugarske od završetka skadarske krize maja 1913. do sarajevskog atentata," *Jugoslovenski narodi pred Prvi svetski rat*, pp. 825–28.
28. Giesl to Berchtold, 26 August 1913, *OUA*, VII, No. 8481.
29. Berchtold to Weinzetl, 8 August 1913, *OUA*, VII, No. 8285; Berchtold to Giesl, 8 September 1913, No. 8560; Ambrózy to Berchtold, 1 September 1913, No. 8527.

30. Giesl to Berchtold, 6 September 1913, *OUA*, VII, No. 8548.

31. Delaroche-Vernet to Pichon, 16 October 1913, *DDF*, 3, VIII, No. 336.

32. Delaroche painted a very black portrait of Nicholas, calling him "an egoist, an autocrat, accustomed for half a century to look upon Montenegro as his own personal property to be ruled and directed according to his own personal will." He said the Montenegrin people would not tolerate this kind of abuse any longer. Delaroche-Vernet to Pichon, 11 October 1913, cited in Vujović, *Crna Gora i Francuska*, pp. 371–73. Theo. Russell, the British ambassador in Vienna, characterized such allegations about an Austro-Montenegrin rapprochement as typical of "Russian and French tales as to [Austria's] ulterior designs" in the Balkans, and especially Albania. He believed they were trying to subvert Britain's good working relationship with Austria. Grey responded: "Austria will be of little use to us as a friend, if she falls to pieces. One cannot steer with confidence by a star that may dissolve." Russell to Nicolson, 21 November 1913, *BD*, X/1, No. 316. Neratov, for one, never took the reports seriously. He told the French chargé in St. Petersburg that an Austro-Montenegrin reconciliation would cause the Montenegrin people to rise up and dethrone Nicholas. Doulcet to Pichon, 7 October 1913, *DDF*, 3, VIII, No. 281. See also Giesl to Berchtold, 10 October 1913, *OUA*, VII, No. 8817.

33. Akers-Douglas to Grey, 9 October and 4 December 1913, PRO, FO 371/1681/48316 and 55632; Grey to Rodd, 18 December 1913, 371/1681/55672.

34. Grey to Rodd, 15 December 1913, PRO, FO 371/1681/57288. While in London, Plamenac queried the British about their willingness to propose border rectifications in Montenegro's behalf. Grey advised him to see Austria about such matters. Grey to Akers-Douglas, 12 December 1913, 371/1681/56775.

35. See, for example, Heath (Treasury) to foreign office, 19 August 1914, PRO, FO 371/2041/33166. For a study of the loan question based on French documents, see Vujović, *Crna Gora i Francuska*, pp. 400–406.

36. The British representative remarked that "the King and some of the members of the Royal Family have barely concealed, during the past year, their antipathy to the . . . Minister, whose alleged hostility towards Montenegro they have considered being largely the cause of what is held to be the unfriendly attitude of his Government. Baron Giesl's position has thus been rendered a disagreeable one." Akers-Douglas to Grey, 8 November 1913, PRO, FO 371/1681/52169. Cf. Giesl, *Zwei Jahrzehnte*, p. 249.

37. Upon hearing of Giesl's transfer, Nicholas and his minions maintained a coolness towards him that bordered on frigidity. At an official reception on 16 November, held to commemorate the 100th anniversary of Njegoš's birth, the royal family, in particular Queen Milena, made a special point of ignoring Giesl. Montenegrin officials refrained from wearing Austro-Hungarian decorations on their tunics—an omission which irritated Giesl. The slight became even more annoying when Prince Peter appeared, sporting a Turkish star, despite the fact that Montenegro was

still formally at war with Turkey. Giesl advised his staff not to attend that evening's celebration in the theater, at which they would normally be obligated to wear their Montenegrin awards. Giesl to Berchtold, 17 November 1913, *OUA*, VII, No. 9007.

38. Otto to Berchtold, 30 December 1913 and 27 January 1914, *OUA*, VII, Nos. 9139, 9248; Hubka, "König Nikolaus," Pt. 1, p. 25; Obnorsky to Sazonov, 25/12 January 1914, *IB*, I/1, No. 102.

39. Obnorsky to Sazonov, 25/12 January, 2 February/20 January and 8 February/26 January 1914, *IB*, I/1, Nos. 102, 162, 203. Months later, the Powers sought to facilitate "freedom of movement" for the Klementi, whom the Montenegrins were denying access to their traditional pasturage. See HHStA, PA XII/Albanien, Karton 45, Liasse IL/1.

40. Hubka to Conrad, 18 February 1914, *OUA*, VII, No. 9386.

41. Conrad, *AMD*, III:579.

42. Halla to Berchtold, 3 June, 10 and 17 July 1914, HHStA, PA XII/Albanien, Karton 45, Liasse IL/1, Nos. 103/P, 356, 367; Egger to Berchtold, 29 June 1914, No. 44; Berchtold to Otto, 10 July 1914, No. 3238.

43. Potapov to Dept. of Russian Gen. Quartermaster, 15/2 April 1914, *IB*, I/1, No. 230; Sazonov to Obnorsky, 21/8 April 1914, No. 248.

44. Aide-mémoire of the British embassy to Sazonov, 22/9 April 1914, *IB*, I/2, No. 260; aide-mémoire, Sazonov to Buchanan, 23/10 April 1914, No. 274; *GP*, XXXVI/2, No. 14438. Cf. Delaroche-Vernet to Doumergue, 29 April 1914, *DDF*, 3, X, No. 179.

45. Sazonov to Obnorsky, 21/8 April 1914, *IB*, I/2, No. 248.

46. Obnorsky to Sazonov, 25/12 April 1914, *IB*, I/2, No. 293; Sazonov to Izvolsky, 26/13 April 1914, No. 298.

47. *GC*, 3 March 1914 O.S.; *CV*, 26 February 1914 O.S.; de Salis to Grey, 10 March 1914, PRO, FO 371/2041/10577; Hartwig to Sazonov, 8 March/23 February 1914, *IB*, I/1, No. 395. Despite the seriousness of the incident, there is a striking dearth of relevant documents in the published Austrian collection. In fact, Sjenokos is explained only in a footnote, Otto to Berchtold, 18 March 1914, *OUA*, VII, No. 9486. For comprehensive Austrian accounts, see HHStA, PA XVII/Montenegro, Karton 50, Liasse XIV.

48. Stevanović to Pašić, March 1914 (n.d.), SSIP. Cf. Otto to Berchtold, 13 March and 4 April 1914, HHStA, PA XVII/Montenegro, Karton 50, Liasse XIV, Nos. 39, 51; war ministry to Berchtold, 31 March 1914, Abt. 5, No. 1879; Giesl to Berchtold, 8 April 1914, No. 52; *CV*, 26 February, 5, 12, and 19 March 1914 O.S. See also *Stenografske bilješke o radu Crnogorske narodne skupštine, 1906–1914*.

49. Rakočević, "Odnosi izmedju Crne Gore i Austro-Ugarske," p. 843. Initially, the Montenegrins blamed Schreiber. Otto to Berchtold, 9 March 1914, HHStA, PA XVII/Montenegro, Karton 50, Liasse XIV, No. 35. But Berchtold reminded Otto that bureaucrats did not give orders to Austria's military. Berchtold to Otto, 10 March 1914, No. 26.

50. De Salis to Grey, 11 May 1914, *BD*, X/1, No. 363; Otto to Berchtold, 8 and 27 March 1914, HHStA, PA XVII/Montenegro, Karton 50, Liasse XIV, Nos. 14, 47; 20 May 1914, No. 32.

51. Hartwig to Sazonov, 25/12 March, cited in Obnorsky to Sazonov, 23/10 March 1914, *IB*, I/2, No. 68, n. 1.

52. For a discussion of border negotiations and Austrian attitudes concerning the delimitation of the border, see Rakočević, "Odnosi izmedju Crne Gore i Austro-Ugarske," pp. 833–38.

53. Giesl to Berchtold, 10 June 1913, *OUA*, VI, No. 7321.

54. Giesl to Berchtold, 17 November 1913, *OUA*, VII, No. 9006.

55. Giesl to Berchtold, 4 November 1913, *OUA*, VII, No. 8952. Plamenac told the British chargé in Cetinje that his purpose in going to St. Petersburg was not just to secure the loan, but also to improve Russo-Montenegrin relations. Akers-Douglas to Grey, 22 October 1913, PRO, FO 371/1681/48902.

56. Giesl to Berchtold, 17 November 1913, *OUA*, VII, No. 9006.

57. Nicholas subsequently made several efforts to arrange special missions to St. Petersburg, led either by himself or Montenegrin generals. Obnorsky to Sazonov, 5 February/23 January 1914, *IB*, I/1, Nos. 185; 9 April/27 March 1914, I/2, No. 194. Regarding Obnorsky's refusal to open a Montenegrin mission in St. Petersburg, see Giesl to Berchtold, 17 November 1913, *OUA*, VII, No. 9006.

58. De Salis, "Montenegro: Annual Report, 1913," PRO, FO 371/2041/424; Otto to Berchtold, 20 May 1914, *OUA*, VIII, No. 9696.

59. Otto to Berchtold, 27 January 1914, *OUA*, VII, No. 9248; *CV*, 24 January 1914 O.S.

60. Akers-Douglas to Grey, 6 February 1914, *BD*, X/1, No. 342.

61. Hubka to Conrad, 18 February 1914, *OUA*, VII, No. 9386; Obnorsky to Sazonov, 23/10 February 1914, cited in 23/10 March 1914, *IB*, I/2, No. 67. Although the Russo-Montenegrin détente had its own rationale, it was perceived by some to be part of a general Russian effort to improve relations with all parties in the Balkans. See Crackanthorpe to Grey, 25 January 1914, *BD*, X/1, No. 330.

62. Pašić to Peter, 2 February/20 January 1914, *APS*, I, No. 399. Cf. Tschirschky to Bethmann Hollweg, 15 February 1914, *GP*, XXXVIII, No. 15536; Conrad, *AMD*, III:575–76.

63. Szápáry to Berchtold, 28/15 February 1914, *OUA*, VII, Nos. 9426–27; Sazonov to Hartwig, 5 March/20 February 1914, *IB*, I/1, No. 380. See also Tschirschky to Bethmann Hollweg, 15 February 1914, *GP*, XXXVIII, No. 15536; Akers-Douglas to Grey, 6 February 1914, *BD*, X/1, No. 342.

64. Pallavicini to Berchtold, 11 February 1914, *OUA*, VII, No. 9339; Berchtold to Mérey, 13 February 1914, No. 9355; Gellinek to Conrad, 14 February 1914, No. 9360. The Turkish ambassador to Austria combined fact with rumor in fanciful speculation as to what was blowing in the Balkan wind. See report on a conversation with the Turkish ambassador, 14 February 1914, No. 9364. Hartwig, for his part, discussed widespread fears that the Bulgarians and Turks were on the verge of concluding a military pact to be directed against Serbia and Greece. Sazonov to Hartwig, 10 February/28 January 1914, *IB*, I/1, No. 224. Rome was disturbed by the Balkan rumors, once more giving Berchtold an opportunity to forge an agreement with San Giuliano concerning Montenegro. As in the past, he left it up to Mérey to bring the matter up, but the ambassador never

found the right moment. Berchtold to Mérey, 13 February 1914, *OUA,* VII, No. 9355.

65. Gellinek to Conrad, 14 February 1914, *OUA,* VII, No. 9360.

66. Giesl to Berchtold, 24 February 1914, *OUA,* VII, No. 9418. Local Serbian circles seemed inclined to accept as gospel rumors about imminent unification. See report of Hoflehner, 3 March 1914, No. 9440.

67. See, for example, Hartwig to Sazonov, 30/17 March and 7 April/ 25 March 1914, *IB,* I/2, Nos. 119, 170.

68. Conference reports on the question of a Montenegrin subsidy, 3 February/21 January 1914, *IB,* I/1, No. 165; 13 April/31 March 1914, I/2, No. 209; Sazonov to Obnorsky, 5 February/23 January 1914, I/1, No. 180. Danilov's attitude lent credence to Conrad's accusation that the Russo-Montenegrin rapprochement was directed principally against Austria-Hungary. Conrad, *AMD,* III:579, 582.

69. It was understood that Pašić himself had originally suggested using Serbian instructors when he visited St. Petersburg in February, officially for the baptism of King Peter's new grandson, but he did not pursue the matter subsequently. See, inter alia, Sazonov to Obnorsky, 5 February/ 23 January 1914, *IB,* I/1, No. 180; 15/2 April 1914, I/2, No. 223; Sazonov to Hartwig, 29/16 March 1914, No. 111; Neratov to Hartwig, 30/17 April 1914, No. 329; Obnorsky to Sazonov, 26/13 March 1914, No. 98. Giers, who returned to Cetinje in the spring, feared Nicholas's adventurism in Albania and had grave reservations about the rapprochement. Giers to Sazonov, 23/10 March and 9 April/27 March 1914, Nos. 69, 195; Sazonov to Giers, 28/15 March 1914, No. 108.

70. Obnorsky to Sazonov, 22/9 May 1914, *IB,* I/3, Nos. 65–66.

71. Sazonov to Izvolsky and Benckendorff, 24/11 May 1914, *IB,* I/3, No. 72; Sazonov to Obnorsky, 24/11 May 1914, No. 73; Benckendorff to Sazonov, 27/14 May 1914, No. 79; Giers to Sazonov, 27/14 June 1914, No. 397.

72. Giers to Sazonov, 28/15 and 29/16 May 1914, *IB,* I/3, Nos. 113, 120. Otto to Berchtold, 20 May 1914, *OUA,* VIII, No. 9696; Delaroche-Vernet to Doumergue, 19 and 30 May 1914, *DDF,* 3, X, Nos. 249, 311; *CV,* 20 May 1914 O.S.

73. For an overview of the unification question, see Albertini, *Origins of the War,* I:509–23; Heilbronner, "Merger Attempts," pp. 281–91; Novica Rakočević, "Crna Gora i ujedinjenje," *Politički život Jugoslavije, 1914–1945,* ed. Aleksandar Acković (Belgrade: Radio-Beograd, 1973), pp. 75–92; Vojislav Bogićević, "Odnos Austro-Ugarske prema nameravanom ujedinjenju Srbije i Crne Gore," *IZ,* V, Knj. VIII, Nos. 1–3 (1952): 62–68; Nikola Petrović, "Zajednički Austro-Ugarski kabinet i jugoslovensko pitanje, 1912–1918," *Jugoslovenski narodi pred Prvi svetski rat,* pp. 727–60. For a review of political conditions in the spring, see Hartwig to Sazonov, 7 April/25 March 1914, *IB,* I/2, No. 169; Akers-Douglas to Grey, 6 February 1914, PRO, FO 371/2041/10053; Griesinger to Bethmann Hollweg, 11 March 1914, *GP,* XXXVIII, No. 15539.

74. For a superb study of the election and Vukotić's governmental program, see Novica Rakočević, "Izbori za Crnogorsku narodnu skupštinu

u januaru 1914. godine i program vlade generala Janka Vukotića," *IZ,* XXV, Knj. XXX, Nos. 3–4 (1972): 413–30. The old assembly had been in session only two months of its three-year existence. The "parties" that made up both the old and new assemblies were merely rough groupings. See also *GC,* 12 October 1913 O.S.; Akers-Douglas to Grey, 25 October 1913, PRO, FO 371/1681/49396.

75. Jovanović, *Stvaranje Crnogorske države,* p. 408; Rakočević, "Izbori," pp. 424–28.

76. Rakočević, "Crna Gora i ujedinjenje," p. 77.

77. Akers-Douglas to Grey, 12 February 1914, PRO, FO 371/2041/10054; Rakočević, "Izbori," p. 423. See also Rakočević, "Crna Gora i ujedinjenje," pp. 76–77; Obnorsky to Sazonov, 23/10 March 1914, *IB,* I/2, No. 67; *CV,* 29 and 31 January 1914 O.S.

78. Eckardt to Bethmann Hollweg, 25 February 1914, *GP,* XXXVIII, No. 15537.

79. Despite the sentiment for a closer relationship with Serbia, the Montenegrin skupština went about the business of formally incorporating the newly acquired territories, creating four new oblasts: Peć, Berane, Bijelo Polje, and Pljevlja. Jovanović, *Stvaranje Crnogorske države,* p. 408.

80. Nicholas to Peter, "Nekoliko dokumenata iz 1913. do 1915. godine," *Z,* X, Knj. XVIII, No. 1 (1937), No. 4, pp. 50–51; Vuković, *Rat Crne Gore,* pp. 139–40; Hartwig to Sazonov, 7 April/25 March 1914, *IB,* I/2, No. 169; Hartwig to Sazonov, 25/12 March 1914, cited in Obnorsky to Sazonov, 23/10 March 1914, No. 68, n. 1.

81. Obnorsky to Sazonov, 26/13 March 1914, *IB,* I/2, No. 97; Paléologue to Doumergue, 22 April 1914, *DDF,* 3, X, No. 141. Cf. Giers to Sazonov, 30/17 May 1914, cited in Giers to Sazonov, 12 May/29 April 1914, *IB,* I/2, No. 412, n. 1.

82. Hartwig to Sazonov, 30/17 March and 7 April/25 March 1914, *IB,* I/2, Nos. 119, 169–70; Vuković, *Rat Crne Gore,* pp. 140–41; Rakočević, "Crna Gora i ujedinjenje," pp. 77–78. Mijušković was a good choice to represent Nicholas's interests. A devotee of the dynasty, he was personally opposed to complete amalgamation. See Storck to Berchtold, 3 July 1914, *OUA,* VII, No. 10003.

83. Giesl to Berchtold, 6 March 1914, *OUA,* VII, No. 9445.

84. Gellinek to Conrad, 5 April 1914, *OUA,* VII, No. 9554. Cf. Giesl to Berchtold, 12 March 1914, HHStA, PA XVII/Montenegro, Karton 50, Liasse XIV, No. 39.

85. One Marković, a Montenegrin subject, suddenly reappeared after a long absence and told the skupština that in 1879 a wealthy Russian had given his fortune so that dowries could be provided Montenegrin girls. The entire fortune, an estimated two hundred fifty thousand rubles, was alleged to have been paid to Nicholas—in cash. The question was: what had happened to the money? Otto to Berchtold, 18 March 1914, *OUA,* VII, No. 9486. Hubka and Conrad blamed the Russians for the revelations and interpellations before the skupština. Conrad, *AMD,* III:581. The latest scandals regarding Mirko concerned his relationship with one Mlle. Fritsch, a Swiss woman, whom he had allegedly seduced years before when she

had served as a teacher at the Russian institute, and who had unexpectedly reappeared as a "sister of mercy" during the Balkan wars, sharing Mirko's tent and champagne. It was also reported that the prince, for reasons unknown, had sent blackmail letters to his sister, the queen of Italy, and her husband. Nicholas was encouraged to deprive Mirko of a right of succession. Giesl to Berchtold, 6 March 1914, *OUA*, VII, No. 9445; 13 June 1914, VIII, No. 9851. Cf. Conrad, *AMD*, III:578.

86. Szápáry to Berchtold, 28/15 February 1914, *OUA*, VII, Nos. 9426–27.

87. Hubka to Conrad, 15 July 1914, Conrad, *AMD*, IV:93–94.

88. Giers to Sazonov, 12 May/29 April 1914, *IB*, I/2, No. 412; Hartwig to Sazonov, 19/6 May 1914, I/3, No. 35; 30/17 June 1914, I/4, No. 25; Otto to Berchtold, 20 May 1914, *OUA*, VIII, No. 9695.

89. Heilbronner, "Merger Attempts," p. 288.

90. Sazonov to Hartwig, 24/7 July 1914, *IB*, I/4, No. 112; Hartwig to Sazonov, 26/9 July 1914, No. 148.

91. Quadt to foreign ministry, 2 April 1914, *GP*, XXXVIII, No. 15540; Bethmann Hollweg to Tschirschky, 6 April 1914, No. 15541; Conrad, *AMD*, III:661–62.

92. Albertini asked "how could the Kaiser lend an ear to such a cock-and-bull story as that Russia, who had not gained the right even for her own navy to pass out of the Black Sea, could have hopes of a port on the Adriatic and of gaining it in this childish fashion." Albertini, *Origins of the War*, I: 516–16.

93. Bethmann Hollweg to Tschirschky, 6 April 1914, *GP*, XXXVIII, No. 15541; Tschirschky to Bethmann Hollweg, 23 April 1914, No. 15546.

94. Discussed in Bethmann Hollweg to Tschirschky, 6 April 1914, *GP*, XXXVIII, No. 15541.

95. Ibid.

96. Tschirschky to Bethmann Hollweg, 15 February 1914, *GP*, XXXVIII, No. 15536.

97. Tschirschky to Bethmann Hollweg, 23 April 1914, *GP*, XXXVIII, No. 15546. The Austrians also proposed that in the event of union, Serbia should cede Ištip and Kočana to Bulgaria, and Prizren and Djakovica to Albania, thus forcing a major revision of the decisions of the London conference and the Bucharest peace conference. As far as Treutler's gratuitous admonition about achieving a Serbo-Austrian *modus vivendi*, Berchtold tartly observed: "I do not think that we can include such a combination in our policy."

98. Led by *Le Temps*, European newspapers kept the Lovćen question before the general public, repeatedly printing stories about nonexistent Austro-Montenegrin negotiations or Austrian preparations to seize the mountain. Hubka was falsely accused of negotiating for Lovćen behind Berchtold's back. See, for example, Gellinek to Conrad, 5 April 1914, *OUA*, VII, No. 9554; de Salis to Grey, 11 May 1914, *BD*, X/1, No. 363; Delaroche-Vernet to Doumergue, 8 May 1914, *DDF*, 3, X, No. 213; *CV*, 26 March, 3 and 10 April 1910 O.S. San Giuliano did little to play down the bellicose soundings of Italy's press and warned Flotow that if Vienna ac-

quired Lovćen he might be forced to turn to Russia or some other power for assistance. Once more Flotow remarked that Montenegro might provide the spark for world war. Flotow to Bethmann Hollweg, 9 April 1914, *GP*, XXXVIII, Nos. 15542–43. Conrad heard rumors that Italy was already giving Montenegro money and guns to improve Lovćen's defenses. This was not the case, although Cetinje was in the process of transferring a few Turkish cannon to the mountain and installing barbed wire and searchlights. Conrad to Berchtold, 8 May 1914, HHStA, PA XVII/Montenegro, Karton 50, Liasse XV, Res. Gstb. No. 1663; Berchtold to Mérey and Otto, 10 June 1914, Nos. 2628–29; Mérey to Berchtold, 2 July 1914, No. 30; Otto to Berchtold, 15 July 1914, No. 50. Cf. Conrad, *AMD*, III:665.

99. Berchtold's notes on his meeting with San Giuliano, 18 April 1914, *OUA*, VII, No. 9592; *GP*, XXXIX, Nos. 15729–30. See also Hantsch, *Berchtold*, II:534–39. San Giuliano had already told Flotow he believed that union could not be prevented by force, but in view of Austria's hostility vis-à-vis Serbia, there seemed little choice but to assign the Montenegrin coastal strip to Albania. Flotow to Bethmann Hollweg, 9 April 1914, *GP*, XXXVIII, Nos. 15542–43. See Bosworth, *Italy*, pp. 249–51; *CV*, 10 April 1914, O.S.

100. Bethmann Hollweg to Tschirschky, 8 May 1914, *GP*, XXXVIII, No. 15550.

101. Flotow to Bethmann Hollweg, 4 May 1914, *GP*, XXXVIII, No. 15548.

102. Bethmann Hollweg to Jagow, 8 May 1914, *GP*, XXXVIII, No. 15549; Tschirschky to Jagow, 17 May 1914, No. 15553.

103. The state of Francis Joseph's health was a matter of great concern to the German emperor, who suggested that Bethmann, then in Corfu, return to Berlin via Vienna to consult with Berchtold and the heir to the throne. Jagow advised against such a trip which might have been seen in Austrian eyes to be motivated less by compassion for the venerable Francis Joseph than by interest in the effects of a possible change of sovereigns. Bethmann Hollweg to foreign office, 21 April 1914, *GP*, XXXVIII, No. 15544; Jagow to Bethmann Hollweg, 22 April 1914, No. 15545.

104. Tschirschky to Bethmann Hollweg, 4 July 1914, *GP*, XXXVIII, No. 15554, n.

105. Crackanthorpe to Grey, 10 July 1914, *BD*, X/1, No. 375. Crackanthorpe had reported a union plan as early as November, 1913.

106. Flotow to Bethmann Hollweg, 12 May 1914, *GP*, XXXVIII, No. 15551.

107. Tschirschky to Bethmann Hollweg, 4 July 1914, *GP*, XXXVIII, No. 15554.

108. See also Flotow to Bethmann Hollweg, 4 and 12 May, 10 July 1914, *GP*, XXXVIII, Nos. 15548, 15551, 15555.

109. Leo Valiani, "Italian-Austro-Hungarian Negotiations, 1914–1915," *Journal of Contemporary History*, I (July 1966): 113–36; Bosworth, *Italy*, p. 249.

110. Flotow to Bethmann Hollweg, 10 July 1914, *GP*, XXXVIII, No. 15555.

CHAPTER TEN

1. See Vladimir Dedijer, *The Road to Sarajevo* (New York: Simon and Schuster, 1966); Joachim Remak, *Sarajevo: The Story of a Political Murder* (New York: Criterion Books, 1959); Uebersberger, *Österreich zwischen Russland und Serbien*, pp. 239–314. For a provocative account, see also Friedrich Würthle, *Die Spur führt nach Belgrad: Die Hintergründe des Dramas von Sarajevo 1914* (Vienna, Munich, and Zurich: Verlag Fritz Molden, 1975).
2. For Robert A. Kann's views on this subject, see *Erzherzog Franz Ferdinand Studien* (Munich: R. Oldenbourg Verlag, 1976), pp. 36, 39, 42–43, and passim.
3. Nikola Škerović, *Crna Gora za vrijeme Prvog svjetskog rata* (Titograd, 1963), p. 9; Delaroche-Vernet to Viviani, 4 July 1914, *DDF*, 3, X, No. 474; *CV*, 17 and 20 June 1914 O.S.
4. At the same time, Nicholas told Egger, the Austrian chargé, that Danilo probably would be unable to attend the funeral because of illness. Later the same day he told Gavrilović, the Serbian minister, he had no intention of sending Danilo. Novica Rakočević, *Crna Gora u Prvom svjetskom ratu, 1914–1918* (Cetinje: Obod, 1969), p. 25. In the end, it was academic: no foreign countries were invited to send representatives.
5. "Spannung und Entladung: Reminiszenzen aus Montenegro," *Grazer Tagespost*, 26 November 1914, cited in Rakočević, *Crna Gora u Prvom svjetskom ratu*, p. 25.
6. Note of the war ministry, 3 July 1914, *OUA*, VIII, No. 10033; Berchtold to Egger, 4 July 1914, No. 10040.
7. Otto to Berchtold, 6 July 1914, *OUA*, VIII, No. 10077.
8. Otto to Berchtold, 7 July 1914, *OUA*, VIII, No. 10078; Gavrilović to Pašić, 17 July/24 June 1914, SSIP.
9. Note of the war ministry, 9 July 1914, *OUA*, VIII, No. 10162.
10. Miro Božović, "Crna Gora i njena uloga od 15. jula 1914. do kapitulacije," *Slobodna Misao*, 19 April 1936.
11. *GC*, 21 June 1914 O.S. Similarly, the *Vjesnik* denounced "the act of terrorism." *CV*, 19 June 1914 O.S.
12. Hubka, "Kritische Tage," p. 39.
13. Egger to Berchtold, 29 June and 4 July 1914, *OUA*, VIII, Nos. 9944, 10044; Delaroche-Vernet to Viviani, 30 June 1914, *DDF*, 3, X, No. 464.
14. Egger to Berchtold, 4 July 1914, *OUA*, VIII, Nos. 10042–44; Müller to Grey, 14 July 1914, *BD*, XI, No. 70; Delaroche-Vernet to Viviani, 6 and 7 July 1914, *DDF*, 3, X, Nos. 478, 480; *CV*, 25 June 1914 O.S. The anti-Serb demonstrations had repercussions as far away as Kiev. Hein to Berchtold, 4 July 1914, *OUA*, VIII, No. 10045.
15. Egger to Berchtold, 5 July 1914, *OUA*, VIII, No. 10061.
16. Otto to Berchtold, 6 July 1914, *OUA*, VIII, No. 10131.
17. The demonstrations would have been even worse if the leaders had known that Austro-Hungarian authorities had turned back Montenegrin students in Serbia, who had wanted to return to their homeland via the Monarchy. Both Plamenac and Mijušković sought Austrian assist-

ance in redressing this error. Egger to Berchtold, 4 July 1914, *OUA*, VIII, No. 10041; Otto to Berchtold, 6 July 1914, No. 10131.

18. Jovan Ivović, "Atentator Muhamed Mehmedbašić u Nikšiću," *IZ*, II, Knj. III, Nos. 1–2 (1949): 35–49; Milan Popović, "Boravak atentatora Muhameda Mehmedbašića u Crnoj Gori nakon atentata 1914. g." *IZ*, II, knj. III, Nos. 5–6 (1949): 280–85; "Dokumenta o atentatoru Muhamedu Mehmedbašiću," *IZ*, II, Knj. III, Nos. 1–2 (1949): 95–103.

19. Telegram of the presidium of the provincial government of Bosnia and Hercegovina, 13 July 1914, *OUA*, VIII, No. 10224; Berchtold to Otto, 13 July 1914, No. 10241; Directive to Cetinje, 17 July 1914, No. 10329.

20. Otto to Berchtold, 15 and 22 July 1914, *OUA*, VIII, Nos. 10279, 10487.

21. Otto to Berchtold, 19 and 20 July 1914, *OUA*, VIII, Nos. 10381, 10404.

22. Otto to Berchtold, 25 July 1914, *OUA*, VIII, No. 10669. Mehmedbašić was never recaptured in connection with the murder of the archduke, but lived to fight another day. Although he was arrested and tried along with "Apis," the mastermind behind the Sarajevo assassination, in the famous Salonica trial of 1917, he was pardoned in 1919, whereupon he returned to Sarajevo, where he died during the Second World War. Remak, *Sarajevo*, pp. 248, 261. As a point of interest, he was interviewed by Albertini. Albertini, *Origins of the War*, II:46.

23. Otto to Berchtold, 15 and 22 July 1914, *OUA*, VIII, Nos. 10279, 10487.

24. Otto to Berchtold, 15 July 1914, *OUA*, VIII, No. 10279. While in custody, Mehmedbašić told of his participation at a meeting of conspirators in Tours, France. Citing Dedijer's sources, Würthle insists that this meeting actually took place. In defense of this position, he notes messages from the French minister to Paris, and from the Serbian minister to Belgrade, both mentioning the Tours "disclosures." This, of course, does not prove the veracity of Mehmedbašić's boast. Moreover, Würthle seems to neglect the French minister's own conclusion that Mehmedbašić's story was untrue. Würthle, *Die Spur*, pp. 65, 302; Dedijer, *Road to Sarajevo*, p. 284. Remak, on the other hand, who chooses not to "distract" his readers with footnotes, concludes that Mehmedbašić's story was "an invention that was to become the basis for one of the several myths about the origins of the conspiracy." Remak, *Sarajevo*, p. 191.

25. Even after Mehmedbašić's escape, Austria-Hungary and Montenegro wrangled over his possible extradition. On the one hand, Vienna wanted him to stand trial in Sarajevo, in accordance with the Austro-Montenegrin convention on extradition of 1872. On the other hand, Cetinje preferred to try him in Montenegro, following the precedent established by Austria in bringing to justice several men inculpated in the Bomb Affair of 1907. Otto to Berchtold, 15 and 25 July 1914, *OUA*, VIII, Nos. 10279, 10666.

26. Remak, *Sarajevo*, p. 197. Delaroche-Vernet to Bienvenu-Martin, 20 July 1914, *DDF*, 3, X, No. 537.

27. Otto to Berchtold, 22 July 1914, *OUA*, VIII, No. 10487.
28. Note to Conrad, 2 July 1914, *OUA*, VIII, No. 9995.
29. Berchtold to Otto, 8 July 1914, *OUA*, VIII, No. 10130.
30. Berchtold to Otto, 16 July 1914, *OUA*, VIII, No. 10300.
31. Otto to Berchtold, 18 July 1914, *OUA*, VIII, No. 10352.
32. Szécsen to Berchtold, 19 July 1914, *OUA*, VIII, No. 10386; Otto to Berchtold, 20 July 1914, No. 10405; *CV*, 4 July 1914 O.S. The other part of the rumor was that Montenegro had already collected 10,000 men to repulse the attack. An Italian newspaper contended that "Italy cannot allow the strategical situation in the Adriatic to be altered to her disadvantage. Lovćen must remain as it is . . . Montenegrin." De Salis to Grey, 26 July 1914, *BD*, XI, No. 652. Cf. Delaroche-Vernet to Bienvenu-Martin, 17, 18, 19, 20 and 22 July 1914, *DDF*, 3, X, Nos. 523, 524, 527, 532, 534, 561.
33. Berchtold to Otto, 21 July 1914, *OUA*, VIII, No. 10449. Cf. Delaroche-Vernet to Bienvenu-Martin, 21 July 1914, *DDF*, 3, X, No. 544; 24 July 1914, XI, No. 31.
34. Otto to Berchtold, 21 July 1914, *OUA*, VIII, No. 10450.
35. Otto to Berchtold, 22 July 1914, *OUA*, VIII, No. 10486.
36. Storck to Berchtold, 5 July 1914, *OUA*, VIII, No. 10057. The Serbian chargé in Berlin did his part to muddy the waters by talking indiscreetly about the "imminent" union of his country and Montenegro. Sazonov, who was trying to keep Austria and Serbia at arm's length, was outraged by the chargé's remarks, calling the Serbian a fool and suggesting his immediate recall. Sazonov assured Ottokar Czernin, the Habsburg minister in Bucharest, that no union was in the works and that Serbia intended to maintain the status quo. Rumania's King Carol shared this appraisal, suggesting that a union was at least a decade away. Czernin to Berchtold, 6 and 10 July 1914, *OUA*, VIII, Nos. 10086, 10174, 10176. Cf. the greek government's attitude. Szilassy to Berchtold, 9 July 1914, No. 10147; Berchtold to Szilassy, 10 July 1914, No. 10165.
37. Italy's mid-July call-up of the class of 1891 worried Vienna because it was feared that the young troops might be used to take advantage of complications in the Balkans. In this regard, the surprise visit of Vukotić and Martinović to Rome had a disquieting effect at the Ballhausplatz. Otto to Berchtold, 25 July 1914, *OUA*, VIII, No. 10667; Mérey to Berchtold, 13 and 16 July 1914, Nos. 10246, 10308. San Giuliano's hesitance to commit himself to Berchtold and the nature of Italy's demands confounded Vienna. See, for example, Mérey to Berchtold, 21 July 1914, No. 10460; Report on Avarna's visit, 26 July 1914, No. 10715; Berchtold to Mérey and Szögyény, 26 July 1914, Nos. 10746–47. See Dragan R. Živojinović, "San Djuliano i italijanske pretenzije na Jadranu na početku svetskog rata 1914–1915. godine," *Istorijski Časopis*, XX (1973), pp. 307–17.
38. Otto to Berchtold, 25 July 1914, *OUA*, VIII, No. 10667.
39. Note of Conrad, 16 July 1914, *OUA*, VIII, No. 10316.
40. Hubka to Conrad, 17 July 1914, *OUA*, VIII, No. 10330; Note of Conrad, 18 July 1914, No. 10375.
41. Circular telegram to Albanian posts, 23 July 1914, *OUA*, VIII, No. 10533; Halla to Berchtold, 24 July 1914, No. 10621; Kral to Berch-

told, 28 July 1914, Nos. 10888–89. By 29 July, Halla, the consul general in Scutari, reported that the Malissori chiefs were ready to send one or two thousand men into the field against Montenegro. Halla to Berchtold, 29 July 1914, No. 11005. On 28 July, a correspondent for the *Times* reported Isa Boletin's intention to raise a rebellion among the Albanian tribes of Kosovo. Their goal was to recapture Dibra and possibly Djakovica and Peć. *LT*, 30 July 1914, p. 8; Negrotto Cambiaso to San Giuliano, 1 August 1914, *I Documenti diplomatici italiani, 1861–1914* (hereafter cited as *DDI*), ed. commissione per la pubblicazione dei documenti diplomatici (Rome, 1952—), 4, XII, No. 837. Cf. Delaroche-Vernet to Viviani, 1 August 1914, *DDF*, 3, XI, No. 531.

42. Directive to Belgrade, 20 July 1914, *OUA*, VIII, No. 10395; Circular telegram, 23 July 1914, No. 10529. For an English translation of the ultimatum, see Fay, *Origins of the World War*, II: 269–73; Albertini, *Origins of the War*, II:286–89. See also Bridge, *Sadowa to Sarajevo*, pp. 374–78.

43. Circular directive, 25 July 1914, *OUA*, VIII, No. 10654. Despite Berchtold's assiduous efforts to justify the tough ultimatum, many people then and later believed that the ultimatum was too demanding and that Austria never really intended the Serbians to accept it.

44. Berchtold to Otto, 23 July 1914, *OUA*, VIII, No. 10531.

45. Otto to Berchtold, 24 July 1914, *OUA*, VIII, No. 10594; *CV*, 11 July 1914 O.S. Such was also the assessment of the German minister in Cetinje. See Szögyény to Berchtold, 26 July 1914, No. 10719.

46. Otto to Berchtold, 25 July 1914, *OUA*, VIII, No. 10668. Cf. Delaroche-Vernet to Bienvenu-Martin, 24 July 1914, *DDF*, 3, X, Nos. 17, 24.

47. Hubka to Conrad, 24 July 1914, *OUA*, VIII, No. 10595.

48. Note of Conrad, 25 July 1914, *OUA*, VIII, No. 10702.

49. According to one authority, "the Serbian reply was a masterpiece of diplomatic language, especially considering the speed with which it was composed. The Serbs had been advised by everybody to be conciliatory, and they were; butter remained visibly unmelted in their mouths." Laurence Lafore, *The Long Fuse: An Interpretation of the Origins of World War I* (Philadelphia: J. B. Lippincott, 1965), p. 234.

50. See Albertini, *Origins of the War*, II:346–89.

51. Otto to Berchtold, 28 July 1914, *OUA*, VIII, No. 10882. In this respect, Plamenac was proved right. Berchtold concluded that Europe's sympathetic response to Serbia was the result of Belgrade's "deception and manipulation of the press." Circular telegram, 29 July 1914, No. 10951. See, for example, *LT*, 28 July 1914. Fay and Lafore gave similar but distinct explanations. Fay, *Origins of the World War*, II:343; Lafore, *Long Fuse*, p. 235.

52. Even Kaiser William was struck by the reasonableness of Serbia's response: "A brilliant performance for a time-limit of only 48 hours. This is more than one could have expected! A great moral success for Vienna; but with it every reason for war drops away, and Giesl ought to have remained quietly in Belgrade! After such a thing, *I* should never have ordered mobilization." Cited in Fay, *Origins of the World War*, II:348.

53. Less than thirty minutes after Pašić had delivered his government's note to the Austrian legation, Giesl and his entire staff were on a train out of Belgrade. Clearly, they had packed in advance.

54. For one, Conrad had decided to order a partial mobilization of the army according to Plan B (for Balkans), which as its name implied was directed primarily against Serbia and Montenegro. The subsequent mobilization of the third corps was designed to keep Italy honest. Conrad's note, 24 July 1914, *OUA*, VIII, No. 10632. Secondly, Vienna inquired whether Germany would be willing to assume Austro-Hungarian interests in Belgrade as was done in 1909 with Serbia and 1913 with Montenegro. Telegram to Berlin, 13 July 1914, No. 10236. Jagow, however, obviously cognizant of larger possibilities, indicated that although Germany would ordinarily be prepared to honor such a request, in the prevailing circumstances, especially in the event of war between Austria and Serbia, Germany would probably have to recall her own representatives from Belgrade and Cetinje. Szögyény to Berchtold, 14 July 1914, No. 10259. Berchtold acknowledged the German position, but wired back his belief that even in the event of war with Serbia, Montenegro would probably not be a belligerent. Telegram to Berlin, 16 July 1914, No. 10295. On the other hand, Redlich's diary reveals that more than one Austrian diplomat, including Count Hoyos, was for war, and fully anticipated that it would not remain localized: "That Russia will go with Serbia is as good as understood." Redlich, *Das politische Tagebuch*, I, 15 July 1914, p. 237; 24 July 1914, p. 238.

55. Otto to Berchtold, 29 July 1914, *OUA*, VIII, No. 10963; de Salis to Grey, 27 July 1914, *BD*, XI, No. 255; Hubka, "Kritische Tage," p. 40; Warren, *Montenegro,* p. 13.

56. Berchtold to Otto, 27 July 1914, *OUA*, VIII, No. 10799.

57. Telegram No. 136 of 25 July 1914, cited in Otto to Berchtold, 28 July 1914, *OUA*, VIII, No. 10882. Cf. Delaroche-Vernet to Bienvenu-Martin, 26 July 1914, *DDF*, 3, XI, No. 105.

58. Redlich and Hoyos seemed to hold a slightly different opinion: "We do not want to dissolve Serbia, but only to reduce her—and to take northern Albania." Redlich, *Das politische Tagebuch*, I, 24 July 1914, p. 238.

59. Berchtold, to Otto, 27 July 1914, *OUA*, VIII, No. 10800.

60. Otto to Berchtold, 29 July 1914, *OUA*, VIII, No. 10959; *CV*, 16 July 1914 O.S.; *LT*, 28 July 1914; *NYT*, 28 July 1914; Sinclair to Grey, 28 July 1914, *BD*, XI, No. 214; de Salis to Grey, 28 July 1914, No. 292; Barrère to Viviani, 1 August 1914, *DDF*, 3, XI, No. 540. On mobilization see E. Czega, "Die Mobilmachung Montenegros im Sommer 1914," *Berliner Monatshefte*, XIV (January 1936): 3–23.

61. Otto to Berchtold, 29 July 1914, *OUA*, VIII, No. 10962; Mérey to Berchtold, 28 July 1914, No. 10913.

62. *LT*, 29 July 1914, p. 3; 30 July 1914, p. 7.

63. Otto to Berchtold, 26 July 1914, *OUA*, VIII, No. 10727. Cf. Delaroche-Vernet to Bienvenu-Martin, 25 July 1914, *DDF*, 3, XI, No. 41.

64. Berchtold to Otto, 27 July 1914, *OUA*, VIII, No. 10800.

65. Berchtold to Otto, 31 July 1914, *OUA*, VIII, No. 11145.

66. Montenegro's official protest note: 28/15 July 1914, *OUA*, VIII, No. 10886. One of the first "selected" to leave Montenegro was one of Otto's closest friends, the representative of the Austro-Hungarian Telegraph Correspondence Bureau. Cf. Delaroche-Vernet, 28 July 1914, *DDF*, 3, XI, No. 182.
67. Otto to Berchtold, 27 July 1914, *OUA*, VIII, No. 10801.
68. Ibid. See supplement No. 1 of same report.
69. Ibid.; *CV*, 14 July 1914 O.S.
70. Ibid. See also supplements 2, 3, and 4; Otto to Berchtold, 28 July 1914, No. 10885.
71. Otto to Berchtold, 28 July 1914, *OUA*, VIII, No. 10884. One other measure was Austria's seizure of some three hundred thousand crowns en route to the Montenegrin treasury. See Otto to Berchtold, 29 July 1914, No. 10963; Berchtold to Otto, 30 July 1914, No. 11048; Barrère to Viviani, 1 August 1914, *DDF*, 3, XI, No. 540; Beguin Billecocq to Viviani, 30 July 1914, No. 314.
72. Berchtold to Otto, 29 July 1914, *OUA*, VIII, No. 10958.
73. Otto to Berchtold, 30 July 1914, *OUA*, VIII, No. 11052.
74. Berchtold to Otto, 30 July 1914, *OUA*, VIII, No. 11048.
75. Berchtold to Otto, 31 July 1914, *OUA*, VIII, No. 11145.
76. Otto to Berchtold, 29 July 1914, *OUA*, VIII, No. 10862.
77. Otto to Berchtold, 29 July 1914, *OUA*, VIII, No. 10961. Initially, the startled Serbians did not want to believe that a declaration of war had been made. As late as midnight on the twenty-ninth, the Serbian chargé in Bucharest told the Rumanian foreign minister that Serbia did not consider herself at war for two reasons: first, Austria-Hungary had not initiated hostilities; second, the telegram received by Pašić could be a mistake. Czernin to Berchtold, 29 July 1914, No. 10954. Unfortunately for Serbia, Austria soon followed up her declaration by seizing Serbian ships in the Danube and then bombarding Belgrade, the Russian answer to which, according to many, was general mobilization. See *LT*, 29 July 1914, p. 8; 31 July 1914, p. 8; *NYT*, 28 July 1914, p. 1; *NFP*, 1 August 1914, pp. 3–4; Crackanthorpe to Grey, 29 and 30 July 1914, *BD*, XI, Nos. 269, 291.
78. Otto to Berchtold, 30 July 1914, *OUA*, VIII, No. 11051; Note of Plamenac, 30/17 July 1914, No. 11053.
79. Telegram to Cetinje, 31 July 1914, *OUA*, VIII, No. 11143. Cf. Berchtold to Otto, 30 July 1914, No. 11049.
80. Berchtold to Otto, 31 July 1914, *OUA*, VIII, No. 11143.
81. Otto to Berchtold, 28 July 1914, *OUA*, VIII, No. 10884. See also Sinclair to Grey, 28 July 1914, *BD*, XI, No. 214.
82. Halla to Berchtold, 29 July 1914, *OUA*, VIII, No. 11004. While Count Forgách, the Austro-Hungarian undersecretary, reported that he was not sure what his government intended to do with its military contingent in Scutari, Whitehall, acting on the assumption that war between Austria-Hungary and Montenegro was inevitable, gave orders for the immediate withdrawal of Col. Phillips and the British detachments from Scutari and Lezhë. Minute to note from de Salis to Grey, 27 July 1914, *BD*, XI, No. 255; Grey to Bertie, 30 July 1914, No. 308; de Bunsen to Grey, 31

July 1914, No. 360; Avarna to San Giuliano, 31 July 1914, *DDI*, 4, XII, No. 801.

83. Berchtold to Otto, 31 July 1914, *OUA*, VIII, No. 11144; *LT*, 29 July 1914, p. 3.

84. *NYT*, 31 July 1914, p. 2.

85. Otto to Berchtold, 28 July 1914, *OUA*, VIII, No. 10884.

86. Hubka, "Kritische Tage," p. 40.

87. Otto to Berchtold, 31 July 1914, *OUA*, VIII, No. 11147.

88. Ibid. On August 1, Plamenac said the same thing to Giers. *IB*, I/5, p. 436. Giers, however, recognized Nicholas's reluctance to join the fight. The king of Italy and San Giuliano both shared Plamenac's outlook. Berchtold to Otto, 30 July 1914, *OUA*, VIII, No. 11050; Mérey to Berchtold, 30 July 1914, No. 11087.

89. At an official level, Montenegro's relations with Russia were still troubled. There was still no sign of the promised military subsidy. Unlike Belgrade, Cetinje hardly remarked upon the passing of Hartwig, Russia's pan-Slav minister to Serbia, and the principal architect of the original Balkan alliance. De Salis to Grey, 23 July 1914, *BD*, XI, No. 651. Hartwig died suddenly, in Giesl's arms no less, on a visit to the Austrian legation. See Giesl to Berchtold, 10 and 11 July 1914, *OUA*, VIII, Nos. 10170, 10191.

90. See Albertini, *Origins of the War*, II:528–81, 651–86; III: 1–65, 112–65; *CV*, 18 July 1914 O.S.

91. Hubka, "Kritische Tage," p. 41; *CV*, 19 July 1914 O.S.; Rakočević, *Crna Gora u Prvom svjetskom ratu*, pp. 38–39.

92. See Otto to Berchtold, 13 July 1914, *OUA*, VIII, No. 11148. The skupština immediately notified the Serbian and Russian parliaments of its decision. *GC*, 22 July 1914 O.S.

93. Hubka, "Kritische Tage," p. 41.

94. Francis Joseph assured the safe passage of Danilo, Peter, and Vera. Paar to Hubka, 28 July 1914, ibid.; Hubka, "König Nikolaus," p. 178.

95. Hubka, "Kritische Tage," p. 42.

96. Hubka, "König Nikolaus," p. 179; *CV*, 25 July 1914 O.S. The text of the Montenegrin note, published only in 1929, read as follows: "On 24 (sic) July last the Austro-Hungarian Government handed the Serbian Government a note in which it demanded nothing less than the alienation of Serbia's sovereignty to the benefit of the Monarchy. To save the peace of Europe and spare it the horrors of war, the Government of Serbia in reply to the note made all the concessions compatible with the dignity of an independent State. The Austro-Hungarian Government was not willing to declare itself satisfied with this unprecedented condescension and on 28 July declared war on Serbia and for the last week has been trying to invade her territory, threatening her independence and that of the whole Serb nation. On 1 August Germany, the ally of the Austro-Hungarian Monarchy, also declared war on Russia, Montenegro's protectress. Bound to Serbia by solid ties of consanguinity, attached to Russia by indissoluble bonds of age-old gratitude, menaced in her own turn, as is proved by all

the aggressive measures taken by Austria-Hungary for the last fortnight along her Dalmatian and Herzegovinian frontier, the expulsion of Montenegrins from the Monarchy, the seizure of sailing vessels, the armed attack on the Sanjak frontier—Montenegro finds herself forced to declare that she cannot remain neutral in this struggle and that she must herself resort to arms in order to contribute to the defence of the freedom of the Serb people." Alfred Rappaport, "Montenegros Eintritt in den Weltkrieg," *Berliner Monatshefte,* VII (October 1929):962–63, translated in Albertini, *Origins of the War,* III:660–61.

97. Hubka, "Kritische Tage," p. 43; Hubka, "König Nikolaus," p. 179, translated in Albertini, *Origins of the War,* III:661.

CONCLUSION

1. Askew, "Austro-Italian Antagonism," p. 212.
2. Milovan Djilas, *Njegoš: Poet, Prince, Bishop,* trans. Michael B. Petrovich (New York: Harcourt, Brace & World, 1966), p. 103.
3. Ibid., p. 137.
4. Fischer, *War of Illusions,* pp. 209-12; Fischer, *World Power or Decline: The Controversy over Germany's Aims in the First World War,* trans. Lancelot L. Farrar, Robert Kimber, and Rita Kimber (New York: W. W. Norton, 1974), p. 22.

Bibliography

Archival and Manuscript Sources

Austria-Hungary
 Vienna: Haus-, Hof- und Staatsarchiv, Politisches Archiv
Great Britain
 London: Public Record Office
  Foreign Office correspondence, series 371, political
  The Public Papers of Viscount Grey of Fallodon
United States
 Washington, D.C.: National Archives
  Department of State correspondence, Record Group 59
Yugoslavia
 Belgrade: Savezni sekretarijat za inostrane poslove
 Cetinje: Državni Archiv
  Ministarstvo inostranih djela
  Ministarstvo unutrašnjih djela
 Cetinje: Državni Muzej
  Papers of Nicholas I
  Prinovljeni spisi (rukopisi)

Published Documents

Austro-Hungarian

Austria-Hungary. Ministerium des Äussern. *Österreich-Ungarns Aussenpolitik von der bosnischen Krise 1908 bis zum Kriegsausbruch 1914. Diplomatische Aktenstücke des österreichisch-ungarischen Ministeriums des Äussern.* Edited by Ludwig Bittner and Hans Uebersberger. 8 vols. and index. Vienna: Österreichischer Bundesverlag für Unterricht, Wissenschaft und Kunst, 1930.

Austria. *Reichsgesetzblatt für die im Reichsrate vertretenen Königreiche und Länder.* Vienna, 10 March 1912.

Pribram, Alfred F. *The Secret Treaties of Austria-Hungary, 1879–1914.* Translated by Denys P. Myers and J. G. D'Arcy Paul. 2 vols. Cambridge, Mass.: Harvard University Press, 1920–21.

British

Great Britain. Foreign Office. *British Documents on the Origins of the War, 1898–1914.* Edited by G. P. Gooch and Harold Temperley. 11 vols. London: H. M. Stationery Office, 1926–38.

Bulgarian

Kesiakov, B. D. *Prinos kŭm diplomaticheskata istoriia na Bŭlgariia.* 4 vols. Sofia: T. L. Klisarov, 1925–35.

French

France. Ministère des Affaires étrangères. *Documents diplomatiques français, 1871–1914.* Edited by the commission de publication des documents relatifs aux origines de la guerre de 1914. 2d and 3d series. Paris: Alfred Costes, 1929–59.

German

Germany. Auswärtiges Amt. *Die Grosse Politik der europäischen Kabinette, 1871–1914.* Edited by Johannes Lepsius, Albrecht Mendelssohn Bartholdy, and Friedrich Thimme. 40 vols. Berlin: Deutsche Verlagsgesellschaft für Politik und Geschichte, 1922–27.

Italian

Italy. Ministero degli Affari Esteri. *I Documenti diplomatici italiani, 1861–1914.* Edited by the commissione per la pubblicazione dei documenti diplomatici. Rome, 1952–.

Montenegrin

Stenografske bilješke o radu Crnogorske narodne skupštine 1906–1914. Cetinje, 1906–1914.

"Balkanski rat."
Zapisi, VIII, Knj. XIII, No. 1 (1935), pp. 42–53; No. 2, pp. 113–19; No. 3, pp. 168–75; No. 4, pp. 239–46; No. 5, pp. 300–305, No. 6, pp. 359–63; Knj. XIV, No. 1 (1935), pp. 51–55; No. 2, pp. 118–22; No. 3, pp. 184–89; No. 4, pp. 244–49; No. 5, pp. 310–15; No. 6, pp. 377–82; IX, Knj. XV, No. 1 (1936), pp. 55–61; No. 2, pp. 119–24; No. 3, pp. 178–85; No. 4, pp. 239–41; No. 6, pp. 364–68; Knj. XVI, No. 1 (1936), pp. 43–45; No. 2, pp. 108–11; No. 3, pp. 165–67; No. 4, pp. 236–39; No. 5, pp. 292–94; No. 6, pp. 358–62; X, Knj. XVII, No. 1 (1937), pp. 39–41.

"Dokumenta o atentatoru Muhamedu Mehmedbašiću."
Istorijski Zapisi, II, Knj. III, Nos. 1–2 (1949), pp. 95–103.

"Gradja iz borbe oko Skadra 1913. godine."
Istorijski Zapisi, III, Knj. V, Nos. 1–3 (1950), pp. 107–30.

"Izveštaji o malisorskim bunama 1911. godine."
Zapisi, XIV, Knj. XXV, No. 1 (1941), pp. 42–56; No. 2, pp. 113–21.

"Nekoliko dokumenata iz aneksije Bosne i Hercegovine."
Zapisi, X, Knj. XVII, No. 4 (1937), pp. 239–47; No. 5, pp. 302–15.

"Nekoliko dokumenata iz Balkanskog rata."

Zapisi, XIV, Knj. XXV, No. 4 (1941), pp. 246–50.

"Nekoliko dokumenata iz 1913. do 1915. godine."
Zapisi, X, Knj. XVIII, No. 1 (1937), pp. 43–52; No. 2, pp. 108–20.

"Nekoliko dokumenata o projektu željezničke pruge Cetinje-Vir."
Zapisi, XIII, Knj. XXIII, No. 2 (1940), pp. 114–19.

"Ruski car Nikola II imenuje kralja Nikolu za feldmaršala."
Zapisi, XII, Knj. XXII, No. 5 (1939), p. 294.

"Uvod u evropski rat."
Zapisi, X, Knj. XVIII, No. 3 (1937), pp. 171–80.

In German Translation:

"Montenegrinische Dokumente zur Annexionskrise."
Berliner Monatshefte, XV (August 1937), pp. 702–6.

"Neue montenegrinische Dokumente."
Berliner Monatshefte, XV (September 1937), pp. 796–98.

Russian

Russia. Komissiia po izdaniiu dokumentov epokhi imperializma. *Mezhdunarodnie otnosheniia v epokhu imperializma: Dokumenti iz arkhivov tsarskogo i vremennogo pravitel'stv 1878–1917 gg.* Edited by A. P. Bol'shemennikov, A. S. Erusalimskii, A. A. Mogilevich, and F. A. Rotshtein.

2d series: 1900–1913, vols. XVIII-XX. Moscow: Gospolizdat, 1938–40.

3d series: 1914–1917, vols. I-X. Moscow: Gosudarstvennoe Sotsial'no-Ekonomicheskoe Izdatel'stvo, 1931–38.

Most of the volumes in the 2d and 3d series have been translated into an authorized German-language edition: *Die internationalen Beziehungen im Zeitalter des Imperialismus. Dokumente aus den Archiven der zarischen und der provisorischen Regierung, 1878–1917.* Edited by Otto Hoetzsch. Berlin, 1931—.

Siebert, Benno von, ed. *Graf Benckendorffs diplomatischer Schriftwechsel.* 3 vols. Berlin and Leipzig: Verlag von Walter de Gruyter & Co., 1928.

Stieve, Friedrich, ed. *Der diplomatische Schriftwechsel Iswolskis, 1911–1914. Aus den Geheimakten der russischen Staatsarchive.* 4 vols. Berlin: Deutsche Verlagsgesellschaft für Politik und Geschichte, 1925.

Serbian

Boghitschewitsch, Milosch [Bogićević, Miloš]. *Die auswärtige Politik Serbiens, 1903–1914.* 3 vols. Berlin: Brückenverlag, 1928–31.

Bittner, Ludwig; Hajek, Alois; Uebersberger, Hans, eds. *Serbiens Aussenpolitik 1908–1918: Diplomatische Akten des serbischen Ministeriums des Äussern in deutscher Übersetzung.* Vienna: A. Holzhausens Nachfolger, 1945.

Newspapers Most Frequently Used

Cetinjski Vjesnik (Cetinje)
Glas Crnogorca (Cetinje)
Neue Freie Presse (Vienna)
New York Times (New York)
The *Times* (London)

Secondary Sources, Reminiscences, etc.

Acković, Aleksandar, ed. *Politički život Jugoslavije, 1914–1945*. Belgrade: Radio-Beograd, 1973.

Albertini, Luigi. *The Origins of the War of 1914*. Translated and edited by Isabella M. Massey. 3 vols. London: Oxford University Press, 1952–57.

Albrecht-Carrié, René. *A Diplomatic History of Europe since the Congress of Vienna*. New York: Harper, 1958.

Aleksić-Pejković, Ljiljana. *Odnosi Srbije sa Francuskom i Engleskom, 1903–1914*. Jugoslovenske zemlje u XX veku, Vol. LXXXIII. Belgrade: Istorijski Institut, 1965.

Almanach de Gotha; annuaire généalogique, diplomatique et statistique. Gotha: J. Perthes, 1908–14.

Anderson, Matthew S. *The Eastern Question, 1774–1923: A Study in International Relations*. London: Macmillan, 1966.

Arnaoutovitch [Arnautović], Dragomir. *Histoire des Chemins de fer yugoslaves, 1825–1937*. Paris: Dunod, 1937.

Askew, William C. "The Austro-Italian Antagonism, 1896–1914." *Power, Public Opinion and Diplomacy: Essays in Honor of Eber Malcolm Carroll by His Former Students*, edited by Lillian Parker Wallace and William C. Askew, pp. 172–221. Durham, N.C.: Duke University Press, 1959.

―――. *Europe and Italy's Acquisition of Libya, 1911–1912*. Durham, N.C.: Duke University Press, 1942.

Avarna, Carlo. *L'ultimo rinnovo della Triplice (5 dicembre 1912)*. Milan: Alpes, 1924.

Babić, Branko. "'Moskovke' u naoružanju Crnogorske vojske." *Glasnik Cetinjskih Muzeja*, I (1968), pp. 95–101.

―――. "Ruski poklon berdanki Crnoj Gori." *Glasnik Cetinjskih Muzeja*, I (1968), pp. 95–101.

Bach, August. "Die November und Dezemberkrise 1912: Ein Vorspiel zum Weltkrieg." *Berliner Monatshefte*, XIII (February 1935), pp. 101–22.

Barker, J. Ellis. "War in the Balkans." *Fortnightly Review*, n.s., XCII (November 1912), pp. 813–25.

Baerlein, Henry. "The First and Last King of Montenegro." *Contemporary Review*, CLXXXVIII (August 1955), pp. 170–74.

Baernreither, Josef M. "Aehrenthal und Milovanovitch: Ein Tagebuchblatt." *Deutsche Revue*, XLVII (January 1922), pp. 84–89.

_____. *Fragmente eines politischen Tagebuches: Die südslawische Frage und Österreich-Ungarn vor dem Weltkrieg.* Edited by Joseph Redlich. Berlin: Verlag für Kulturpolitik, 1928.

Balkanicus [Stojan M. Protić]. *Das albanische Problem und die Beziehungen zwischen Serbien und Österreich-Ungarn.* Translated by L. Markowitsch. Leipzig: O. Wigand, 1913.

_____. *Serbien und Bulgarien im Balkankriege 1912/13.* Translated by L. Markowitsch. Leipzig: O. Wigand, 1913.

Batowski, Henryk. "Crna Gora i balkanski savez 1912. g." *Istorijski Zapisi*, X, Knj. XIII, Nos. 1–2 (1957), pp. 47–60.

_____. "Die drei Trialismen." *Österreichische Osthefte*, IV (July 1965), pp. 265–74.

_____. "Teritorijalni razvoj Crne Gore." *Zapisi*, X, Knj. XVIII, No. 2 (1937), pp. 74–78.

Beaver, Stanley H. "Railways in the Balkan Peninsula." *Geographical Journal*, XCVII (May 1941), pp. 273–94.

Beer, Adolf. *Die orientalische Politik Österreichs seit 1774.* Prague: F. Tempsky, 1883.

Belić, Vladimir J. *Ratovi srpskog naroda u XIX i XX veku (1788–1919).* Belgrade: G. Kohn, 1937.

Benna, A. H. "Studien zum Kultusprotektorat Österreich-Ungarns in Albanien im Zeitalter des Imperialismus (1888–1918)." *Mitteilungen des österreichischen Staatsarchivs*, LXXIII, No. 7 (1954), pp. 13–47.

Berchtold, Leopold. "Russia, Austria and the World War." *Contemporary Review*, CXXXIII (April 1928), pp. 422–32.

Bestuzhev, Igor' Vasil'evich. *Bor'ba v Rossii po voprosam vneshnei politiki, 1906–1910 gg.* Moscow: Akademia Nauk SSSR, 1961.

Bethmann-Hollweg, Theobald von. *Reflections on the World War.* Translated by George Young. London: T. Butterworth, 1920.

Bickel, Otto. *Russland und die Entstehung des Balkanbundes 1912: Ein Beitrag zur Vorgeschichte des Weltkrieges.* Königsberg and Berlin: Osteuropa-Verlag, 1933.

Bissolati, Leonida. *La Politica estera dell'Italia dal 1897 al 1920*. Milan: Fratelli Treves, 1923.

Blumenthal, Johann Heinrich. "Österreichische und russische Balkanpolitik 1853–1914." *Donauraum*, VIII, No. 3 (1963), pp. 117–30.

Boghitschewitsch [Bogićević], M[iloš]. *Causes of the War: An Examination into the Causes of the European War, with Special Reference to Russia and Serbia*. London: G. Allen & Unwin, 1920.

Bogićević, Vojislav. "Odnos Austro-Ugarske prema nameravanom ujedinjenju Srbije i Crne Gore." *Istorijski Zapisi*, V, Knj. VIII, Nos. 1–3 (1952), pp. 62–68.

Bojović, J. "Radnička klasa i njeno organizovanje u Crnoj Gori do 1914." *Prvo radničko društvo u Jugoslavenskim zemljama*, pp. 317–39. Slavonski Brod, 1969.

Bosworth, R. J. B. *Italy, the Least of the Great Powers: Italian Foreign Policy before the First World War*. Cambridge: Cambridge University Press, 1979.

Bourchier, J[ames] D. "Montenegro." *Encyclopaedia Britannica*, 11th ed., XVIII, pp. 766–73.

──────. "Nicholas." *Encyclopaedia Britannica*, 11th ed., XIX, p. 651.

Božović, Miro. "Crna Gora i njena uloga od 5. jula 1914. do kapitulacije." *Slobodna Misao*, 19 April 1936.

Božović, Vukašin B. *Krvavi kamen: Crna Gora u drugom balkanskom ratu sa Bugarskom, 1913*. Belgrade: Štamparija 'Privredni pregled,' 1932.

Braičić, Radul. "Operacije Zetskog odreda crnogorske vojske oko Skadva 1912. i 1913. godine." *Zapisi*, VI, Knj. X, No. 3 (1932), pp. 172–77.

Bridge, F. R. *From Sadowa to Sarajevo: The Foreign Policy of Austria-Hungary, 1866–1914*. London and Boston: Routledge and Kegan Paul, 1972.

──────. *Great Britain and Austria-Hungary, 1906–1914: A Diplomatic History*. London: Weidenfeld and Nicolson, 1972.

Brković, Savo. *O postanku i razvoju Crnogorske nacije*. Titograd: Grafički Zavod, 1974.

Bulajić, Žarko. *Agrarni odnosi u Crnoj Gori (1878–1912)*. Titograd, 1959.

Bülow, Bernard von. *Memoirs of Prince von Bülow*. Translated by Geoffrey Dunlop. 4 vols. Boston: Little, Brown, and Co., 1931.

Burke's Royal Families of the World. London: Burke's Peerage, 1977–.

Cailler, Claude Alexandre. *La Politique balkanique de l'Italie entre 1875 et 1914*. La Tour de Peilz: Stalder-Vodoz, 1951.

Calleo, David. *The German Problem Reconsidered: Germany and the World Order, 1870 to the Present*. Cambridge: Cambridge University Press, 1979.

Campbell, Spencer. "The Dissolution of the Balkan Allies." *Fortnightly Review*, n.s., XCIII (June 1913), pp. 1063–70.

Carlgren, Wilhelm Mauritz. *Isvolsky und Aehrenthal vor der bosnischen Annexionskrise: Russische und österreich-ungarische Balkanpolitik 1906–1908.* Uppsala: Almqvist & Wiksells, 1955.

Cary, Joyce. *Memoir of the Bobotes.* Austin: University of Texas Press, 1960.

Cataluccio, Francesco. *Antonio di San Giuliano e la Politica estera italiana dal 1910 al 1914.* Florence: F. le Mounier, 1935.

Ćetković, Jovan. *Borbe oko Skadra 1912–1913.* Belgrade: Prosveta, 1954.

―――――. *Ujeditelji Crne Gore i Srbije.* Dubrovnik, 1940.

Challener, Richard D. "Montenegro and the United States: A Balkan Fantasy." *Journal of Central European Affairs*, XVII (October 1957), pp. 236–42.

Charmatz, Richard. *Geschichte der auswärtigen Politik Österreichs im 19. Jahrhundert.* 2 vols. Leipzig: B. G. Teubner, 1912–14.

―――――. *Österreichs äussere und innere Politik von 1895 bis 1914.* Leipzig and Berlin: B. G. Teubner, 1918.

Chastenet, Jacques. *Raymond Poincaré.* Paris: R. Julliard, 1948.

Chekrezi, Constantine A. *Albania: Past and Present.* New York: Macmillan, 1919.

Chlumecký, L. von. "Die Italo-Albanesen und die Balkanpolitik." *Österreichische Rundschau*, V (November 1905-January 1906), pp. 331–52.

―――――. "Die Jungtürken und Albanien." *Österreichische Rundschau*, XXVI (January-March 1911), pp. 268–74.

Collins, Doreen. *Aspects of British Policies, 1904–1919.* Oxford: Oxford University Press, 1965.

Conrad von Hötzendorf, Franz. *Aus meiner Dienstzeit, 1906–1918.* 5 vols. Vienna: Rikola Verlag, 1921–25.

―――――. *Private Aufzeichnungen: Erste Veröffentlichungen aus den Papieren des k.u.k. Generalstabs-Chefs.* Vienna and Munich: Amalthea-Verlag, 1977.

Coon, Carleton S. *The Mountain of Giants: A Racial and Cultural Study of the North Albanian Mountain Ghegs.* Papers of the Peabody Museum of American Archaeology and Ethnology, Harvard University, Vol. XXIII, No. 3. Cambridge, Mass.: The Museum, 1950.

Cooper, M. B. "British Policy in the Balkans, 1908–9." *Historical Journal*, VII, No. 2 (1964), pp. 258–79.

Ćorović, Vladimir. *Istorija Jugoslavije.* Belgrade: Narodno Delo, 1933.

―――――. *Odnosi izmedju Srbije i Austro-Ugarske u XX veku.* Belgrade: Štampa Drž. štamparije Kraljevine Jugoslavije, 1936.

―――――. "Srpsko-bugarski odnosi," *Politika*, 1–4 May 1937.

Crampton, R. J. "The Decline of the Concert of Europe in the Balkans, 1913–1914." *Slavonic and East European Review*, LII (July 1974), pp. 393–419.

_____. *The Hollow Detente: Anglo-German Relations in the Balkans, 1911–1914*. Atlantic Highlands, N.J.: Humanities Press, 1980.

Čubrilović, Vasa, ed. *Jugoslovenski narodi pred prvi svetski rat*. Srpska Akademija Nauka i Umetnosti, Posebna Izdanje, Vol. CCCCXVI; Odeljenje Društvenih Nauka, Vol. LXI. Belgrade: Naučno Delo, 1967.

Cvijić, Jovan. *L'Annexion de la Bosnie-Hercégovine et la Question serbe*. Paris: Hachette, 1909.

Cvjetković, Marko. "Poštanska služba u Crnoj Gori." *Istorijski Zapisi*, XII, Knj. XVI, Nos. 3–4 (1959), pp. 59–78.

_____. "Prevoz pošte na Skadarskom jezeru." *Istorijski Zapisi*, XVII, Knj. XXI, No. 1 (1964), pp. 152–60.

_____. "Telegrafska i telefonska služba u Crnoj Gori." *Istorijski Zapisi*, IX, Knj. XII, Nos. 1–2 (1956), pp. 165–90.

Czega, E. "Die Mobilmachung Montenegros im Sommer 1914." *Berliner Monatshefte*, XIV (January 1936), pp. 3–23.

Danev, Stoian. *Balkánský svaz a válka s Tureckem, 1912–1913*. Prague: Orbis, 1935.

Darby, H. C. "Montenegro." *A Short History of Yugoslavia*, edited by Stephen Clissold, pp. 73–86. Cambridge: Cambridge University Press, 1968.

Dedijer, Vladimir. *The Road to Sarajevo*. New York: Simon and Schuster, 1966.

_____, et al. *History of Yugoslavia*. Translated by Kordija Kveder. New York: McGraw-Hill, 1974.

Denton, William. *Montenegro: Its People and Their History*. London: Daldy, Isbister & Co., 1877.

Devine, Alexander. *Montenegro in History, Politics and War*. New York: Frederick A. Stokes, 1918.

Dillon, E. J. "The Albanian Tangle." *Fortnightly Review*, n.s., XCVI (July 1914), pp. 565–84.

_____. "Foreign Affairs." *Contemporary Review*, CII (April 1913), pp. 565–84.

_____. "Foreign Affairs." *Contemporary Review*, CIII (May 1913), pp. 718–36.

Djilas, Milovan. *Land without Justice*. New York: Harcourt, Brace and Co., 1958.

_____. *Njegoš: Poet, Prince, Bishop*. Translated by Michael B. Petrovich. New York: Harcourt, Brace & World, 1966.

Djonović, Jovan. *Ustavne i političke borbe u Crnoj Gori, 1905–1910.* Belgrade: K. J. Mihailović, 1939.

Djonović, Nikola. *Crna Gora pre i posle ujedinjenja.* Belgrade: Politika, 1939.

Djonović, Svetozar. "Crnogorke na evropskim dvorima." *Verčernje novosti,* 13 February–13 March 1969.

Djordjević, Dimitrije. *Carinski rat Austro-Ugarske i Srbije, 1906–1911.* Jugoslovenske zemlje u XX veku, Vol. I. Belgrade: Istorijski Institut, 1962.

_____. "Italijansko-turski rat 1911–1912 godine i njegov uticaj na Balkanu." *Istoriski Pregled,* I, No. 4 (1954), pp. 46–54.

_____. *Izlazak Srbije na Jadransko more i konferencija ambasadora u Londonu 1912.* Belgrade: Slobodan Jović, 1956.

_____. *Milovan Milovanović.* Belgrade: Prosveta, 1962.

_____. "Les mouvements pour l'indépendence nationale et économique des Balkans au XIXe et XXe siècle (jusqu'a 1914)." *Rapports* du XXe Congrès International des Sciences Historiques 1965, Vol. IV, pp. 237–54. Vienna: Berger Horn, 1965.

_____. "Projekt Jadranske železnice u Srbije 1896–1912." *Istorijski Glasnik,* III/IV (1956), pp. 3–35.

_____. *Revolutions nationales des peuples balkaniques, 1804–1914.* Belgrade: Istorijski Institut, 1965.

Djordjević, Vladan. *Arnauti i velike sile.* Belgrade, 1913.

_____. *Crna Gora i Austrija 1814–1894.* Srpska Kraljevska Akademija Nauka i Umetnosti, Posebna Izdanja, Vol. CLIX, Društveni Istorijski Spisi, Vol. XIX. Belgrade: Radoljub, 1924.

_____. *Crna Gora i Rusija 1784–1814.* Belgrade, 1914.

Djurišić, Mitar. *Prvi Balkanski rat, 1912–1913 (Operacije Crnogorske vojske).* Belgrade: Istoriski institut Jugoslovenske narodne armije, 1960.

_____. "Uloga kralja Nikole u Prvom balkanskom ratu." *Istorijski Zapisi,* XIII, Knj. XVII, No. 1 (1969), pp. 69–92.

Djurović, Mirčeta. *Crnogorske finansije, 1860–1915.* Titograd, 1960.

_____. "Formiranje akcionarskih društava u Crnoj Gori početkom XX vijeka (u pojedinim privrednim granama)." *Istorijski Zapisi,* XII, Knj. XVI, Nos. 3–4 (1959), pp. 79–111.

_____. *Trgovački kapital u Crnoj Gori u drugoj polovini XIX i pocetkom XX vijeka.* Cetinje: Obod, 1958.

Dragićević, Risto J. "Djevojački institut na Cetinju." *Istorijski Zapisi;* Pt. 1: II, Knj. IV, Nos. 4–6 (1949), pp. 130–51; Pt. 2: III, Knj. V, Nos. 1–3 (1950), pp. 40–61.

_____. "Malisorske bune 1910. i 1911. godine." *Zapisi,* XIII, Knj. XXIV, No. 3 (1940), pp. 144–59; No. 4, pp. 202–22; No. 5, pp. 274–89.

_____. *Tajni ugovor Crne Gore i Austrije*. Cetinje: Obod, 1968.

Dragnich, Alex N. *Serbia, Nikola Pašić, and Yugoslavia*. New Brunswick, N.J.: Rutgers University Press, 1974.

Drljević, Sekula. "Crna Gora u balkanskom ratu: poslijedna velika inicijativa kralja Nikole." *Godišnjak matice srpske*, (1938), pp. 148–53.

Dumba, Constantin. *Memoirs of a Diplomat*. Translated by Ian F. D. Morrow. Boston: Little, Brown, and Company, 1932.

Durham, Mary Edith. *High Albania*. London: E. Arnold, 1909.

_____. "King Nikola of Montenegro." *Contemporary Review*, CXIX (April 1921), pp. 471–77.

_____. "The Serb and Albanian Frontiers." *Contemporary Review*, XCV (January 1909), pp. 15–23.

_____. "The Story of Essad Pasha." *Contemporary Review*, CXVIII (August 1920), pp. 207–15.

_____. *The Struggle for Scutari (Turk, Slav, and Albanian)*. London: E. Arnold, 1914.

_____. *Twenty Years of Balkan Tangle*. London: G. Allen and Unwin, 1920.

Efremov, P. N. *Vneshniaia politika Rossii (1907–1914 gg.)*. Moscow: Institut Mezhdunarodnykh otnoshenii, 1961.

Egli, Karl. *Drei Monate vor Skutari*. Bern, 1913.

Enciklopedija Jugoslavije. Zagreb: Leksikografski Zavod FNRJ, 1955–57.

Engel-Jánosi, Friedrich. *Geschichte auf dem Ballhausplatz: Essays zur österreichischen Aussenpolitik, 1830–1945*. Graz: Verlag Styria, 1963.

Erdeljanović, Jovan. *Stara Crna Gora: etnička prošlost i formiranje Crnogorskih plemena*. Belgrade, 1925.

Fabricius. "Austria, Disturber of the Peace." *Fortnightly Review*, n.s., XCIII (February 1913), pp. 249–64.

Faissler, Margareta. "Austria-Hungary and the Disruption of the Balkan League." *Slavonic and East European Review*, XIX (1939), pp. 141–57.

_____. *European Diplomacy in the Balkan Peninsula, August 10, 1913–June 28, 1914*. Chicago: University of Chicago Library, 1938.

Fay, Sidney Bradshaw. *The Origins of the World War*. 2d ed. rev. 2 vols. New York: Macmillan, 1939.

Feis, Herbert. *Europe, the World's Banker, 1870–1914: An Account of European Foreign Investment and the Connection of World Finance with Diplomacy before the War*. New Haven, Conn.: Yale University Press, 1930.

Fellner, Fritz. *Der Dreibund: Europäische Diplomatie vor dem Ersten Weltkrieg*. Vienna: Verlag für Geschichte und Politik, 1960.

Fischer, Fritz. *Germany's Aims in the First World War.* New York: W. W. Norton, 1967.

―――. *War of Illusions: German Politics from 1911 to 1914.* Translated by Marian Jackson. London: Chatto and Windus, 1975.

―――. *World Power or Decline: The Controversy over Germany's Aims in the First World War.* Translated by Lancelot L. Farrar, Robert Kimber, and Rita Kimber. New York: W. W. Norton, 1974.

Ford, Emmett B., Jr. "Montenegro in the Eyes of the English Traveler, 1840–1914." *Südostforschungen,* XVIII (1959), pp. 350–80.

Franetović, D. *Historija pomorstva i ribarstva Crne Gore do 1918. godine.* Titograd, 1960.

Franz, Georg. *Erzherzog Franz Ferdinand und die Pläne zur Reform der Habsburger Monarchie.* Munich: G. D. W. Callwey, 1943; Brünn: R. M. Rohrer, 1943.

Freundlich, Leo, ed. *Albaniens Golgatha: Anklageakten gegen die Vernichter des Albanervolkes.* Vienna: J. Roller, 1913.

Friedjung, Heinrich. *Das Zeitalter des Imperialismus 1884 bis 1914.* 3 vols. Berlin: Neufeld & Henius, 1919–22.

Gasic, Dragan. "Die Presse Serbiens 1903–1914 und Österreich-Ungarn." Ph.D. Dissertation: University of Vienna, 1971.

Geiss, Imanuel. *Germany Foreign Policy, 1871–1914.* Boston: Routledge and Kegan Paul, 1976.

Gerhardt, Heinz. *War in der bosnischen Annexionskrise die deutsche Demarche vom 22. März 1909 ein Ultimatum?* Berlin: E.-Reuter Gesellschaft, 1965.

Gesemann, Gerhard. *Der montenegrinische Mensch.* Prague: Kommissionsverlag der J. G. Calveschen Universitäts-Buchhandlung, 1934.

Giesche, Richard. *Der serbische Zugang zum Meer und die europäische Krise 1912.* Stuttgart: W. Kohlhammer, 1932.

Giesl, Wladimir. *Zwei Jahrzehnte im Nahen Orient.* Edited by Eduard Ritter von Steinitz. Berlin: Verlag für Kulturpolitik, 1927.

Giolitti, Giovanni. *Memoirs of My Life.* Translated by Edward Storer. London: Chapman and Dodd, 1923.

Gooch, G. P. *Before the War: Studies in Diplomacy.* 2 vols. London: Longmans, Green & Co., 1936–38.

Gooss, Roderich. *Das österreichisch-serbische Problem bis zur Kriegserklärung Österreich-Ungarns an Serbien, 28. Juli 1914.* Berlin: Deutsche Verlagsgesellschaft für Politik und Geschichte, 1930.

Gopčević, Spiridon. *Geschichte von Montenegro und Albanien.* Gotha: F. A. Perthes, 1914.

―――. *Montenegro und die Montenegriner.* Leipzig: H. Fries, 1877.

―――――. *Russland und Serbien von 1804–1915*. Munich: H. Schmidt, 1916.

Gosses, Frans. *The Management of British Foreign Policy before the First World War*. Leiden: A. W. Sijthoff, 1948.

Great Britain. Admiralty. Intelligence Division. *A Handbook of Serbia, Montenegro, Albania and Adjacent Parts of Greece*. London, 1916.

―――――. Foreign Office. Historical Section. *Montenegro*. London: H.M.S. Stationery Office, 1920.

Grey, Sir Edward. *Speeches on Foreign Affairs, 1904–1914*. Edited by Paul Knaplund. London: G. Allen and Unwin, 1931.

―――――. *Twenty-five Years, 1892–1916*. 2 vols. New York: Frederick A. Stokes, Co., 1925.

Grogan, Ellinor. *The Life of J. D. Bourchier*. London: Hurst and Blackett, 1926.

Grothe, Hugo. *Durch Albanien und Montenegro*. Munich: M. Mörike, 1913.

Geshov, Ivan. *The Balkan League*. Translated by Constantine C. Mincoff. London: J. Murray, 1915.

Hanotaux, Gabriel. *La guerre des Balkans et l'Europe 1912–1913*. Études diplomatiques, 2d series. 2d ed. Paris: Plon-Nourrit et Cie, 1914.

Hantsch, Hugo. *Leopold Graf Berchtold: Grandseigneur und Staatsmann*. 2 vols. Graz and Cologne: Styria-Verlag, 1963.

―――――. "Die Tagebücher und Memoiren des Grafen Leopold Berchtold." *Südostforschungen*, XIV (1955), pp. 205–15.

Heilbronner, Hans. "The Merger Attempts of Serbia and Montenegro, 1913–1914." *Journal of Central European Affairs*, XVIII (October 1958), pp. 281–91.

Helmreich, Ernst C. "The Conflict between Germany and Austria over Balkan Policy, 1913–1914." *Essays in the History of Modern Europe*, edited by Donald C. McKay, pp. 130–48. New York: Harper, 1936.

―――――. *The Diplomacy of the Balkan Wars, 1912–1913*. Cambridge, Mass.: Harvard University Press, 1938.

―――――. "Montenegro and the Formation of the Balkan League." *Slavonic Review*, XV (January 1937), pp. 426–34.

―――――. "Russlands Einfluss auf den Balkanbund im Oktober 1912." *Berliner Monatshefte*, XI (March 1933), pp. 217–45.

―――――. "The Serbian-Montenegrin Alliance of September 23/October 6, 1912." *Journal of Central European Affairs*, XIX (January 1960), pp. 411–5.

―――――. "Die tieferen Ursachen der Politik Berchtolds im Oktober 1912." *Berliner Monatshefte*, X (March 1932), pp. 28–44.

———. "An Unpublished Report on Austro-German Military Conversations of November, 1912." *Journal of Modern History,* V (June 1933), pp. 197–207.

Henderson, W. O. "German Economic Penetration in the Middle East, 1870–1914." *Economic History Review,* XVIII (1948), pp. 54–64.

Herre, Paul. *Die kleinen Staaten Europas und die Entstehung des Weltkrieges.* Munich: C. H. Beck'sche Verlagsbuchhandlung, 1937.

Hiller, Gerhard. *Die Entwicklung des österreichisch-serbischen Gegensatzes, 1908–1914.* Halle: Akademischer Verlag, 1934.

Hinsley, F. H., ed. *British Foreign Policy under Sir Edward Grey.* New York, London, and Cambridge: Cambridge University Press, 1977.

Hoffmann, John Wesley. *The Austro-Russian Rivalry in the Balkans, 1909–1912: A Part of a Dissertation Submitted to the Faculty of the Division of the Social Sciences in Candidacy for the Degree of Doctor of Philosophy.* Chicago: University of Chicago Libraries, 1940.

Hoijer, Olof. *Le Comte d'Aehrenthal et la Politique de la violence.* Paris, 1922.

Holdege, K. *Frankreichs Politik im Nahen Orient und im Mittelmeer in der Zeit vom Ausbruch des italienisch-türkischen Krieges bis zum Zusammentritt der Londoner Botschafterkonferenz Oktober 1911–Dezember 1912.* Dresden: Risse Verlag, 1934.

Hoyos, A. *Der deutsch-englische Gegensatz und sein Einfluss auf die Balkanpolitik Österreich-Ungarns.* Berlin and Leipzig: Vereinigung wissenschaftlicher Verleger, 1922.

Hrabak, Bogumil. "Arbanaški prvak Isa Boljetinac i Crna Gora 1910–1912. godine." *Istorijski Zapisi,* XXX, Knj. XXXIV, No. 1 (1977), pp. 177–92.

———. "Crna Gora i Srbija na početku nove ere u južnoslovenskoj povesti (1903–1904)." *Istorijski časopis,* XX (1973), pp. 319–58.

Hubka, Gustav von. "Diplomatum in Montenegro." *Berliner Monatshefte,* XIV (August 1936), pp. 657–62.

———. "König Nikolaus von Montenegro." *Deutsche Revue,* XLVI (April; June 1921), pp. 23–31, 174–84.

———. "Kritische Tage in Montenegro." *Berliner Monatshefte,* IX (January 1931), pp. 27–45.

Huebner, Hans. *Österreich-Ungarns Balkanpolitik vor dem Ersten Weltkrieg; Deutschlands Polenpolitik vor dem Zweiten Weltkrieg.* Bregenz: Eugen-Russ-Verlag, 1964.

Ippen, Th. A. "Das religiöse Protectorat Österreich-Ungarns in der Türkei." *Kultur,* III (1902), pp. 298–316.

Istorija Crne Gore. 8 vols. projected. Titograd: Istorijski Institut i Istorijska Komisija Centralnog Komiteta Saveza Komunista Jugoslavije, 1967–.

Ivanova, Yu. B. *Severnaia Albaniia v XIX-nachale XX v. Obshchestvennaia zhizn'*. Moscow: Nauka, 1973.

Ivović, Jovan. "Atentator Muhamed Mehmedbašić u Nikšiću." *Istorijski Zapisi*, II, Knj. III, Nos. 1–2 (1949), pp. 35–49.

Izvolsky, Alexander P. *The Memoirs of Alexander Isvolsky*. Translated and edited by C. L. Seeger. London: Hutchinson and Co., 1920.

Janković, Dragoslav and Krizman, Bogdan, eds. *Gradja o stvaranju Jugoslovenske države*. 2 vols. Institut Društvenih Nauka, Odeljenje za Istorijske Nauke, Serija III: Gradja. Belgrade, 1964.

Jelavich, Barbara. *A Century of Russian Foreign Policy, 1814–1914*. Philadelphia and New York: J. B. Lippincott, 1964.

―――. *The Habsburg Empire in European Affairs, 1914–1918*. Chicago: Rand McNally, 1969.

Jelavich, Charles. "Nikola Pašić: Greater Serbia or Yugoslavia?" *Journal of Central European Affairs*, XI (July 1951), pp. 133–52.

Jelavich, Charles and Jelavich, Barbara. *The Establishment of the Balkan National States, 1804–1920. A History of East Central Europe*, Vol. VIII. Seattle and London: University of Washington Press, 1977.

―――, eds. *The Balkans in Transition: Essays on the Development of Balkan Life and Politics since the Eighteenth Century*. Hamden, Conn.: Archon Books, 1974.

Jenkins, R. *Asquith*. London, 1967.

Jireček, Jovan. *Projekat željeznice Dunav-Niš-Jadransko More*. Belgrade, 1908.

Jovanović, Jagoš. *Stvaranje Crnogorske države i razvoj Crnogorske nacionalnosti: Istorija Crne Gore od početka VIII vijeka do 1918. godine*. Cetinje: Obod, 1947.

―――. "Veze Crne Gore sa Rusijom od druge polovine XVI veka do danas." *Istorijski Zapisi*, I, Knj. II, Nos. 3–4 (1948), pp. 139–60; Nos. 5–6, pp. 248–58; Knj. III, Nos. 3–4, pp. 120–33; Knj. IV, Nos. 1–3, pp. 30–36.

Jovanović, Jovan M. "Austrijska tajna arhiva 1914." *Zapisi*, V, Knj. VIII, No. 1 (1931), pp. 33–35; No. 2, pp. 86–90; No. 3, pp. 160–63.

―――. *Borba za narodno ujedinjenje 1914–1918*. Belgrade: G. Kohn, 1934.

―――. "Crna Gora pred rat." *Zapisi*, IV, Knj. VII, No. 3 (1930), pp. 162–65.

―――. "Crna Gora za ujedinjenje." *Zapisi*, III, Knj. V, No. 3 (1929), pp. 156–59.

―――. "Odgovornost za rat." *Zapisi*, IV, Knj. VII, No. 2 (1930), pp. 97–99.

―――. "Rusija i Crna Gora." *Zapisi*, VII, Knj. XII, No. 2 (1933), pp. 109–13.

Jovanović, Radoman. "Crna Gora i istočna Hercegovina za vrijeme aneksione krize 1908–1909." *Jugoslovenski narodi pred Prvi svetski rat*, edited by Vasa Čubrilović, pp. 289–313. Belgrade: Naučno Delo, 1967.

―――――. "Crna Gora i Srbija za vrijeme aneksione krize (1908–1909). *Zbornik radova prikazanih na Medjunarodnom naučnom skupu Velike sile i Srbija pred prvi svetski rat*, pp. 565–75. Naučni skupovi Srpske akademije nauka i umetnosti, Vol. IV, Odeljenje istoriskih nauka, No. 1. Belgrade. 1976.

―――――. "Jedan inostrani otpor prodiranju italijanskog kapitala u Crnu Goru." *Istorijski Zapisi*, XIV, Knj. XVIII, No. 3 (1961), pp. 417–42.

―――――. "Pokušaj Austro-Ugarske da dobije koncesiju za izgradnju željeznice u Crnogorskom primorju." *Istorijski Zapisi*, XVI, Knj. XX, No. 2 (1963), pp. 311–15.

―――――. "Stav Crne Gore prema aneksiji Bosne i Hercegovine." *Istorijski Zapisi*, XVI, Knj. XX, No. 1 (1963), pp. 91–121.

Jovanović, Slobodan. *Moji Savremenici*. 6 vols. in 1. Windsor, 1962.

―――――. "Nicholas Pašić: After Ten Years." *Slavonic and East European Review*, XV (July 1937), pp. 368–76.

Kalbskopf, Willy. *Die Aussenpolitik der Mittelmächte im Tripoliskrieg und die letzte Dreibunderneuerung: Eine Studie zur Bündnispolitik der europäischen Grossmächte vor dem Weltkrieg*. Erlangen: K. Döres, 1932.

Kann, Robert A. "Die Prochaska Affäre vom Herbst 1912: zwischen kaltem und heissem Krieg," *Österreichische Akademie der Wissenschaften. Philosophisch-Historische Klasse*. Sitzungsbericht No. 319, Vienna 1977.

―――――. *Erzherzog Franz Ferdinand Studien*. Munich: R. Oldenbourg Verlag, 1976.

―――――. "Erzherzog Franz Ferdinand und Graf Berchtold als Aussenminister, 1912–1914." *Mitteilungen des österreichischen Staatsarchivs*, XXII (1969), pp. 246–78.

―――――. *The Multinational Empire*. 2 vols. New York: Columbia University Press, 1950.

Kanner, Heinrich. *Kaiserliche Katastrophenpolitik*. Vienna, 1922.

Kapidžić, Hamdija. "Skadarska kriza i izuzetne mjere u Bosni i Hercegovini u maju 1913. godine." *Godišnjak Društva Bosne i Hercegovine*, XIII (1962), pp. 5–51.

Kašanin, Ratimir. "Srpsko-bugarski odnosi 1903–1913." Ph.D. Dissertation: University of Belgrade, 1960.

Khitrova, N. I. "Sotsial'no-ekonomicheskoe razvitie Chernogorii v kontse XIX-nachale XX v. i konstitutsiia 1905 g." *Kratkie Soobshcheniia Instituta Slavianovedeniia*, XX (1956), pp. 85–94.

Kiderlen-Wächter, Alfred von. *Kiderlen-Wächter: Der Staatsmann und Mensch: Briefwechsel und Nachlass.* 2 vols. Edited by Ernst Jäckh. Stuttgart: Deutsche Verlags-Anstalt, 1924.

Kiendl, Hans. *Russische Balkanpolitik von der Ernennung Sasonows bis zum Ende des Zweiten Balkankrieges.* Garmisch: A. Adam, 1925.

Kiszling, Rudolf. *Erzherzog Franz Ferdinand von Österreich-Este: Leben, Pläne und Wirken am Schicksalsweg.* Graz: Hermann Böhlaus Nachf., 1953.

―――――. "Feldmarschall Conrad v. Hötzendorf." *Österreich in Geschichte und Literatur,* VIII, No. 4 (1964), pp. 157–67.

―――――. "Russlands Kriegsvorbereitungen im Herbst 1912 und ihre Rückwirkungen auf Österreich-Ungarn." *Berliner Monatshefte,* XIII (March 1935), pp. 181–92.

Klein, Fritz, ed. *Österreich-Ungarn in der Weltpolitik, 1900 bis 1918.* Berlin: Akademie-Verlag, 1965.

Korać, Milorad. "Sukobi na crnogorsko-turskoj granici u Sandžaku početkom XX vijeka." *Istorijski Zapisi,* XXI, Knj. XXV, No. 2 (1968), pp. 283–91.

Kritt, Robert. "Die Londoner Botschafter Konferenz, 1912–1913." Ph.D. Dissertation: University of Vienna, 1961.

Kutschbach, Albin. *Der Brandherd Europas: 50 Jahre Balkan-Erinnerungen.* Leipzig: E. Haberland, 1929.

Lafore, Laurence. *The Long Fuse: An Interpretation of the Origins of World War I.* Philadelphia: J. B. Lippincott, 1965.

Lainović, Andrija. "Pitanje Skadra u Prvom balkanskom ratu." *Istorijski Zapisi,* II, Knj. IV, Nos. 1–3 (1949), pp. 66–76.

Lalić, Radovan. "O tradicionalnim vezama izmedju Crne Gore i Rusije." *Istorijski Zapisi,* IV, Knj. VII, Nos. 7–9 (1951), pp. 273–93.

Lamouche, Léon. "La naissance de l'état albanais." *Revue politique et parlementaire,* LXXX (10 May 1914), pp. 220–39.

Langer, William L. "The 1908 Prelude to the World War." *Foreign Affairs,* VII (July 1929), pp. 633–49.

Larmeroux, Jean. *La Politique extérieure de l'Autriche-Hongrie, 1875–1914.* 2 vols. Paris: Plon-Nourrit et Cie, 1918.

Lazarević, Djordje. *Istorija Crne Gore.* Belgrade: Privrednik, 1935.

Lee, Dwight. *Europe's Crucial Years: The Diplomatic Background of World War I, 1902–1914.* Hanover, N.H.: University Press of New England, 1974.

Lichnowsky, Karl von. *Heading for the Abyss.* Translated by Sefton Delmer. London: Constable, 1928.

Loeding, Doerte. "Deutschlands und Österreich-Ungarns Balkanpolitik von 1912–1914 unter besonderer Berücksichtigung ihrer Wirtschaftsinteressen." Ph.D. Dissertation: University of Hamburg, 1969.

Lončarević, Dušan. *Jugoslawiens Entstehung*. Zurich: Amalthea-Verlag, 1929.

Lopičić, Stevo. *Cetinjska bombaška afera u vezi sa Zagrebačkim procesom*. Belgrade, 1927.

Lorey, August Louis. *Frankreichs Politik während der Balkankriege, 1912/13*. Dresden: M. Dittert, 1941.

Lützow, Heinrich von. "Is Austria Really the Disturber?" *Fortnightly Review*, n.s., XCIII (May 1913), pp. 598–602.

M. "The Balkan League, History of its Formation." *Fortnightly Review*, n.s., XCIII (March 1913), pp. 430–39.

Magrini, Luciano. *Il Montenegro: La Fine di un Regno*. Milan, 1922.

Maksimović, Vojin. *Rat Srbije protiv Bugarske 1913*. Belgrade, 1921–2.

―――. *Rat Srbije protiv Turske 1912–1913*. Belgrade, 1922.

Mandl, Leopold. *Die Habsburger und die serbische Frage: Geschichte des staatlichen Gegensatzes Serbiens zu Österreich-Ungarn*. Vienna: Moritz Perles, 1918.

―――. *Österreich-Ungarn und Serbien nach dem Balkankrieg: Materialien zum Verständnis der Beziehungen Serbiens zu Österreich-Ungarn*. Vienna: Moritz Perles, 1912.

Marco [Simić, Božin]. "Nikolaus Hartwig: Serbiens Aussenpolitik vor dem Weltkrieg." *Kriegsschuldfrage*, VI (August 1928), pp. 745–69.

Margutti, Albert A. *The Emperor Francis Joseph and His Times*. London: Hutchinson, 1921.

Marriott, J. A. R. *The Eastern Question: An Historical Study in European Diplomacy*. 4th ed. Oxford: Clarendon Press, 1951 (1st ed. 1917).

Martinović, Niko S. "Jedan prilog proučavanju balkanskog rata." *Istorijski Zapisi*, X, Knj. XIII, Nos. 1–2 (1957), pp. 320–25.

―――. "Otpor naroda u Crnoj Gori protiv aneksije Bosne i Hercegovine." *Jugoslovenski narodi pred Prvi svetski rat*, edited by Vasa Čubrilović, pp. 497–512. Belgrade: Naučno Delo, 1967.

―――. "Počeci radničkog pokreta u Crnoj Gori." *Istorijski Zapisi*, XII, Knj. XV, No. 1 (1959), pp. 7–30.

―――. *Razvitak štampe i štamparstva u Crnoj Gori, 1493–1945*. Belgrade, 1965.

Masaryk, Thomas. *Der Agramer Hochverratsprozess und die Annexion von Bosnien und der Herzegovina*. Vienna, 1910.

Massie, Robert K. *Nicholas and Alexandra*. New York: Atheneum, 1967.

May, Arthur J. *The Habsburg Monarchy, 1867–1914*. Cambridge, Mass.: Harvard University Press, 1965.

―――. "The Novibazar Railroad Project." *Journal of Modern History*, X (December 1938), pp. 496–527.

———. "Trans-Balkan Railway Schemes." *Journal of Modern History*, XXIV (December 1952), pp. 352–67.

Medlicott, William N. *The Congress of Berlin and After: A Diplomatic History of the Near Eastern Settlement, 1878–1880*. London: Methuen, 1938.

Michaelis, Herbert. *Die deutsche Politik während der Balkankriege, 1912/13*. Waldenburg: E. Kästner, 1929.

Mijušković, Slavko. "Protivaustrijske demonstracije u Kotoru juna 1914. godine." *Istorijski Zapisi*, XVII, Knj. XXI, No. 3 (1964), pp. 573–87.

Miller, William. *The Balkans: Roumania, Bulgaria, Servia, and Montenegro*. London: T. Fisher Unwin, 1923.

Milošević, Pavle. "Operacije Istočnog odreda crnogorske vojske u Sandžaku, Gornjem Polimlju i Metohiji 1912. godine." *Istorijski Zapisi*, XXV, Knj. XXX, Nos. 3–4 (1972), pp. 279–382.

Molden, Berthold. *Alois Graf Aehrenthal: Sechs Jahre äussere Politik Österreich-Ungarns*. Stuttgart and Berlin: Deutsche Verlagsanstalt, 1917.

Mosely, P. E. "Russian Policy in 1911–1912." *Journal of Modern History*, XII (March 1940), pp. 69–86.

Mousset, Albert. *L'Albanie devant l'Europe 1912–1929*. Paris, 1930.

Murray, Beaven. *Austrian Policy since 1868*. London, 1914.

Murray, G. *The Foreign Policy of Sir Edward Grey, 1906–1915*. Oxford, 1915.

Musulin, Alexander von. *Das Haus am Ballplatz: Erinnerungen eines österreichisch-ungarischen Diplomaten*. Munich: Verlag für Kulturpolitik, 1924.

MacKenzie, David. *The Serbs and Russian Pan-Slavism, 1875–1878*. Ithaca: Cornell University Press, 1967.

Nekliudov, A. V. *Diplomatic Reminiscences before and during the World War*. Translated by Alexandra Paget. London: J. Murray, 1920.

Nicolson, Harold. *Sir Arthur Nicolson, Bart., First Lord Carnock: A Study in the Old Diplomacy*. London: Constable, 1930.

Nikčević, Tomica. *Političke struje u Crnoj Gori u procesu stvaranja države u XIX vijeku*. Cetinje: Narodna knjiga, 1958.

Nikola I Petrović Njegoš. *Cjelokupna djela Nikole I Petrovića Njegoša*. Cetinje: Obod, 1969.

Nintchitch, Momtchilo [Ninčić, Momčilo]. *La Crise bosniaque (1908–1909) et les puissances européennes*. 2 vols. Paris: A. Costes, 1937.

Nola, Carlo di. "4 Documenti." *Risorgimento*, XII, No. 2 (1960), pp. 118–26.

Pagliano, Emilio. *La Constituzione del Montenegro*. Rome, 1906.

Pavičević, Branko. *Stvaranje Crnogorske države*. Belgrade: Rad, 1955.

Pavlović, Živko. *Opsada Skadra 1912–1913*. Belgrade, 1926.

———. *Pedeset godina na prestolu Crne Gore.* Cetinje, 1910.
Peacock, Wadham. "The Future of Albania." *Fortnightly Review*, n.s., XCIII (May 1913), pp. 920–32.
———. "Nicholas of Montenegro and the Czardom of the Serbs." *Nineteenth Century and After*, LXXII (November 1912), pp. 879–88.
———. "The 'Wild Albanian.' " *Fortnightly Review*, n.s., XCIX (February 1913), pp. 322–34.
Pejović, Djordjije D. *Iseljavanja Crnogoraca u XIX vijeku.* Titograd: Obod, 1962.
———. *Razvitak prosvjete i kulture u Crnoj Gori, 1852–1916.* Cetinje: Obod, 1971.
———. "Uzroci masovnog iseljavanja stanovništva iz Crne Gore (1878–1916)." *Istorijski Zapisi*, XV, Knj. XIX, No. 2 (1962), pp. 209–53.
Perović, Branko, et al. *Prvi balkanski rat, 1912–1913.* Belgrade: Vojnoistorijski institut, 1959–75. Vol. I, Branko Perović, et al., *Operacije Srpske vojske;* Vol. II, Borislav Ratković. *Operacije Srpske vojske;* Vol. III, Mitar Djurišić, *Operacije Crnogorske vojske.*
Petrović, Nikola. "Zajednički Austro-Ugarski kabinet i jugoslovensko pitanje, 1912–1918." *Jugoslovenski narodi pred Prvi svetski rat*, edited by Vasa Čubrilović, pp. 725–60. Belgrade: Naucno Delo, 1967.
Petrovich, Michael Boro. *A History of Modern Serbia, 1804–1918.* 2 vols. New York and London: Harcourt Brace Jovanovich, 1976.
Pilcher, George. "The Future of Montenegro." *Fortnightly Review*, n.s., XCIV (July 1913), pp. 82–95.
Pinon, René. "Austrija i Balkanski rat." *Delo*, LXVI, No. 3 (1913).
———. "Le Monténégro and son prince." *Revue des deux mondes*, 5th période, LVI (March-April 1910), pp. 76–111.
Pisarev, Jurij Aleksejević. "Neki aspekti odnosa Rusije sa Crnom Gorom i Srbijom početkom Prvog svjetskog rata." *Istorijski Zapisi*, XX, Knj. XXIV, No. 2 (1967), pp. 229–53.
Poincaré, Raymond. *Au Service de la France: Neuf Années de Souvenirs.* Vol. II: *Les Balkans en Feu 1912;* Vol. III: *L'Europe sous les Armes 1913.* Paris, 1926–33.
———. *The Origins of the War.* London, 1922.
Politicus. "The Problem of Austria-Hungary." *Fortnightly Review*, n.s., XCIII (June 1913), pp. 1047–62.
Pollak, Rudolph. *Gerichtsorganisation und Rechtspflege Österreich-Ungarns in Montenegro und Albanien.* Jena, 1918.
Popov, Radoslav. "Balkanskite dŭrzhavi i kraiat na krizata ot 1908–1909 g." *V chest na akademik Dimitŭr Kosev*, edited by Evlogi Buzhashki, et al., pp. 253–63. Sofia: BAN, 1974.

———. "Serbiia, velikie derzhav' i vopros o kompensatsiiah v period bosniiskogo krizisa 1908–1909 g.g." *Zbornik radova prikazanih na Medjunarodnom naučnom skupu Velike sile i Srbija pred prvi svetski rat*, pp. 151–70. Naučni skupovi Srpske adademije nauka i umetnosti, Vol. IV; Odeljenje istoriskih nauka, No. 1. Belgrade, 1976.

Popović, Bogdan. "Jedna ponuda kralja Nikole Amerikancima." *Prilozi za književnost, jezik, istoriju i folklor*, I/2 (1960), pp. 110–18.

Popović, Dimitrije. *Borba za narodno ujedinjenje od 1908 do 1914*. Belgrade: G. Kohn 1936.

Popović, Djorde. *Istorija Crne Gore*. Belgrade: P. Burčić, 1896.

Popović, Milan. "Boravak atentatora Muhameda Mehmedbašića u Crnoj Gori nakon atentata 1914 g." *Istorijski Zapisi*, II, Knj. III, Nos. 5–6 (1949), pp. 280–85.

Popović. Pavle. *Le Monténégro et la question de Scutari*. Geneva, 1919.

Popović, Pavle, et al. *Spoljašanja i unutrašnja politika Crne Gore od 1851 do 1918*. 2 vols. Belgrade, 1937.

Popović. Vasilj. *Evropa i srpsko-pitanje u periodu oslobodjenja 1804–1918*. Belgrade: G. Kohn 1938.

Popovitch, Pavle. "Bulgaria and the Balkan Alliance." *Balkan Review*, I (April 1927), pp. 174–87.

Pribram, Alfred Francis. *Austria-Hungary and Great Britain, 1908–1914*. Translated by Ian R. D. Morrow. Oxford: Oxford University Press, 1951.

———. *Austrian Foreign Policy, 1908–1918*. London: George Allen and Unwin, 1923.

Pržić, Ilija. *Spoljašna politika Srbije (1804–1914)*. Belgrade, 1939.

Raabe, Ingrid. *Beiträge zur Geschichte der diplomatischen Beziehungen zwischen Frankreich und Österreich-Ungarn 1908–1912*. Vienna: Verlag Notring, 1971.

Radosavović, Ilija. *Medjunarodni položaj Crne Gore u XIX vijeku*. Belgrade, 1960.

Radović, Andrija. *The Question of Scutari*. Paris, 1919.

Rakočević, Novica. "Bombaška afera i crnogorska narodna skupština." *Istorijski Zapisi*, XXX (L), Knj. XXXIV, No. 1 (1977), pp. 167–75.

———. "Crna Gora i ujedinjenje." *Politički život Jugoslavije, 1914–1945*, edited by Aleksandar Acković, pp. 75–92. Belgrade: Radio-Beograd, 1973.

———. *Crna Gora u Prvom svjetskom ratu 1914–1918*. Cetinje: Obod, 1969.

———. "Izbori za Crnogorsku narodnu skupštinu u januaru 1914, godine i program vlade generala Janka Vukotića." *Istorijski Zapisi*, XXV, Knj. XXX, Nos. 3–4 (1972), pp. 413–30.

―――――. "Nabavka oružja od strane Crne Gore u balkanskom i prvom svjetskom ratu." *Istorijski Zapisi*, XIV, Knj. XVIII, No. 1 (1961), pp. 143–53.

―――――. "Nacionalna politika i politička misao u Crnoj Gori u ustavnom periodu 1905–1914. godine." *Simpozijum oslobodilački pokreti jugoslovenskih naroda od XVI veka do početka prvog svetskog rata*, edited by Danica Milić, pp. 311–17. Istoriski Institut, Zbornik radova, Vol. 1. Belgrade, 1976.

―――――. "O jugoslovenskoj misli u Crnoj Gori do Prvog svjetskog rata." *Historijski Zbornik*, XXIX-XXX (1976–1977), pp. 439–46.

―――――. "Odnosi Crne Gore i Srbije u periodu 1912–1914. godine." *Zbornik radova prikazanih na Medjunarodnom naučnom skupu Velike sile i Srbija pred prvi svetski rat*, pp. 577–86. Naučni skupovi Srpske akademije nauka i umetnosti, Vol. IV, Odeljenje istoriskih nauka, No. 1. Belgrade, 1976.

―――――. "Odnosi izmedju Crne Gore i Austro-Ugarske od završetka skadarske krize maja 1913. do sarajevskog atentata." *Jugoslovenski narodi pred Prvi svetski rat*, edited by Vasa Čubrilović, pp. 819–45. Belgrade: Radio-Beograd, 1973.

―――――. "Oslobodjenje Pljevalja i Kamene Gore u Balkanskom ratu 1912. godine." *Simpozijum "Seoski dani Sretena Vukosavljevića" VII*, pp. 137–47. Prijepolje, 1979.

―――――. "Politička osnova proglašenja Crne Gore za kraljevinu 1910. godine." *Balcanica*, VIII (1977), pp. 455–60.

―――――. " 'Radničke novine' i Crna Gora 1903–1914." *Počeci socijalističke štampe na Balkanu*, edited by Milo Popović, et al., pp. 479–88. Belgrade, 1974.

―――――. "Sandžak na stranicama 'Cetinjskog Vjesnika' od ustava jula 1908. do Balkanskog rata. *Simpozijum "Seoski dani Sretena Vukoslavljevića" VI*, pp. 131–44. Prijepolje, 1978.

―――――. "Stanje na crnogorsko-turskoj granici uoči balkanskog rata (1908–1912)." *Istorijski Zapisi*, XV, Knj. XIX, Nos. 3–4 (1962), pp. 485–515.

Rappaport, Alfred. "Albaniens Werdegang." *Kriegsschuldfrage*, V (September 1927), pp. 815–44.

―――――. "Montenegros Eintritt in den Weltkrieg." *Berliner Monatshefte*, VII (October 1929), pp. 941–66.

Ratković, Borislav. *Prvi Balkanski rat, 1912–1913 (Operacije Srpske vojske)*. Belgrade: Vojnoistorijski institut, 1975.

―――――, et al. *Srbija i Crna Gora u balkanskim ratovima 1912–1913*. Belgrade: Izdavačko-grafički zavod, 1972.

Ražnatović, Novak. *Crna Gora i Berlinski kongres*. Cetinje: Obod, 1979.

―――――. "Crnogorsko-srpski odnosi i pitanje prestolonasljedja u Srbiji 1900–1903 godine." *Istorijski Zapisi*, XXX, Knj. XXXIV, Nos. 3–4 (1977), pp. 655–706.

──────. "Rusko posredovanje u crnogorsko-srpskim odnosima od bombaškog procesa do aneksione krize." *Istorijski Zapisi*, XV, Knj. XIX, Nos. 3–4 (1962), pp. 540–62.

──────. "Sprovodjenje XXXIX Čg. Berlinskog ugovora o Crnogorskim primorju i ingerenciji Austro-Ugarske u luci Bar." *Istorijski Zapisi*, XXV, Knj. XXX, Nos. 3–4 (1972), pp. 383–413.

Rechberger Walther. "Zur Geschichte der Orientbahnen: Österreichische Eisenbahnpolitik auf dem Balkan." *Österreichische Osthefte*, II, No. 5 (1960), pp. 348–59; III, No. 2 (1961), pp. 102–12.

Recouly, Raymond. "Les conférences de Londres et la Guerre Balkanique." *Revue politique et parlementaire*, LXXVI (10 January 1913), pp. 136–45.

──────. "La question de Scutari." *Revue politique et parlementaire*, LXXVI (10 May 1913), pp. 337–44.

Redlich, Joseph. *Emperor Francis Joseph of Austria: A Biography.* New York: Macmillan, 1929.

──────. "Habsburg Policy in the Balkans before the War." *Foreign Affairs*, VI (July 1928), pp. 645–57.

──────. *Schicksalsjahre Österreich, 1908–1919: Das politische Tagebuch Josef Redlichs.* Edited by Fritz Fellner. Kommission für neure Geschichte Österreichs, No. XXXIX. Graz: H. Böhlaus Nachf., 1953.

Redlich, Marcellus D. A. von. *Albania, Yesterday and Today.* Worcester, Mass.: The Albanian Messenger, 1936.

Regele, Oskar. *Feldmarschall Conrad: Auftrag und Erfüllung 1906–1918.* Vienna: Verlag Herold, 1955.

Remak, Joachim. "1914—The Third Balkan War: Origins Reconsidered." *Journal of Modern History*, XLIII (September 1971), pp. 353-66.

──────. *The Origins of World War I, 1871–1914.* New York: Holt, Rinehart and Winston, 1967.

──────. *Sarajevo, the Story of a Political Murder.* New York: Criterion Books, 1959.

Remy, Oscar. "Sandschakbahn und Donau-Adriabahn: Ein Kapitel aus der Vorgeschichte des Weltkrieges." *Archiv für Eisenbahnwesen*, L, No. 5 (1927), p. 1189.

Renouvin, Pierre. *The Immediate Origins of the War (28th June-4th August, 1914).* New Haven, Conn.: Yale University Press, 1928.

──────. *La Politique extérieure de la IIIe République de 1904 a 1919.* Paris: Centre de Documentation universitaire, 1949.

Reuning, Wilhelm. "The Sanjak Railroad: A Reply to Italian Economic Penetration." *Susquehanna University Studies*, IX (June 1973), pp. 149–76.

Robbins, Keith. *Sir Edward Grey: A Biography of Lord Grey of Fallodon.* London: Cassell, 1971.

Rossos, Andrew. *Russia and the Balkans: Inter-Balkan Rivalries and Russian Foreign Policy, 1908–1914.* Toronto: University of Toronto Press, 1981.

Ružić, Jevto A. *Crna Gora u ratovima 1912–1918 i u poratnoj istoriji.* Windsor, Canada, 1955.

Salvemini, Gaetano. *La Politica estera dell'Italia dal 1871 al 1915.* 2nd ed. rev. Florence, 1950.

Salvatorelli, Luigi. *La Triplice Alleanza, Storia diplomatica 1877–1912.* Milan: Instituto per gli studi di politica internazionale, 1939.

Sasse, Heinz Günther. *War das deutsche Eingreifen in die Bosnische Krise im März 1909 ein Ultimatum?* Stuttgart, W. Kohlhammer, 1936.

Sazonov, Sergei D. *Fateful Years 1909–1916: the Reminiscences of Serge Sazonov.* New York: Frederick A. Stokes Co., 1928.

Schanderl, Hans Dieter. *Die Albanienpolitik Österreich-Ungarns und Italiens, 1877–1908.* Albanische Forschungen, No. IX. Wiesbaden: Otto Harrassowitz, 1971.

Schargl, Ludwig. "Die Affäre des österreichisch-ungarischen Konsuls Prohaska im Ersten Balkankriege, 1912." *Berliner Monatshefte,* VII (April 1929), pp. 345–54.

Schiemann, Theodor. *Deutschland und die grosse Politik.* Berlin: G. Reimer, 1902–15.

Schinner, Walter. *Der österreichisch-italienische Gegensatz auf dem Balkan und an der Adria von seinen Anfängen bis zur Dreibundkrise, 1875–1896.* Stuttgart: W. Kohlhammer, 1936.

Schmidt, H. T. "Österreich-Ungarn und Bulgarien, 1908–1913." *Jahrbücher für Kultur und Geschichte der Slawen,* n.s., XI (1935), pp. 503–609.

Schmitt, Bernadotte. *The Annexation of Bosnia, 1908–1909.* Cambridge: Cambridge University Press, 1937.

―――――. *The Coming of the War: 1914.* 2 vols. New York: Charles Scribner's Sons, 1930.

―――――. *Triple Alliance and Triple Entente.* New York: H. Holt and Co., 1934.

Schröder, Werner. *England, Europa und der Orient: Untersuchung zur englischen Vorkriegspolitik in Vorgeschichte und Verlauf der Balkankrise 1912.* Stuttgart: W. Kohlhammer, 1938.

Schurman, Jacob Gould. *The Balkan Wars, 1912–1913.* Princeton: Princeton University Press, 1914.

Schwendemann, Karl. "Grundzüge der Balkanpolitik Österreich-Ungarns von 1908–1914." *Berliner Monatshefte,* VIII (March 1930), pp. 203–26.

Segre, Roberto. *Vienna e Belgrado, 1876–1914*. Milan: Edizioni Corbaccio, 1935.

Senkevich, I. G. "Mladoturetskaia revoliutsiia 1908 goda i albanskoe natsional'noe dvizhenie." *Sovetskoe vostokovedenie*, I (1958), pp. 31–41.

Seton-Watson, Robert William. "Austria-Hungary as a Balkan Power." *Contemporary Review*, CII (December 1912), pp. 801–6.

_____. *The Balkans, Italy and the Adriatic*. London: Nisbet & Co., 1912.

_____. *The Emancipation of South-Eastern Europe*. London, 1912.

_____. "Les relations diplomatiques Austro-Serbes." *Le Monde slave*, III (1926), pp. 273–88.

_____. *The Rise of Nationality in the Balkans*. London: Constable, 1917.

_____. "The Role of Bosnia in International Politics, 1875–1914." *Proceedings of the British Academy*, 1931.

_____. *Sarajevo: A Study in the Origins of the Great War*. London: Hutchinson & Co., 1926.

_____. *The Southern Slav Question and the Habsburg Monarchy*. London: Constable, 1911.

_____. "William II's Balkan Policy." *Slavonic Review*, VII (June 1928), pp. 1–29.

Sforza, Carlo. *Fifty Years of War and Diplomacy in the Balkans: Pashich and the Union of the Yugoslavs*. New York: Columbia University Press, 1940.

Shaw, Stanford, and Shaw, Ezel Kural. *History of the Ottoman Empire and Modern Turkey*. Vol. 2: *Reform, Revolution, and Republic: The Rise of Modern Turkey, 1808-1975*. Cambridge: Cambridge University Press, 1977.

Skendi, Stavro. *The Albanian National Awakening, 1878–1912*. Princeton: Princeton University Press, 1967.

Škerović, Nikola P. *Crna Gora na osvitku XX vijeka*. Srpska Akademija Nauka i Umetnosti, Posebna Izdanja, Vol. CCCLXIX. Belgrade, 1964.

_____. *Crna Gora za vrijeme Prvog svjetskog rata*. Titograd: Obod, 1963.

_____. "Iz odnosa Crne Gore i Rusije: Vojna konvencija iz 1910." *Istorijski Zapisi*, XII, Knj. XVI, Nos. 3–4 (1959), pp. 113–23.

Skoko, Savo. *Drugi Balkanski rat 1913. godine*. Belgrade: Vojnoistorijski Institut, 1968.

Šoć, Marko F. "Austrijska tajna arhiva 1914 i g. J. Jovanović." *Zapisi*, V, Knj. IX, No. 4 (1931), pp. 228–31.

_____. "Crna Gora u balkanskom ratu." *Balkan*, XXII (1938), No. 344.

Sosnosky, Theodor von. *Die Balkanpolitik Österreich-Ungarns seit 1866*. 2 vols. Stuttgart and Berlin: Deutsche Verlagsanstalt, 1913.

Spalajković, Miroslav. "O aneksiji Bosne i Hercegovine sa diplomatskog gledišta." *Politika,* 7 January 1938.

Stanojević, Gligor. "Prilozi za diplomatsku istoriju Crne Gore od Berlinskog kongres do kraja XIX veka." *Istorijski Časopis,* XI (1960), pp. 149–73.

Stanojević, St[anoje], ed. *Narodna Encikopedija Srpsko-Hrvatsko-Slovenačka.* 4 vols. Zagreb, Bibliografski zavod, 1925–29.

Stavrianos, L. S. *Balkan Federation: A History of the Movement Toward Balkan Unity in Modern Times.* Smith College Studies in History, XXVII, Nos. 1–4. Northampton, Mass., 1944.

―――. *The Balkans since 1453.* New York: Rinehart, 1958.

Steed, Henry Wickham. *The Habsburg Monarchy.* 4th ed. London: Constable, 1919.

Steiner, Zara. *The Foreign Office and Foreign Policy, 1898–1914.* Cambridge: Cambridge University Press, 1969.

Steinhart, Harold. "The Balkan Question after the Storm." *Fortnightly Review,* n.s., XCIV (September 1913), pp. 546–54.

Steinitz, Eduard Ritter von. "Berchtolds albanische Politik." *Berliner Monatshefte,* X (February 1932), pp. 152–67.

―――. "Berchtolds Politik gegen den Balkanbund." *Berliner Monatshefte,* X (April 1932), pp. 331–45.

―――. "Berchtolds Politik während des Ersten Balkankrieges." *Berliner Monatshefte,* IX (March 1931), pp. 229–48.

―――. "Berchtolds Politik während des Waffenstillstandes auf dem Balkan." *Berliner Monatshefte,* IX (August 1931), pp. 723–46.

―――. "Berchtolds Politik während des Zweiten Balkankrieges." *Berliner Monatshefte,* X (July 1932), pp. 660–74.

―――. "Berchtolds Politik zu Beginn der Balkankrise 1912." *Berliner Monatshefte,* IX (January 1931), pp. 45–57.

―――, ed. *Rings um Sasonow: Neue dokumentarische Darlegungen zum Ausbruch des Grossen Krieges durch Kronzeugen.* Berlin: Verlag für Kulturpolitik, 1928.

Stevenson, Francis Seymour. *A History of Montenegro.* London: Jarrold & Sons, 1912.

Stoianov, Anastas. *Die Handelspolitische Situation der Balkanstaaten gegenüber Österreich-Ungarn.* Vienna: M. Perles, 1914.

Stone, Norman. "Conrad von Hötzendorf, Chief of Staff in the Austro-Hungarian Army." *History Today,* XIII (July 1963), pp. 480–89.

Swire, Joseph. *Albania: the Rise of a Kingdom.* London: Williams and Norgate, 1929.

Szilassy, Gyula von. *Der Untergang der Donau-Monarchie: Diplomatische Erinnerungen.* Berlin: Verlag Neues Vaterland, E. Berger & Co., 1921.

Tadić, Dj. "Bura na Balkanu." *Večernje novosti,* 20 September-4 October, 1967.

Taylor, A. J. P. *The Habsburg Monarchy 1809–1918: A History of the Austrian Empire and Austria-Hungary.* Rev. ed. London: H. Hamilton, 1951.

──────. *The Struggle for Mastery in Europe, 1848–1918.* Oxford: Clarendon Press, 1954.

Terzić, Velimir. "Napad Austro-Ugarske na Srbiju i Crnu Goru 1914. godine." *Istorijski Zapisi,* XVII, Knj. XXI, No. 3 (1964), pp. 397–401.

Thaden, Edward C. "Montenegro: Russia's Troublesome Ally, 1910–1912." *Journal of Central European Affairs,* XVIII (July 1958), pp. 111–33.

──────. *Russia and the Balkan Alliance of 1912.* University Park, Pa.: Pennsylvania State University Press, 1965.

Tittoni, Tommaso. *Italy's Foreign and Colonial Policy.* London, 1914.

Tomanović, Lazar. *Iz moga ministrovanja.* Novi Sad, 1921.

──────. "Povodom memoara Barona Gisla." *Zapisi,* II, Knj. II, No. 6 (1928), pp. 346–60.

Tomić, Jaša. *Rat u Albaniji i pod Skadrom, 1912–1913. godine.* Novi Sad: S. Miletić, 1913.

Tomljenović, L. "Austrija i Crna Gora." *Nova Evropa,* XX, No. 5 (1925).

Tommasini, Francesco. *L'Italia alla vigilia della guerra: La politica estera di Tommaso Tittoni.* 2 vols. Bologna, Nicola Zanichelli, 1934.

Toshev, Andrei. *Balkankite voini.* 2 vols. Sofia, Fakel', 1929–1931.

Tošković, Janko. *Memoari: Bilješka iz ustavne vladavine Kralja Nikole i njenog tragičnog svršetka od 1905. do 1918 godine.* Cetinje, 1974.

Traylor, Idris Rhea, Jr. "The Double-Eagle and the Fox: The Dual Monarchy and Bulgaria, 1911–1913." Ph.D. Dissertation, Duke University, 1965.

Treadway, John D. "Temperate Coercion: Aehrenthal's Balkan Diplomacy at the Outbreak of the Turco-Italian War." *Essays in History,* XVIII (1974), pp. 5–32.

Trevelyan, George Macaulay. *Grey of Fallodon.* Boston: Houghton Mifflin, 1937.

Trevor, Roy [Chadburn, William Roy]. "An Englishman in Montenegro." *Fortnightly Review,* n.s., XCIII (January 1913), pp. 37–50.

──────. *Montenegro: A Land of Warriors.* London: Adam and Charles Black, 1913.

Tukim, Cemal. *Die politischen Beziehungen zwischen Österreich-Ungarn und Bulgarien von 1908 bis zum Bukarester Frieden.* Hamburg: H. Christian, 1936.

Uebersberger, Hans. *Österreich zwischen Russland und Serbien: Zur südslawischen Frage und der Entstehung des Ersten Weltkrieges.* Cologne and Graz: Verlag Hermann Böhlaus Nachf., 1958.

Valiani, Leo. "Italian-Austro-Hungarian Negotiations 1914–1915." *Journal of Contemporary History.* I (July 1966), pp. 113–36.

Vešović, R. *Pleme Vasojevići u vezi sa istorijom Crne Gore i plemenskim životom susjednih Brda.* Sarajevo, 1935.

Vinogradov, Kirill Borisovich. *Bosniiskii Krizis, 1908–1909.* Leningrad, 1964.

Vivian, Herbert. "Montenegro." *Fortnightly Review,* n.s., XCIV (November 1912), pp. 852–60.

V[lora] E. *Die Wahrheit über das Vorgehen der Jungtürken in Albanien.* Vienna and Leipzig, 1911.

Vojvodić, Mihailo. "Akcija Nemačke za zajedničku politiku sila Trojnog saveza u vreme prvog balkanskog rata." *Glasnik Cetinjskih Muzeja,* III (1970), pp. 171–76.

————. "Bugarsko-crnogorski pregovori i sporazum 1912. godine." Belgrade University *Zbornik filozofskog fakulteta,* VIII (1964), pp. 741–51.

————. "Crna Gora početkom XX veka." *Glasnik Cetinjskih Muzeja,* IV (1971), pp. 19–27.

————. "Jedan neuspeli pokušaj Austro-Ugarske da sklopi carinsku uniju sa Crnom Gorom." *Jugoslovenski narodi pred Prvi svetski rat,* edited by Vasa Čubrilović, pp. 117–25. Belgrade: Naučno Delo, 1967.

————. *Skadarska kriza 1913. godine.* Belgrade: Zavod za izdavanje udžbenika Socijalističke Republike Srbije, 1970.

————. "Velike sile i balkanska inicijativa Austro-Ugarske u avgustu 1912. godine." Belgrade University *Zbornik filozofskog fakulteta,* X-1 (1968), pp. 413–28.

Volpe, Gioacchino. *L'Italia nella Triplice Alleanza, 1882–1915.* 2nd ed. Milan: Instituto per gli studi di politica internazionale, 1941.

Vucinich, Wayne S. *Serbia between East and West: The Events of 1903–1908.* Stanford: Stanford University Press, 1954.

Vučković, Vojislav. "Diplomatska pozadina ujedinjenja Crne Gore i Srbije." *Revija za medjunarodno pravo,* No. 2 (1959).

Vujošević, Dragić. "Operacije crnogorskog Primorskog odreda u ratu 1912. godine." *Istorijski Zapisi,* VII, Knj. X, No. 2 (1954), pp. 458–73.

Vujović, Dimitrije-Dimo. *Crna Gora i Francuska 1860–1914.* Cetinje: Obod, 1971.

———. "Francuski dokumenti o crnogorsko-bugarskim odnosima, 1879–1912." *Istorijski Zapisi*, XVIII, Knj. XXII, No. 2 (1965), pp. 330–60.

———. "Molba donjih Vasojevića 1860. da se pripoje Crnoj Gori." *Istorijski Zapisi*, XVI, Knj. XX, No. 2 (1963), pp. 303–7.

———. *Ujedinjenje Crne Gore i Srbije*. Titograd, 1962.

Vukčević, Luka. "Diplomatska aktivnost Crne Gore na dobijanju Spiča za vrijeme aneksione krize (1908–1909)." *Istorijski Zapisi*, XXV, Knj. XXX, Nos. 3–4 (1972), pp. 463–73.

Vukosavljević, Sreten. *Organizacija dinarskih plemena*. Srpska Akademija Nauka, Posebna izdanja, Vol. CCLXX; Etnografski Institut, Vol. VII. Belgrade, 1957.

Vuković, Božidar-Božo. *Rat Crne Gore protiv Turske i Bugarske 1912–1913 i Rad Crne Gore na uniji i saradnji sa Srbijom*. Cetinje: Obod, 1971.

Vuković, Gavro. *Memoari Vojvode Gavra Vukovića: Iz diplomatskih odnosa Crne Gore sa Engleskom, Francuskom, Bugarskom, Austrijom i Turskom*. Cetinje, 1929.

Vuksan, Dušan. *Pregled štampe u Crnoj Gori, 1834–1934*. Cetinje: Obod, 1934.

———. "Što je prethodilo tituli knjaza Nikole 'kraljevsko visočanstvo.'" *Zapisi*, VIII, Knj. XIII, No. 1 (1935), pp. 14–16.

Vuletić, Savo P. "Crna Gora i Skadar." *Zapisi*, V, Knj. VIII, No. 2 (1931), pp. 90–101.

———. "Crna Gora za ujedinjenje." *Zapisi*, III, Knj. V, No. 5 (1929), pp. 285–90.

Wank, Solomon. "Aehrenthal and the Policy of Action." Ph.D. dissertation: Columbia University, 1961.

———. "Aehrenthal and the Sanjak of Novibazar Railway Project: A Reappraisal." *Slavonic and East European Review*, XLII (June 1964), pp. 353–69.

———. "Aehrenthal's Programme for the Constitutional Transformation of the Habsburg Monarchy: Three Secret *Mémoires*." *Slavonic and East European Review*, XLI (June 1963), pp. 513–36.

———. "The Appointment of Count Berchtold as Austro-Hungarian Foreign Minister." *Journal of Central European Affairs*, XXIII (July 1962), pp. 143–51.

———. "Some Reflections on Conrad von Hötzendorf and His Memoirs Based on Old and New Sources." *Austrian History Yearbook*, I (1965), pp. 74–88.

Ward, A. W. and Gooch, G. P. *The Cambridge History of British Foreign Policy*, Vol. III: 1866–1919. Cambridge: Cambridge University Press, 1923.

Warren, Whitney. *Montenegro: The Crime of the Peace Conference.* New York: Brentano's, 1922.

Wedel, Oswald Henry. *Austro-German Diplomatic Relations, 1908–1914.* Stanford: Stanford University Press, 1932.

Wegerer, Alfred von. *Der Ausbruch des Weltkrieges, 1914.* Hamburg: Hanseatische Verlagsanstalt, 1939.

⸺. "Graf Berchtolds Interview über den Kriegsausbruch." *Berliner Monatshefte,* XIII (June 1935), pp. 518–28.

Wendel, Hermann. *Die Habsburger und die südslawische Frage.* Belgrade: G. Kohn, 1924.

William II. *The Kaiser's Memoirs.* Translated by Thomas R. Ybarra. New York: Harper and Bros., 1922.

Wilson, Orme. "The Belgrade-Bar Railroad: An Essay in Economic and Political Geography." *Eastern Europe: Essays in Geographical Problems,* edited by George W. Hoffmann, pp. 365–89. New York: Praeger, 1971.

Wittich, A. von. "Die Rüstungen Österreich-Ungarns von 1866 bis 1914." *Berliner Monatshefte,* X (September 1932), pp. 861–79.

⸺. "Feldmarschall Conrad und die Aussenpolitik Österreich-Ungarns." *Berliner Monatshefte,* X (February 1932), pp. 116–36.

Woods, H. Charles. "The Situation in Albania." *Fortnightly Review,* n.s., XCVI (March 1914), pp. 460–72.

⸺. "The Armies of the Balkan League." *Fortnightly Review,* n.s., XCII (December 1912), pp. 1060–70.

Würthle, Friedrich. *Die Spur führt nach Belgrad: Die Hintergründe des Dramas von Sarajevo 1914.* Vienna, Munich, and Zurich: Verlag Fritz Molden, 1975.

Wyon, Reginald and Prance, Gerald. *The Land of the Black Mountain.* London: Methuen and Co., 1903.

Zambaur, Hortense von. *Die Belagerung von Scutari (10 Oktober 1912 bis 22 April 1913): Ein Tagebuch.* Berlin: G. Stilke, 1914.

Zhogov, Pavel V. *Diplomatiia Germanii i Avstro-Vengrii i pervaia balkanskaia voina 1912–1913 gg.* Moscow: Nauka, 1969.

Živanović, M. Ž. "Jugoslovensko pitanje: Austro-Ugarska uoči balkanskog rata 1912." *Zadarska Revija,* VII, No. 4 (1957), pp. 314–28.

Živanović, Živan. *Politička istorija Srbije u drugoj polovini devetnaestog veka.* 4 vols. Belgrade, 1923–25.

Živković, Dragoje. "Konflikt izmedju Crne Gore i Vatikana oko ustoličenja privremenog nasljednika barskog biskupa Milinovića." *Glasnik Cetinjskih Muzeja,* II (1969), pp. 183–97.

Živković, Miloš. *Pad Crne Gore*. Nikšić, 1935.

Živojinović, Dragan R. "San Djuliano i italijanske pretenzije na Jadranu na početku svetskog rata 1914–1915. godine." *Istorijski Časopis*, XX (1973), pp. 307–17.

———. "Ustanak Malisora 1911. godine i američka pomoć Crnoj Gori." *Istorijski Zapisi*, XX, Knj. XXIV, No. 2 (1967), pp. 323–38.

Index

A

Abdul Hamid II (Turkish sultan, 1876–1909), 69, 102, 167
Abdullah Pasha (Turkish general), 78
Ada Kaleh (island), 257 n.27, 276 n.115
Aegean Sea, islands in, 130, 131
Aehrenthal, Alois Lexa von (baron, after 1909 count; Austro-Hungarian foreign minister, 1906–1912), 163; and origins of annexation crisis, 19–21; policies after annexation, 22–24, 28–29; intervenes for release of Vukotić, 31; policy of regarding Spič, 33–35; and Conrad, 37–39, 94–95; decision to make peace with Turkey, 40–41; efforts to resolve annexation crisis, 43–47, 231 n.56; dealings with Tittoni, 47–49; and Kolašin conspiracy, 54; and visit of Austro-Hungarian fleet, 56, 59; and Austro-Montenegrin trade negotiations, 59; and Nicholas's jubilee celebration, 64; and Malissori revolt of 1910, 71, 73; and Malissori crisis of 1911, 79–80, 82–83; comments on Sazonov and Neratov, 84; and Turco-Italian War, 86–90, 247 n.24; on Ržanica, 92; strengthens Austrian forces along Montenegrin border, 94; and reform of Montenegrin judiciary, 247 n.26; and Nicholas's visit to St. Petersburg, 96; death of, 97–98; compared to Berchtold, 98
Albania, 99; and annexation crisis, 37–38, 68; Conrad's description of, 66; Roman Catholics in, 66–68, 120, 133, 140, 161 (*see also* Malissori); Muslims in, 69–70, 73, 133, 161, 251 n.83; Austro-Italian rivalry in, 66–67; and Turkey, 68–70 (*see also* Malissori uprisings); and First Balkan War, 108–13, 116; independence of, 126, 130; and border commissions for, 162, 204; and frontier disputes with Montenegro, 68, 162, 165, 167–68, 188–89, 204, 251 n.83; and frontier dispute with Serbia, 162; and Italy, 208, 275 n.114. *See also* Scutari Crisis
Albertini, Luigi (historian), 122, 157, 175, 177, 210, 230 n.44, 279 n.14
Alexander I (Russian tsar, 1801–1825), 12
Alexander II (Russian tsar, 1855–1881), 9, 13
Alexander III (Russian tsar, 1881–1894), 14
Alexander III (pope, 1159–1181), 249 n.44
Alexander Karadjordjević (prince, later prince regent of Serbia), 17, 62, 63, 191
Alexander I Obrenović (king of Serbia, 1889–1903), 17
Anastasija (Montenegrin princess, wife of Russian Grand Duke Nicholas Nikolaievich; known as "Stana"), 13, 217 n.14
Anglo-Montenegrin Trading Company, 16
Anna (Montenegrin princess, wife of Prince Francis Joseph of Battenberg), 217 n.14
Annexation Crisis, 13; origins of, 19–21; outbreak of, 22; Montenegro's initial response to, 22–27; and Montenegrin demands for

327

Annexation Crisis *(cont.)*
compensation, 22, 25, 28, 32–36; and proposed international conference, 24–25, 29–30; Montenegrin popular protests against, 25–27, 222 n.11; Austria-Hungary bans Montenegrin newspapers during, 27; Montenegro imposes economic sanctions during, 27, 222 n.22; Montenegrin activities in Hercegovina, 27; first efforts toward Austro-Montenegrin negotiations, 28–30; and Serbo-Montenegrin rapprochement, 30–32, 223 n.36; and Montenegro's efforts to acquire Spič, 32–36; and Albanians, 37–38, 231 n.56; Austrian and Montenegrin military preparations during, 36–39, 45, 47, 50; policy dispute between Aehrenthal and Conrad concerning, 37–39, 45, 47; Turkish response to, 40; Austro-Hungarian renunciation of occupation rights in Sandžak, 40; Austro-Turkish protocol during, 40–41, 42; Austria's relations with Serbia and Montenegro worsen, 41; Russia urges Serbian cooperation, 42–43; Serbia's demands for compensation, 42; Serbia's capitulation, 42–47; Montenegrin response to Russian démarche, 44; German plan to approve annexation, 45–46; Serbian pledges to Austria, 46–47; Montenegro's capitulation, 47–50; Austrians and Muslims of Sandžak, 222 n.19; Italy and Russia restrict arms shipments to Montenegro during, 226 n.67. *See also* names of countries involved in the crisis
Arseniev, Sergei Vasilievich (Russian minister at Cetinje, 1910–1912), 73, 79, 81, 82, 84
Article 7. *See* Triple Alliance
Article 25. *See* Berlin, Treaty of
Article 29. *See* Berlin, Treaty of
Askew, William C. (historian), 261 n.68
Aspern (Austrian cruiser), 264 n.8
Asquith, Herbert Henry (British prime minister, 1908–1916), 139, 140
Augusta Charlotte (of Mecklenburg-Strelitz, wife of Crown Prince Danilo), 171, 217 n.14
Austria-Hungary: and South Slavs, 11, 202; mobilization plans of, 38, 45, 109, 113–14, 292 n.54; policy of keeping Montenegro and Serbia apart, 94; and Aehrenthal's successor as foreign minister, 97–98; railroad policies of, 122, 123–24; Post and Telegraph Administration of, 193;
—and Albania: during annexation crisis, 37–38; "religious protectorate" and sphere of influence in, 67–68; and Serb expansionism, 114, 118–19, 121–22, 162; and separate Albanian entity, 118–19, 208; and large Albanian state, 133; offers of financial and military aid, 189, 197; on eve of world war, 195–96;
—and Bulgaria: 100, 160;
—and Germany: relations in the Balkans, 16, 209; and Malissori uprisings, 242 n.85; and Turco-Italian War, 92, 98; and Austrian plan for Albania, 118; and Berchtold's 1913 ultimatum to Serbia, 162; and question of Serbo-Montenegrin union, 177–81; and Scutari Crisis, 144, 157, 277 n.125; and hostility between Giesl and Eckardt, 273–74 nn.100 and 101;
—and Italy: 208–9; rivalry in Montenegro, 34; during annexation crisis, 47–49, 227 n.3, 232 n.53; in Albania, 66–67, 71, 118, 208, 237 n.5, 260 n.52; and Turco-Italian War, 87–88, 94–95; and Triple Alliance, 237 n.9; and First

Austria-Hungary *(cont.)*
Balkan War, 118, 119, 126, 131; and Scutari-Lovćen exchange, 122, 126, 131–32; possible joint action of, during Scutari Crisis, 148–50, 153, 157–58, 263 n.80, 264 n.10, 271 n.68, 275 n.107; and question of Serbo-Montenegrin union, 163, 177–81, 283 n.64; after assassination of Francis Ferdinand, 188, 196;

—and Montenegro: relations between, to 1908, 8–12, 14, 218–19 n.22; border conflicts between, 9, 11, 59, 64, 85, 114, 168–69, 192–94, 204, 232 n.64; and possible customs union, 34, 91, 114, 122, 203; and coinage convention, 85, 204; and trade treaty, 59, 97, 123, 204; and annexation crisis, 22, 24–50; and Kolašin conspiracy, 53–55; and 1910 détente, 55–59; and Danilo's overtures of friendship, 59–61; and proclamation of Montenegrin kingdom, 63–64, 204–5; and visit of Austrian fleet, 56, 59; and Malissori uprisings, 72–73, 76, 79–80, 83–84; relations after 1911 uprising, 84–86; and Turco-Italian War, 90–92, 99; and Austrian loan, 91, 93, 96; and proposed reform of Montenegrin institutions, 97, 247 n.26; and Nicholas's trip to Vienna, 100–101, 251 n.77; and outbreak of First Balkan War, 113–16; efforts to restrict Montenegrin military operations, 119–20; and Austrian proposals for better relations during the First Balkan War, 120, 122–26, 128–29; and Montenegrin proposals regarding Albania and Scutari, 127–29; and Mijušković at the London conference, 131–32; and Hungarian commercial show, 251 n.80; and question of Serbo-Montenegrin union, 112, 114, 163; and improved relations after Balkan wars, 164–65; and Giesl's departure, 166–67; and Sjenokos incident, 168–69; and Russo-Montenegrin relations, 1913–1914, 169–73; efforts at accommodation after Sarajevo, 186, 189–192, 194–95, 204; military buildup along frontier, 192–93, 197–98; declaration of war, 198–99; summary of relations between, 201–7;

—and Rumania: 100;

—and Russia: relations before 1908, 11–14; and annexation crisis, 20, 31–32, 41–47; and Malissori uprisings, 83–84; and Russo-Montenegrin rapprochement, 169–73; and outbreak of First World War, 197–99;

—and Serbia: and Pig War, 18; and annexation crisis, 31–32, 41–47; and Turco-Italian War, 93; and First Balkan War, 114, 118, 119; and Prochaska affair, 121; and Austrian attempt to reach accommodation with Belgrade, 121–22; 1913 ultimatum to Serbia, 162; and question of Serbo-Montenegrin union, 163; and assassination of Francis Ferdinand, 182–83; 1914 ultimatum to Serbia, 189–92; outbreak of war, 191, 194;

—and Turkey: early relations, 8–9; and Young Turk revolution, 19–20; and annexation crisis, 26, 40–41; and Malissori uprisings, 79–80, 242 n.85; and Turco-Italian War, 88–89, 92–93; and Turkish prisoners in First Balkan War, 116; and Turco-Montenegrin boundary disputes, 248 n.35, 251 n.83

—*See also* Annexation crisis, Malissori uprisings, Scutari Crisis, and Cetinje Bomb Affair

Avarna di Gualtieri, Giuseppe (duke; Italian ambassador at Vienna,

Avarna di Gualtieri *(cont.)*
1904–1915), 60, 100, 153, 154, 181
Aynard, Joseph Raymond (French minister at Cetinje, 1912–1913), 261 n.63

B

Baernreither, Josef Maria (Austrian parliamentarian), 119
Balkan Alliance, origins of, 105–8, 203
Balkan wars (1912–1913), 7;
—First Balkan War, 203; initial Montenegrin military operations, 111–13; Austria and Montenegro at outset of, 113–16; Russian attitudes in early stages of, 116–17; Austro-Hungarian relief efforts in Montenegro, 116; Serbian claim for Adriatic port, 118; Austrian attempts to restrict military activities along Albanian coast, 119; Nicholas rejects Austrian and Italian démarches, 120; and question of Albania, 118–21; Austro-Hungarian military preparations, 119, 121, 129; Russian military activity during, 121, 129; Great-Power decision to hold conference concerning, 121; Austrian attempt to reach accommodation with Serbia during, 121–22; Serbian occupation of Adriatic coast, 121; Prochaska affair, 121; Austro-Hungarian overtures to Montenegro, 122–26; initial armistice concluded, 129; peace conferences, 129, 130; renewal of conflict, 130; Treaty of London ending, 159; atrocities during, 256–57 n.19. *See also* Conference of Ambassadors; Scutari Crisis
—Second Balkan War, 159–61
Bar (town): as commercial center, 2, 11, 16, 244 n.120, 234 n.29; strike in, 4; first Montenegrin radio-telegraph station in, 15; and annexation crisis, 10, 26, 33, 36, 45, 47, 49; naval demonstration at, 135–36, 156; threatened occupation of, 139; and question of Serbo-Montenegrin union, 163; on eve of world war, 197; and bishopric of, 249 n.44
Barclay, Colville Adrian de Rune (British chargé d'affaires at Belgrade, 1911–1913), 63, 75
Bastriku (village), 189
Beaumont, Henry H. D. (British legation secretary at Athens, 1910–1913; occasional chargé d'affaires at Cetinje), 53, 54, 61, 233 n.4
Bedri Pasha (vali of Scutari), 240 n.51
Belgrade (city), 17; Vukotić visits, 30–32, 37; demonstrations in during jubilee, 63. *See also* Serbia
Belgrade, Treaty of (1739), 12
Berane (town), 90, 115, 239 n.40, 285 n.79; protests in during annexation crisis, 26, 27; frontier incident, 103–4, 107
Berchtold von and zu Ungarschitz, Leopold (count; Austro-Hungarian ambassador at St. Petersburg, 1906–1911; foreign minister, 1912–1915): appointed foreign minister, 98; compared to Aehrenthal, 98; and Nicholas's trip to Vienna, 100–101, 106; and First Balkan War, 108–20; wartime policies toward Balkans and Albania, 113–14, 118, 119, 133, 203, 260 n.52; addresses Austrian parliamentary delegation, 119; seeks accommodation with Serbia, 121–22; and Lovćen-Scutari exchange proposal, 122–26, 131–32; and Scutari Crisis, 135–57, 278 n.125; and Italy, 148–50, 153, 283 n.64; and Treaty of

Berchtold *(cont.)*
Bucharest, 160; ultimatum to Serbia regarding withdrawal from Albania, 162; policy toward Serbo-Montenegrin union, 163, 179, 204; and Obnorsky's plan, 171; Opatija conference, 179–81; and Metaljka incident, 184; and demonstrations in Cetinje, 185–86; and Mehmedbašić's escape, 185; overtures to Nicholas, 187, 190, 195–96, 198; offers aid to Albanians, 189, 197; issues ultimatum to Serbia, 189–90, 204; justifies declaration of war on Serbia, 191–92; and border incidents, 192, 194; final attempt to win Montenegrin neutrality, 195–96, 198; orders full mobilization, 197; German comment on policy of, 286 n.97
Berlin, Congress of (1878), 7, 10, 11, 13, 20, 33, 68, 249 n.44. *See also* Berlin, Treaty of
Berlin, Treaty of (1878), 10, 13, 218 n.19; Article 25, 46, 49; Article 29, 10, 24, 25, 28, 30, 33, 47, 48, 54
Berliner Tageblatt (German newspaper), 228 n.11
Berlin-to-Baghdad railway, 16
Bethmann Hollweg, Theobald von (German chancellor, 1909–1917), 178, 180, 209–10, 287 n.103
Bijela Gora (town), 192
Bijelo Polje (town), 27, 112, 115, 161, 285 n.79
Bileća (town), 192, 193
Bilinski, Leon von (Austro-Hungarian finance minister, 1912–1915), 273 n.91
Birzhevye vedomosti (Russian newspaper), 155
Bitola (town), 108, 160
Black Hand (Serb nationalist group), 90, 182, 189
Boden-Credit-Anstalt (Austrian bank), 91

Bojana River, 11, 15, 25, 132, 165, 188
Boletin, Isa (Albanian leader), 73, 108, 291 n.41
Boris (crown prince of Bulgaria), 96
Bošković, Blažo (Montenegrin general), 110, 122
Bosnia-Hercegovina, 8, 182; Austro-Hungarian administration of, 20. *See also* Annexation Crisis
Božović, Mašan (Montenegrin army officer), 115
Brda (region), 7
Bregalnica, battle of, 160
Breslau (German cruiser), 135
"Brotherhood of Prince Ivan Crnojević," 227 n.80
Brown Mobilization, 38
Buchanan, Sir George W. (British ambassador at St. Petersburg, 1910–1918), 148
Bucharest, Treaty of (1913), 160–62
Buchlau Bargain, 20, 46
Budva (town), 10
Bulgaria, 100, 172, 249 n.52; possible Montenegrin revolutionaries in, 96; and Balkan Alliance, 104, 106–7, 252 n.107; and First Balkan War, 118, 130; and Second Balkan War, 159–60
Bülow, Bernhard von (prince; German chancellor, 1900–1909), 46
Burián von Rajecz, Stephan von (baron; Austro-Hungarian finance minister, 1903–1912; minister at court, 1913–1915), 98
Burney, Sir Cecil (British admiral), 136, 155, 156, 274 n.101

C

Čajniče, 168
Čakor, height of, 248 n.35
Cambon, Paul (French ambassador at London, 1898–1920), 145

Index

Canada: Montenegrin emigré organization in, 227 n.80
Cap d'Antibes, 211
Carol I (king of Rumania, 1881–1914), 100, 290 n.36
Cartwright, Sir Fairfax (British ambassador in Vienna, 1908–1913), 75, 76, 80, 143, 152
Catherine II (Russian empress, 1762–1796; known as "the Great"), 12
Cetinje (capital of Montenegro), 1, 2, 4, 6, 11, 12, 17, 132, 201; protests in during annexation crisis, 25, 26, 222 n.11; jubilee celebration in, 63; electric lighting in, 235 n.48; Austro-Hungarian naval delegation visits, 56; and First Balkan War, 111, 123; Russian cadet school in, 111; pro-Russian demonstrations in, 117; Hungarian commercial show in, 251 n.80; celebrations in, after fall of Scutari, 142, 144; mood in, after surrender of Scutari, 150; anti-Austrian demonstrations in wake of Francis Ferdinand's assassination, 185; end as capital, 211
Cetinje Bomb Affair (1907), 19, 29, 30, 51, 52, 53, 153, 154, 210, 224 n.39, 233 n.4, 235 n.48
Cetinjski Vjesnik (Montenegrin newspaper), 27, 53, 99; hostile response to *Neue Freie Presse* article, 101; and Balkan Alliance, 106; and First Balkan War, 120
Chataldja (Turkish defensive line), 118, 130
Colombani, Franz (Austro-Hungarian legation secretary at Cetinje, 1912–1914), 193, 194
Committee of Union and Progress, 69. *See also* Young Turks
Compagnia di Antivari, 15, 16
Concert of Europe, 9, 46, 105, 130. *See also* names of major European powers
Conference of Ambassadors (London), 159, 162, 166, 203, 208, 209–10; convened, 130; difficulties agreeing to Albanian frontiers, 133; proposed naval demonstration, 133; and Scutari Crisis, 158. *See also* Scutari Crisis
Conrad von Hötzendorf, Franz (baron; chief of the Austro-Hungarian general staff, 1906–1911, 1912–1917; army inspector, 1911–1912), 72, 109, 205, 241 n.72, 268 n.49; and annexation crisis, 31, 37–39, 40, 41, 42, 45, 47, 50, 231 n.53; and disputes with Aehrenthal, 37–39, 82–83; and origins of First World War, 54; description of Albania, 66–67; claims Austria's right of occupation in Sandžak, 83; and Turco-Italian War, 89, 94–95; temporarily dismissed, 94; reappointed chief of staff, 129; and Scutari Crisis, 146, 157, 262 n.80, 275 n.107; and Montenegrin-Albanian border, 167–68; after death of Francis Ferdinand, 185, 187, 189, 190; on Russo-Montenegrin détente, 284 n.68; and Austria's interest in Lovćen, 287 n.98
Constantinople, 118, 129
Corriere della Sera (Italian newspaper), 131, 187
Crackanthorpe, Dayrell E. M. (British legation secretary at Belgrade, 1912–1915), 181
Crampton, R. J. (historian), 271 n. 67
Crete, 130
Crimean War, 9
Crmnica valley, 4
Crna Ruka. *See* Black Hand
Crnogorac (Montenegrin newspaper), 13
Crnojević, Ivan (ruler of Zeta, 1465–1490), 6
Crnojević dynasty, 15
Čubrović, Pavle (Bosnian), 26–27
Czernin von und zu Chudenitz, Ot-

Czernin *(cont.)*
tokar (count; Austro-Hungarian minister at Bucharest, 1913–1916), 290 n.36

D

Dalmatia, 10, 38, 39, 192
Danev, Stoian (president of Bulgarian sŭbranie, 1911–1913; delegate to peace conference, 1912–1913; premier and foreign minister, 1913), 107
Danilo (Montenegrin crown prince), 17, 102, 164, 171, 176, 183, 184, 217 n.14, 244 n.120, 274 n.101; and jubilee, 57–59, 60; and 1910 Malissori uprising, 72; expresses pro-Austrian sentiments, 86; and annexation crisis, 222 n.8; visits Sofia, 96; departs for Italy, 108; named general in Russian army, 235 n.51; on Montenegrin intentions in 1911 Malissori crisis, 75; and First Balkan War, 112, 124, 127; and Scutari Crisis, 139, 142, 144
Danilo I (Montenegrin prince-bishop, 1696–1737), 6, 7
Danilo II (Montenegrin prince-bishop, 1851; reigning prince, 1852–1860), 6, 9
Danilov, Yuri (Russian general), 173
Danubian principalities, 9
Danzers Armee-Zeitung (Austrian newspaper), 41
Darby, H. C. (historian), 1
De Salis, John Francis Charles. *See* Salis, John Francis Charles de
Dečić (small mountain), 77
Delaroche-Vernet, P. H. (French minister at Cetinje, 1913–1921, including court in exile), 15, 165, 185, 186, 208, 289 n.24
Diachenko, Nikolai (Russian chargé d'affaires at Cetinje, 1910), 54–55

Dibër Mountains, 74
Dibra (town), 133, 278 n.126
Djakovica (town), 161, 275 n.113, 286 n.97
Djavid Pasha (Turkish general), 69, 103
Djevojački Institut (girls' school), 14, 111, 133, 164
Djinović, Petar (Montenegrin army officer), 52
Dnevne Novosti (Montenegrin newspaper), 190
Dnevni List (Serbian newspaper), 53
Dobrečić, Nikola (Roman Catholic archbishop of Bar), 249 n.44
Dobrudja, 160
Doda, Prenk Bib (Albanian member of Young Turk central committee), 109
Dožić, Gavrilo (metropolitan of Prizren), 93–94
Draga (queen of Serbia, wife of Alexander I), 17
Drin River, 121, 136, 188
Dubrovnik (town), 8, 9, 29, 39, 198
Dumba, Konstantin Theodor (Austro-Hungarian minister at Belgrade, 1903–1905), 233 n.18
Durham, Mary Edith (English writer and adventurer): on Russo-Montenegrin ties, 12; predicts war over Albania, 66; on Austria and Catholic Albanians, 67, 68; and 1911 Malissori uprising, 76, 81, 82; on the Balkan situation early in 1912, 98–99; on Balkan-Montenegrin entente, 106; on Hartwig, 105; on eve of First Balkan War, 110–11; on Young Turks, 238 n.25; on Montenegrin hospital preparations, 112; on Serbian occupation of Prizren, 113; on Nicephor, 249 n.44; on readiness of Montenegrin army for war, 254 n.118; on Russia's role in Montenegrin war preparation, 254 n.129; on outbreak of hostilities in 1912, 254 n.134

334 *Index*

Durrës (town), 121, 130, 136, 152
Dušan, Stephen. *See* Stephen Dušan
Dvrsnik, Mount, 11, 234 n. 31

E

Eastern Crisis (1875–1878), 9, 13
Eckardt, Heinrich von (German minister at Cetinje, 1911–1914), 167, 174, 178, 258 n.40; and Turco-Italian War, 90; and Scutari Crisis, 141, 144, 150, 151, 152; and Giesl, 272 n.75, 273–74 n.100, 274 n.101
Edirne (town), 130
Egger von Möllwald, Lothar (ritter; Austro-Hungarian legation secretary at Cetinje, 1914), 183, 288 n.4
Emirghian (suburb of Constantinople), 102
Empress of the Balkans (play by Nicholas I), 63
Essad Pasha Toptani (Albanian-born Turkish commander at Scutari), 141–42, 265 n. 17

F

Fay, Sidney Bradshaw (historian), 229 n.44
Ferdinand (tsar of Bulgaria, 1908–1918), 63, 100, 106, 107, 234 n.29, 159, 160
Fifteenth Army Corps (Austro-Hungarian), 38
Figaro, Le (French newspaper), 180
First World War: Austria and Montenegro in, 212
Fischer, Fritz (historian), 157, 178, 210
Fiume and Zara (Rijeka and Zadar) resolutions, 221 n.38
Flotow, Hans von (German ambassador at Rome, 1913–1915), 149, 180, 181, 287 n.99, 286 n.98

Forgách von Ghymes und Gács, Johann (count; Austro-Hungarian minister at Belgrade, 1907–1911; later section chief in foreign ministry), 32, 166, 293 n.82
France: relations with Montenegro before 1908, 9, 16; and annexation crisis, 25, 222 n.11, 228 n.14; and visit of fleet to Montenegro, 54–55; and proclamation of Montenegrin kingdom, 61, 63; and Malissori uprisings, 72; and First Balkan War, 119; and Scutari Crisis, 136, 138–40, 145, 264 n.10, 267 n.26; relations with Montenegro after Scutari, 165–66, 173, 208
Francis Ferdinand (Austro-Hungarian archduke and heir presumptive), 38, 57–58, 59, 60, 98, 176, 180–81, 182–83, 232 n.70, 278 n.126
Francis Joseph (emperor of Austria and king of Hungary, 1848–1916): autograph letter of, to Nicholas, 63–64; and Nicholas's trip to Vienna, 100–101, 106; names Nicholas commandant of an Austrian infantry regiment, 100; and First Balkan War, 121; and Scutari Crisis, 146, 151; mentioned, 7, 11, 22, 29, 49, 57, 96, 98, 129, 179, 180, 204, 205, 247 n.26, 287 n.103
Francis Joseph (prince of Battenberg, husband of Princess Anna), 217 n.14
Fremdenblatt (Austrian newspaper), 79–80, 119, 187
Fritsch, Mlle. (Swiss teacher), 285 n.85

G

Gäa (Austro-Hungarian warship), 100
Garibaldi Association, 239 n.47

Garibaldi, Ricciotti (Italian general), 239 n.47
Gavrilović, Milan (Serbian minister at Cetinje, 1910–1914), 288 n.4
Geiss, Imanuel (historian), 178
Gellinek, Otto (major; Austro-Hungarian military attaché at Belgrade, 1910–1914), 89, 176
George V (king of Great Britain, 1910–1936), 155, 244 n.120
George Karadjordjević (until 1909 Serbian crown prince), 223 n.36, 231 n.52
Gerče memorandum, 78
Germany: and annexation crisis, 45–46; and proclamation of Montenegrin kingdom, 63; and Malissori uprisings, 80; and First Balkan War, 119–20; and Scutari Crisis, 135, 144, 145, 150, 151, 152, 157–58, 264 n.10; and Vermosh incident, 167; and Italy, 92, 98, 177–81, 209; and Russia, 45–46, 198; and Turkey, 71, 80. *See also* Austria *and* Germany
Geshov, Ivan E. (Bulgarian premier and foreign minister, 1911–1913), 104, 106, 107
Giers, Alexander Alexandrovich (Russian minister at Cetinje, 1912–1916): and First Balkan War, 111, 114, 116–17, 132; and Scutari Crisis, 144; and relations with Montenegro, 1913–1914, 164, 165, 170, 171, 192, 207–8, 284 n.69, 294 n.88
Giers, Nikolai Karlovich (Russian foreign minister, 1882–1895), 59
Giers, Nikolai Nikolaievich (Russian ambassador at Vienna, 1910–1913), 110
Giesl von Gieslingen, Wladimir (baron, Austro-Hungarian minister at Cetinje, 1909–1913, minister at Belgrade, 1913–1914), 93, 103, 165, 250 n.63, 258 n.40, 294 n.89; and jubilee preparations, 55–61; and 1910 border incident, 64; and Malissori uprisings, 72; criticized by Izvolsky, 84; and Turco-Italian War, 90–91, 247 n.24; suspicions concerning Nicholas's trip to St. Petersburg, 95–96; and Nicholas's trip to Vienna, 100, 101, 106; and Berane incident, 104; visits Lovćen, 104–5; and First Balkan War, 108–11, 115–16, 117, 119, 254 n.118, 261 n.66; and Lovćen-Scutari exchange proposal, 124–26, 131; and Montenegrin proposals regarding Albania and Scutari, 127–29; and Scutari Crisis, 138–39, 141, 142, 144, 145, 150–52; comments on Nicholas, 129; appointment as minister at Belgrade, 166; and Obnorsky, 170, 171; and Serbo-Montenegrin union, 175–76; and ultimatum to Serbia, 189–91; and Eckardt, 272 n.75, 273–74 n.100, 274 n.101; character of, 205–6
Giolitti, Giovanni (Italian prime minister, 1906–1909, 1911–1914), 246 n.3
Gladstone, William Ewart (British prime minister), 2
Glas Crnogorca (Montenegrin newspaper), 13, 27, 189
Goeben (German warship), 263 n.3
Goluchowski von Goluchowo, Agenor (count; Austro-Hungarian foreign minister, 1895–1906), 163
Gooch, George Peabody (historian), 88
Gorski vjenac (Montenegrin epic poem), 7
Govedje Brod, 102
Grahovo (town), 97; fortifications outside of, 36
Grahovo, battle of (1858), 7
Grahovo-Krivošije, district of, 11, 59, 247 n.26
Great Britain: British investments in Montenegro, 16; and annexation crisis, 25, 35, 42, 47, 48; and

Great Britain *(cont.)*
proclamation of Montenegrin kingdom, 61, 63; and Malissori uprisings, 72, 80; and Scutari Crisis, 135, 136, 139, 144–48, 151, 152; and Vermosh incident, 167; and Montenegrin offer of port, 244 n.120; and Turkey, 103, 104.

Great Powers. *See* individual countries

Great Serbian Idea, 76. *See also* Serbia

Greece: and Balkan alliance, 107; and démarche to Powers, 109; and First Balkan War, 130; and Scutari Crisis, 136, 138; and Second Balkan War, 159–60

Gregović, Dušan (Montenegrin chargé d'affaires at Constantinople, 1907–1910; foreign minister, 1911–1912; afterwards court marshal), 85, 86, 90, 165; and annexation crisis, 227 n.9, 231 n.63; and Turco-Italian War, 91; and Turco-Montenegrin relations, 93; on Nicholas's visit to St. Petersburg, 97; and Nicholas's trip to Vienna, 251 n.77; and Balkan alliance, 106–7; and Scutari Crisis, 145, 151, 156

Grey, Sir Edward (British secretary of state for foreign affairs, 1905–1916): and annexation crisis, 25, 35, 42, 47, 48, 208, 228 n.18, 230 n.45, 231 n.54, 281 n.32; and 1911 Malissori uprising, 80; and Turco-Montenegrin frontier incident at Berane, 103; and First Balkan War, 126; and Conference of Ambassadors, 130, 132–33; and Scutari Crisis, 132–33, 136, 145–47, 150–52, 155, 158, 275 n.107; on Treaty of Bucharest, 160

Gruda (village), 124

Grudi (Malissori tribe), 71, 167–68, 244 n.110. *See also* Malissori uprisings

Guchkov, Alexander (Russian parliamentarian), 46

Günther, Alexander von (ritter, Austro-Hungarian court official), 273 n.91

Gusinje (town), 68, 77, 112, 167

H

Halla, Karl (Austro-Hungarian consul general at Scutari, 1913–1915), 291 n.41

Hammer and Thomson (British company), 16

Hartwig, Nikolai Henrikovich (Russian minister at Teheran, 1906–1909; at Belgrade, 1909–1914), 105, 172, 175, 177–78, 283 n.64, 294 n.89

Heilbronner, Hans (historian), 280 n.21

Helmreich, Ernst C. (historian), 107, 253 n.112, 256 n.17

Hercegovina, 4, 9, 10, 21, 22, 24; citizens of, working in Montenegro, 4, 26; protests in during annexation crisis, 27 *See also* Annexation Crisis; Bosnia-Hercegovina

Heron (Russian ship), 226 n.67

Hohenberg, Duchess of. *See* Sophie

Hohenzollern dynasty, 175

Hoti (Malissori tribe), 71, 167–68, 244 n.110. *See also* Malissori uprisings

Hoyos, Alexander (count; Austro-Hungarian legation secretary at London, 1908–1911; at foreign ministry, 1911–1914), 118, 181, 292 nn.54 and 58

Hubka, Gustav von (captain, later major; Austro-Hungarian military attaché at Cetinje, 1912–1914): and Scutari Crisis, 137, 141, 150, 151, 184, 185, 189, 190, 197, 199, 274 n.101; and Montenegrin activity regarding Albania, 167; and rumors of coup at-

Hubka *(cont.)*
tempt, 176; and eleventh-hour plan for accommodation with Montenegro, 195
Hungary, 183; revolution of 1848 in, 9; Slavs in, 20. *See also* Austria-Hungary

I

Iaşi, Treaty of (1792), 12
Ibar (town), 115
Illyria, 9
Imperiali di Francavilla, Guglielmo (marquis; Italian ambassador at Constantinople, 1904–1910; at London, 1910–1920), 155, 271 n.68
Ioánnina (town and vilayet), 108, 130, 268 n.46
Ionian Sea, 114
Ismail Kemal Bey Vlora (Turkish parliamentarian; Albanian leader; president of provisional Albanian government, 1912–1914), 78, 126
Ištip (town), 286 n.97
Italia irredenta, 181
Italy: Chamber of Deputies of, 34, 237 n.5; investments in Montenegro, 15–16, 232 n.70; and annexation crisis, 24, 34, 35, 43, 44, 47; and proclamation of Montenegrin kingdom, 60–61, 63; and Malissori uprisings, 72; and First Balkan War, 114–15, 120; and Scutari Crisis, 135, 138, 139, 148–50, 153, 267 n.26; and advance on international loan for Montenegro, 166, 173; and Vermosh incident, 167; and Russia, 167. *See also* Turco-Italian War and names of other countries
Ivović, Djuro (Montenegrin), 26
Izvolsky, Alexander Petrovich (Russian foreign minister, 1906–1910; ambassador at Paris, 1910–1917), 108, 268 n.49; general aims of, 20; and annexation crisis, 20, 24, 43, 46, 49, 228 n.14, 229–30 n.44, 230 n.45; berated by Nicholas, 59; compared to Sazonov and Neratov, 84; criticizes Montenegro's policies, 84; visited by Mijušković, 25, 224 n.47, 225 n.64; and first Balkan War, 117; and financial practices of Montenegrin royal family, 253 n.112

J

Jagow, Gottlieb von (German ambassador at Rome, 1909–1912; secretary of state for foreign affairs, 1913–1916), 180, 209, 277–78 n.127, 287 n.103, 292 n.54
Jelena (queen of Italy, wife of Victor Emmanuel III), 15, 217 n.14, 237 n.6
Jergović, Filip (Montenegrin financial official), 234 n.30
Jezerski Vrh (district in northeastern Montenegro), 92
Joseph II (Austrian emperor, 1780–1790), 12
Jovanović, Jovan (historian), 30, 232 n.2, 244 n.120
Jovanović, Miloje (Montenegrin official), 234 n.30
Jovanović-Bjeloš, Ilija, 223 n.38

K

Kanner, Heinrich (Austrian editor), 98
Karadjordjević dynasty, 17, 128; mausoleum at Topola, 99. *See also* Serbia, Peter I Karadjordjević, Alexander Karadjordjević
Kastrati (Malissori tribe), 71, 168, 244 n.110. *See also* Malissori uprisings
Kavalla (town), 160

Kennedy, Sir Robert John (British representative at Cetinje, 1893–1905), 218 n.22
Kiamil Pasha (Turkish grand vizier, 1908–1909), 40
Kiderlen-Waechter, Alfred von (German secretary of state for foreign affairs, 1910–1912), 80, 104, 118, 229–30 nn.44 and 45
Kirk Kilisse, battle of, 118
Klementi (Albanian tribe), 244 n.110, 282 n.39
Klubaši (Montenegrin political group), 18, 19, 52, 53, 128, 174, 235 n.48
Kočana (town), 286 n.97
Kolašin (town), 237 n.12
Kolašin conspiracy, 52–55, 62, 210, 235 n.48
Köller, Walter (Austro-Hungarian cadet officer), 236 n.59
Koloman, Gustav (official of Hungarian trade ministry), 234 n.30
Kolushev, N. (Bulgarian minister at Cetinje, 1910–1913), 104, 107, 260 n.58
Kosovo, battle of (1389), 6, 95, 99, 108, 161, 180, 182, 251 n.8, 291 n.41
Kosovo (vilayet): and 1910 Malissori revolt, 69, 70, 71; and 1911 Malissori uprising, 77; and First Balkan War, 112
Kotor (town), 9, 10, 11, 12, 34, 36, 39, 193, 194, 197, 198; and First Balkan War, 123, 125, 141
Kotor, Bay of, 192
Kovačević, Stojan (Hercegovinian), 26
Kral, August von (ritter; Austro-Hungarian consul general at Scutari, 1905–1909; at Salonica, 1911–1913; later member of international control commission for Albania), 189, 231 n.56
Kramář, Karel (Czech political leader), 119

Krobatin, Alexander von (general; Austro-Hungarian war minister, 1912–1917), 273 n.91, 277 n.125
Krstac (ridge), 11, 125, 126
Kruff, Baron de (Dutch journalist), 106
Krusi, battle of (1796), 7
Ksenija (Montenegrin princess), 26, 115, 217 n.14
Kuchuk Kainardji, Treaty of (1774), 12
Kuhn von Kuhnenfeld, Otto von (baron; Austro-Hungarian minister at Cetinje, 1903–1909), 206; and annexation crisis, 22, 24, 28–29, 30, 33–35, 43–44, 49–50, 222 n.11
Kumanovo, battle of, 118

L

Laurin and Klement (Bohemian firm), 10–11
League of the Three Emperors, 13
Lee, Dwight (historian), 230 n.44
Lezhë (town), 120–21, 241 n.69, 293 n.82
Libre Parole (French newspaper), 253 n.112
Ličeni Hotit (arm of Lake Scutari), 276 n.115
Lichnowsky, Karl Max (prince; German ambassador at London, 1912–1914), 145, 277 n.125
Lim River, 167
Lloyd line, 11
London, Treaty of (1913), 159
Loti, Pierre (French writer), 2
Lovćen, Mount, 6, 11, 34, 36, 50, 57, 63, 104, 163, 176, 179, 181, 187, 192, 197, 203, 204, 209; and Austrian desire for border change, 114; and proposed exchange of for Scutari, 122–26, 131, 144; Italian fear of Austrian designs on, 149

Index   341

N

Napoleon I (French emperor, 1804–1815), 9
Napoleon III (French emperor, 1852–1870), 9, 16
Narodna Odbrana, 189
Natalija Konstantinović (wife of Prince Mirko), 17, 176, 217 n.14
Nekliudov, Anatol Vasilievich (Russian minister at Sofia, 1911–1913), 105
Neratov, Anatol Anatolievich (Russian deputy foreign minister, 1911–1914), 81, 84
Neue Freie Presse (Austrian newspaper), 29, 36, 54, 101, 152, 224 n.39; on Albanian revolt, 70; on Aehrenthal's criticism of Turkey, 79–80; on Conrad's dismissal, 95; and Scutari Crisis, 134
Nicephor (archimandrite), 94, 249 n.44
Nicholas I (prince of Montenegro, 1860–1910, king, 1910–1918): accession of, 1, 7; marriage, politics of, 7, 13–14, 15, 17, 201, 217 n.14; expansionism of, 7–8, 11–12, 21, 76, 210–11; and rival Serb dynasties, 17; and Peter I, 17, 30, 51, 61–62, 99, 160, 172, 175, 176, 210, 211; plots against, 19, 51–53, 55, 57, 96–97, 128, 176 (*see also* Cetinje Bomb Affair); and annexation crisis, 22, 24–25, 28–30, 32–36, 43–44, 228 n.10, 232 n.72; and Kolašin conspiracy, 51–53; and jubilee, 51–52, 63, 204, 235 n.48; named Russian field marshal, 235 n.51; and visit of Austro-Hungarian fleet, 56, 59; desires better Austro-Montenegrin ties, 58–59, 120, 128–29; and Russian military convention, 64–65; and Malissori uprisings, 66, 72–75, 79–82; visits Vienna, 11, 100 –101, 205–6; and Turco-Italian War, 90–93, 247 n.24, 248 n.44, 250 n.63; visits St. Petersburg, 95–97; and Durham, 99; and Avarna, 100; proposes judiciary reform, 97, 247 n.26; rejects Great-Power démarche, 111; and outbreak of First Balkan War, 104–11; and designs on Albania, 113, 116, 119–20, 127, 167–68, 203; and Lovćen-Scutari exchange proposal, 124–26, 144–47, 151–52; threatens to abdicate, 129, 228 n.10; reported to have abdicated, 150; and Scutari Crisis, 134–42, 157, 276 n.116; offers port to United States, 245 n.120; appoints new cabinet, 153–54; and Second Balkan War, 159–60; and Sjenokos incident, 169; and foreign policy after Scutari, 165–67, 171–78; twenty-fifth anniversary as honorary Russian commander, 173; and assassination of Francis Ferdinand, 183, 185; and anti-Austrian demonstrations in Cetinje, 185, 187; courted by Berchtold, 187; broaches Scutari question again, 188; reacts to Austrian ultimatum to Serbia, 190; exchanges telegrams with Alexander, 191; and declaration of war, 196–99; overtures to Austria to secure throne, 204; exile and death, 211; character of, 206–7
Nicholas I (Russian tsar, 1825–1855), 13
Nicholas II (Russian tsar, 1894–1917), 18, 151, 173, 235 n.51
Nicholas Nikolaievich (Russian grand duke; husband of Princess Anastasia), 63, 171, 217 n.14
Nicolson, Sir Arthur (British ambassador at St. Petersburg, 1906–1910; permanent undersecretary of state for foreign affairs, 1910–1916), 135, 136, 139, 140, 152, 269 n.51

Nikšić (town), 2, 4, 97, 185–86; annexation crisis protests in, 26; and First Balkan War, 116; suggested as Montenegrin capital, 132
Ninković, Leontije (Bosnian), 226 n.77
Njeguši (town), 141
Northern Albania Border Commission, 167, 204
Nova Varoš (town), 27
Novi Pazar (town), 27
Novi Pazar, Sandžak of. *See* Sandžak of Novi Pazar.
Novoe vremia (Russian newspaper), 117, 155, 228 n.11

O

O'Beirne, Hugh James (British chargé d'affaires at St. Petersburg, 1906–1915), 164
Obnorsky, Nikolai (Russian legation secretary at Cetinje, often chargé d'affaires, 1912–1914), 170–73, 175, 176, 247 n.24
Obod (town), 15
Obrenović dynasty, 17, 34
Ohrid (town), 160
Old Serbia. *See* Kosovo
Onogošt brewery, 4
Opatija (town), 181
O'Reilly, William (British chargé d'affaires at Cetinje, 1908–1909), 35, 41, 50
Orthodox Church, 2, 6
Otranto, Strait of, 66, 188
Otto, Eduard (Austro-Hungarian minister at Cetinje, 1913–1914), 206; appointment as minister to Montenegro, 166–67; and Sjenokos incident, 169; and Russo-Montenegrin reconciliation, 171; and outbreak of World War I, 183, 186–88, 190–94, 196, 198
Ottoman Empire. *See* Turkey
Ottomanization, 69, 71. *See also* Malissori uprisings

P

Paget, Sir Ralph Spencer (British minister at Belgrade, 1910–1913; assistant of undersecretary of state for foreign affairs, 1913–1915), 259 n.48
Paléologue, Maurice (political director at French foreign ministry, 1912–1914; ambassador at St. Petersburg, 1914–1917), 175
Palić, Luigi (Franciscan), 140, 151
Pallavicini, Johann von (count; Austro-Hungarian ambassador at Constantinople, 1906–1918), 70–71, 76, 91, 98, 109
Pan-Serbism, 8. *See also* Serbia *and* Montenegro
Pan-Slavism, 13, 105, 117, 135, 171, 228 n.11, 268
Panther (German gunboat), 88
Paris Peace Conference (1856), 9
Pašić, Nikola (Serbian prime minister and foreign minister, 1906–1908; prime minister, 1909–1911; prime minister and foreign minister, 1912–1918), 55, 99, 161; and annexation crisis, 224 nn.44 and 47; and Kolašin conspiracy, 53; and proclamation of Montenegrin kingdom, 62; and First Balkan War, 122, 126, 130; and Scutari Crisis, 137; and Sjenokos incident, 169; and question of Serbo-Montenegrin union, 172, 175, 176, 284; and Austro-Hungarian ultimatum, 190
Peć (town), 133, 160, 161, 239 n.40, 285 n.79
People's Party. *See* Klubaši
Perper (Montenegrin currency), 5
Peter (Montenegrin prince, youngest son of Nicholas), 111, 120, 217 n.14, 223 n.36, 281–82 n.37
Peter I (Russian tsar, 1682–1725; known as "the Great"), 12
Peter II (Russian tsar, 1762), 12

Index 343

Peter I Karadjordjević (king of Serbia, 1903–1921), 17, 30, 31, 51, 88, 99, 160, 161, 210, 211, 217 n.14, 284 n.69; and Nicholas's jubilee, 61–63; and Serbo-Montenegrin union, 172, 175, 176; visit to Turkey, 234 n.29

Peter II Njegoš (Montenegrin prince-bishop, 1830–1851), 7, 9, 207

Peter Nikolaievich (Russian grand duke; husband of Princess Milica), 63, 117, 217 n.14

Petković, Todor (Serbian minister at Cetinje, 1909–1911), 54, 55, 62

Petrović-Njegoš family, 6, 7, 21, 86, 102, 126, 188, 196, 217 n.14; financial practices of 253 n.112; scandals relating to, 176. *See also* names of individual family members

Phillips, G. F. (colonel; commander of British delegation at Scutari), 168, 293 n. 82

Pichon, Stephen J. M. (French foreign minister, 1906–1911, 1913, 1917–1920), 25, 138, 231 n.54

Pig War (Austro-Serbian), 18

Pilgrim-Baltazzi, Gisbert von (German minister at Cetinje, 1906–1911), 225 n.51

Plamenac, Jovan (Montenegrin interior minister, 1912–1913), 115

Planenac, Petar (Montenegrin chargé d'affaires at Constantinople, 1912; foreign minister, 1913–1915), 164; appointed Montenegrin representative in Constantinople, 99; and Turkish frontier incidents, 102, 103; appointed foreign minister, 154, 155; submits memorandum to Nicholas, 165–66; and Metaljka incident, 184; and anti-Austrian demonstrations, 185; and Mehmedbašić incident, 186; on Austro-Hungarian ultimatum to Serbia, 190, 191; and border incidents, 192, 193–94; on Montenegrin readiness for war, 197; on eve of First World War, 198; trip to St. Petersburg, 283 n.55

Planinica (hill), 108, 112

Plav (town), 112

Pljevlja (town), 27, 115–16, 161, 285 n.79

Podgorica (town), 2, 11, 15, 52, 111, 167, 168, 243 n.95; Bosnian annexation protests in, 26; and 1911 Malissori uprising, 75, 77, 81, 82; and Kolašin conspiracy, 52

Podgorica declaration of 1911, 77

Politika (Serbian newspaper), 142, 228 n.11

Poincaré, Raymond (French premier and foreign minister, 1912–1913; president, 1913–1920), 107–8, 117, 119

Popović, Jovo (Montenegrin chargé d'affaires at Constantinople, 1909–1912), 24–25, 99, 129, 269 n.51, 266 n.22; and Scutari Crisis, 135, 139, 146, 151

Potapov, Nikolai (colonel, later general; Russian military attaché at Cetinje, 1913–1914), 81, 117, 252 n.107

Potiorek, Oskar (general; governor of Bosnia-Hercegovina, 1911–1914), 169

Pravaši (Prava Narodna Stranka), 174

Pravda (Belgrade newspaper), 99, 224 n.39, 228 n.11

Prijepolje (town), 27

Princip, Gavrilo (Bosnian), 182

Priština (town), 70

Prizren (town), 8, 76, 94, 111, 133, 160, 201, 286 n.97; goal of Montenegro in First Balkan War, 112, 113; and Prochaska affair, 121

Prochaska, Oskar (Austro-Hungarian consul in Prizren, 1906–1912), 121

Protić, Stojan (Serbian finance minister, 1909–1912), 55

Provincia di Padova, La (Italian newspaper), 131
Pruth, Treaty of (1711), 12
Puglia line, 15
Pula (town), 100, 262 n.80

R

Racconigi: Russo-Italian agreement at (1909), 94
Radenković, Vasilije (Serbian candidate for archbishopric of Prizren), 94
Radović, Andrija (Montenegrin prime minister, 1907), 18, 19, 235 n.48
Radulović, Marko (Montenegrin prime minister, 1906–1907), 18
Railroads: in Balkans, 11, 16, 234 n.29, 244 n.120
Ramadanović, S. (Montenegrin court marshal), 251 n.77
"Red Book" (Albanian). *See* Gerče memorandum
Red Cross: American, 243 n.95; Austrian, 116, 256 n.18; Italian, 256 n.18; Montenegrin, 36, 197
Redlich, Josef (Austrian professor and parliamentarian), 39, 40, 42, 122, 245 n.127, 275 n.107, 292 nn.54 and 58; and Scutari Crisis, 276 n.116
Regia Co-interessata dei Tabacchi del Montenegro, 15
Reichspost (Austrian newspaper), 95
Reichstadt (Russo-Austrian agreement, 1876), 13
Reitzes (Austrian bank), 253 n.112
Reshid Bey (director of political affairs, Turkish foreign ministry), 169
Riedl, Richard (official of Austrian trade ministry), 234 n.30
Rifaat Pasha (Turkish foreign minister, 1909–1911), 241 n.79
Rijeka (city), 30

Rijeka Crnojevića (town), 11, 26, 50, 120, 127
Risan (town), 97
Riz(a) Ahmed (president of Turkish parliament) 238 n.18
Riz(a) Bey, Ali (colonel; Turkish head of Turco-Montenegrin boundary commission), 103, 251 n.83
Riz(a) Bey, Hussan (vali of Scutari), 113
Rizov, Dimitŭr (Bulgarian minister at Cetinje, 1903–1905; at Rome, 1909–1915), 107
Rodd, Sir James Rennell (British ambassador at Rome, 1908–1919), 149, 232 n.70
Romanovsky, Prince (first husband of Princess Anastasia), 217 n.14
Rožaje (town), 27
Rumania, 100, 159–60
Russell, Theo W. O. (British legation secretary at Vienna, 1908–1914), 281 n.32
Russia: Asiatic Office in Foreign Ministry, 13; duma (assembly) of, 14, 18, 34, 173; and wars with Turkey, 12; and desire for Balkan alliance, 105, 107–8; and Bulgaria, 106; and Italy, 94, 181; —and Montenegro, 94, 165, 167; relations before annexation crisis, 9, 12–15, 18; and annexation crisis, 22, 25, 34, 42, 50, 228 n.11; Nicholas's resentment at Russian influence, 14, 82, 84–86; and Kolašin conspiracy, 53–54; and visit of French fleet, 54–55; and proclamation of Montenegrin kingdom, 63; and military convention between, 64–65, 73, 81, 171, 173, 175, 207, 294 n.89; and Malissori uprisings, 72–73, 79–82, 84–86; and Nicholas's trip to St. Petersburg, 95–97; and First Balkan War, 111, 116–17, 132; and Scutari Crisis, 135–37, 138, 144–47, 153, 164, 275 n.107, 276 n.115; and Second Balkan War, 159–61;

Russia *(cont.)*
  and Russian subsidies, 12–14, 164; and question of Serbo-Montenegrin union, 117, 164, 170, 172, 173, 175–77; relations after Scutari Crisis, 169–73, 174, 190;
  —and Serbia, and ascendancy of Karadjordjević dynasty, 18; during annexation crisis, 42–43, 44, 45, 46; Russian support for Serbian port, 119.
  —*See also* names of other countries.
Russo-Japanese War, 20
Rustem Bey (Turkish minister at Cetinje, 1911–1912), 102–3
Ržanica (town and region), 92, 101

S

Sadreddin Bey (Turkish minister at Cetinje, 1910–1911), 74, 80, 102
St. James Conference (London), 129, 131, 132
St. Vitus's Day (Vidov dan), 182, 184
Salis, John Francis Charles de (count; British minister at Cetinje, 1911–1916), 85, 99, 101, 104, 244 n.120; and First Balkan War, 126; and Scutari Crisis, 139, 151
Salonica (city), 11, 37, 108, 122, 160, 289 n.22
Salvo, Giovanni di (Italian monk), 249 n.44
Sandžak of Novi Pazar, 20, 32, 35, 106, 150, 157, 162, 165, 195, 196, 197, 202, 203, 204, 266 n.24; and annexation crisis, 27, 40, 222 n.19; Conrad claims right of occupation in, 83; and Turco-Italian War, 89–90, 247 n.24; and First Balkan War, 113–16, 128; division of, between Serbia and Montenegro, 161
San Giuliano, Antonio di (marquis; Italian foreign minister, 1905–1906; ambassador at London, 1906–1910), 260 n.52, 279 n.14, 294 n.88; and Malissori uprising of 1910, 71; and Turco-Italian War, 87; and First Balkan War, 110, 118, 119, 132; and Scutari Crisis, 138, 148–49, 153, 155, 263 n.80; and Opatija conference, 179–80; and desire for accord with Austria, 181; after death of Francis Ferdinand, 188; and inability to agree with Austria on Montenegro, 283 n.64; and Austria's interest in acquiring Lovćen, 286–87 n.98; and question of Serbo-Montenegrin union, 287 n.99
San Stefano, Treaty of (1878), 10
Sarajevo (city), 38, 182, 185
Sava (Montenegrin prince-bishop, 1735–1781), 12
Šavnik (district), 7
Sazonov, Sergei Dimitrievich (Russian foreign minister, 1910–1916), 81, 84, 253 n.112; on successor for Aehrenthal, 98; and Balkan alliance, 106, 107, 108; and First Balkan War, 109, 110, 117; and Scutari Crisis, 135, 138, 146, 147–48, 153, 275 n.107; on Treaty of Bucharest, 161; and question of Serbo-Montenegrin union, 172–73, 175, 176, 290 n.36; and outbreak of First World War, 197
Scanderbeg (Albanian national hero, fifteenth century), 71, 156
Schemua, Blasius (general; chief of the Austro-Hungarian general staff, 1911–1912), 109, 121
Schreiber, Eduard (Austro-Hungarian president of Čajniče district, Bosnia), 168
Scutari (city), 6, 37, 76, 90, 97, 188, 293 n.82; as center of Austro-Italian rivalry, 67; and Malissori uprisings, 71, 75, 77; as Montenegrin war aim, 112–13, 119, 120, 128, 130–31, 203; proposed exchange for Lovćen, 122–26, 131,

Scutari *(cont.)*
144; disputed at Conference of Ambassadors, 133; international occupation of, 155–56; Austrian and Italian relief units in, 156. *See also* Scutari Crisis
Scutari (province), 71, 108, 240 n.51
Scutari Crisis, 203, 205; outbreak of, 132–34; and Montenegrin compensation, 132, 155; and Austrian demands for military force, 133; Nicholas refuses to abandon siege, 134; naval demonstration and blockade, 135–37, 156, 262 n.80; Serbia's pullback from Scutari, 137–38; and question of compensation to Montenegro, 138–40, 144, 154–55; worsening situation inside Scutari, 139–40; Palić and Hubka affairs, 140–41; Montenegrin occupation of Scutari and reaction in Belgrade and Vienna, 141–43; Great-Power deliberations, 143–48; possibility of joint Austro-Italian action, 148–50, 263 n.80, 264 n.10, 271 n.68, 275 n.107; Austro-Hungarian council agrees to prepare for military intervention, 149–50; Montenegro capitulates, 150–52; in perspective, 156–58. *See also* Conference of Ambassadors
Scutari, Lake, 6, 11, 15, 81, 132, 232 n.72
Serbia: as potential Piedmont of South Slav state, 20–21, 182; and Balkan démarche to Powers, 109; and claim to Adriatic port, 118, 119, 122, 130; withdrawal from Scutari theater, 137–38; and Second Balkan War, 159–61; in First World War, 211; assembly (skupština) of, 279 n.6;
—and Bulgaria, 105–8, 159–60;
—and Greece, 107, 136, 138;
—and Montenegro, 128, 310; relations to 1908, 16–18; Montenegrin students in Serbia, 4, 5, 19, 23, 53; rivalry between, for dominance in Serb world, 16, 17, 18, 21; and Cetinje Bomb Affair, 19; during annexation crisis, 30–32, 38, 41–42, 44; relations between, 1908–1909, 51; and Kolašin conspiracy, 53–55, 57; and proclamation of Montenegrin kingdom, 61–63; possibility of joint action in Macedonia, 75; continued enmity, 1911–1912, 93–95, 99; and Dožić affair, 93–94; improved relations and alliance, 99, 107–8; and Serbia's pullback from Scuturi, 137–38; and fall of Scutari, 142–143; and division of Sandžak, 155, 161, 162; and question of union, 157, 161, 163, 164, 173–77, 212; and Second Balkan War, 160; and pro-Serbian activity in Montenegro, 188, 191, 198;
—and Turkey: relations before 1908, 16–17; and annexation crisis, 31.
—*See also* names of other countries
Sercey, R. de (count; French minister at Cetinje, 1904–1911), 53, 54, 55, 222 n.11
Servizi Marittimi line, 15
Shali (Malissori tribe), 71. *See also* Malissori uprisings
Shëngjin (town), 113, 119, 120, 125, 136
Shevket Turgut Pasha (Turkish general), 71, 77–78, 93, 243 n.100
Shreti (Malissori tribe), 244 n.110
Sjenica (town), 27
Sjenokos (village), 168–69, 176, 204
Skodra affair, 133
Skopje (city), 108
Skreli (Albanian tribe), 168
Skupština. *See* Montenegro, assembly of; Serbia, assembly of
Slavophiles, 13. *See also* Pan-Slavism
Società Commerciale d'Orientale, 15

Sofija (Sophia; Montenegrin princess), 217 n.14
Sophie (duchess of Hohenberg; wife of Francis Ferdinand), 180, 182
Spalajković, Miroslav (first section-chief in Serbian foreign ministry to 1911; minister at Sofia, 1911–1913; delegate to Bucharest peace conference, 1913; director of foreign ministry, 1913; later minister at St. Petersburg), 70
Spič (height), 10, 25, 32–36, 45
Squitti, Nicola (baron; Italian minister at Cetinje, 1908–1913; at Belgrade, 1913–1916), 60 95, 270 n.64; and annexation crisis, 35, 43, 44, 48, 49; Nicholas complains to, about Russia, 82, 84; and Turco-Montenegrin frontier incidents, 103; and First Balkan War, 114, 120; and Scutari Crisis, 145
Stanojević, Stanoje (Serbian professor), 256 n.15
Stavrianos, L.S. (historian), 2
Steamship transportation, 15. *See also* names of individual lines
Steed, Wickham (British correspondent), 259 n.48
Stephen Dušan Nemanja (Serb king, 1335–1346), 5, 8, 16, 76
Stephen Mali (Montenegrin ruler, eighteenth century), 12
Stolac (town), 185
Stolypin, Peter A. (Russian prime minister, 1906–1911), 236 n.61
Storck, Wilhelm von (ritter; Austro-Hungarian legation counsel in Belgrade), 188
Stürgkh, Karl (Count; Austrian prime minister, 1911–1916), 273 n.91
Switzerland, 107
Szápáry von Szápár, Friedrich (count; Austro-Hungarian ambassador at St. Petersburg, 1913–1914), 172
Szécsen von Temerin, Nikolaus (count; Austro-Hungarian ambassador at Paris, 1911–1914), 98

T

Tarabosh (height), 141
Tarnowski von Tarnow, Adam (count; Austro-Hungarian minister at Sofia, 1911–1917), 252 n.107
Taylor, A. J. P. (historian), 229–30 n.44
Teleszky, Johann (Hungarian finance minister, 1912–1917), 273 n.91
Temperley, Harold (historian), 88
Temps, Le (French newspaper), 187, 286 n.98
Thaden, Edward (historian), 252 n.107
Thurn und Valasássina, Duglas (count; Austro-Hungarian diplomatic agent at Sofia, 1905–1909; after 1909, minister; ambassador at St. Petersburg, 1911–1913), 253 n.112
Times (of London), 122, 192, 254 n.118
Tisza de Boros-Jenö, Stephen (count; Hungarian prime minister, 1904, 1913–1914), 178–79, 181
Tittoni, Tommaso (Italian foreign minister, 1903–1905, 1906–1909; ambassador at Paris, 1910–1917), 24, 47–49, 60, 227 n.3, 231 n.53, 237 n.5
Tobacco, 4, 5
Tomanović, Lazar (Montenegrin prime minister, 1907–1911), and annexation crisis, 19, 24, 25, 34, 41, 49, 50; and Malissori revolt of 1910, 72; and Malissori revolt of 1911, 81, 85; on Russo-Montenegrin relations, 96; replaced as

Tomanović *(cont.)*
  prime minister, 101; and Nicholas's trip to Vienna, 251 n.77; and offer to United States, 245 n.120
Topola (town), 99
Tošković, Janko (Montenegrin parliamentarian), 198
Trans-Balkanic railroad, 16, 244 n. 120
Trebinje (town), 198
Trentino (region), 181, 196, 209
Treutler, Carl Georg (foreign office representative at imperial German court), 178, 286 n.97
Tribuna (Italian newspaper), 54
Trieste (city), 100, 106, 183
Triple Alliance, 94, 98, 129, 131, 148, 158, 201, 208; renewal of in 1887, 237 n.9; and proposed Serbo-Montenegrin union, 177–81. See also member countries
Triple Entente, 201. *See also* member countries
Tripoli (city), 87, 88, 90
Trubel (town), 97
Tschirschky und Boegendorff, Heinrich von (German ambassador at Vienna, 1907–1916), 143, 146, 179, 181, 277 n.125
Turco-Italian War (1911–1912), 87–91, 98, 105, 203
Turgut Pasha. *See* Shevket Turgut Pasha
Turkey, 172; program for internal reform, 108, 109, 110; military preparations before First Balkan War, 109; coup in, 130; and Sjenokos, 169; and Second Balkan War, 159;
—and Montenegro: relations to 1908, 1, 6, 7, 8, 9, 11; and annexation crisis, 31; and Ržanica question, 92–93, 101; and sale of Montenegrin residence, 102; and boundary commission, 97, 101, 103; and Nicholas's visit to Russia, 97; and deteriorating relations before First Balkan War, 98–99, 101–5, 108–11.
—*See also* Annexation Crisis, Malissori uprisings, Turco-Italian War, and names of other countries
Turkish Straits, 20
Tuzi (town), 68, 75, 77, 108, 116, 168

U

Ugron zu Ábránfalva, Stephan von (Austro-Hungarian minister at Belgrade, 1911–1913; afterwards at foreign ministry), 89, 122, 142
Ulcinj (town), 2, 7, 10, 15, 26, 68, 139, 163, 197, 244 n. 120
Ungaro-Croata line, 11
United States, 4, 96, 129, 227 n.80, 245 n.120

V

Vasilije (Montenegrin prince-bishop, eighteenth century), 12
Vasojević clan, 27, 103
Vatican, 248–49 n.44
Velika (district in northeastern Montenegro), 92
Venice, 6, 15
Venizelos, Eleutheros (Greek prime minister, 1910–1915), 264 n.11
Vermosh (town and region), 167, 168
Vešović, Radomir (Montenegrin general), 112
Victor Emmanuel III (king of Italy, 1900–1946), 15, 63, 98, 118, 217 n.14, 237 n.6, 294 n.88
Virpazar (town), 15, 119
Vjera (Montenegrin princess), 26, 217 n.14
Vladike (prince-bishops), 6
Vlorë (town), 66, 67, 120, 126, 149

Vojnović, Lujo (count; adviser to Nicholas), 129, 265 n.12
Vraka (village), 276 n.115
Vršuta (village), 64
Vukotić, Dušan (Montenegrin acting foreign minister, 1913), 144
Vukotić, Janko (general/serdar; Montenegrin envoy to Belgrade and Constantinople, 1908; chief of the general staff, 1912; interim foreign minister, 1913; prime minister and war minister, 1913–1919), 240 n.53; and annexation crisis, 30–32, 37, 224 n.42; and Malissori uprisings 72, 75, 81; and First Balkan War, 110–11, 112, 115, 128; and Scutari Crisis, 146; appointed prime minister, 153–54; and Sjenokos incident, 169; and closer ties with Serbia, 174; and Metaljka incident, 184; and visit to Rome, 290 n. 37; returns to Montenegro, 192, 197
Vukotić, Mme., 111

W

Wagner, Violet Emily (wife of Prince Peter), 217 n.14
Weinzetl, Rudolf (consul general attached to Austro-Hungarian legation in Cetinje, often chargé d'affaires, 1911–1913), 92, 103, 161, 164–65
Wellington, duke of, 235 n.51
Whitehead, Sir James B. (British minister at Belgrade, 1906–1910), 62
Wiesinger, Leo (Austro-Hungarian infantry officer), 236 n.59

William II (German emperor, 1888–1918), 98, 118, 177–79, 181, 201, 287 n.103, 291 n.52; and Scutari Crisis, 270 n.61, 277–78 n.125
Wittelsbach dynasty, 175
Würthle, Friedrich (historian), 289 n.24

Y

Yellow Mobilization, 45, 109, 113–14, 292 n.54
Young Bosnia (Mlada Bosna), 182, 183
Young Turk Revolution (1908), 19–20, 69
Young turks, 40, 69, 70

Z

Zagreb (city), 30, 32
Zalesky, Wenzel von (ritter; Austrian finance minister, 1911–1913), 273 n.91
Zambaur, Alfred von (ritter; Austro-Hungarian consul general at Scutari, 1909–1913), 150
Zara and Fiume (Zadar and Rijeka) resolutions, 221 n.38
Zeit, Die (Austrian newspaper), 62, 98
Zeta (medieval state), 4, 5, 6, 26, 76, 141
Zorka (Montenegrin princess; wife of Peter Karadjordjević, later Peter I of Serbia), 17, 99, 217 n.14
Zumbi (village), 189

www.ingramcontent.com/pod-product-compliance
Lightning Source LLC
Chambersburg PA
CBHW071649160426
43195CB00012B/1409